William Mathews

Getting on in the World

Hints on Success in Life

William Mathews

Getting on in the World
Hints on Success in Life

ISBN/EAN: 9783744724494

Printed in Europe, USA, Canada, Australia, Japan

Cover: Foto ©ninafisch / pixelio.de

More available books at **www.hansebooks.com**

GETTING ON IN THE WORLD;

OR,

HINTS ON SUCCESS IN LIFE.

BY

WILLIAM MATHEWS, LL. D.,

PROFESSOR OF RHETORIC AND ENGLISH LITERATURE IN THE UNIVERSITY
OF CHICAGO.

Fungar vice cotis, acutum
Reddere quæ ferrum valet, exsors ipsâ secandi.
HORACE.

Do not shun this maxim as commonplace. On the contrary take the
closest heed of what observant men, who would probably like to show originality, are yet constrained to repeat. Therein lies the marrow of the wisdom of the world.—ARTHUR HELPS.

TORONTO:

BELFORD BROTHERS.

MDCCCLXXVI.

Quit yourselves like men.—1 Samuel iv. 9.

A sacred burden is the life ye bear,
Look on it, lift it, bear it solemnly,
Stand up and walk beneath it steadfastly.
Fail not for sorrow, falter not for sin,
But onward, upward till the goal ye win.
—FRANCES ANNE KEMBLE.

In general I have no patience with people who talk about "the thoughtlessness of youth" indulgently ; I had infinitely rather hear of thoughtless old age, and the indulgence due to *that*. When a man has done his work, and nothing can any way be materially altered in his fate, let him forget his toil, and jest with his fate if he will ; but what excuse can you find for wilfulness of thought at the very time when every crisis of fortune hangs on your decisions? A youth thoughtless, when all the happiness of his home forever depends on the chances or the passions of an hour ! A youth thoughtless, when the career of all his days depends on the opportunity of a moment ! A youth thoughtless, when his every action is a foundation-stone of future conduct, and every imagination a fountain of life or death ! Be thoughtless in *any* after years, rather than now—though, indeed, there is only one place where a man may be nobly thoughtless, his deathbed. Nothing should ever be left to be done there.—RUSKIN.

There is no fault nor folly of my life which does not rise up against me, and take away my joy and shorten my power of possession, of sight, of understanding. And every past effort of my life, every gleam of rightness or good in it, is with me now, to help me in my grasp of this art and its vision.—*Ib.*

For of all sad words of tongue or pen,
The saddest are these "It might have been !"
.   —WHITTIER.

The well-known, worn-out topics of consolation and of encouragement are become trite *because they are reasonable.*—RICHARD SHARP.

PREFACE.

THE origin of this book, which will account for some of its peculiarities of style, is as follows. In the early part of 1871 the author wrote for the Chicago *Tribune* a series of articles on the subject here treated, after the publication of which a considerable number of persons in different parts of the Northwest expressed a wish that they should be gathered into a volume. This led to their revision, and the addition of nearly twice as much new matter, the whole forming the work which is now offered to the public.

That the book has many imperfections, the author is well aware; they are due partly to the fact that it has been written by economizing moments of leisure snatched from professional labours, and, to use a phrase of Milton, with his left hand. Upon a subject which so many pens have discussed, it is, of course, hardly possible to say anything absolutely new; the most that a writer can hope to do is to recombine and present in novel and attractive forms, with fresh illustrations, so as to impress persons who have not been impressed before, thoughts which have substantially been repeated from the days of Solomon to those of Smiles and "Titcomb." Some of the topics, however, have been less hackneyed than others; as, for example, the important one of "Reserved Power,"—in writing the chapter upon which the author has been materially aided by some of the suggestions contained in "The Army of the Reserve," an eloquent and scholarly address delivered at Bowdoin College, in 1862, by Hon. B. F. Thomas, LL.D.

If this book shall serve to rouse to honourable effort any young man who is wasting his time and energies through indifference to life's prizes,—to cheer, stimulate, and inspire with enthusiasm any one who is desponding through distrust of his own abilities,—or to reveal to any one who is puzzled to discover the path to success and usefulness the art of "getting on" to the goal of his wishes,—the author will feel himself abundantly repaid for his labours. Doubtless there are many persons who are better qualified by their worldly knowledge to discuss the subject here considered ; but, unhappily, the most successful men do not reveal the secret of their successes ; and if we do not reject criticisms on paintings from men who have never handled a brush, nor refuse to follow the directions of a guide-post though it has never hopped off upon its one leg and travelled the road to which it points, a young man who is beginning life may accept the hints of a well-wisher whose knowledge of his needs has been derived from observation, rather than from experience.

CHICAGO.

CONTENTS.

CHAPTER I.

Success and Failure 9   **Page.**

CHAPTER II.

Good and Bad Luck 25

CHAPTER III.

Choice of a Profession 39

CHAPTER IV.

Physical Culture 55

CHAPTER V.

Concentration, or Oneness of Aim 66

CHAPTER VI.

Self-Reliance 82

CHAPTER VII.

Originality in Aims and Methods 95

CHAPTER VIII.

Attention to Details 104

CHAPTER IX.

Practical Talent 112

CHAPTER X.

Decision 123

CONTENTS.

CHAPTER XI.

Manner 136

CHAPTER XII.

Business Habits 153

CHAPTER XIII.

Self-Advertising 171

CHAPTER XIV.

The Will and the Way 180

CHAPTER XV.

The Will and the Way (continued) 210

CHAPTER XVI.

Reserved Power 226

CHAPTER XVII.

Economy of Time 253

CHAPTER XVIII.

Money,—its Use and Abuse 264

CHAPTER XIX.

Mercantile Failures 286

CHAPTER XX.

Overwork and Under-Rest 309

CHAPTER XXI.

True and False Success 324

Index 331

GETTING ON IN THE WORLD.

CHAPTER I.

SUCCESS AND FAILURE.

Let every man be occupied, and occupied in the highest employment of which his nature is capable, and die with the consciousness that he has done his best.—SYDNEY SMITH.

Men must know that in this theatre of man's life it remaineth only to God and to angels to be lookers-on.—BACON.

Toil alone could never have produced the " Paradise Lost " or the " Principia." The born dwarf never grows to the middle size.—REV. R. A. WILLMOTT.

The talent of success is nothing more than doing what you can do well, without a thought of fame.—HENRY W. LONGFELLOW.

IN attending a concert in one of our large cities, did you ever observe the wide chasm that separates the first and second violinists of the orchestra ? One is all pomp, fire, bustle, enthusiasm, energy. Now waving his bow high in the air, he silently guides the harmony ; now rapidly tapping on the rest-board, he hurries the movement ; and again, bringing the violin to his shoulder, he takes the leading strain, and high above the crash of sound, above the shrill blast of the trumpet, the braying of horns, the ear-piercing notes of the fife, the sobbing of oboes, the wailing of violoncellos, and all the thun ders of the orchestra, are heard, distinct and clear, the shrieking notes of the first violin. Dressed in unimpeachable broadcloth, with kids and linen of immaculate purity, stamping his feet, wagging his head, nodding earnestly to the right and to the left, and beating time with mad energy, he enters heart and soul into the music, oblivious of all things else ; and all because he is the leader, and plays the first violin. Standing by his side, but upon a lower platform, and before a lower music-rest, is a patient, care-worn man, who saws quietly on the strings, with the air rather of the hired labourer than of the enthusiast. His eye you never see in a fine frenzy rolling, glancing from heaven to earth, from earth to heaven, nor does his facile hand run off in roulades of melody ; he never wags his head, nor stamps his foot, nor labours to wreak his thoughts upon expression, but steadily and conscientiously he pours a rich undercurrent of harmony into the music, which few hear, fewer care for, but without which, losing the charm of contrast, it would be as dreary as the droning of a bagpipe—as monotonous as a picture which is all lights and no shadows. With his eye fixed on the notes, he scrapes away with diligence, not with enthusiasm ; he is moved, not by the inspiration of a master, but by the reflection that he is exchanging his notes for dollars, and that, with each quaver, he earns so much bread and butter for his family. Yet this automaton—this musical machine, that plays its part so mechanically, with apparently as little interest in the result as Babbage's calculating-machine in the solution of a mathematical problem—may have been endowed by nature with as much genius and fire as that thundering Jupiter of the orchestra, the leader ; but, alas ! he plays second fiddle.

The world is an orchestra, and men are players. All of us are playing some part in the production of life's harmony—some wielding the baton, and fired by the sympathy of lookers-on ; others feeling that they are but second fiddles, humbled by conscious inferiority, and drudging on as the treadmill horse plods through his monotonous task. Our object will be, in this series of papers, to show the reason of this inequality, and especially how, whether one plays first or second fiddle, or is gifted with talents that qualify him only to strike the cymbals or beat the drum, he may magnify his calling, and act well his part, " where all the honour lies."

We purpose, in this volume, to discuss the subject of success in life ; or, in other words, to answer the question which every young man, as he enters upon his career of self-dependence, is likely to ask of himself or others, " How shall I get on in the world ?" The theme is as old as the human race ; yet, though volumes have been written on it, it is still new to each successive generation, and assuming, as it does, new phases with the ceaseless changes in society, must be inexhaustible. Out of the thousand topics which it offers for consideration, we shall select only those of vital interest, just notions of which are indispensable to every young man who would act well his part in the great drama of life. To the mass of men, and especially to those who are about embarking on the voyage of active life, no theme can be of deeper interest than this. A man sailing on that voyage has been compared to a vessel of war leaving port under sealed orders. He knows not, but as the ways of Providence are disclosed, to what ports he must go, or on what seas he must sail. The dangers of the voyage—the sunken reefs, the icebergs, or the stormy capes, which may be his ruin—are unknown. Through perilous storms and treacherous calms must he steer his unknown course, nor is there any exact chart laid down for the voyage. No man ever sailed over exactly the same route that another sailed over before him; every man who starts on the ocean of life arches his sails to an untried breeze. Like Coleridge's mariner, "he is the first that ever burst into that lonely sea."

In looking about among the circle of our acquaintances, we are surprised to see how few have made the voyage successfully, that fewer still have reached the ports for which they sailed. Many a shallop, which sailed out of harbour noiselessly and unnoticed, has anchored at last safely in port; many a noble argosy, freighted with precious hopes, and launched with streamers flying, amid the salvos of artillery and the huzzas of thousands, has sunk beneath the waves. To what impotent conclusions, indeed, do young men of brilliant parts frequently come! What becomes of the foremost boy at the academy, of the "senior wrangler" of the university, of the champion of the debating club, the law school, or the lyceum? Where are to be found, in the various walks of life, all of the geniuses to which almost every village periodically gives birth? All along the shores of the great ocean, on whose currents we are borne with resistless sweep, are strewn the wrecks of those whose embarkation was seemingly under the very star of hope. On whatever shoals or hidden rocks they may have struck, it matters not to them; only one voyage is vouchsafed, and failure is irretrievable; but to all who come after them, an explanation of the causes of disaster is of deep interest, and may save many from a similar fate.

Before discussing, however, the causes of shipwreck, **let us**
anticipate **a** few of the objections that may meet us **at** the
threshold.   And, first, there are those who deny that success
is pre-eminently desirable, or that it is by any means identical
with happiness.   No doubt there are many enjoyments outside of worldly success.   After all, it is pleasant to lie in bed
till eight o'clock in the morning, instead of turning out at five ;
it is pleasant to hug the chimney-corner, instead of breasting
the pitiless storm ; it is pleasant to pass one's evenings in the
bosom of a family ; pleasant, too, to taste the difference between winter and spring, fine sunsets and storms, town and
country.   The path of success, never "a primrose path of dal-
liance," is steeper and more thorny to-day than ever before.
Never before in the world's history was competition in every
calling and pursuit so fierce as now ; never did success, in more
than a moderate degree, demand for its attainment such a union
of physical and intellectual qualities,—of alertness, activity,
prudence, persistence, boldness, and decision,—as in this latter
half of the nineteenth century.   Carlyle truly says that "the
race of life has become intense ; the runners are treading upon
each other's heels ; woe be to him who stops to tie his shoe-
strings !"   This fact alone is sufficient to show the absurdity
of the opinion sometimes advanced, that success is not, as a
general thing, a test of merit.   In spite of the occasional triumphs of mediocre men and charlatans, the rule still holds,
that the men who make their way to the front, becoming rich
or famous by force of their personal characters, must have
something more in them than impudence, and even the Hud-
sons and Fisks could not have won their positions without
some sterling qualities, however alloyed with their opposites.

Again, it must be confessed that success does not always
yield the happiness expected ; that the prizes of life, like the
apples of Sodom, often turn to ashes in the grasp.   Of every
object of human pursuit, however dazzling in the distance, it
may be said, as the poet has said of woman,—

> The lovely toy, so fiercely sought,
> Hath lost its charm by being caught."

But persons who reason thus concerning human happiness forget its true nature.   They forget that it does not consist in

the gratification of the desires, nor in that freedom from care, that imaginary state of repose, to which most men look so anxiously forward, and with the prospect of which their labours are lightened, but which is more languid, irksome, and insupportable than all the toils of active life. True, the objects we pursue with so much ardour are insignificant in themselves, and never fulfil our extravagant expectations ; but this by no means proves them unworthy of pursuit. Properly to estimate their value, we must take into view all the pleasurable emotions they awaken prior to attainment.

"Man never is, but always to be blest,"

says the poet. That is, his true happiness consists in the *means*, and not in the *end ;* in *acquisition*, and not in *possession* The principle and source of it is not the gratification of the desires, nor does its amount depend on the frequency of such gratifications. He who cultivates a tree derives far more satisfaction from the care he bestows upon it than from the fruit. Give the huntsman his game, and the gambler the money that is staked, that they both may enjoy, without care or perplexity, the objects they pursue, and they will smile at your folly. "If my son," said a certain wealthy man, whose wasteful heir was fast dissipating the fruits of his exertions, " can take as much pleasure in spending my property as I have derived from acquiring it, I will not complain." Lessing declared that if he had been offered the choice between the possession of truth and the pleasure of seeking for it, he would unhesitatingly have preferred the latter. A state of constant fruition would be, according to our present notions, a state truly lamentable, since it would preclude, in a great degree, the pleasing emotions that spring from hope and expectation, and thus extinguish the lights that principally serve to cheer our path through life. Were all our desires satiated at their birth, or were we always satisfied with our present condition, in either case, as there would be nothing to draw forth our active energies, life would stagnate. In short, man was made for action, and life is a mere scene for the exercise of the mind and the engagements of the heart,—a scene where the most important occupations are, in a sense, but graver species of amusement, and where, so long as we take pleasure in the pursuit of an object, it matters but little that we attain it not, or that it fades when acquired. Hope is, indeed, a deceitful enchantress; but she sheds a sweet radiance on the stream of life, and never exerts her magic except to our advantage. We seldom attain what she beckons us to pursue; but her deceptions resemble those which the dying husbandman in the fable practised upon his sons, who, by telling them of a hidden mass of wealth, which he had buried in a secret place in his vineyard, led them so sedulously to delve the ground, and turn up the earth about the roots of the vines, that they found, indeed, a treasure—though not in gold, in wine.

The truth is, we owe a large part of our happiness to our mistakes. As, in the natural world, it would be only necessary to improve our vision to a higher degree of acuteness to make the sublimest scenes in nature and the most magnificent works of art appear horrid and deformed; so in the moral, too nicely to consider the intrinsic worth of the objects we pursue, will infallibly lead to a wrong estimate of the value of human life.

But whatever the views we may take of this subject, one thing is quite certain, and that is, that if happiness is not found in success, it is not found in failure. It is a sad thing to feel, even when we have done our best—when the stinging sense of time and talents wasted is absent—that we have foundered in our earthly voyage; to feel that we have ingloriously stranded, while those who set sail with us pass by with streamers flying and swelling sail. Mediocre men often mistake aspiration for inspiration; they have first-class ambition along with third-rate powers; and these coming together make a most ill-matched pair of legs, which bear a person along awkwardly in his path of life, and expose him to endless mortifications. Philosophy or religion may take the sting out of disappointment; but generally the impossibility of connecting the ideas of felicity and failure is so great, that though examples abound to show that success is not happiness, it is yet clear that it is essential to it. The moments in a man's life when, Alexander-like, he feels that the world has no more prizes to be coveted, are few indeed. It has been truly said that an object to be desired is at once the pleasure and the torment of life; sometimes a great object to be steadily pursued, all else being made subservient to it; or, more commonly, a succession of minor objects, rising, one after another, in endless succession. If Keats did somewhat exaggerate when he declared that "there is no fiercer hell than the failure in a great attempt," yet it must be admitted that the pleasure of a long-sought, ardently-desired success, dreamed of by night and toiled for by day, is, probably, as complete as anything this side of heaven; and it is universally felt to be a compensation for all toil or hardship; it is well, if not for any sin.

Again, while success is necessary to happiness, it must be remembered that the term is a relative one; in other words, that there are many degrees of success, among which the highest are neither attainable by all, nor essential to felicity. A man may be a very successful lawyer, though he should fail of becoming Chief Justice of the Supreme Court of the United States; a successful physician, though far inferior in skill to a Brodie or Magendie; a successful merchant, though he may never accumulate a tithe of the wealth of a Stewart, a Girard, or an Astor. All this, we are aware, is obvious enough; and we should not think of repeating such truisms, were not the contrary so often explicitly or implicitly taught in so many "Young Men's Own Books," "Student's Manuals," and articles in popular newspapers. As if restlessness, dissatisfaction with its lot, contempt for reasonable and attainable successes, were altogether wanting in Young America, our youth are hardly out of their jackets ere they are urged by a certain class of writers and lecturers to look with scorn upon, and to struggle out of, the sphere or place in life to which, if a lowly one, Providence has assigned them, and to become "great men," that is, governors, members of Congress, foreign ministers, major-generals, railroad kings, *et id omne*, which they are told they may become, if they only *will* to do it. Forgetting that all callings are alike honourable, if pursued with an honourable spirit; that it is the *heart* only which degrades, the intention carried into the work, and not the work a man does; that the most despised calling may be made honourable by the honour of its professors; that a blacksmith may be a man of polished manners, and a millionnaire a clown; that a shoemaker may put genius and taste into his work, while a lawyer may cobble; —these writers are continually pointing to the Herschels and the Stevensons, the Astors and the Angelos, and telling the

young that *they*, too, may shine as stars in the firmament of
art, science, or mammon, provided that they will scorn delights,
" outwatch the bear," concentrate their energies, and convert
their intellectual diamond dust into a diamond.

From the general spirit of these appeals, one would suppose
the writers to believe that every human being at birth is poten-
tially a Shakespeare or a Newton, and that, provided he is
educated properly, and labours long and hard enough, he may
astonish the world with " Hamlets" and " Principias." Genius
these writers are fond of defining with Buffon as " patience,"
and they will quote to you with gusto the saying of Newton,
that, if he differed from other men, it was only by " patient
thought."   A great orator, like Clay or Chatham; a wondrous
musical composer, like Handel or Rossini; a great architect
of buildings, like Wren, or a more marvellous architect of
periods, like De Quincey,—all the great lights of physical science,
the superior intelligences of art and literature,—have attained
to eminence by steps easily traceable by themselves, and which
all other men may follow, if they will but concentrate their
efforts upon one point, and not fritter away their resources in
a variety of pursuits.   Let us, it is said, but search into and
analyze the causes of that excellence which in its intensity has
dazzled and confounded us,—let us but trace it through the
various minor stages through which it has passed to its present
summit of power,—and we shall find that to labour unceasing
does it owe its splendour, and that under similar circumstances,
with equal advantages of culture, equal incentives, and as firm
a will, there are few persons who could not present the same
result.   Shelley, we may infer, hardly exaggerated when he
said that the Almighty had given men arms long enough to
reach the stars, if they would only put them out. *If* the young
man will but exert himself to the utmost, say these writers,
there is no height of greatness to which he may not soar.   Ah !
but how immense is that " if !"   It is the castle in which these
possible Mirabeaus, unlike the thunderer of the French tribune,
are always confined.   " If my aunt had been a man, she would
have been my uncle !"   They forget, who talk thus, that the
power of patient labour was the very *essence* of Newton's genius ;
that continuity and concentration of thought are in exact proportion to the size and vitality of the thinking principle.

What a man *does* is the real test of what a man *is ;* and to talk of what great things one would accomplish, *if* he had more activity of mind, is to say how strong a man would be if he only had more strength ; or how swiftly a steamer would cut the waves, if she only had a bigger boiler, or could generate steam fast enough !

It is easy to theorize as to what men might become, *if* they were something different from what they are. Give a man the mental energy, the spiritual force of Newton, and he may unquestionably do as great things as Newton. Give a dog the muscular strength, the physical qualities of the lion, and he will be as terrible as the monarch of the forest ; or, *vice versa,* make the lion cease to be carnivorous in his instincts, and he will be a pleasant playfellow for your dogs and children.

All experience shows that it is the nature of genius to labour patiently, and hence it is easy to leap to the conclusion that genius is but patient labour. But though genius is essentially active, and will labour, though not always by square, rule and compass, it is the falsest of notions that will can do the work of intellect, that effort can supply genius, and that mere intensity of desire can give intensity of power. As well might the tortoise hope, by intense striving, to run as fast as the greyhound, the truck-horse to rival Dexter in fleetness, or the monkey to acquire the strength of the elephant. It is perhaps doubtful whether any great intellectual thing was ever done by great effort ; a great thing can be done only by a great *man,* and he does it without effort. Hazlitt goes so far as to say that "an *improving* actor never becomes a great one. I have known such in my time, who were always advancing by slow and sure steps to the height of their profession ; but in the meantime some man of genius rose, and, passing them, at once seized on the topmost round of ambition's ladder, so that they still remained in the second class." As the same acute writer further adds, a volcano does not give warning when it will break out, nor a thunderbolt send word of its approach. Kean stamped himself the first night in Shylock ; he never did it any better. A man of genius is *sui generis ;* to be known, he needs only to be seen ; you can no more dispute whether he is one, than you can dispute whether it is a panther that is shown you in a cage.

Neither do great occasions make great men,—as our late civil war and the struggle of France with Prussia too painfully prove. Great occasions are the necessities only for which great men are the supplies. Great men even make great occasions ; nay more, they *are* great occasions, the great events of history ; " not merely the beacon lights on the line of human progress, but the efficient motive-powers, the *causæ causantes ;* they make, they constitute history." There was never a truer sentiment uttered than that quoted some years ago, at a scientific meeting in England, by Professor Owen, from the note-book of the late Dr. Hunter, namely, that no man was ever a great man who *wanted* to be one. To achieve any species of greatness, we must be utterly unconscious of the way we arrive at it. It is not to be acquired by " malice prepense." As well might one by taking thought add a cubit to his stature. Great works do not make greatness ; they only reveal it. They are the outgoings of an inward being ; they are the embodiments of the soul, which was *born great.* The greatest works of human genius were written, not to immortalize their authors, but to provide for some practical need. Homer sang, partly to kindle patriotism in his countrymen, partly, perhaps, to get a good night's lodging as he wandered on the shores of Greece and Asia ; Shakespeare wrote his dramas, not for glory, but to " put money in his purse ;" Hooker's great work was composed to quiet the strifes of his time ; and the masterpiece of Burke, on which he lavished such a prodigality of thought, was thrown out as a bastion to protect the British citadel from French republicanism. So in all other callings. When the Duke of Wellington carried out any of his great strategetical operations in Spain, or put the keystone to the arch of his glory at Waterloo, think you he was dreaming of a star and a garter ? No ; he thought only of giving the French a sound thrashing.

It is well known that hero-worshippers are almost universally disappointed in President Grant. The closest scrutiny of his features or manner fails to detect any signs of genius in him. Senator Yates well observed in a speech, that the genius of General Grant " is not ostentatious nor dramatic. It is *the genius of accomplishment* that he has. When his work is done, there it is, done ; and there is the man, except for the work, ordinary as before." Such men are content *to do,* and leave their glory to take care of itself.

Paradoxical as this may all seem, it is nevertheless true, nor does it offer any encouragement to idleness, or flatter the conceit of heaven-descended genius in turn-down collars, that labour may be dispensed with. It simply says that the crow is not the eagle, and that no amount of sun-starings will make it one; therefore, as an able writer, himself a man of brilliant genius, has said, "It is no man's business whether he has genius or not; work he must, whatever he is, but quietly and steadily, and the natural and unforced results of such work will be always the things that God meant him to do, and will be his best. No agonies, nor heart-rendings, will enable him to do any better! If he be a great man, they will be great things; if he is a small man, small things; but always, if thus peacefully done, good and right; always, if restlessly and ambitiously done, false, hollow, and despicable."

The writers who talk of the great things that may be achieved by a determined will—by an intense, continuous act of volition to do and to be such and such things—forget that this power of willing strongly is, to a large extent, a gift of nature, and as rare as any other good thing in the world. Again, while some pre-eminently successful men have pursued paths previously marked out, many have proposed to themselves no distant goal to be reached. As a sensible writer says: "A man starts on his career with a tacit understanding with himself that he is to rise. It is a step-by-step progress. He probably has no distinct aim. It is only in books that he resolves from the first dawning of ambition to become owner of such an estate, or bishop of such a see. But he *means to get on*, and devotes all his powers to that end. He fixes his thought beyond immediate self-indulgence, chooses his friends as they will help the main design, falls in love on the same principle, and, habitually deferring to a vague but glowing future, learns to work towards it, and for its sake to be self-denying and long-sighted. His instincts quicken; he puts forth feelers, which men who take their pleasure from hand to mouth have no use for; he lives in habitual caution, with an eye always to the main chance. Thus he refines and enhances that natural discretion which doubles the weight and value of every other gift, and yet keeps them on an unobtrusive level, leaving itself the most notable quality, till he is universally pronounced the man made to get on by people who do not know that it is a steady will that has made and kept him what he is."

The truth is, men differ from birth in mind as they differ in body, though in each case the differences may be modified to a certain degree by training, regimen, and so forth. But is there anything in this truth to discourage the young man who is anxious to get on in the world? By no means. No man knows what are his powers, whether he is capable of great or only of little things, till he has tested himself by actual trial. Let every beginner in life put forth his whole strength, without troubling himself with the question whether he has genius or not; then, as Sir Joshua Reynolds says, "if he has great talents, industry will improve them; if he has but moderate abilities, industry will supply their deficiency." The more limited your powers, the greater need of effort; the smaller the results of your efforts, the greater need that they should be repeated. The mediocre capacity must be eked out by brave resolve and persistent effort. The Spartan youth who complained to his mother that his sword was too short, was told to add a step to it; and so must your scant capacity be increased by redoubled diligence and a more earnest determination. If it be not true that, as Sir Joshua Reynolds says, "nothing is denied to well-directed labour," it is certain that, as he further says, "nothing is to be obtained without it." To large extent, as William Penn declares, "industry supplies the want of parts; patience and diligence, like faith, remove mountains." "There lives not a man on earth, out of a lunatic asylum," says Sir Edward Bulwer Lytton, and the words should ring in every young man's ears, "who has not in him the power to do good. What can writers, haranguers, or speculators do more than that? Have you ever entered a cottage, ever travelled in a coach, ever talked with a peasant in the field, or loitered with a mechanic at the loom, and not found that each of those men had a talent you had not, knew some things you knew not? The most useless creature that ever yawned at a club, or counted the vermin on his rags, under the suns of Calabria, has no excuse for want of intellect. What men want is, not talent, it is purpose; in other words, not the power to achieve, but the will to labour."

There is, perhaps, no mistake of the young more common than that of supposing that, in the pursuits of life, extraordinary talents are necessary to one who would achieve more than ordinary success. To minds that lack energy, it seems impossible to believe that those persons who have made themselves a place in history by their connection with striking events, and whose influence has been felt through ages in the changes they have produced in the destinies of nations, have been men of ordinary intellectual calibre, and not possessed of that comprehensive grasp of the wholeness of things which embraces all their bearings and relations, and places a man in advance of the philosophy of his age. But the experience of the world is not so discouraging to its mediocre men. The spectacle of triumphant mediocrity is exhibited daily; and every man of great intellectual capacity, who has made the observation of his fellow-creatures his business during an extended career, must have had frequent occasion to be forcibly struck by the successes of eminent persons whose abilities, in comparison with his own, appeared to striking advantage. The wants of society raise thousands to distinction who are not possessed of uncommon endowments. The utility of actions to mankind is the standard by which they are measured, and not the intellectual supremacy which is established by their performance. But very ordinary abilities will suffice to make a man eminently useful; and surpassing talents have frequently been unserviceable in proportion as they were objects of admiration. Nor has it escaped the notice of any close observer of human affairs, that, in numerous instances, men are pushed forward by events over which they have no control. It often happens that schemes work out their own execution, and that benignant fortune obviates astounding deficiencies and extravagant blunders. Besides, worldly success depends less on the general superiority of one's intellectual powers, than on their peculiar adaptation to the work in hand. A moderate talent well applied will achieve more useful results, and impose more on mankind, than minds of the highest order, whose temper is too fine for the mechanical parts of a profession. The astonishing variety of talents which some men display is purchased at the dear price of comparative feebleness in every part. The highest reputation in every department of human exertion is reserved for minds of one faculty, where no rival powers divide the empire of the soul, and where there is no variety of pursuits to distract and perplex its energies.

The life of Sir Francis Horner strikingly illustrates the truth we have tried to enforce. "The valuable and peculiar light in which Horner stands out," says Cockburn in his Memorials of this eminent Scotchman, "the light in which his history is calculated to inspire every right-minded youth, is this : he died at the age of thirty-eight, possessed of greater public influence than any other private man, and admired, beloved, trusted, and deplored by all except the heartless or the base. No greater homage was ever paid in Parliament to any deceased member. Now, let every young man ask, How was this attained ? By rank ? He was the son of an Edinburgh merchant. By wealth ? Neither he nor any of his relatives ever had a superfluous sixpence. By office ? He held but one, and only for a few years, of no influence, and with very little pay. By talents ? His were not splendid, and he had no genius; cautious and slow, his only ambition was to be right. By eloquence ? He spoke in calm good taste, without any of the oratory that either terrifies or seduces. By any fascination of manner ? His was only correct and agreeable. By what, then, was it ? Merely by sense, industry, good principles, and a good heart,—qualities which no well-constituted mind need ever despair of attaining. It was the force of his character that raised him, and this character not impressed upon him by nature, but formed out of no peculiarly fine elements by himself. Horner was born to show what moderate powers, unaided by anything whatever except culture and goodness, may achieve, even when these powers are displayed amidst the competition and jealousy of public life."

It is indeed wonderful with what slender qualifications one may, under favourable circumstances, attain success, and even fill a large space in society. The high reputation of many persons is acquired in a great measure by mere dexterity and cunning, by siding with prevailing opinions, or by flattering the prejudices of a powerful party. Besides, there is a discretion more valuable than the most extensive knowledge or the highest intellectual endowments. There are some men who give excellent advice touching the affairs of others, but who, from some inexplicable reason, show a total want of judgment in directing their own. They are useful when under able guidance, but, if let alone, plunge into some quagmire, and render useless the services they have already performed. We see other men, who, with comparatively slender talents, are the instruments of achieving more important results than are effected by men of far greater endowments. They know precisely the extent of their faculties, and never aim at objects beyond their reach. They carefully survey their means of success, and never fix their attention so strongly upon one point as to overlook others equally important. Never struggling obstinately against the stream, they are constantly ready, as the aspect of things changes, to vary their plans or remit their exertions, yet in all their variations they keep one object steadily in view. Preferring to play a small game rather than to stand out, and content with petty advances when a more rapid progress is impossible, they quicken their pace and enlarge their schemes as fortune favours, and, though unnoticed by the world, exert a more important influence over its destinies than many who have filled a larger space in the eye of mankind.

A still greater source of discouragement than the consciousness of mediocre abilities, to many beginners, is the feeling that there is no place for them in the great beehive of society. Looking about in the world, they see, or fancy they see, every place filled,—a complement of hands in every department of the great workshop, and, even if a vacant place for them could be found, a skilful workman has anticipated their best efforts ; so, like the rustic who waited for the river to run by, they hesitate to embark in any business, or embark without spirit or hope. Had they lived a little earlier or a little later in the world's history, they could have "got on" without difficulty, but not at this epoch. They could have won fame or a fortune half a century ago, could win it, perhaps, half a century later, but not at this unlucky time. Success, always a coy maiden, is now, when crowds of wooers have made her saucy, harder than ever to win. The would-be poet, it is said, is always labouring under this disorder. He always somehow falls on evil days. The good time is either past or to come ; it is never *now*. The truth is, however, that there is no occasion for these croakings, nor ever was at any period of the world's history. The world is a hard world, but in the long run it is an eminently just one. It is always groping about for men of ability and integrity to fill its places of responsibility, and those who have these qualifications, if they do not hide them from shyness, are almost sure to find employment. It always has been, and always will be, more difficult to find talents for the places than places for the talents. Human selfishness, where there are no other agencies at work, will not suffer men of ability to languish in idleness.

Do not despair, then, because to win the prizes of life you must struggle against many competitors. Dryden says that no man ever need fear refusal from any lady, if he only gives his heart to getting her; and the same is true of success. As Lady Mary Wortley Montagu used to say, "If you wish to get on, you must do as you would to get in through a crowd to a gate all are equally anxious to reach. Hold your ground and push hard. To stand still is to give up your hope." Give your energies to "the highest employment of which your nature is capable;" be alive; be patient; work hard; watch opportunities; be rigidly honest; hope for the best; and if you fail to reach the goal of your wishes, which is possible in spite of the utmost efforts, you will die with the consciousness of having done your best, which is, after all, the truest success to which man can aspire.

CHAPTER II.

GOOD AND BAD LUCK.

Le bien, nous le faisons ; le mal, c'est la fortune ;
On a toujours raison, le Destin toujours tort.—LA FONTAINE.

People do not very readily blame themselves. They call in a third party, like the mysterious sleeping partner of a money-lender, who always finds the money ; this third party is Fate or Destiny.—J. H. FRISWELL, *The Gentle Life.*

Quand il vous arrivera quelque grand malheur, examinez vous bien, et vous verrez qu'il y aura toujours un peu de votre faute.—LE SAGE.

Burden not the back of Aries, Leo, or Taurus with thy faults ; nor make Saturn, Mars, or Venus guilty of thy follies.—SIR THOMAS BROWNE.

Untoward accidents will sometimes happen ; but, after many, many years of thoughtful experience, I can truly say, that nearly all those who began life with me have succeeded or failed as they deserved.—RICHARD SHARP.

BEFORE proceeding to inquire what are the elements of success in life, it may be well briefly to discuss a question which starts up at the very threshold, namely, How far do men owe their success to their own merits, and how far to favouring circumstances or luck ? There are some persons who proverbially never get on in the world, whom Fortune seems to persecute with unrelenting cruelty from the cradle to the grave. If they were born rich, they contrive to become poor ; and if they begin poor, they have a knack of always remaining so, "holding their own" with remarkable steadiness through life. Perhaps they were born blockheads ; yet, even in that case, their blunders are so gross and glaring that it seems as if, like those of Foresight in one of Congreve's comedies, they must have required infinite study, consideration, and caution,— caution, lest by any chance they should deviate into sense. Dr. Johnson graphically described these persons in his account of the conversation of the elder Sheridan : "Why, sir, Sherry is dull, naturally dull ; but it must have taken him a great deal of pains to become what we now see him. Such an excess of stupidity is not in nature." Yet never will you extort from such persons the admission that their ill-success is their own fault. They ascribe it to their hard luck, to the rascality of the men they have confided in, to the improper organization of society, to anything but their own folly, indolence, or lack of brains.

Indeed, there is hardly a word in the vocabulary which is more cruelly abused than the word "luck." To all the faults and failures of men, their positive sins and their less culpable shortcomings, it is made to stand a godfather and sponsor. We are all Micawbers at heart, fancying that "something" will one day "turn up" for our good, for which we have never striven. Go talk with the bankrupt man of business, who has swamped his fortune by wild speculation, extravagance of living, or lack of energy, and you will find that he vindicates his wounded self-love by confounding the steps which he took indiscreetly with those to which he was forced by "circumstances," and complacently regarding himself as the victim of ill-luck. Go visit the incarcerated criminal, who has imbrued his hands in the blood of his fellow-man, or who is guilty of less heinous crimes, and you will find that, slumping the temptations which were easy to avoid with those which were comparatively irresistible, he has hurriedly patched up a treaty with conscience, and stifles its compunctious visitings by persuading himself that, from first to last, he was the victim of circumstances. Go talk with the mediocre in talents and attainments, the weak-spirited man who, from lack of energy and application, has made but little headway in the world, being outstripped in the race of life by those whom he had despised as his inferiors, and you will find that he, too, acknowledges the all-potent power of luck, and soothes his humbled pride by deeming himself the victim of ill-fortune. In short, from the most venial offence to the most flagrant, there is hardly any wrong act or neglect to which this too fatally convenient word is not applied as a palliation. It has been truly said that there is a fine generality in the expression,—a power of any meaning or no meaning,—which fits it for all purposes alike. It is the great permanent, non-papal, and self-granted indulgence of all mankind.

Now, that there is such a thing as luck—meaning by it the occasional operation of causes over which we have no control, though their influence is greatly exaggerated—is not to be denied. True as it may be generally that, as Shakespeare says,

> "It is not in our stars,
> But in ourselves, that we are underlings,"

yet it is equally true, as the same great moralist has qualified the sentiment, that

> "There's a divinity that shapes our ends,
> Rough-hew them how we will."

A De Moivre may calculate, with mathematical nicety, what he calls the "doctrine of chances;" but experience will falsify the calculation in perhaps five cases out of ten. The profound mathematician tells you that, if you throw the dice, it is thirty to one against your turning up a particular number, and a hundred to one against your repeating the same throw three times running; and so on, in an augmenting ratio. You take the box, and throw. At the first cast up comes the unlucky number, that beggars you, if a gambler; and you repeat it ten times running. An unskilful commander sometimes wins a victory; and again a famous warrior finds himself, "after a hundred victories, foiled." Some of the skilfullest sea-captains lose every ship they sail in ; others, less experienced, never lose a spar. Some men's houses take fire an hour after the insurance expires ; others never insure, and never are burned out. Some of the shrewdest men, with indefatigable industry and the closest economy, fail to make money ; others, with apparently none of the qualities that ensure success, are continually blundering into profitable speculations, and, Midaslike, touch nothing but it turns to gold. Beau Brummell, with his lucky sixpence in his pocket, wins at every gaming-table, and bags £40,000 in the clubs of London and Newmarket ; he loses his magic talisman and with it his luck, is plucked of his fortune, and obliged to fly to the Continent. The experience of a character in one of Cumberland's plays hardly burlesques an actual truth. "It is not upon slight grounds," says he, "that I despair. I have tried each walk, and am likely to starve at last. There is not a point to which the art and faculty of man can turn, that I have not set mine to, but in vain. I am beat through every quarter of the compass. I have blustered for prerogative ; I have bellowed for freedom ; I have offered to serve my country; I have engaged to betray it. Why, I have talked treason, writ treason; and if a man can't live by that, he can't live by anything. Here I set up as a bookseller, and people immediately leave off reading. If I were to turn butcher, I believe, o' my conscience, they'd leave off eating." On the other hand, the crazy-headed Lord Timothy Dexter sends a cargo of warming-pans to the West Indies, and lo! while everybody is laughing at him, it proves a brilliant adventure.

A writer in the " Edinburgh Review," in speaking of success at the bar, says, with much truth, that, when there is not legal business enough for all the profession, some must starve. An overstocked profession is like a crew trying to save themselves upon a raft scarcely large enough to carry half of them; or like the inmates of the Black Hole at Calcutta, where all who could not get near the aperture in the wall were suffocated, the survivors owing their safety as much to position and selfishness as to strength. Erskine once declared in Parliament that success oftener depended upon accident and certain physical advantages, than upon the most brilliant talent and the most profound erudition. A high-spirited and popular leader lately illustrated the matter thus: " When I look round upon my competitors, and consider my own qualifications, the wonder to me is, how I ever got the place I now occupy. I can only account for it by comparing the forensic career to one of the crossings in our great thoroughfares. You arrive just when it is clear, and get over at once; another finds it blocked up, is kept waiting, and arrives too late at his destination, *though the better pedestrian of the two.*"

So powerfully does Fortune appear to sway the destinies of men, putting a silver spoon into one man's mouth, and a wooden one into another's, that some of the most sagacious of men, as Cardinal Mazarin and Rothschild, seem to have been inclined to regard luck as the first element of worldly success; experience, sagacity, energy, and enterprise as nothing, if linked to an unlucky star. Whittington, and his cat that proved such a source of riches; the man who, worn out by a painful disorder, attempted suicide, and was cured by opening an internal imposthume; the Persian, condemned to lose his tongue, on whom the operation was so bunglingly performed

that it merely removed an impediment in his speech; the
painter who produced an effect he had long toiled after in vain,
by throwing his brush at the picture in a fit of rage and
despair; the musical composer, who, having exhausted his
patience in attempts to imitate on the piano a storm at sea,
accomplished the precise result by angrily extending his hands
to the two extremities of the keys, and bringing them rapidly
together,—all these seem to many fit types of the freaks of
Fortune by which some men are enriched or made famous by
their blunders, while others, with ten times the capacity and
knowledge, are kept at the bottom of her wheel. Hence we
see thousands fold their arms and look with indifference on the
great play of life, keeping aloof from its finest and therefore
most arduous struggles, because they believe that success is a
matter of accident, and that they may spend their heart's
choicest blood and affection on noble ends, yet be baulked of
victory, cheated of any just returns.

There is one curious fact noticeable in regard to this thing
called " luck," which is, that while it is made responsible for
any turn of affairs that we feel to be discreditable to us, it
rarely has credit for an opposite state of things; but, like most
other faithful allies in victory, comes poorly off. Every good
deed we do, every triumph we achieve, either in the battle-
field of the world or of our own hearts, is due to ourselves
alone. Stoutly as we may affirm that our disasters and vices
are chargeable to luck, we never dream of ascribing our meritorious deeds, in the slightest degree, to its agency. In such
cases we quite unconsciously blink out of sight the magic power
of the latter principle, so wondrous and all-controlling in its
influence at other times, and coolly appropriate to ourselves
not merely the lion's share, but the whole glory of our position.
We would, in fact, persuade the world, that, throughout, all
the circumstances were actually against us, but that by our
own stern resolve and heroic energy we crushed our way
through them. In cases like this, we act very much like the
English sailor in Joe Miller. Falling from the ship's topmast
upon deck without injury, he instantly jumped up, and, springing to the side of the vessel, called out to the crew of a Dutch
vessel near by, one of whom had performed some wonderful
feats in leaping, " Can any of you lubbers do anything like
that ?

The sum of the whole matter is this. Man is, to a considerable extent, the child of opportunity. Estimate as highly as we may the power of the individual in the achievement of success, there is yet another factor in the product, the power of circumstances, which we cannot wholly ignore. It has been remarked that the same tree that is soft and spongy in a fat swamp, with its heavy air, grows hard and noble on the hill-side. Spitzbergen forests are breast high, and Nova Scotia hemlocks mourn their cold wet sky in long weird shrouds of white moss As the acute French writer, M. Taine, says: "Nature, being a sower of men, and constantly putting her hand in the same sack, distributes over the soil regularly and in turn about the same proportionate quantity and quality of seed. But in the handfuls she scatters as she strides over time and space, not all germinate. A certain moral temperature is necessary to develop certain talents; if this is wanting, these prove abortive. Consequently, as the temperature changes, so will the species of talent change ; if it turn in an opposite direction, talent follows ; so that, in general, we may conceive moral temperature as *making a selection* among different species of talent, allowing only this or that species to develop itself, to the more or less complete exclusion of others."

Gray's musings on the Cromwells and Miltons of the village only exaggerate a real truth. There are times in every man's life when, if he were a pagan, he would incline to believe that his career is directed by an ironical fate which finds a certain pleasure in mocking his best plans and most strenuous efforts by an unexpected reverse ; when, finding himself baffled at every turn, he sits down in despair and says to himself, " It is useless to struggle in the meshes in which I am entangled ; all things have conspired against me ; I can never extricate myself, and the sooner I cease to fight against destiny the better." The ancients fully believed in destiny. "Some people," says Pliny, " refer their successes to virtue and ability; but it is all fate." Alexander depended much upon his luck, and Plutarch tells us that Sulla was so lucky that the surname of " Fortunate" was given him. Cicero speaks of the luck of Fabius Maximus, Marcellus, Scipio, and Marius as a settled thing. "It was not only their courage," he says, "but their fortune, which induced the people to entrust them with the command of their armies. For there can be little doubt but that, besides their great abilities, there was a certain *Fortune* appointed to attend upon them, and to conduct them to honour and renown, and to uncommon success in the management of important affairs." Cæsar believed in his own good luck, and told the Pilot in the storm, *Cæsarem portas et fortunam ejus,* —" You carry Cæsar and his good fortune." Some of the greatest modern generals have agreed with Bacon that " outward accidents conduce much to fortune." Marlborough, who planned his battles so carefully, talked more than once about his destiny, Cromwell had his lucky days, of which his birthday, when he gained two great battles, was one ; and Nelson had his white days and his black ones.

When we see Mahomet flying from his enemies, saved by a spider's web ; when we think that a Whig Ministry was hurled from power in England by the spilling of some water on a lady's gown ; when we find a Franklin ascribing his turn of thought and conduct through life to the accident of a tattered copy of Cotton Mather's " Essays to do Good" falling into his hands, and Jeremy Bentham attributing similar effects to a single phrase, " The greatest good of the greatest number," that caught his eye at the end of a pamphlet ; when we see a Bruce pass through a series of perils greater than any which the most daring romance-writer or melodramatist ever imagined for his hero, and then perish from a fall in handing a lady down stairs after dinner, and a Speke accidentally shoot himself in England, after escaping innumerable dangers in penetrating to the furtive and reedy fountains of the Nile ; when we find that one man may suck an orange and be choked by a pip, another swallow a penknife and live ; one run a thorn into his hand and die, in spite of the utmost efforts of medical skill, another recover, after a shaft of a gig has run completely through his body,—we cannot help believing, with Solomon, who, doubtless, had himself witnessed many such grim antitheses of life and death, that time and chance happen to all men, and that circumstances have much to do with every man's career in life. " We talk of life as a journey," says Sydney Smith ; " but how variously is that journey performed ! There are those who come forth girt, and shod, and mantled, to walk on velvet lawns and smooth terraces, where every gale is

arrested and every beam is tempered. There are others who walk
on the Alpine paths of life, against driving misery, and through
stormy sorrows, over sharp afflictions ; walk with bare feet and
naked breast, jaded, mangled, and chilled.''

The degree in which fame—one of the prizes of life for which
men struggle—is dependent on accident, sometimes the result
even of ill-luck, is strikingly illustrated by the fate of Sir John
Moore. " He had fought," says a writer in the "Dublin University Magazine," " as other generals had, had his successes as
well as his reverses, and had just kept his head above water
before the advancing army of Soult. On the walls of Corunna
he met his fate, and might have lain there, as hundreds of others
did, in an unrecorded grave, to this hour and to all future ages,
had not an ordinary Irish parson, from a remote country parish,
and from amid common prosaic pursuits, caught a glance, in his
imagination, of the lifeless warrior, as he was hurried to a hasty
grave, in the silence of the night, within the sound of the advancing enemy's guns. The look was enough,—the picture was
taken, with its full significance of pathos, into the heart of the
poet; and, when it reappeared, it was found to have been incrusted with amber, thereafter never more to pass away. It is
true, little ceremony was observed at that burial—

' Not a drum was heard, nor a funeral note ; '

but the lyre was struck, and the echoes went forth to the ends
of the earth ; and so Sir John Moore passed, by the narrow
channel of those few hasty and careless stanzas, from the shores
of oblivion, where he would have wandered till doomsday with
thousands of unrecorded comrades, to those same Isles of the
Blest, wherein, as we have already observed, the favourite
heroes of all ages have pitched their tents and exalted their
standard."

It cannot be denied, therefore, that there is, in the sense
already explained, an element of chance in human affairs to
which success or failure is sometimes owing. But, while
circumstances may make or mar a man, it is equally true that
he may often make his circumstances. Admitting that luck or
fortune, which are but other names for unforeseen and uncontrollable circumstances, does sometimes shape our destinies, yet
it would be easy to show that, in nine times out of ten, it is a

mere bugbear of the idle, the languid, and the self-indulgent. Two men may seem to adopt the same means to attain the same end, and, because one succeeds and the other fails, we say that the one is more fortunate than the other. But the one succeeds and the other fails because they do not really adopt the same means towards the same end. Of the two pilgrims who started on their journey each with peas in his shoon, it has been justly said that "the one was not more fortunate than the other; he was simply more wise. The man who sank by the way, toil-worn and foot-sore, with drops of agony on his forehead, groaning with pain, may have been the better walker of the two. The race is not always to the swift, nor the battle to the strong. It is by the right application of your swiftness or your strength to the particular object in view that you make your way to success." It is not enough to do the right thing, but we must do it in the right way, and at the right time, if we would achieve great triumphs in life. Again, the "circumstances," of which so many complain, should be regarded as the very tools with which we are to work, the stepping-stones we are to mount by. They are the wind and tide in the voyage of life, which the skilful mariner always calculates upon, and, generally, either takes advantage of or overcomes. The true way to conquer circumstances is to be a greater circumstance to yourself. As Burke says, "You have only to get into the trade-wind, and you will sail secure over the Pactolean sands." "Common sense," says Wendell Phillips, "plays the game with the cards it has. Common sense bows to the inevitable, and makes use of it. It does not ask an impossible chess-board, but takes the one before it, and plays the game." Instead of bemoaning our hard lot, or the unfavourable circumstances under which we are compelled to act, we must put forth the *vivida vis animi* of him

> " Who breaks his birth's invidious bar,
>   And grasps the skirts of happy chance,
>   And breasts the blows of circumstance,
>   And grapples with his evil star."

We must place ourselves *en rapport* with the circumstances ; strike with, not against, the forces of nature, as the pile-driver does when it deals its mighty blows.

Mr. Galton, in his work on Hereditary Genius, observes : "I believe that if the 'eminent' men of any period had been changelings when babies, a very fair proportion of those who survived and retained their health up to fifty years of age would, notwithstanding their altered circumstances, have equally risen to eminence. Thus, to take a strong case, it is incredible that any combination of circumstances could have repressed Lord Brougham to the level of undistinguished mediocrity. If a man is gifted with vast intellectual power, eagerness to work, and power of working, I cannot comprehend how such a man should be repressed. The world is always tormented with difficulties waiting to be solved, struggling with ideas and feelings to which it can give no adequate expression. If, then, there exists a man capable of solving those difficulties, or of giving a voice to those pent-up feelings, he is sure to be welcomed with universal acclamation. We may almost say that he has only to put his pen to paper and the thing is done."

The part which luck plays in relation to human success is strikingly illustrated in the case of the celebrated advocate, Thomas Erskine. When he began his career, his prospects were far from encouraging. Without means, and without professional or social connections, he looked forward probably to a weary probation upon the back benches of the court, among the horde of nameless and briefless juniors, lingering like ghosts upon the banks of the Styx, waiting wearily for a passage over the river. He had scarcely a shilling in his pocket when he got his first retainer ; and that he would not have received, and consequently might not have risen to be Lord Chancellor, but for the fortunate sprain which caused him hastily to relinquish an intended visit, and return home, where he was waited on by a maritime gentleman, Captain Baillie, whose case he took up, mastered, and triumphantly conducted before Lord Mansfield. Even after the brief was handed to him, he might have had no opportunity to display his powers, had not a series of lucky circumstances favoured him. When the case came on, he found in the list of barristers retained the names of four senior counsel, and, despairing of being heard after so many predecessors, he gave himself no more trouble about the matter. But, fortunately, the affidavits

were so long, and some of the counsel so tedious—a tedious-
ness aggravated by the circumstance that one of them was
afflicted with strangury, and had to retire once or twice in
the course of his argument—that Lord Mansfield adjourned
the cause till the next morning, thus giving the young advocate a whole night to arrange his thoughts, and enabling him
to address the Court when its faculties were awake and fresh-
ened.   In alluding to this lucky incident, by which he was
enabled to make what Lord Campbell calls "the most wonderful forensic effort of which we have any account in British an-
nals," Erskine says: "I have since flourished, but I have
always blessed God for the providential strangury of poor
Hargrave."   Rarely has a brilliant start in life—perhaps the
whole success of a life—been owing to so many lucky accidents ; but who does not see that all these would have been of
no advantage to the young barrister, had he been unequal to
the occasion; had he not, by previous hard study, self-train-
ing, and self-sacrifice, prepared himself to take advantage of
the accidents which brought him into notice ?
In the life of the most unlucky person there are always
some occasions when, by prompt and vigorous action, he may
win the things he has at heart.   Raleigh flung his laced jacket
into a puddle and won a proud queen's favour.   A village
apothecary chanced to visit the state apartments at the Pavi-
lion, when George the Fourth was seized with a fit.   He bled
him, brought him back to consciousness, and, by his genial
and quaint humour, made the king laugh.   The monarch took
a fancy to him, made him his physician, and made his fortune.
Probably no man ever lives to middle age to whom two or
three such opportunities do not present themselves.   "There
is nobody," says a Roman Cardinal, "whom Fortune does not
visit once in his life; but when she finds he is not ready to
receive her, she goes in at the door, and out through the window."   Opportunity is coy.   The careless, the slow, the unob-
servant, the lazy, fail to see it, or clutch at it when it is gone.
The sharp fellows detect it instantly, and catch it when on the
wing.   It is not enough, however, to seize opportunity when
it comes.   We must not be content with waiting for "something to turn up ;" we must try to *make* something turn up.
"We must not only strike the iron while it is hot, but strike
it till it is made hot."

It is a popular idea that great inventions are the result of what is called "lucky hits," that chance has more to do with them than head-work. It is true that the very greatest inventions are the simplest, and that the truths on which they are founded seem obvious. But familiar and commonplace as they may appear, we must remember that the veil, flimsy and transparent as it may now seem, when a school-boy's hand can lift it, was yet sufficient to conceal these truths for centuries. As Professor Whewell has truly said, "No man who fairly considers the real nature of great discoveries, and the intellectual processes which they involve, can seriously hold the opinion of their being the effect of accident. Such accidents never happen to common men. Thousands of men, even the most inquiring and speculative, had seen bodies fall; but who, except Newton, ever followed the accident to such consequences?" Buffon, another competent authority, tells us that invention, so far from being accidental, depends on patience. "Contemplate your subject long. It will gradually unfold itself, till a sort of electric spark convulses the brain for a moment, and sends a glow of irritation to the heart. Then comes the luxury of genius."

Cardinal Richelieu was not glaringly wrong, therefore, in the opinion that an unfortunate and an imprudent person are synonymous terms. Every man is placed, in some degree, under the influence of events and of other men; but it is for himself to decide whether he will rule, or be ruled by them. They may operate powerfully against him at times; but rarely so as to overwhelm him, if he bears up manfully, and with a stout, dogged will. In the battle of life we may be drawn as conscripts, but our courage or our cowardice, our gentleness or our cruelty, depends upon ourselves. "The Admiralty," wrote Nelson, when expecting to command the finest fleet in the world, "may order me a cock-boat, but I will do my duty." It is now admitted that the English were not lucky in the Russian war, simply because they hesitated. A gunboat with a will behind it, according to high military authority, would at one time have settled the matter; England had a fleet, but not a will. "In one respect," said the French Admiral Coligni, "I may claim superiority over Alexander, over Scipio, over Cæsar. They won great battles, it is true; I have lost four great battles, and yet I show to the enemy a more formidable front than ever." The man who shows this spirit will triumph over fortune in the end. Like cork, he may be submerged for a while, but he cannot be kept down. De Quincey justly remarks of Cæsar, that the superb character of his intellect throws a colossal shadow, as of predestination, over the most trivial incidents of his career. But it was simply through the perfection of his preparations, arrayed against all conceivable contingencies, and which make him appear like some incarnate providence, veiled in a human form, ranging through the ranks of the legions, that he was enabled to triumph over Pompey, whom Cicero had pronounced " the *semper felix*,"—always lucky,—when he recommended him to the Roman Senate as the best man to crush the pirates.

No doubt that, as Byron said, sometimes

> " Men are the sport of circumstances, when
> The circumstances seem the sport of men."

" Favour, opportunity, the death of others, and occasion fitting virtue," have often been, as Bacon says, stepping-stones to success. Sulla thought it better to be lucky than great. Really " lucky fellows " there have always been in the world ; but in a great majority of cases they who are called such will be found on examination to be those keen-sighted men who have surveyed the world with a scrutinizing eye, and who to clear and exact ideas of what is necessary to be done unite the skill necessary to execute their well-approved plans. If now and then a crazy-headed man, as in the instance already mentioned, sends a cargo of warming-pans to the West Indies, which, while everybody is laughing at his folly, proves a brilliant venture, the very fact that such a freak of fortune excites remark proves its infrequency. It is an interesting fact that Wellington, who never lost a battle, never spoke of luck, though no man guarded more carefully against all possible accidents, or was prompter to turn to account the ill-fortune of an adversary. Napoleon, on the other hand, believed in his star. He was the Man of Destiny, the picked, the chosen. " People talk of my crimes," said he ; " but men of my mark do not commit crimes. What I did was a necessity ; I was the child of destiny !" But who can doubt that it was for that very reason, that, when once the

tide of fortune turned against him, a few years of trouble sufficed to kill him, where such a man as Wellington would have
melted St. Helena rather than have given up the ghost with a
full stomach?

Let no one, then, repine because the fates are sometimes
against him; but when he trips or falls, let him, like Cæsar when
he stumbled on the shore, stumble forward, and, by escaping
the omen, change its nature and meaning. Remembering that
those very circumstances which are apt to be abused as the pal-
liative of failure are the true test of merit, let him gird up his
loins for whatever in the mysterious economy of the world
may await him. Thus will he gradually rise superior to ill-
fortune, and becoming daily more and more impassive to its attacks, will learn to force his way in spite of it, till at last he
will be able to fashion his luck to his will. "Life is too short,"
says a shrewd thinker, "for us to waste its moments in deplor-
ing bad luck; we must go after success, since it will not come
to us, and we have no time to spare."

CHAPTER III.

CHOICE OF A PROFESSION.

It is an uncontroverted truth, that no man ever made an ill-figure who understood his own talents, nor a good one who mistook them.—SWIFT.

The crowning fortune of a man is to be born with a bias to some pursuit, which finds him in employment and happiness.—R. W. EMERSON.

Be what nature intended you for, and you will succeed ; be anything else, and you will be ten thousand times worse than nothing.—SYDNEY SMITH.

I cannot repeat too often that no man struggles perpetually and victoriously against his own character ; and one of the first principles of success in life is so to regulate our career as rather to turn our physical constitution and natural inclinations to good account, than to endeavour to counteract the one or oppose the other.—SIR H. L. BULWER.

IT is almost a truism to say that the first thing to be done by him who would succeed in life is to make a wise choice of a profession. Of the thousands of men who are continually coming upon the stage of life, there are few who escape the necessity of adopting some profession or calling ; and there are fewer still who, if they knew the miseries of idleness, tenfold keener and more numerous than those of the most laborious profession, would ever desire such an escape. In this age of intense activity when hundreds of men in every community are killing themselves by overwork, it is hardly necessary to show that there can be no genuine happiness without labour. All sensible men admit, and none more readily than those who have tried the experiment of killing time in a round of amusements, that the happiest life is made up of alternations of toil and leisure, of work and play. So necessary is labour of some kind to make existence tolerable, that those men who attempt to live a life of idleness are forced eventually *to make* work for themselves ; they turn their very pleasures into toil, and, from mere lack of something to do, engage in the most arduous and exhausting pastimes. To escape from the miseries of ennui, they resort to the most pitiful contrivances to cheat themselves into the illusion that they are busy. Their very amusements

are encumbered by regulations, and their pleasures, which are
converted into tasks, are made formal and heavy. The most
trifling acts and occurrences are treated as of the gravest importance; and the rules of etiquette are enforced by the severest
penalties. The man of leisure is thus transformed into the
most bustling, anxious repository of little paltry cares and
petty crotchets; and when the night comes it is with a sense
of relief, but very different from that of the worker, that he
reflects that

> "Be the day weary, or be the day long,
> At length it ringeth to evensong."

It is true that not a few men kill themselves by overwork;
but the portion of such is small to the number who die from
violating the laws of health; and death from excessive activity
is far preferable to death from rust. The spirits may be
exhausted by employment, but they are utterly destroyed by
idleness. Burton, in his quaint old work, in summing up the
causes of melancholy, reduces them to two, solitariness and
idleness. When Charles Lamb was set free from the desk in
the India Office, to which he had been chained for years, he
was in an ecstacy of joy. "I would not go back to my prison,'
he exclaimed to a friend, "for ten years longer, for ten thousand pounds." "I am free! free as air!" he wrote to Bernard
Barton; "I will live another fifty years. . . . . Positively the
best thing a man can do is—nothing; and next to that, perhaps, good works." Two weary years passed, and Lamb's feelings had undergone a complete revolution. He had found that
leisure, though a pleasant garment to look at, is a very bad one
to wear. He had found that his humdrum task, the seemingly
dreary drudgery of desk-work, was a blessing in disguise. "I
assure you," he again writes to Barton "*no* work is worse than
overwork; the mind preys on itself, the most unwholesome of
food. I have ceased to care for almost anything." Persons of
naturally active minds, whose "quick thoughts like lightning
are alive," are the first to feel the pernicious effects of indolence.
How many such, cursed with too much leisure, take too much
of something else to make their gloom deeper and their mis-
fortunes more! An old divine says truly that the human
heart is like a millstone; if you put wheat under it, it grinds

the wheat into flour; if you put no wheat, it grinds on, but then it is itself it wears away. Colton observes that ennui made more gamblers than avarice, more drunkards than thirst, and more suicides than despair. Muley Ismail, a famous tyrant, always employed his troops in some active and useful work when not engaged in war, to keep them, he said, "from being devoured by the worm of indolence." Count de Caylus, a French nobleman, being born to wealth and princely idleness, turned his attention to engraving, and made many fine copies of antique gems. "I engrave," said he, "that I may not hang myself." Old Dumbiedikes wisely charged his son to be "aye sticking in a tree when he had nothing else to do;" and in the same vein is the advice of an Elizabethan poet :—

> "Eschew the idle vein,
> Flee, flee from doing naught!
> For never was there idle brain
> But bred an idle thought."

It is not easy, however, for a young man to realize this; and hence the time when they shall leave their father's house, and minister with their own hands to their necessities, is looked forward to by many with dislike and dread. Yet it will come, and it is highly important that he who would make the most of life should lose no time in indecision, but promptly determine to what calling he will give his energies.

The Latin poet, Horace, advises authors, in choosing a subject to write upon, to select one just equal to their strength, and to ponder long and deeply what their shoulders will bear. Equally essential is it to worldly success in general, that one should choose a calling to which his abilities are fitted. Without going the length of Hazlitt, who affirms that, if a youth shows no aptitude for languages, but dances well, it would be better to give up ideas of scholarship for him, and hand him over to the dancing-master, we yet deem that profession best for every man which chords most nearly with the bent of his mind, and which he can embrace without compromise of his social standing. To no other cause, perhaps, is failure in life so frequently to be traced as to a mistaken calling. A youth who might become a first-rate mechanic chances to have been

D

born of ambitious parents, who think it more honourable for their son to handle the lancet than the chisel, and so would make him a doctor. Accordingly he is sent to college, pitch-forked through a course of Latin and Greek, attends lectures, crams for an examination, gets a diploma, and, with "all his blushing honours thick upon his vacant head," settles down to kill people scientifically,—to pour, as Voltaire said, drugs of which he knows little into bodies of which he knows less,—till his incapacity is discovered, when he starves. In another case, a boy is forced by unwise parents to measure tape and calico, when writs and replevins are written in every lineament of his physiognomy, and Nature shows by his intellectual acumen,—by his skill in hair-splitting, his adroitness at parry and thrust, his fertility of resources in every exigency, and a score of other signs,—that she designed him not to handle the yard-stick, but to thunder in the forum. Or, again, a skilful engineer is spoiled in a shoemaker, or a lad designed for a shoemaker is trained for the literary profession, reminding you of Lessing's sarcasm :—

> " Tompkins forsakes his last and awl
>   For literary squabbles ;
>   Styles himself poet ; but his trade
>   Remains the same,—he cobbles."

In no other calling is the proportion of failures to successes so great as in that of trade, the mercantile profession. Persons who have been at pains to collect statistics on this subject in our large towns have found that only three out of a hundred merchants are successful ; all the others becoming bankrupt, or retiring in disgust. Why is this ? Is it, in every case, because they are overwhelmed by sudden disaster, which no sagacity could have anticipated or warded off? because they are dishonest, and, after long overreaching others, are overreached themselves? because after many brilliant winnings at the gaming-table, they stake all, and lose all ? because, after partial success, they expect greater, and build marble palaces, drive "two-forty" horses, and make larger investments in champagne suppers than in bonds and mortgages ? Is it because Shylock eats them up with his two per cent., or because of the exploded folly in some new form of investing in eternal lottery tickets, and drawing eternal blanks? No; these causes are only the result of a more radical cause, namely, that they have gone into business without business brains. No father, as a general thing, educates his son to be a musician, without first making sure that he has a natural ear for music. But hundreds and thousands of fathers make merchants of their sons, who have no more actual fitness for trade than has a man to play at the Academy of Music who cannot distinguish a flat from a sharp, or the "Heroic Symphony" from the tune of "Old Hundred."

Above all, the notion that the "three black graces," Law, Physic, and Divinity, must be worshipped by the candidate for respectability and honour, has done incalculable damage to society. It has spoiled many a good carpenter, done injustice to the sledge and the anvil, cheated the goose and the shears out of their rights, and committed fraud on the corn and the potato field. Thousands have died of broken hearts in these professions,—thousands who might have been happy at the plough, or opulent behind the counter; thousands, dispirited and hopeless, look upon the healthful and independent calling of the farmer with envy and chagrin; and thousands more, by a worse fate still, are reduced to necessities which degrade them in their own estimation, rendering the most brilliant success but a wretched compensation for the humiliation with which it is accompanied, and compelling them to grind out of the miseries of their fellow-men the livelihood which is denied to their legitimate exertions. The result of all this is, that the world is full of men who, disgusted with their vocations, getting their living by their weakness instead of by their strength, are doomed to hopeless inferiority. "If you choose to represent the various parts in life," says Sydney Smith, "by holes in a table of different shapes,— some circular, some triangular, some square, some oblong,—and the persons acting these parts by bits of wood of similar shapes, we shall gene- rally find that the triangular person has got into the square hole, the oblong into the triangular, while the square person has squeezed himself into the round hole." A French writer on agriculture observes that it is impossible profitably to im- prove land by trying forcibly to change its natural character, —as by bringing sand to clay, or clay to sand. The only true

method is to adapt the cultivation to the nature of the soil.
So with the moral or intellectual qualities. Exhortation, self-
determination, may do much to stimulate and prick a man on
in a wrong career against his natural bent; but, when the
crisis comes, this artificial character thus laboriously induced
will break down, failing at the very time when it is most
wanted.

The sentiment, " Our wishes are presentiments of our capabilities," is a noble maxim, of deep encouragement to all true
men ; and it is not more encouraging than it is true. Can anything be more reasonable than to suppose that he who, in attending to the duties of his profession, can gratify the predominant
faculty, the reigning passion of the mind, who can strike

" The master-string
That makes most harmony or discord in him,"

will be, *cæteris paribus*, the most successful ? The very fact
that he has an original bias, a fondness and a predilection for a
certain pursuit, is the best possible guaranty that he will follow
it faithfully. His love for it, aside from all other motives, will
ensure the intensest application to it as a matter of course. No
need of spurs to the little Handel or the boy Bach to study
music, when one steals midnight interviews with a smuggled
clavichord in a secret attic, and the other copies whole books of
studies by moonlight, for want of a candle, churlishly denied.
No need of whips to the boy-painter, West, when he begins in
a garret, and plunders the family cat for bristles to make his
brushes. On the other hand, to spend years at college, at the
work-bench, or in a store, and then find that the calling is a
wrong one, is disheartening to all but men of the toughest fibre.
The discovery shipwrecks the feeble, and plunges ordinary minds
into despair. Doubly trying is this discovery when one feels
that the mistake was made in defiance of friendly advice, or to
gratify a freak of fancy or an idle whim. The sorrows that
come upon us by the will of God, or through the mistakes of
our parents, we can submit to with comparative resignation ;
but the sorrows which we have wrought by our own hand, the
pitfalls into which we have fallen by obstinately going our own
way, these are the sore places of memory which no time and no
patience can salve over.

And yet what "trifles, light as air," often decide a young man's calling, leading one to choose that for which nature designed him, another to choose the very one for which he has the least aptitude! It has been said of our race that we are "not only pleased, but turned by a feather; the history of man is a calendar of straws." The force of early impressions in determining the choice of a profession is often deep and controlling. Thus David Hume, who in his youth was a believer in Christianity, was appointed in a debating society to advocate the cause of infidelity, and thus familiarizing himself with the subtle sophisms of scepticism, became a life-long deist. Voltaire, it is said, at the age of five committed to memory a sceptical poem, and the impressions made upon his mind were never obliterated. There was an intimate connection between the little cannon and the mimic armies with which the boy Napoleon amused himself, and the martial achievements of the Emperor; between the miniature ship which Nelson, when a boy, sailed on the pond, and the victories of the Nile and Trafalgar; between the tales and songs about ghosts, fairies, witches, warlocks, wraiths, apparitions, etc., with which the mind of Burns was fed in his boyhood by the superstitious old woman domesticated under the same roof with himself, and the tale of Tam O'Shanter; between the old traditions and legends which formed the staple of Scott's early reading, and the brilliant fictions with which the "Wizard of the North" charmed the world; between the story of a farmer's son who went away to seek his fortune and came home after many years a rich man,—which George Law, a farmer's boy, found in an old, stray volume,—and the subsequent career of George Law the steamboat king and millionaire.

It is said of the great philanthropist, Thomas Clarkson, that when he was a competitor for a prize for an essay at Cambridge, he had never thought upon the subject to be handled, which was, "May one man lawfully enslave another?" Chancing one day to pick up in a friend's house a newspaper advertising a, History of Guinea, he hastened to London, bought the work, and there found a picture of cruelties that filled his soul with horror. "Coming one day in sight of Wade's mill, in Hertfordshire," he says, "I sat down disconsolate on the turf by the roadside, and held my horse. Here a thought came into my mind, that, if the contents of this essay were true, *it was time that some person should see those calamities to their end."* It was but a straw that decided the destiny of Demosthenes, when, burning with shame, he rushed from the Athenian assembly, resolved, doubtless, never again to ascend the *bema.* He met Satyrus, learned the art of elocution, and when he next addressed the people, his lip was roughened by no grit of the pebble. Again, Socrates, meeting Xenophon in a narrow gateway, checks his course by placing a stick across the path, and addresses to him a question in morals. Xenophon cannot answer, and the philosopher, bidding him follow, becomes thenceforward his master in ethics. "These incidents were shadows of leaves on the stream ; but they conducted Demosthenes into the temple of eloquence, and placed Xenophon by the side of Livy."

Let every one, then, who would get on in the world, study his aptitudes,—for what calling he is naturally fit. We are aware that some men, and men of sagacity, too, have denied this doctrine of natural tendencies, and held that any person, by dint of energy, may become whatever he chooses. Lord Chesterfield held this view. Any young man, he declared, if he will but take the pains, may become as learned, eloquent, graceful and agreeable as he pleases. Without the slightest reference to natural aptitude, he may confidently set about making himself a courtier, a diplomatist, an orator, in short, anything but a poet, and he need not utterly despair of success in verse. Acting on these principles, his Lordship laboured for years to mould his dull, heavy, loutish son, Stanhope, into a graceful man of fashion. A more absurd scheme was never attempted, and the result was what might have been expected, —utter failure. There are thousands of such cases where a parent might as well tell a son to be six feet high as to be eloquent, to have a Roman nose as to be graceful, to write like Hawthorne as to bow like the Duc de Richelieu. As Sainte-Beuve says : "On est toujours l'esclave de son premier talent." Doubtless the natural bent is sometimes hard to discern ; but as the boy is father of the man, so he generally shows what sort of a man he is likely to turn out. Talents for special kinds of work are congenital, and men have often their callings forecast in the very sockets of their eyeballs and in the bulgings of their thumbs. Even if we deny the whole doctrine of inborn aptitudes, and believe that the differences in men's capabilities, tastes, and tendencies are the effects of external circumstances, yet it must be admitted that these differences are fixed too early to be removed. Michael Angelo neglected school to copy drawings which he dared not bring home. Murillo filled the margin of his school book with drawings. Dryden read " Polybius" before he was ten years old. Le Brun, in childhood, drew with a piece of charcoal on the walls of the house. Pope wrote excellent verses at fourteen. Pascal composed at sixteen a tractate on the Conic Sections. Lawrence painted beautifully when a mere boy. Madame de Staël was deep in the philosophy of politics at an age when other girls were dressing dolls. Nelson had made up his mind to be a hero before he was old enough to be a midshipman ; and Napoleon was already at the head of armies when pelting snowballs at Crienne.

Dryden, who was an illustration of his own theory, has aptly marked the three steps in the career of most men of genius :—

" What the child admired,
The youth *endeavoured*, and the man ACQUIRED."

In many cases so early is the preference manifested, that it would seem as if the callings, impatient to be chosen, selected their own agents, and storming heart, hands, and brain, made them captive to their will. " We are not surprised," says a writer, " to hear from a schoolfellow of the Chancellor Somers that he was a weakly boy, who always had a book in his hand, and never looked up at the play of his companions ; to learn from his affectionate biographer that Hammond at Eton sought opportunities of stealing away to say his prayers ; to read that Tournefort forsook his college class, that he might search for plants in the neighbouring fields; or that Smeaton, in petticoats, was discovered on the top of his father's barn in the act of fixing the model of a windmill which he had constructed. These early traits of character are such as we expect to find in the cultivated lawyer, who turned the eyes of his age upon Milton ; in the Christian, whose life was one varied strain of devout praise ; in the naturalist, who enriched science by his discoveries ; and in the engineer, who built the Eddystone lighthouse."

When that prodigy of genius and precocity, Chatterton, "the marvellous boy, the sleepless soul, that perished in his pride," was but eight years old, a manufacturer, desiring to present him with a cup, asked him what device should be inscribed on it. "Paint me an angel," was the reply, "with wings and a trumpet, to trumpet my name over the world." So Ferguson's wooden clock; Davy's laboratory at Penzance; Faraday's electric machine, made with a bottle; Claud Lorraine's flour and charcoal pictures on the walls of the baker's shop; John Leyden's secret studies in the country church; Bacon's exposure of the defects of Aristotle's philosophy, made at the age of sixteen; Calhoun's subtle disputations in the class-room, with the President of Yale College; Chantrey's carving of his schoolmaster's head in a bit of pine wood,— were all hints of the future man. It is said that when Rachel, the actress, threw a tablecloth round her person, she was draped on the instant with a becomingness which all the *modistes* that ever fractured stay-lace, or circumlocuted crinoline, never imparted to the female figure before. She had a genius for it, as Brummell had for tying his cravat. Thousands choked themselves in imitating the Beau's knot, but in vain; the secret died with him, and is now among the lost arts.

Everybody knows what miracles of success were once achieved by the Jesuits in the education of youth. What was the secret of the astonishing influence they exercised over the world, but the sagacity they showed in placing each of their pupils in the sphere for which nature had specially organized him? Who can doubt that such a system of education, if adopted among us, would add immensely to the moral power of the republic? When the Scotch dominie concluded that David Wilkie "was much fonder of drawing than of reading, could paint much better than he could write," did he not show far more sagacity than if, possessed of the insane idea that Greek and Latin only can make a man, he had drilled and flogged until the youthful spirit had become soured and incapacitated for its themes of humour? If the boy Carnot, who cried out his disapprobation of some poor tactics in a military show on the stage, had been sent into a mine, we might never have known of the man who could direct, at one and the same time, the movements of fourteen armies. Had Mendelssohn's father discouraged, instead of carefully nurturing, that musical genius which, at the age of eight, detected, in a concerto of Bach, six of those dread offences against the grammar of music, consecutive fifths, we should never have believed that the tricksiness of Puck, the delicate grace of Titania, and the elvish majesty of Oberon could be so translated into music, as to form a perfect tone-picture of Shakespeare's dream. There is hardly any person who is not qualified to shine in *some* profession, and it is far better to be at the head of an inglorious calling than at the foot of one which the world calls respectable. Better be the Napoleon of boot-blacks, or the Alexander of chimney-sweeps, than a briefless and shallow-pated attorney, who, like necessity, " knows no law," watching vainly for victims in an unswept chamber, where " cobwebs in dusty magnificence hang," with no companions but the gaunt spider, a few dog-eared, bilious-looking volumes, and a stale political newspaper ; or become partner with Death, as the sulky rattles and squeaks on the highway, with barely acquirement enough in it to pass for doctor. Whatever nature intended you for, that be, if only a counter or tail-piece. Never desert your true sphere, your own line of talent. If Providence qualified you only to write couplets for sugar-horns, or to scribble editorials for the " Bunkumville Spread-Eagle," stick to the couplets or the editorials ; a good couplet for a sugar-horn is more respectable than a villanous epic poem in twelve books.

The fact that a youth who fails in one calling and at one kind of business may be eminently successful in another is well illustrated by an incident related in " Macmillan's Magazine." A young man, whose bluntness was such that every effort to turn him to account in a linen-drapery establishment was found unavailing, received from his employer the customary note that he would not suit, and must go. " But I'm good for something," remonstrated the poor fellow, loath to be turned out into the street. " You are good for nothing as a salesman," said the principal, regarding him from his selfish point of view. " I am sure I can be useful," repeated the young man. " How ? tell me how." " I don't know, sir ; I don't know." " Nor do I." And the principal laughed as he saw the eagerness of the lad displayed. "Only don't put me away, sir; don't put me away. Try me at something besides selling. I cannot sell, I know I cannot sell." "I know that, too; that is what is wrong." "But I can make myself useful somehow; I know I can." The blunt boy, who could not be turned into a salesman, and whose manner was so little captivating that he was nearly sent about his business, was accordingly tried at something else. He was placed in the counting-house, where his aptitude for figures soon showed itself, and in a few years he became not only chief cashier in the concern, but eminent as an accountant throughout the country.

It is true, as we have said before, that the proclivities of men are not always glaringly manifest in youth. Even the phœnixes of the race do not always come into the world under conditions prophetic of their particular and salient gifts. There are few millionaires who were born with "silver spoons in their mouths;" few warriors who can boast with Owen Glendower, that, at their nativity, "the front of Heaven was full of fiery shapes;" few jockeys, who, if asked whether they can ride on horseback, can answer with Mark Meddle, the dashing gentleman in "London Assurance," that they were born on horseback. Nor is unfitness for a calling marked, in all cases, as unmistakably as in that of John Adams, when his father, a shoemaker, undertook to teach him that craft. It is said that his parent one day gave him some "uppers" to cut out by a pattern that had a three-cornered hole in it, by which it had hung upon a nail; and it was found that the lad had followed the pattern exactly, triangular hole and all! It is true also, that vanity is apt to fool men here; and that young persons are exceedingly apt to overrate their abilities, or to mistake their quality; and you will, perhaps, cite the scores of prosaic youths who annually come to town with their carpet-bags bursting with romances or epics in twenty-four books, or will perhaps ask, Did not Liston imagine that he was born to play "Macbeth?" and did not Douglas Jerrold project a treatise on natural philosophy? Did not David, the painter, fancy he was cut out for a diplomatist? Did not Jonquil, who painted flowers and fruits so exquisitely, begin with enormous cartoons? And where is the Jones who has spouted in a debating club that does not imagine himself an embryo Clay, destined to electrify the United States Senate by his tremendous outbursts against some future Jackson or Van Buren? Doubtless mistakes are made, even more egregious than these; yet, after all deductions, the general truth remains that men are designed for particular callings, and that it is unwise to neglect those callings for others. Some boys are fitted for mechanical pursuits, others just as evidently for commercial. Scholastic pursuits disgust some, who yawn over every book in spite of the pedagogue's frown; while others, who have no taste for farming, or trading, or mechanical labour, are all alive when bending over a volume of history, or following pious Æneas in his wanderings, or watching the revelations of the microscope. Even where nature's indications are obscure, it is not safe to neglect them. The proclivities of the mind may be none the less strong, though latent, and it is the parent's duty to watch long and patiently till he is certain what they are. With the skill of a chemist, he must apply all the intellectual tests till they are exhausted; sometimes watching the mind's unrestrained seekings, sometimes bringing the world's stores, and laying them at its feet for a choice. The head of the Caxtons, in Bulwer's novel, will furnish him a hint here, worthy of a more practical head than that of a cloistered student. While directing his son's studies, he recollects that he had read, in a certain Greek writer, how some man, to save his bees a troublesome flight to Hymettus, cut their wings, and placed before them the finest flowers he could select. But the poor bees made no honey; so he determined that his young Pisistratus should search for his own honey.

Fortunately for the world, in men of great genius the bent of the mind is so strong that it is not in the power of foolish fathers to resist it. Long even before manhood, their souls are haunted by a certain object, which, like the ghost of Miltiades in the case of the Athenian statesman, will not let them sleep. They choose a particular pursuit, not because they deem it the best, because it promises the most glory, money, or happiness, but because they cannot help it, and for the same reason they adhere to it while life lasts. All they know is, that they love what they are about, and they give their whole souls to it accordingly. You may chain down their genius, for a while, to ungrateful, to menial tasks; but there comes a time at last, perhaps without any warning of revolt, when it will no longer consent " to harrow the valleys, or be bound with the band in the furrow ; " when "it laughs at the multitude of the city, and regards not the crying of the driver ; " when, sternly refusing longer to make ropes out of sand, it carves a statue, or paints a picture, or "builds the lofty rhyme," and you have an Apollo, a Madonna, or a Divine Comedy, as fate or inspiration directs. There was Hogarth, there was Correggio ; what enabled these great artists to gain the perfection, in their several ways, which afterward surprised and ravished mankind ?   " Not a mother's approving smile, nor a father's frown ; not the help of teachers, nor the world's premature applause ; but the vivid, tingling delight with which the one seized upon a grotesque incident or expression, 'the rapt soul sitting in the eyes ' of the other, as he drew a saint or an angel from the skies."

We cannot close our observations on this topic without adding a caution touching the importance of adhering to the profession which one has deliberately chosen.   In hours of despondency, or when smarting under some disappointment, a young man is apt to fancy that in some other calling he would have been more successful.   It is so easy, while regarding it at a distance, to look at its bright side only, shutting the eyes at what is ugly and disagreeable,—it is so easy to dream of the resolution and tenacity of purpose with which he would follow it, and to mount up in imagination to its most dazzling honours, and clutch them in defiance of every rival,—that it is not strange that men abandon their professions for others for which they are less fitted.   But when we reflect that the *man* remains the same, whatever his calling,—that a mere change of his position can make no radical change of his mind, either by adding to its strength or diminishing its weakness,—we shall conclude that in many cases what he is in one calling, that he would be, substantially, in any other, and that he will gain nothing by the exchange.

Of course, as we have already shown, one may err so egregiously in the choice of his calling that to abandon it and choose anew is a necessity.   Again, hundreds find themselves out of place through accident, early associations, the unwise choice of parents, a boyish freak or whim.   But a young man should be slow to believe this of himself, especially after he has acquired much valuable experience, and should try another calling only after repeated failures in the most desperate attempts to succeed. No man will work with heart and energy while he is haunted by the idea that in some other vocation he might do better. It is by no means certain that had you chosen your calling, instead of your parents choosing it for you, you would have chosen well. Have you never noted the fact mentioned by a shrewd writer, "In a masquerade, where people assume what characters they like, how ill they often play them ?" The great weakness of our young men is fickleness ; and, where one of them perseveres in a calling which he ought to abandon, a dozen abandon their callings who ought to stick to them. The better the profession, the more likely they are to do this ; for all those kinds of business which are surest in the end, which pay best in the long run, are slowest in beginning to yield a return. It is natural, too, when one sees lions in his way, to fancy that all the other roads are clear of them. But nothing can be achieved without tenacity of purpose ; do not, therefore, give up your deliberately chosen calling, unless the arguments for retreating are far weightier than those for going on.

Finally, we would say to every young man, whatever calling you feel compelled to pursue do not affect to despise it. Do not boast of the heights to which your genius might have soared, had it not been tethered to the earth; of the brilliant things you might have done, had you not been " cabined, cribbed, and confined " in a mean and narrow sphere. Such talk may seem to you very fine, and you may fancy that those who hear it will regard it as an index of a high and noble spirit, conscious of grander powers than it has had an opportunity of exhibiting. But you can scarcely make a more egregious mistake. What you say may be true ; but the world, which deems success the only test of merit, and that ninety-nine men out of a hundred find their just level, will ascribe it to vanity. The popular opinion will always be, that, wherever extraordinary ability exists, it will find out some way to make itself known ; and wherever there is not this pre-eminent force of genius, the injustice done to a man's powers will, in the long run, scarcely be perceptible. Is your calling a humble one ? Ennoble it by the manner in which you discharge its duties, and you will

challenge the respect of all whose good opinion is worth having.
The day has long gone by when a man needed to hang down
his head because of the humbleness of his vocation, however
useful.   Lord Townsend, who introduced the culture of the
turnip into England, was nicknamed "Turnip Townsend" by
the wits of a licentious court; but there are few persons to-day
who would not admit that he did more for his country thereby
than was done by all the popinjays that have spread their butterfly wings in the sunshine of the British Court from the days
of Charles II. to those of Victoria.   Dr. Johnson said of some
one sneeringly, that his conversation "savoured of bullocks;"
yet the world could as well have dispensed with a Johnson as
with a Colling or a Bakewell.   It is not the calling or station
in life that gives dignity or nobility to the man, but the man
that dignifies the station or calling.   It is with real life as with
the mimic life of the stage.   All the players cannot have the
principal parts, even when all are fitted for them; but the play
never goes off more finely, nor elicits more enthusiastic applause,
than when the characters, even down to the most unimportant,
have been personated by men of far greater ability than they
have been required to display.

CHAPTER IV.

PHYSICAL CULTURE.

To the strong hand and strong head, the capacious lungs and vigorous frame, fall, and will always fall, the heavy burdens : and where the heavy burdens fall, the great prizes fall too.—LAWS OF LIFE.

It is said that the Duke of Wellington, when once looking on at the boys engaged in their sports in the playground at Eton, made the remark, "It was there that the battle of Waterloo was won."—SAMUEL SMILES.

No man is in true health who cannot stand in the free air of heaven, with his feet on God's free turf, and thank his Creator for the simple luxury of physical existence.—T. W. HIGGINSON.

THE first element of success needed by him who has wisely chosen his calling is constitutional talent. By constitutional talent we mean the warmth and vigour imparted to a man's ideas by superior bodily stamina, by a stout physical constitution. Till within a recent period, bodi-culture, if it may be so called, has been neglected, and almost despised, in this country. Our books for the young have been full of praises of the midnight oil; our oracles of education have urged unsparing study; and *Nocturna manu versate, versate diurna,* has been the favourite motto in all our colleges. It has been truly said that all the influences under which the young American, especially the student, of the last generation lived, taught him to despise the body, while the mind was goaded to a preternatural activity. They led him to associate muscle with rowdyism, ruddy cheeks with toddies, longwind-edness with profane swearing, and broad shoulders with neg-lect of the ordinances of revealed religion. Tallness was the only sign of virtue tolerated. Width and weight were held to indicate a steady tendency toward the State Prison, and the model young man became pale, lanky, dyspeptic, desiring to be all soul, and regarding his body as the source of all his wretch-edness. It is true the majority of youth protested against this theory, and refused to be goaded to suicidal study ; but not a

few responded to the whip, with the results that are familiar
to all. But within a few years a revolution has taken place in
the public sentiment on this subject. We are beginning to
see that the body, as well as the mind, has rights that must be
respected. We are learning by bitter experience that if the
mind, which rules the body, ever forgets itself so far as to trample on its slave, the slave will not forgive the injury, but will
rise and smite the oppressor. We are discovering that though
the pale, sickly student may win the most prizes in college, it
is the tough, sinewy one who will win the most prizes in life ;
and that in every calling, other things being equal, the most
successful man will be the one who has slept the soundest and
digested the most dinners with the least difficulty. The doctrine of Pascal, that " disease is the natural state of Chris-
tians," has now few believers. We cannot believe that the
Creator thinks so ; else health would be the exception, and
disease the rule. We rather hold the opinion of Dr. J. W.
Alexander, who, when asked if he enjoyed the full assurance
of faith, replied, "I think I do, except when the wind is from
the east."

It is now conceded on all hands that the mind has no right
to build itself up at the expense of the body ; that it is no more
justifiable in abandoning itself without restraint to its cravings,
than the body in yielding itself to sensual indulgence. The
acute stimulants, the mental drams, that produce this unnatural
activity or overgrowth of the intellect, are as contrary to nature,
and as hurtful to the man, as the coarser stimulants that unduly
excite the body. The mind, it has been well said, should be a
good, strong, healthy feeder, but not a glutton. When unduly
stimulated, it wears out the mechanism of the body, like fric-
tion upon a machine not lubricated, and the growing weakness
of the physical frame nullifies the power it encloses. " It is
now generally conceded," says Henry Ward Beecher, in one of his
late admirable lectures to the theological students of Yale College,
" that there is an organization which we call the nervous system
in the human body, to which belong the functions of emotion,
intelligence and sensation, and that that is connected intimately with the whole circulation of the blood, with the condition of the blood as affected by the liver, and by aëration in the
lungs ; that the manufacture of the blood is dependent upon the

stomach ; so *a man is what he is, not in one part or another, but all over;* one part is intimately connected with the other, from the animal stomach to the throbbing brain ; and when a man thinks, he thinks the whole trunk through. Man's power comes from the generating forces that are in him, namely, the digestion of nutritious food into vitalized blood, made fine by oxygenation ; an organization by which that blood has free course to flow and be glorified; a neck that will allow the blood to run up and down easily ; a brain properly organized and balanced; the whole system so compounded as to have susceptibilities and recuperative force ; immense energy to generate resources and facility to give them out ;—all these elements go to determine what a man's working power is."

To do his work cheerfully and well, every professional man needs a working constitution, and this can be got only by daily exercise in the open air. The atmosphere we breathe is an exhalation of all the minerals of the globe, the most elaborately finished of all the Creator's works,—the rock of ages disintegrated and prepared for the life of man. Draughts of this are the true stimulants, more potent and healthful than champagne or cognac, "so cheap at the custom-house, so dear at the hotels." The thorough aëration of the blood by deep inhalations of air, so as to bring it in contact with the whole breathing surface of the lungs, is indispensable to him who would maintain that full vital power on which the vigorous working-power of the brain so largely depends. Sydney Smith tells public speakers that if they would walk twelve miles before speaking, they would never break down. The English people understand this, and hence at the Universities boat-races, horseback rides, and ten-mile walks are practically a part of the educational course. English lawyers and members of Parliament acquire vigour of body and clearness of head for their arduous labours by riding with the hounds, shooting grouse on the Scottish moors, throwing the fly into the waters of Norway, or climbing the Alpine cliffs. Peel, Brougham, Lyndhurst, Campbell, Bright, Gladstone,—nearly all the great political and legal leaders, the prodigious workers at the bar and in the senate,—have been full-chested men, who have been as sedulous to train the bodies as to train their intellects. If our American leaders accomplish less, and die earlier, it is because they neglect the care of the body, and put will-force in the place of physical strength.

It is no exaggeration to say that health is a large ingredient in what the world calls talent. A man without it may be a giant in intellect, but his deeds will be the deeds of a dwarf. On the contrary, let him have a quick circulation, a good digestion, the bulk, thews, and sinews of a man, and the alacrity, the unthinking confidence inspired by these, and, though having but a thimbleful of brains, he will either blunder upon success or set failure at defiance. It is true, especially in this country, that the number of centaurs in every community—of men in whom heroic intellects are allied with bodily constitutions as tough as those of horses—is small; that, in general, a man has reason to think himself well off in the lottery of life, if he draws the prize of a healthy stomach without a mind, or the prize of a fine intellect with a crazy stomach. But of the two, a weak mind in a herculean frame is better than a giant mind in a crazy constitution. A pound of energy with an ounce of talent will achieve greater results than a pound of talent with an ounce of energy. The first requisite to success in life is to be a good animal. In any of the learned professions a vigorous constitution is equal to at least fifty per cent. more brain. Wit, judgment, imagination, eloquence, all the qualities of the mind, attain thereby a force and splendour to which they could never approach without it. But intellect in a weak body is "like gold in a spent swimmer's pocket." A mechanic may have tools of the sharpest edge and highest polish; but what are these, without a vigorous arm and hand? Of what use is it that your mind has become a vast granary of knowledge, if you have not strength to turn the key?

The effects of the culture of the body are strikingly seen in the nations of antiquity, with whom gymnastics and calisthenics were a part of the regular school education. Ancient philosophy, instead of despising the body as a mere husk or vile outside of human nature, regarded it as a true part of the man, the contempt or neglect of which would provoke a fearful retaliation upon the whole being. The gymnastics of the Greeks were not practised by the boxers and wrestlers only, the drill-sergeants and corporals of that day, but went on under the solemn sanction of sages. The orators, philosophers, poets, warriors, and statesmen of Greece and Rome gained strength of mind as well as of muscle by the systematic drill of the palæstra. The brain was filled thereby with a quick-pulsing and finely oxygenated blood, the nerves made healthy and strong, the digestion sharp and powerful, and the whole physical man, as the statues of antiquity show, developed into the fullest health and vigour. It is told of Cicero that he became, at one period of his life, the victim of that train of maladies expressed by the word " dyspepsia,"—maladies which pursue the indolent and the overworked man as the shark follows in the wake of the plague-ship. The orator hastened, not to the physicians, which might have hastened his death, but to Greece ; flung himself into the gymnasium ; submitted to its regimen for two entire years ; and returned to the struggles of the forum as vigorous as the peasants that tilled his farm. Who doubts that, by this means, his periods were rounded out to a more majestic cadence, and his crushing arguments clinched with a tighter grasp ? Had he remained a dyspeptic, he might have written beautiful essays on old age and friendship, but he never would have pulverized Catiline, or blasted Antony with his lightnings. So the intellectual power of those giants of antiquity, Aristotle and Plato, was owing in a large degree to that harmonious education in which the body shared as well as the mind. That the one ruled the world of thought down to the time of Bacon, and that the other is stimulating and quickening the mind of the nineteenth century, are owing in part to the fact that they were not only great geniuses, but, as one has well said, geniuses most happily set, and that no dyspepsia broke the harmony of their thought, no neuralgia twinged the system with agony, and no philosopher's ail infected the throat with bad blood or an ulcerated mucous membrane.

The success of men gifted, apparently, with nothing but constitutional talent, and the frequency with which men endowed with the finest intellectual powers, but powers supported by a couple of spindle-shanks and a weak body, have disappointed the expectations of their admirers, have led some persons almost to regard the stomach as the seat of intellect, and genius and eupepsy as convertible terms. Ridiculous as this may seem, it is certain that the brain is often credited with achievements that belong to the digestion. Everything shows that the greatness of our great men is as much a bodily affair as a mental one. Nature presented our Websters, Clays, and Calhouns, not only with extraordinary minds, but—what has quite as much to do with the matter—with wonderful bodies. Above all, our Grants, Shermans, and Sheridans, what would they be without nerves of whipcord and frames of iron? Let Napoleon answer. The tortures of hereditary disease, united with the pangs of fever, wrung from that great captain, in one of the most critical days of his history, the exclamation that the first requisite of good generalship is good health. The efficiency of the common soldier, too, he knew depended, first of all, upon his being in perfect health and splendid condition; and hence he tried to bring up all his troops to the condition of pugilists when they fight for the championship. This was the secret of their prodigious efforts, their endurance of fatigues that would have killed common men. Even in literature, a robust frame has become absolutely indispensable to great and lasting success. Time was when an author wrote only with his head,—with the superior and intellectual part,—the essence of his being. But to-day, owing to the enormous labour which he imposes upon himself, or which society imposes on him at short notice,—owing, also, to the necessity he is under of striking quick and telling blows, he has no time to be so platonic and delicate. A writer's works in this nineteenth century are the offspring, not merely of his brain, but of his blood and muscles. His physiology and hygiene,—his entire organization,—have become an indispensable chapter in every analysis of his talent.

Look, again, at the pulpit. Who can estimate the accession of energy, of intellectual and moral power, which it would receive if our clergymen, instead of remaining the pale, ghostly-looking, over-read, over-fed, intellectually *blasé* spectres they so often are, should spend a part of their time in getting up animal power to back up their attenuated intellectual power? John Knox was not a dwarf nor a dyspeptic. Latimer and Luther were stalwart men, who could have knocked down an opponent first, and put him down in argument afterward. Isaac Barrow was a vigorous pugilist in his youth; Andrew Fuller, when a farmer's boy, was skilled in boxing; and Adam Clarke, when a lad, could "roll large stones about" as easily as he could afterwards roll over a theological adversary in manhood.

The success of the English people—their victories on the field, in the mart, and in the study—has been largely owing to physical training. John Bull is a large feeder, but he is a hard worker too; he loves the open air, and keeps mind and body vigorous by constant exercise. The effect of this upon the efficiency of men is strikingly seen in the achievements of the British army and navy, whose soldiers and sailors are surpassed in toughness and powers of endurance by no others in the world. That the splendid empires which England has founded in every quarter of the globe have had their origin largely in the football contests at Eton, the boat-races on the Thames, and the cricket-matches on her downs and heaths, who can doubt? The race so widely dominant,—" whose morning drum-beat, following the sun, and keeping company with the hours, circles the earth with one continual, unbroken strain of the martial airs of England,"—is dominant because its institutions cultivate self-reliance, and its breeding develops endurance, courage and pluck. There are some croakers who talk much of England's decline, and predict that she will prove an easy prey whenever any of the continental vultures choose to swoop down upon her. But there is little danger of this while " the silver-coasted isle" is defended by the stalwart men she yet produces. In allusion to the fears of some Englishmen on this subject, a London paper some years ago indulged in the following well-founded boast:—" If any of the home-keeping denizens of London are alarmed by the extraordinary naval preparations which Louis Napoleon is said to be making, we would advise them to go down and take a look at the Imperial yacht which is now lying at Deptford. As a vessel, she is in every respect a match for our royal yacht, the Victoria and Albert. But look at her sailors. They have been strolling about our streets for some days past, exciting wonder wherever they have gone. What pretty little fellows they are! What dandy shirts they wear! what natty enamelled hats! How they remind us of ballet girls, dressed out for a hornpipe in a nautical pantomime. Pretty, truly; but their slender knees are not made to cling to a giddy maintop in a gale. Their delicate fingers are not designed to grasp a rough, tarred rope, and hold on, like grim death, when the fate of the ship and its crew rests upon the strength, the daring, and the rugged skill of one man. There they trip along, a batch of French ' able seamen,' looking, at the best, like the apprentices of an English war-ship. The big, burly, hard-fisted British tar, who comes lumbering down the street, looks as if he could eat one of them with ease. They are like a litter of Italian greyhounds by the side of that huge English mastiff. Our rivals, then, whoever they may be, may build as many iron-cased ships as they please. They cannot build sailors like ours. In that respect Nature and our insular position will always give us the advantage, if we only exercise the most ordinary vigilance in keeping the material of our fleet up to the requirements and exigencies of the time."

It is true there have been men who, despite of frail and miserable health, have done immortal things. Great and heroic were the achievements of Paul, "in bodily presence weak;" of the blind Milton; of Pascal, a confirmed invalid at eighteen; of Johnson, bravely carrying through life the weight of a diseased and tortured body; of Nelson, little and lame; of Channing, with his frail, clayey tabernacle; of the pale Lawrence, weighing from day to day the morsels of bread which alone his dyspeptic stomach could bear. It is true that Julius Cæsar was troubled with epilepsy, and never planned a great battle without going into fits; that the great Suwarrow stood but five feet one in his boots; that Pope was a hunchback and an invalid; and that Aristotle was a pygmy in body, though a giant in intellect. But these are brilliant exceptions, which only prove the rule. The general fact still remains that it is the man of tough and enduring fibre, of elastic nerve, of comprehensive digestion, who does the great work of life. It is Scott, with his manly form; it is Brougham, with his superhuman power of physical endurance. It is Franklin, at the age of seventy, camping out, on his way to arouse the Canadas, as our hardiest boys of twenty now camp out in the Adirondacks. It is Napoleon, sleeping four hours, and in the saddle twenty. Rarely does the world behold such a spectacle as that presented in 1693, at Neerwinden, in the Netherlands, when, among the one hundred and twenty thousand soldiers who were marshalled under the banners of all Europe, the two feeblest in body were the hunchbacked dwarf who urged on the fiery onset of France and the asthmatic skeleton who covered the slow retreat of England.

Fven the greatest poets have been those who, like Burns, have combined athletic bodies with souls of Æolian tones, who were blessed with good digestion as well as brains. The Greek poet, Æschylus, fought nobly for his country at Salamis ; and the trumpet that woke his countrymen to battle that morning still rings in his verse. Chaucer was a sturdy bard, as ready to fight as to write ; and, when some Londoners had accused him of untruth, " prepared his body for Mars his doing, if any contrairied his saws." There is no calling in which men do not need that sturdy vigour, that bodily strength and agility, without which all mental culture is but a preparation for disap pointment and mortification. But, in the learned professions, a good constitution is doubly indispensable. There is nothing else which so taxes, tries, and exhausts the life-force as mental effort. Instead of being pale, delicate, feeble and sickly, the thinker, whether in the law-office, the pulpit, the editorial room, the counting-room, or the hall of legislation, needs to be stalwart and hardy. He should have tougher thews and stronger sinews, and a more vigorous pulse than the man who holds the plough or shoves the foreplane. It has been said with not a little truth, that a small body has comparatively small chances of success ; " people will yield that to mere physical largeness which they will refuse to, or at least dispute with, littleness of body and self-distrust." No matter how true the rifle or the aim, a light ball will not carry far ; heavy men, like heavy bullets, do the most execution, and win the battle at long range. See Palmerston at fourscore still handling the helm of empire with the firm grasp of thirty ! Look at Lord Brougham ! That the King never dies, and that Brougham never sleeps, used to be the two leading features of English constitutional doctrine. One would think from his toughness, when almost ninety, that he was a son of old McDonald of Keppoch, the Scotch chieftain of whom it is told that, camping out one night with a portion of his clan, he went and kicked the snow from under his son's head—which the youth had piled together so as to form a sort of pillow—declaring that " the young rascal, by his degenerate effeminacy, would bring disgrace on the clan." The life of Brougham was a perpetual series of mental feats and triumphs over the frail *physique* of humanity. It is told that he once worked six days on a stretch—one hundred and forty-four hours—without sleep ;

then ran down from London into the country, slept from Saturday night till Monday morning, and returned and buckled to his work again, as fresh and elastic as ever. Is it not an immense advantage to have such a working constitution as this? —to be able, if a professional man, to endure for a whole week a perpetual strain on your brain, and, amid confinement and close air, with heaps of confused papers, law books, and books of reference to get through, to go on daily and nightly extracting therefrom liquid and transparent results, and find yourself, when you rise from your task, as elastic as a rubber ball? Is not a lawyer doubly sure of success who, after a fortnight's laborious attention to a suit, can rise up to address a jury with all his faculties as vigorous and eager for the contest as on the first day of the term, while his wilted and exhausted opponent has hardly more vitality than a bag of sand?

On the other hand, of what avail are brilliant talents and a splendid education to a young man just entering manhood, who has a feeble constitution? It is Ulysses' bow in the hands of the suitors. He brings into the arena of life, to meet its fierce contests, to bear its hard shocks, to persevere in its long-continued enterprises, and to subdue its impetuous oppositions, a shrivelled, puny body, limbs trembling with weakness and palsied with pain. His feeble system is borne down to the bed of sickness even by the operations of his own over-cultivated mind. The spirit is too strong for its tenement. The sword has worn through the scabbard. He hears the trumpet sound, and the busy hum of preparation—his soul is " up in arms and eager for the fray "—but he cannot arise and equip himself for the battle. Opportunities of usefulness and of winning an honourable reputation crowd thick upon him; but he feels a prostrating weakness, which, like an invisible enemy, creeps through his veins, and drinks the life-blood from his heart; and he languishes in pain and wretchedness, like Ivanhoe in the castle of Front de Bœuf, unable to perform a solitary act in the fray on whose results hang all his most cherished hopes.

Horace Mann, in a letter of advice to a law student, justly remarks that a spendthrift of health is one of the most reprehensible of spendthrifts. " I am certain," continues he, " I could have performed twice the labour, both better and with greater ease to myself, had I known as much of the laws of health and life at twenty-one as I do now. In college I was taught all about the motions of the planets, as carefully as though they would have been in danger of getting off the track if I had not known how to trace their orbits ; but about my own organization, and the conditions indispensable to the healthful functions of my own body, I was left in profound ignorance. Nothing could be more preposterous. I ought to have begun at home, and taken the stars when it should come to their turn. The consequence was, I broke down at the beginning of my second college year, and have never had a well day since. Whatever labour I have since been able to do, I have done it all on credit instead of capital—a most ruinous way either in regard to health or money. For the last twenty-five years, so far as it regards health, I have been put, from day to day, on my good behaviour; and during the whole of this period, as an Hibernian would say, if I had lived as other folks do for a month, I should have died in a fortnight."

Let, then, the man who is stripping for the race in life account no time or money as wasted that contributes in any way to his physical health—that gives tone to the stomach, or development to the muscles. The life of the present day is lived so often at fever-heat, is so swift and restless, that the mental wear and tear is enormous. Never before were men devoured by so insatiable an ambition, or scourged by so merciless an activity, as in this latter half of the nineteenth century. It is the pace that kills. We need, therefore, all the vigour, all the "healthy animalism," that can be drawn from sport or play, to strengthen us for the struggle. It is true the professional or business man needs health rather than strength. He need not boast the brawn of the gladiator. He need not be a Heenan or a Spartacus ; he need not lift a thousand pounds, nor walk a hundred miles in twenty-four hours. It is a sound constitution that most men want to do their work—in short, that condition of body and that amount of vital power which shall enable them to pursue their callings with the greatest amount of comfort to themselves and usefulness to others. It is true also that physical ability is required more in some callings than in others. But in all it is indispensable to leadership, and he who lacks it, though he may lead a useful and respectable life—may even become a first-rate second-rate man— must not think to command.

CHAPTER V.

CONCENTRATION, OR ONENESS OF AIM.

> One science only will one genius fit ;
> So wide is art, so narrow human wit.—POPE.

"So it comes to pass that now, at last, the measure of a man's learning will be the amount of his voluntary ignorance ; the measure of his practical effectiveness, the amount of what he is content to leave unattempted."

Be not simply good,—be good for something.—THOREAU.

We should guard against a talent which we cannot hope to practise in perfection. Improve it as we may, we shall always, in the end, when the merit of the master has become apparent to us, painfully lament the loss of time and strength devoted to such botching.—GOETHE.

ANOTHER indispensable requisite to success is concentration, or devotion to one object.

The great State of New York, which leads the Union in commerce, has but one port upon the ocean, and none elsewhere of any importance. The State of New Jersey has several ports, but so poor that all of them, with their shallow water and narrow limits, are a miserable substitute for a good one. What is the result ? The universal sea is whitened with the sails of Manhattan, while the voyages of New Jersey are restricted to a visit to the neighbouring emporium, or to the Hudson, that washes her shores. So with human talent. *One,* well cultivated, deepened and enlarged, is worth a hundred shallow faculties. The first law of success at this day, when so many things are clamouring for attention, is concentration— to bend all the energies to one point, and to go directly to that point, looking neither to the right nor to the left. It has been justly said that a great deal of the wisdom of a man in this century is shown in leaving things unknown, and a great deal of his practical sense in leaving things undone. The day of universal scholars is past. Life is short, and art is long. The range of human knowledge has increased so enormously, that no brain can grapple with it : and the man who would know one thing well must have the courage to be ignorant of a thousand other things, however attractive or inviting. As with knowledge, so with work. The man who would get along must single out his speciality, and into that must pour the whole stream of his activity,—all the energies of his hand, eye, tongue, heart, and brain. Broad culture, many-sidedness, are beautiful things to contemplate ; but it is the narrow-edged men—the men of single and intense purpose who steel their souls against all things else—that accomplish the hard work of the world, and who are everywhere in demand when hard work is to be done.

Every beginner in life, therefore, should try early to ascertain the strong faculty of his mind or body, fitting him for some special pursuit, and direct his utmost energies to bring it to perfection. A man, says Emerson, is like a bit of Labrador spar, which has no lustre as you turn it in your hand, until you come to a particular angle; then it shows deep and beauti-ful colours. There is no adaptation or universal applicability in man ; but each has his special talent ; and the mastery of successful men consists in adroitly keeping themselves where and when *that* turn shall need oftenest to be practised. The successful man in every calling, whether literary, scientific or business, is he who is *totus in illo,*—who can say with Paul, " This one thing I do." With the exception of a few great creative minds, the men whose names are historic are identified with some one achievement upon which all their life-force is spent. You think of Watt, and instantly the steam-engine is suggested ; of Arkwright, and the spinning-jenny whirls before you ; of Davy, and the safety-lamp lights up the mine ; of Harvey, and the blood courses the more quickly in your veins ; of Jenner, and you see disease stayed in its progress by the pricking of a lancet ; of Morse, and the electric spark is seen darting from continent to continent, ready, like Puck, to " put a girdle round the earth in forty minutes." " Whatever I have tried to do in my life," said Charles Dickens, " I have tried with all my heart to do it well. What I have devoted myself to, I have devoted myself to completely. Never to put one hand to anything on which I would not throw my whole self, and never to affect depreciation of my work, whatever it was, I find now to have been golden rules."

A man may have the most dazzling talents, but if they are scattered upon many objects, he will accomplish nothing. Sir Joshua Reynolds used to say that a painter should sew up his mouth; that is, he must not shine as a talker, if he would excel in his art. Strength is like gunpowder,—to be effective, it needs concentration and aim. The marksman who aims at the whole target will seldom hit the centre. The literary man or philosopher may revel among the sweetest and most beautiful flowers of thought, but unless he gathers and condenses the sweets in the honeycomb of some great thought or work, his finest conceptions will be lost or useless. When Michael Angelo was asked why he did not marry, he replied, "Painting is my wife, and my works are my children." "Mr. A. often laughs at me," said a learned American chemist, "because I have but one idea. He talks about everything,—aims to excel in many things; but I have learned that if I wish ever to make a breach, I must play my guns continually upon *one point*." His gunnery was successful. Beginning life as an obscure schoolmaster, and poring over "Silliman's Journal" by the light of a pine-knot in a log-cabin, he was ere long performing experiments in electro-magnetism to English earls, and has since been at the head of one of the chief scientific institutions of his country.

It was the opinion of William Hazlitt that life is long enough for many pursuits, provided we set about them properly, and give our minds wholly to them. Let one devote himself to any art or science ever so strenuously, he said, and he will still have leisure to make considerable progress in half a dozen acquisitions. "Let a man do all he can in any one branch of study, he must either exhaust himself and doze over it, or vary his pursuit, or else lie idle. All our real labour lies in a nutshell. The mind makes, at some period or other, one Herculean effort, and the rest is mechanical." All this is true enough of a few prodigies of genius that have appeared at rare intervals in the ages. Cicero was master of logic, ethics, astronomy, and natural philosophy, besides being well versed in geometry, music, and all the other fine arts. Bacon took all knowledge for his province. Dante, skilled in all the learning of his times, sustained arguments at the University of Paris against fourteen disputants, and conquered in all. Scipio Africanus was not only a great warrior, but famed for his learning and eloquence. Salvator Rosa was a lutenist and a satirist. The variety of knowledge and accomplishment accumulated by Leonardo da Vinci almost staggers belief. It has been said that if he had stood before the gates of Macedon, he would have tamed Bucephalus; if he had been seated on the magic throne of Comus, he would have broken the wand of the demon; if he had seen the chariot of the King of Phrygia, he would have unravelled the Gordian knot. He was not only a great painter, but a mathematician, metaphysician, musician, poet, sculptor, engineer, architect, chemist, botanist, anatomist, astronomer, besides being skilled in mechanics and natural history. But how many Bacons, Dantes, Salvators, or Da Vincis have there been in the world's history?—nay, among the men of any generation, how many are even Hazlitts? The very rarity of such prodigies is what makes them prodigies. To every such instance of universal accomplishment may be opposed thousands of men who have failed in life by dabbling in too many things. Most men run uncertainly if they have two goals. Hobbes made himself a laughing-stock as a poet; Milton wrote but little good prose, and provokes a smile at himself as a humorist; Bentley's hand forgot its cunning when he laid it on Paradise Lost; Boileau failed almost utterly when he attempted to sweep the strings of the lyre, as did Corneille in comedy and Dryden in tragedy. "Art, not less eloquently than literature," says Willmott, "teaches her children to venerate the single eye. Remember Matsys. His representations of miser-life are breathing. A forfeited bond twinkles in the hard smile. But follow him to an altar-piece. His Apostle has caught a stray tint from his usurer."

Sydney Smith, in an excellent lecture on the Conduct of the Understanding, justly censures what he calls the foppery of *universality*,—of knowing all sciences and excelling in all arts,—chemistry, mathematics, algebra, dancing, history, reasoning, riding, fencing, Low Dutch, High Dutch, natural philosophy, and enough Spanish to talk about Lope de Vega. The modern precept of education, he says, is, very often, be ignorant of nothing. "Now *my* advice, on the contrary, is to have the *courage* to be ignorant of a great number of things, in order to avoid the calamity of being ignorant of everything. I would exact of a young man a pledge that he would never read Lope de Vega ; he should pawn to me his honour to abstain from Bettinelli and his thirty-five original sonneteers ; and I would exact from him the most rigid securities that I was never to hear anything about that race of penny poets who lived in the reigns of Cosmo and Lorenzo di Medici."

The world has few Admirable Crichtons,—few universal geniuses, who are capable of mastering a dozen languages, arts, or sciences, or driving a dozen callings abreast. Beginners in life are perpetually complaining of the disadvantages under which they labour ; but it is an indisputable fact that more persons fail from a multiplicity of pursuits and pretensions than from an absolute poverty of resources. Don Quixote thought that he could have made beautiful bird-cages and toothpicks, if his brain had not been so full of ideas of chivalry ; and many other persons would achieve an easy success in their callings, if they were not distracted by rival ambitions.

" The one prudence in life," says a shrewd American essay-ist, " is concentration, the one evil is dissipation ; and it makes no difference whether our dissipations are coarse or fine—. property and its cares, friends and a social habit, or politics, or music, or feasting. Everything is good which takes away one plaything and delusion more, and drives us home to add one stroke of faithful work." The same essayist felicitously com-pares the culture of a healthy, vigorous mind to that of a tree. The gardener does not suffer the sap to be diverted into a thou-sand channels, merely to develop a myriad of profitless twigs ; he prunes the offshoots, and leaves the vital juices to be absorb-ed by a few vigorous fruit-bearing branches. Racine, we are told, might have rivalled Molière in comedy ; but he gave up the cultivation of his comic talents to devote himself to the tragic muse. If, as the French assert, he thereby attained to the per-fection of comic writing, was not that better than writing come-dies as well as Molière, and tragedies as well as Crebillon ?

It is said that a Yankee can splice a rope in many different ways ; an English sailor knows but one mode, but that mode is the best. The one thing which an Englishman detests with his whole soul is a Jack-of-all-trades, the miscellaneous man who knows a little of everything. England is not a country for average men ; every profession is overstocked, and the only chance of success is for the man of signal ability and address to climb to a lofty position over the heads of a hundred others. America, on the other hand, is full of persons who can do many things, but who do no one thing well. The secret of their failure is mental dissipation,—the squandering of the energies upon a distracting variety of objects, instead of condensing them upon one. To do anything perfectly, there should be an exclusiveness, a bigotry, a blindness of attachment to that one object, which shall make all others for the time being seem worthless. Just as the general who scatters his soldiers all about the country ensures defeat, so does he whose attention is for ever diffused through so innumerable channels that it can never gather in force on any one point. The human mind, in short, resembles a burning-glass, whose rays are intense only as they are concentrated. As the glass burns only when its light is conveyed to the focal point, so the former illumines the world of science, literature or business, only when it is directed to a solitary object. Or to take another illustration, what is more powerless than the scattered clouds of steam, as they rise in the sky? They are as impotent as the dew-drops that fall nightly upon the earth. But, concentrated and condensed in a steam-boiler, they are able to cut through solid rock, to hurl mountains into the sea, and to bring the antipodes to our doors.

"Be a *whole* man at everything," was the advice of a celebrated Englishman to his son at school. It is just the lack of this wholeness which distinguishes the shabby, half-hearted, and blundering—the men who make the mob of life—from those who win victories. In slower times success might have been won by the man who gave but a corner of his brain to the work in hand ; but in these days of keen competition it demands the intensest application of the entire thinking faculty. Exclusive dealing, hateful as it is in politics, is yet, in worldly pursuits, a principle of hundred-headed power. The great linguist of Bologna mastered a hundred languages by attacking them singly, as the lion did the bulls. On the other hand, by dividing his time among too many objects, a man of genius often becomes diamond-dust instead of a diamond. Many men walk as much idly in Broadway or Pall Mall as in a few years could carry them around the globe. Many a person misses of being

a great man by splitting into two middling ones. Enough o
irregular, disconnected and objectless effort is put forth by
amateur artists to secure a commendable, if not an enviable
success, were the effort only systematic and persistent. The
scattered hours wasted in idly drawing the bow by some dream
ing violinist would make, if properly employed, not, indeed, a
Vieuxtemps or a Paganini, but a brilliant performer. The time
spent by many persons in profitless desultory reading, if concentrated upon a single line of study, would make them masters
of an entire literature or science. The toil expended by the
newspaper hack in writing disconnected essays, dissertations,
and sketches, to buy his daily bread, would produce—if directed
with energy for a year to one absorbing object—a volume.
instead of the two-and-fifty or more crude and ephemeral articles which are once read and then for ever forgotten. The
highest ability will accomplish but little, if scattered on a mul
tiplicity of objects ; while, on the other hand, if one has but a
thimbleful of brains, and concentrates them all upon the thing
he has in hand, he may achieve miracles. Momentum in
physics, properly directed, will drive a tallow candle through an
inch board. Just so will oneness of aim and the direction of
the energies to a single pursuit, while all others are waived as
harlotry, enable the veriest weakling to make his mark where
he strikes.

We are aware that it is fashionable in these days, with small
wits, to ridicule men of one idea. But no man has ever yet
made his mark on the world who was not possessed by some
master passion. Now and then we meet with a Fearne, who
writes an " Essay on Contingent Remainders," and is at the
same time profoundly versed in medicine, chemistry, and mathematics, obtains a patent for dyeing scarlet, and produces an
acute treatise on the Greek accent ; with a Mill, who besides
being an able writer on metaphysics and politics, is a fine
pianist, an able archæologist, philologist, and botanist ; or again,
with a Gladstone, who works double tides and excels in both,—
who, though Chancellor of the Exchequer, receives despatches,
makes experiments with Sykes's hydrometer, answers the letters
of financial amateurs, conducts a well-sustained correspondence
with half a dozen Greek scholiasts on Homer, translates some
scores of English hymns into Latin verse, and writes occasional

letters of forty pages to a lawyer on some nice legal point. But the Loyolas and the Luthers, the Cavours and Bismarcks, of every age, have been men of "one idea," which, though their capacious souls have contained many ideas, have subordinated and directed all the rest. An acute observer, who knew intimately the celebrated Canning, said of him that he possessed too many talents; for, betrayed by his rare powers of declamation and sarcasm, he often produced more admiration than conviction, and seldom delivered an important speech without making an enemy for life. Pitt said of the same brilliant orator and statesman, that he might have achieved anything had he but gone straight to the mark. What a contrast between his dazzling but fitful and half-successful career and that of William Pitt! If there was anything divine in this man, whom his contemporaries called a Heaven-born statesman, it was the marvellous gift of concentrating his powers. Whatever he did, he did with all his might. Ever master of himself, he converged all the rays of his mind, as into a focus, upon the object in hand, worked like a horse, and did nothing by halves. Hence with him there was no half vision, no sleepy eyes, no dawning sense. All his life he had his wits about him so intensely directed to the point required, that, it is said, he seemed never to learn, but only to recollect. He gave men an answer before they knew there was a riddle; he had formed a decision before they had heard of a difficulty. His lightning had struck, and done its work, before they had heard the thunder-clap which announced it.

Is it strange that such a man went straightway from college into the House of Commons, and in two years to the Prime Ministership of Great Britain,—reigned, for nearly a quarter of a century, virtual king,—and carried his measures in spite of the opposition of some of the greatest men England ever produced? The simple secret of his success was, that his whole soul was swallowed up in the one passion for political power. So we see him "neglecting everything else,—careless of friends; careless of expenditures, so that with an income of fifty thousand dollars yearly, and no family, he died hopelessly in debt; tearing up by the roots from his heart a love most deep and tender, because it ran counter to his ambition; totally indifferent to posthumous fame, so that he did not take the pains to

F

transmit to posterity a single one of his speeches ; utterly insensible to the claims of art, literature, and belles-lettres ; living and working terribly for the one sole purpose of wielding the governing power of the nation." Again, we all know of the success of Rufus Choate as a lawyer. To what did he owe it but to a similar quality,—his marvellous powers of concentration,—that entire absorption and identification with the interests of his client which led him to burn and freeze with him ; which led him, it has been said, to be as pathetic as the grand lamentations in "Samson Agonistes" over the obstructions of fishways, and to rise into the cathedral music of the universe on the right to manufacture india-rubber suspenders ? His biographer tells us that every important cause took such possession of him that sound sleep was an impossibility. His mind, as he himself said, became a stream that took up the cause, like a ship, and bore it on, night and day, till the verdict or judgment was reached ; and days elapsed before he could enter upon a new case with the full force of his faculties.

Another argument for concentration is, that it is the only way of using strength economically, so as to avoid exhaustion. The man who scatters himself upon many objects soon loses his energy, and with his energy his enthusiasm ; and how is success possible without enthusiasm ? Dr. J. W. Alexander, in counselling young clergymen, exhorted them above all things to throw their force into their sermons. "Many ministers," said he, " are *enthusiastic* about other things, such as art, poetry, authorship, or politics ; but their Sabbath sermon is like a sponge from which all the moisture is squeezed out. Live *for* your sermon,—live *in* your sermon. Get some starling to cry *Sermon, sermon, sermon !*" Rufus Choate, who was so successful with juries, used to say : " Carry the jury at all hazards ; move heaven and earth to carry the jury, and then fight it out with the judges on the law questions as best you can." It was thus that Macdonough, the hero of Champlain, won his victories. He pointed all his guns at the " big ship " of the enemy. No matter how hot the fire from the others ; every ball must be hurled at the " big ship," till her guns were silenced.

Let it not be inferred from all this that by concentration we mean isolation or self-absorption. In a work of art there may be great variety of detail with perfect unity of conception ; and

·~· in the conduct of life. There may be a hundred accessories, provided they but contribute to the one grand result. " Stick to your business, and your business will stick to you," is a golden rule. But what if I accomplish my main ends more rapidly and surely by leaving my office or shop occasionally, and dining with an influential friend ? A late writer justly urged that " social intercourse, of the right kind, is a material aid to success. Often the gain is palpable to you at once, and you count your advantage as you take off your dress-coat. But if not, it will find you out after many days ; you have sown, and in due season you will reap. If you do nothing more than assert your individuality,—make yourself a living presence among men, instead of a myth, a *stat nominis umbra*,—you may be sure that you have done something. Am I more or less likely to read your book, or to buy your picture, or to say a good word for you, if I have a chance, to some man in authority, for sitting next to you at our friend Robinson's, and thinking you a pleasant fellow ?"

Again, in urging the importance of sticking to one thing, we do not mean that any man should be a mere lawyer, a mere doctor, or a mere merchant or mechanic, and nothing more. We would commend to no man the example of Saint Bernard, who was so great a saint that he could keep no flesh on his bones, and knew not the difference between a cake composed of ashes and one composed of meal. A Daniel Lambert, with his elephantine proportions, is hardly more a monstrosity than the intellectually obese Neander, who so far neglects the practical part of his nature that he cannot find the way from his own house to the university where he has lectured nearly a third of a century. Napoleon thought war the sum of all the arts ; a great musician thought the chief value of the Seven Years' War lay in the opportunity it gave for improving wind instruments ; Parson Adams thought a schoolmaster the greatest character in the world ; Vestris, the French dancing-master, believed himself and Voltaire to be the two greatest men in all Europe ; and Dr. George, we are told, shrewdly suspected that Frederick the Great, with all his victories, could not conjugate a Greek verb in *mi*. It is said of Baron Masères, with whom the study of abstract arithmetic was a passion, that "his leading idea seemed to have been to calculate more decimal

places than any one would want, and to print the works of all
who had done the same thing." Douglas Jerrold once knew a
man with twenty-four languages, and not an idea in any of
them ; and it is said that the dying regret of a great German
philologist was, that he had not concentrated his life-labours on
the dative case. Jean Paul says of the Germans that they
determine the course of a zephyr by a sea-compass, and the
heart of a girl by conic sections. To a Lowell cotton manufacturer " the blood of all the Howards " is, doubtless, but so
much crimson fluid, that would make, perhaps, good red ink ;
and if you were to show him the mummy of Potiphar's wife,
he would declare, oracularly, that the wrapper was flax, not
cotton. But these are cases of one-ideaism pushed too far.
There is no more pitiable wretch than the man in whom one
giant faculty has starved the rest, like the dwarf whose large
feet and hands seem to have devoured his stature. And yet
does not the world abound in such dwarfed specimens of humanity ? Has not every profession its peculiar tendencies, that
more or less cripple, mutilate or warp those that devote themselves to it too exclusively, paralyzing this or that mental
or moral faculty, and preventing them from attaining to a
complete, healthful and whole-souled manhood ? Is not the
weaver, in many cases, but an animated shuttle ?—the seam-
stress a living needle ?—the labourer a spade that eats and
sleeps ? Does not the clergyman too often get a white-neck-
cloth ideal of the world, with some twists of dyspepsia in it ?—
and do not his shyness, stiffness, and lack of practicality,
give too much occasion for the jest that the human race is
divided into three classes,—men, women, and ministers ?
Does not the lawyer often become a mere bundle of precedents,
a walking digest of real-estate rules and decisions in law or
chancery ? Are not scholars too often Dominie Sampsons,
—mere bloated encyclopædias of learning ? Is not the time
rapidly drawing near when, to find a perfect man, we must
take a brain from one, a heart from another, senses from a
third, and a stomach from a fourth ?

Surely, man dwarfs himself, if he pushes too far the doctrine
of the subdivision of labour. Success is purchased too dear, if,
to attain it, one has to become a monster of one-sided development, and transformed into a head, an arm, a finger, or a leg,

instead of a man. Every person ought to be something more than a factor in some grand formula of social or economical science,—a cog or pulley in some great machine. Let every one take care, first of all, to be a *man*, cultivating and developing, so far as he can, all his powers on a symmetrical plan, and then let him expend his chief labours on the one faculty which Nature, by making it prominent, has given a hint should be specially cultivated. There is, indeed, no profession upon which a high degree of knowledge will not continually bear. Things which at first view seem most remote from it, will often be brought into close approximation to it; and acquisitions which the narrow-minded might deem a hindrance, will sooner or later yield something serviceable. Nothing is more beautiful than to see a man hold his art, trade, or function in an easy, disengaged way,—wearing it as a soldier his sword, which, once laid aside, the accomplished soldier gives you no hint that he has ever worn. How it exalts our estimate of the genius of Charles James Fox to learn, as Walpole tells us, that after his long and exhausting speech on Hastings' trial, he was seen handing the ladies into the coaches with all the gaiety and prattle of an idle gallant! Too often the shop-keeper smells of the shop, and the scholar, who should remind you, unconsciously, that he has been on Parnassus, only by the odours of the flowers that he has crushed, which cling to his feet, affronts you with a huge nosegay stuck in his bosom.

It is recorded of Braham, the celebrated vocalist, that his voice was equally effective in treble, tenor or bass, but that his individuality was ever distinguishable throughout. So should it be in the conduct of life. The man who would get on need not always pursue the "grand trunk" line; he may "switch off" upon other tracks, provided they lead ultimately to the same terminus. With one object ever in view, he may have many varying activities, conducing to the same result. Singleness of aim by no means necessitates monotony of action; but if we would be felt on this stirring planet, if we would strike the world with lasting force, we must be men of one thing. Having found out the thing we have to do, we must throw into it all the energies of our being, seeking its accomplishment at whatever hazard or sacrifice. What did Edward Everett accomplish in proportion to his rare gifts?

What great work did he leave,—what monument of his fine powers ? What could be expected of a man who dispersed himself nearly over the whole field of knowledge and elegant accomplishment ? Or what impress would Crichton have made upon his age, if, instead of dying in a street brawl, a prodigy of acquisition at twenty-two, he had continued to scatter his energies to the age of seventy ? It is not such men that confer the highest blessings on mankind, and send their names ringing down the ages. No ; it is Bishop Butler, giving twenty years to his " Analogy," and Edward Gibbon, twenty years to the " Decline and Fall ;" it is Kant, working half a century in the quicksilver mines of metaphysics ; it is Isaac Newton, rewriting his " Chronology " seventeen times, and Adam Smith toiling ten years over " The Wealth of Nations,"—who do the work which the world honours. One of the most striking illustrations of this concentration of mind was Chief Justice Marshall. Read what Wirt says of him, and you cease to wonder at the success with which he grappled with the tough-est problems of the law. " Here is John Marshall," he writes in one of his letters, " whose mind seems to be little else than a mountain of barren and stupendous rocks,—an inexhaustible quarry from which he draws his materials and builds his fabrics, rude and Gothic, but of such strength that neither time nor force can beat them down ; a fellow who would not turn off a single step from the right line of his argument, though a paradise should rise to tempt him." And so with the giants of theology and medicine,—it is because they have rigorously limited themselves to a single subject of thought, instead of careering over the whole encyclopædia, that they have made epochs.

The poet Praed, describing a certain vicar, says :—

> " His talk is like a stream which runs
>   With rapid change from rocks to roses
> It slips from politics to puns,
>   It glides from Mahomet to Moses ;
> Beginning with the laws that keep
>   The planets in their radiant courses,
> And ending with some precept deep
>   For skinning eels or shoeing horses."

But persons who thus know a little of everything generally do not know much of anything. Even of Lord Brougham, who, of those aspiring intellects that, like Bacon, take all knowledge to be their province, is the least obnoxious to the charge of being "superficially omniscient," it has been sarcastically observed that "science was his forte, omniscience his foible," and that if his Lordship had only known a little of law, he would have known a little of everything.

Dr. Adam Clarke used to say : "The old adage about 'too many irons in the fire' conveys an abominable lie. Keep them all agoing—poker, tongs, and all !" But all are not Clarkes ; and experience shows that, generally, those who try to heat half a dozen irons at once, either burn their fingers or find the irons cooling faster than they can use them. Distraction of pursuit is the rock on which most unsuccessful persons split in early life. Nine men out of ten lay out their plans on too vast a scale ; and they who are competent to do almost anything, do nothing, because they never make up their minds distinctly as to what they want, or what they intend to be. Hence the mournful failures we see all round us in every walk of life. Behold a De Quincey, with all his wondrous and weird-like powers,—his enormous learning and wealth of thought,—producing nothing worthy of his rare gifts ! See a Coleridge, a man of Shakespearian mould, possessing a creative power of Titanic grasp, and yet, for want of concentration, fathoming among all his vagrancies no foundation, filling no chasms, and of all his dazzling and colossal literary schemes not completing one ! The heir of eternity, scorning to be the slave of time ! Feeling that he has all the ages to work in, he squanders the precious present ; so he lets his dreams go by ungrasped, his magnificent promises unrealized ; and his life may be summed up in the words of Charles Lamb, who writes to a friend : "Coleridge is dead, and is said to have left behind him above forty thousand treatises on metaphysics and divinity —not one of them complete !"

There is probably no more frequent cause of failure in life than that greediness which leads men to grasp at too many of its prizes. There are some the acquisition of which is incompatible with the acquisition of others, and the sooner this truth is realized and acted upon the better the chance of success and happiness. Much material good must be resigned if we would attain to the highest degree of moral excellence, and many spiritual joys must be foregone if we resolve at all risks to win great material advantages. To strive for a high professional position, and yet expect to have all the delights of leisure ; to labour for vast riches, and yet to ask for freedom from anxiety and care, and all the happiness which flows from a contented mind ; to indulge in sensual gratification, and yet demand health, strength, and vigour ; to live for self, and yet to look for the joys that spring from a virtuous and self-denying life, —is to ask for impossibilities. The world is a market, where everything is marked at a settled price ; and whatever we buy with our time, labour, or ingenuity,—whether riches, ease, tranquillity, fame, integrity or knowledge—we must stand by our decision, and not, like children, when we have purchased one thing, repine that we do not possess another which we did not buy. The unreasonableness of many persons in this matter is well illustrated by a passage in one of Lucian's Dialogues— cited by Mrs. Barbauld in one of her essays—where Jupiter complains to Cupid that, though he has had so many intrigues, he was never sincerely beloved. In order to be loved, says Cupid, you must lay aside your ægis and your thunderbolts, and you must curl and perfume your hair, and place a garland on your head, and walk with a soft step, and assume a winning, obsequious deportment. But, replied Jupiter, I am not willing to resign so much of my dignity. Then, returns Cupid, leave off desiring to be loved. He wanted to be Jupiter and Adonis at the same time.

In law, in medicine, in trade, in the mechanical professions, the most successful men have been those who have stuck to one thing. The advice of Dr. Hugh Blair, on a certain occasion, to Boswell, the biographer, contains a lesson for all. Boswell, in his youth, imitated, in the pit of the Drury Lane Theatre, the lowing of a cow so well that there was a general cry in the gallery, " *Encore* the cow ! " As he attempted, with very inferior effect, to vary the performance, Blair, who sat next him, whispered in his ear, " Stick to the cow, mon ! " There are few actors in life that would not do better to " stick to the cow " than to attempt the part of harlequin. Who is the favourite actor at the theatre ? Not he who personates scores of characters, but the Kean, the Booth, the Jefferson, the Warren, who always discovers the same peculiarities, and secures the applause of the audience by never going out of his individuality. When Bully Bottom, the weaver, undertook to do all the parts in the most lamentable comedy of " Pyramus and Thisbe," he no doubt set himself down for a universal genius. Not only would he play *Pyramus* and *Thisbe*, but he put in for the *Lion* and the *Wall*, the *Prologue* and the *Epilogue;* and had there been an orchestra, he would unquestionably have insisted on being the first violin. There are thousands of men in society who exhibit just so absurd and monopolizing an ambition. As Sydney Smith said of Lord John Russell, they are ready to attempt at a moment's notice the most incongruous things—to go up in a balloon, to perform an operation for cataract, or to take command of the Channel fleet. So Pope says of Wharton :—

> " Though wondering Senates hung on all he spoke,
> The club must hail him master of the joke :
> Shall parts so various aim at nothing new ?
> He'll shine a Tully, and a Willmot too."

But in ninety-nine cases out of a hundred the old adage proves true of such, that a Jack-at-all-trades is good at none. A circus-rider may ride five or six horses at a time, and not break his neck ; but a man who drives five or six trades or speculations abreast generally tumbles to the ground. Knives that contain a half-dozen blades,two or three cork-screws, a file, a small saw, a toothpick and a pair of tweezers, are wretchedly adapted to any of these purposes, and are soon thrown away in disgust. " Stick to your business," said Rothschild to a beginner ; " stick to your brewery, and you may be the great brewer of London. Be a brewer and a baker and a merchant and a manufacturer, and you will soon be in the *Gazette.*"

CHAPTER VI.

SELF-RELIANCE.

What men most covet, wealth, distinction, power,
Are bawbles nothing worth : they only serve
To rouse us up, as children at the school
Are roused up to exertion ; our reward
Is in the race we run, not in the prize.
Those few, to whom is given what they ne'er earned,
Having by favour or inheritance
The dangerous gifts placed in their hands,
Know not, nor ever can, the generous pride
That glows in him who on himself relies,
Entering the lists of life. He speeds beyond
Them all, and foremost in the race succeeds.
His joy is not that he has got his crown,
But that the power to win the crown is his.—Rogers.

"Le sentiment de nos forces les augmente."

Every person has two educations—one which he receives from others, and one, more important, which he gives himself.—Gibbon.

I remember when Mr. Locke (of Norbury Park) first came over from Italy, and old Dr. Moore, who had a high opinion of him, was crying up his drawings, and asked me if I did not think he would make a great painter? I said, "No, never!" "Why not?" "Because he has six thousand a year."—Northcote.

"Our motive power is always found in what we lack."

OF all the elements of success none is more vital than self-reliance,—a determination to be one's own helper, and not to look to others for support. It is the secret of all individual growth and vigour, the master-key that unlocks all difficulties in every profession or calling. *Aide toi, et le ciel t'aidera,* as the French have it,—help yourself, and Heaven will help you,—should be the motto of every man who would make himself useful in the world or carve his way to riches or honour. The direst curse that can befall a young man is to be the recipient of charity ; to lean, while his character is forming, on others for support. He who begins with crutches will generally end with crutches. Help from within always strengthens, but help from without invariably enfeebles, its recipient. It is not in the sheltered garden or the hot-house, but on the rugged Alpine cliffs, where the storms beat most violently, that the toughest plants are reared. It is not by the use of corks, bladders, and life-preservers that you can best learn to swim, but by plunging courageously into the wave and buffeting it, like Cassius and Cæsar, " with lusty sinews."

The man who dares not follow his own independent judgment, but runs perpetually to others for advice, becomes at last a moral weakling and an intellectual dwarf. Such a man has no *self* within him, and believes in no self within him, but goes as a suppliant to others, and entreats of them, one after another, to lend him theirs. He is, in fact, a mere element of a human being, and is borne about the world an insignificant cipher, unless he desperately fastens, by accidental cohesion, to some other floating and supplementary elements, with which he may form a species of corporation resembling a man.

It is said that a lobster, when left high and dry among the rocks, has not instinct and energy enough to work his way back to the sea, but waits for the sea to come to him. If it does not come, he remains where he is and dies, although the slightest effort would enable him to reach the waves, which are perhaps tossing and tumbling within a yard of him. The world is full of human lobsters,—men stranded on the rocks of business, who, instead of putting forth their own energies, are waiting for some grand billow of good fortune to set them afloat. There are many young men of vivid imaginations, who, instead of carrying their own burdens, are always dreaming of some Hercules coming to give them " a lift." The vision haunts their minds of some benevolent old gentleman,—a bachelor, with no children, of course, but with a bag full of money, and a trunk full of mortgages and stocks, who, being astonishingly quick to detect merit or genius, will give them a trifle of ten or twenty thousand dollars, with which they will earn a hundred thousand more. Or, perhaps they will have a legacy from some unheard-of relative, who will become conveniently defunct. " I'd rather be a kitten, and cry mew," than one of these charity-mongers. With another, we can say, that to us " one of the most disgusting sights in this world is that of a young man with healthy blood, broad shoulders, presentable calves, and a hundred and fifty pounds, more or less, of good bone and muscle, standing with his hands in his pock-ets, longing for help." In ninety-nine cases out of a hundred, pecuniary help to a beginner is the Devil's blessing,—to be de-precated, not coveted. It is the Upas-tree, that paralyzes and reduces to the last gasp the moral integrity of every man who inhales its poisonous atmosphere. Under the appearance of aiding, it weakens its victims, and keeps them in perpetual slav-ery and degradation. Cold, consequential and patronizing, it freezes the recipient into humiliation, and there leaves him, as firmly wedged as Sir John Franklin amid the thick-ribbed ice of the Arctic Ocean. Money bestowed in this way, in a majority of cases, is more truly wasted than if thrown into the sea.

God never intended that strong, independent beings should be reared by clinging to others, like the ivy to the oak, for support. The difficulties, hardships and trials of life—the obstacles one encounters on the road to fortune—are positive blessings. They knit his muscles more firmly, and teach him self-reliance, just as by wrestling with an athlete who is supe-rior to us, we increase our own strength and learn the secret of his skill. All difficulties come to us, as Bunyan says of tempt-ation, like the lion which met Samson ; the first time we en-counter them they roar and gnash their teeth, but, once subdued, we find a nest of honey in them. Peril is the very element in which power is developed. "Ability and necessity dwell near each other," said Pythagoras. "He who has battled," says Carlyle, "were it only with poverty and hard toil, will be found stronger and more expert than he who could stay at home from the battle, concealed among the provision-waggons, or even rest unwatchfully ' abiding by the stuff.' " Burke, repelling the Duke of Bedford's attack upon his pension, says of himself: "I was not rocked and swaddled and dandled into a legislator. *Nitor in adversum* is the motto for a man like me." Great statesmen in all countries have owed their sagacity, tact and foresight more to their failures than to their successes. The diplomatist becomes master of his art by being baffled, thwarted, defeated, quite as much as by winning his points. Every time he is checkmated he acquires a profounder know-ledge of the political game, and makes his next combination with increased skill and increased chances of success.

It is told of Lord Thurlow, the Chancellor of England, that, on being consulted by a parent as to the best means his son could adopt to secure success at the bar, he thus replied : " Let your son spend his own fortune, marry and spend his wife's, and then go to the bar ; there will be little fear of his failure." Why this recommendation ? Plainly, because Thurlow's observation had taught him that the man who has a sure means of support has not the inducement to put his shoulder to the wheel which stimulates and urges him who feels the pressure of the *res angustæ domi.* *Ibit eo quo vis qui zonam perdidit.* It was for this reason that Thurlow withheld from Lord Eldon, when poor, a commissionership of bankruptcy which he had promised him, saying it was a favour to Eldon to withhold it. " What he meant," says Eldon, " was, that he had learnt (a clear truth) that I was by nature very indolent, and it was only want that could make me very industrious." Nothing, indeed, can be more unwise than the anxiety of parents to accumulate property for the support of their children after their own death. Many a father toils hard and painfully economizes, that he may leave means enough to give his children " a start in the world," when, were he their worst enemy, he could hardly adopt a surer means of keeping them in poverty and obscurity.

Read the history of the rich and the poor in all ages and countries, and you will find, almost invariably, that the " lucky dogs," as they are called, began life at the foot of the ladder, without a finger's lift from Hercules; while the " unfortunates," who flit along life's paths more like scarecrows than human beings, attribute the very first declensions in their fortunes to having been bolstered and propped by others. It is a proverb that rich young men, who begin their fortunes where their fathers left off, leave off where their fathers began. The only money which benefits a man is that which he has himself earned. Inherited wealth, instead of prompting to further acquisition, is " a title-deed to sloth." The ready-made fortune of an ancestor, like his ready-made clothes, rarely fits the man to whom it falls. But why confine ourselves to those who have won distinction in the marts of commerce ? Whence come the great lights of the intellectual firmament—the stars that shine with steady radiance through the ages ? Have they not, in the vast majority of cases, emerged to eminence from the chilling depths of obscurity, destitution, and want? Who are they that

> "Pluck bright glory from the pale-faced moon,
> Or dive into the bottom of the deep,
> Where fathom-line could never touch the ground
> And drag up drowned honour by the locks?"

The scions of noble blood? The sons of the rich, who were dandled in the lap of luxury, whose path was smoothed for them at every step, who were never for an instant compelled to fight against the armed resistance of misfortune, penury, and wrong? No! they are men of humble parentage,—men whose cradles were rocked in lowly cottages, and who have buffeted the billows of fate without dependence, save upon the mercy of God and their own energies,—the gentlemen of nature, who have trodden under foot the "painted lizards" of society, and worked out their own distinction with an ardour that could not be quenched, and a perseverance that considered nothing as done while anything yet remained to be done.

There are many persons who are always looking to government, to reform societies, to improved educational institutions, to working-men's or other associations, to anything and everything but their own hands and brains, to better their condition and make their life-journey easy. But even the best institutions can give a man no active help. Laws, wisely administered, will secure to men the fruits of their industry; but no laws which the wit of man can devise can make the idle industrious, the thriftless provident, or the drunken sober. Nine-tenths of the great social evils which our reformers denounce are but the outgrowth of individual life, and no legislation can extirpate them, unless the axe is also laid at their root. It is said that when Fuseli presided at the Academy of Art in London, he read while his pupils drew, and rarely opened his lips. "I believe he was right," says his great pupil, Leslie; "for those students who are born with powers that will make them eminent, it is sufficient to place works before them. *They* do not want instruction, and those that *do* are not *worth* it. Art may be learned, but cannot be taught." What Leslie affirmed of painting is true of every pursuit under the sun. The world, though rough, is, after all, the best school-master,—better than books, better than study,—for it makes a man his own teacher, and gives him that practical training which no schools, academies, or colleges can ever impart. The great art of education, it has been wisely said, is "to teach others to teach themselves." Nor is there any contradiction to this aphorism in the saying so often quoted, that "a self-taught man had a very ignorant fellow for his master;" for, by "self-taught," is here meant one who, ignorant of all that others have accomplished, makes no use of others' labours in any department of art, science or learning, and is therefore limited to the results of his own discoveries. It has been well said that, "in mind as well as body, we are children first, only that we may afterwards become men ; dependent upon others, in order that we may learn from them such lessons as may tend eventually to our edification on an independent basis of our own .... The in-struction of others, compared with self-instruction, is like the law compared with faith—a discipline of preparation, beggarly elements, a schoolmaster to lead us on to a state of greater worthiness, and there give up the charge of us."

It cannot be too often repeated that it is not helps, but ob-stacles, not facilities, but difficulties, that make men. Beet-hoven said of Rossini, that he had the stuff in him to have made a good musician, if he had only been well flogged when a boy ; but he was spoiled by the *ease* with which he composed. Shelley tells us of certain poets that they

> " Are cradled into poetry by wrong ;
> They learn in suffering what they teach in song ; "

and it would seem that, as flowers need to be crushed before they will give forth all their perfumes, and as the goldfinch is said to sing the most sweetly when a hot needle is thrust into its eye, so pain and anguish are the conditions of some men's success, without which it is impossible to evoke the most brilliant displays of their genius. It was a shrewd remark, therefore, which a great musician once made concerning a promis-ing but passionless cantatrice : "She sings well, but she wants something, and in that something, everything. If I were single, I would court her ; I would marry her ; I would maltreat her ; would break her heart ; and in six months she would be the greatest singer in Europe." It may be doubted whether the thousand helps which men have in this age of steam, electricity, and cheap printing, are not almost as great a disadvantage as blessing. A great statesman once said that the world is governed too much. In our day it is rather doctored too much— takes too many powders, and is treated too much as an invalid. Society is everywhere overslaughed with institutions. Instead of being robust and healthy, it is getting into the condition of a sick man, with limbs bandaged and face poulticed, a nightcap on its head, and pills in its stomach, always trying some new quack medicine, always on the eve of being cured by some new matchless sanative. Like King James I. of England, who was rendered helpless by the weight of his ponderous armour, men are crushed by the very coats of mail, shields and defences by which they guard themselves against their enemies. The very asylums, hospitals and infirmaries, which are the glory of the age, unavoidably aggravate the ills they are intended to cure. Not only are the sense of danger and the fear of penalty— the great checks on transgression—lessened by the helps and reliefs interposed between the sinner and the natural consequences of his sins, but parents are encouraged to neglect the care of their children, knowing, as they do beforehand, that whatever may be their own thriftlessness or neglect of their children's education or morals, their offspring will find a safe retreat and abundant discipline in some Refuge of the Homeless, some Orphan Asylum or Reform School.

The moral feebleness of the time is equalled by the intellectual. Men are gradually ceasing to think; they have their thinking done *for* them—done by machines. " As the native in some parts of the world carries the traveller in a chair on his back over the mountains, so the teacher carries the pupil up the Alpine peaks of knowledge ; as the priest in Siberia puts his devotions into a mill, and grinds out prayers, so we expect our preacher to do our praying for us ; as the steam-whistle whisks us, asleep or awake, to the city or capital, so we expect the book over which we doze or snore to bear us to the metropolis of science." Our logarithms are ground out of a box ; our calculations manufactured by turning a handle ; we learn chemistry by inhaling laughing-gas ; we float on the water with bladders tied under our arms, and call it swimming ; and, from the cradle to manhood, make use of mental go-carts till we have lost the use of our legs. Hardly greater than this mental degeneracy of some classes is the physical, which has reached such a point that in our principal hotels elevators are employed to lift spider-legged dandies and languid females from the dinner-table to the rooms above, without the labour of climbing stairs. It has been suggested that the next contrivance to this by which the human package of dinner and *ennui* is borne, in a few seconds, to the top of the house, will be some machine for putting lazy folks to bed, and a crank-mill through which they will be run in the morning, to come out washed, cravated, brushed, combed, ready for the breakfast-table, or rather the breakfast stuffing-machine, which will have taken its place.

The London "Saturday Review," in an article on "Limp People," draws a vivid picture of the class we have been describing,—men who, lacking the force to hew out a path for themselves, can travel only in a groove already fashioned : "A molluscous man," says the writer, "too suddenly ejected from his long-accustomed groove, where, like a toad imbedded in the rock, he had made his niche exactly fitting to his own shape, presents a wretched picture of helplessness and unshiftiness. In vain his friends suggest this or that independent endeavour , he shakes his head, and says he can't,—it won't do ; what he wants is a place where he is not obliged to depend on himself, where he has to do a fixed amount of work for a fixed amount of salary, and where his fibreless plasticity might find a mould ready formed, into which it may run without the necessity of forging shapes for itself. Many a man of respectable intellectual powers has gone down to ruin, and died miserably, because of his limpness, which made it impossible for him to break new ground, or to work at anything whatsoever, with the stimulus of hope only. He must be bolstered up by certainty, supported by the walls of his groove, else he can do nothing ; and if he cannot get into his friendly groove, he lets himself drift into destruction. In no manner are limp people to be depended on, their very central quality being fluidity, which is a bad thing to rest on."

It was a saying of the late Sir Thomas Fowell Buxton, that " no man ought to be convinced by anything short of assiduous and long-continued labours issuing in absolute failure, that he is not meant to do much for the honour of God, and the good of mankind." This is a noble saying, which all men, especially all young men, should take deeply to heart. While it is true that all men cannot become Raphaels or Shakespeares, and while it is true that the number of " mute, inglorious Miltons" and Newtons, who have Paradise Losts and Principias packed away in their brains, is far smaller than is generally supposed,— it is equally true that every individual mind may contain some germ, some seed, or latent principle, the development of which may sooner or later exert an important influence over the whole widespread world. Do you complain of your feeble abilities? We answer that neither power nor capacity is to be measured by the capacity of the recipient. What ! were not the oak forests of the earth once contained in a single acorn ? Was it not a camel-driver that founded a new religion, and changed the face of empires? Was not Pope Gregory VII. a carpenter's son, Sixtus V. a shepherd, and Adrian VI. a bargeman ? Was not Copernicus the son of a baker, and Kepler the son of a publican ? Was it not an obscure monk who split in twain the Catholic Church, and a still obscurer countryman of his, who, by the invention of the printing-press, revolutionized the whole intellectual aspect of society ? Have you never heard of Clarkson, a man originally of no mark or promise, who, by the accidental reading of a pamphlet, when the slave-trade was at the zenith of its popularity, was led to see its horrors, solemnly dedicated himself to its extinction, and, amid scorn and obloquy, lived to accomplish a purpose which, at its annunciation, was ridiculed as an enthusiast's dream ? Have you not seen Cobden, a manufacturer with no brilliancy of parts, by his stubborn perseverance overthrow, in a few years, the long-established and deeply rooted commercial system of the British Empire ? Have you never read the story of Arkwright, tne barber's apprentice, who received little more than a barbe.'s education, the splendid achievements of whose mechanical genius bore the English nation triumphantly through the wars of the French Revolution, and are now declared to be of greater value than all her colonies, from Hindostan to Labrador ? History teems with such examples, showing that giant deeds may be performed by apparent pigmies, and that, if engaged in a noble cause, there is no social dwarf who may not become a moral Hercules.

There are some men who, instead of making the best use of the facilities they have for achievement, are always telling of what they might do "under happier circumstances." Under happier circumstances !—as if the very seal and sign of greatness were not precisely the regal superiority to circumstances which makes them aids and ministers to success, instead of becoming their slave ; as if it were not the masterful will which subjugates the forces of nature to be the genii of the lamp ; that concentrates twenty years of tireless but unappreciated labour on a great invention ; that forces a life-thought into a pregnant word or phrase, and sends it ringing through the ages. The truth is, the "circumstances" upon which so many faint-hearted men dwell with lugubrious eloquence should be regarded as the very tools with which one is to work—the stepping-stones he is to mount by. As Lewes says in his "Life of Goethe," instead of saying that man is the creature of circumstances it would be nearer the mark to say that man is the architect of circumstances. "Our strength is measured by our plastic power. From the same materials one man builds palaces, another hovels ; one warehouses, another villas ; bricks and mortar are' mortar and bricks until the architect makes them something else. Thus it is that in the same family, in the same circumstances, one man rears a stately edifice, while his brother, vacillating and incompetent, lives forever amid ruins ; the block of granite, which was an obstacle in the pathway of the weak, becomes a stepping-stone in the pathway of the resolute." The difficulties which utterly dishearten one man only stiffen the sinews of another, who looks on them as simply things to be vanquished—or rather as a sort of mental springing-board by which to vault across the gulf of failure on to the sure, solid ground of full success.

Archimedes said, "Give me a standing-place, and I will move the world." Goethe has changed the postulate into the precept, "Make good thy standing-place, and move the world." A reviewer, speaking of the poems of Arthur Clough, says, that he "was one of the prospectuses which never become works,—one of that class whose unwritten poems, undemonstrated discoveries, or untested powers are confidently announced as certain to carry everything before them, when they appear. *Only they never do appear.*" The world is full of such men, who are always very " promising " because they never do more than promise.

It is said that when John C. Calhoun was in Yale College he was ridiculed by his fellow-students for his intense application to study. " Why, sir," he replied, " I am forced to make the most of my time, that I may acquit myself creditably when in Congress." A laugh followed, when he exclaimed, "Do you doubt it ? I assure you, if I were not convinced of my ability to reach the national capital as a representative within the next three years, I would leave college this very day ! " Let every young man thus have faith in himself, and take earnestly hold of life, scorning all props and buttresses, all crutches and life preservers. Let him believe, with Pestalozzi, that no man in God's earth is either willing or able to help any other man. Let him strive to be a creator rather than an inheritor,—to bequeath rather than to borrow. Instead of wielding the rusted sword of valorous forefathers, let him forge his own weapons, and, conscious of the God in him and the Providence over him, let him fight his own battles with his own good lance. Instead of sighing for an education, capital, or friends, and declaring that. " if he only had these, he would be somebody," let him remember that, as Horace Greeley says, he is looking through the wrong end of the telescope ; that if he only *were* somebody, he would speedily have all the boons whose absence he is bewailing. Instead of being one of the foiled potentialities of which the world is so full,—one of the subjunctive heroes, who always might, could, would, or should do great things, but whose not doing great things is what nobody can understand,—let him be in the imperative mood, and do that of which his talents are indicative. This lesson of self-reliance once learned and acted on, and every man will discover within himself, under God, the elements and capacities of usefulness and honour.

We have dwelt at some length on the virtue which is the subject of this chapter, because it is one which, though nowhere easy to practise, is especially difficult to attain in communities like our own, where there is much social tyranny. Americans boast fondly of their independence ; yet nowhere, perhaps, is " Mrs. Grundy " more feared than here. Both men and women are, to a great extent, the moral slaves of the set or circle to which they belong; and it is only the heroic few who dare to step out into the air of freedom, where they may speak "their ain thought" instead of another's. In almost every section except the extreme West, there is an unconscious conspiracy among the members of society against each other's individuality. Custom dictates our amusements, the furniture of our houses, our modes of living, the style of our garments, and the education of our children. It tells us what we shall eat, drink, wear, when we shall go to bed and get up, what we shall give to benevolent objects, where we shall spend the summer months, and almost what we shall think. James Russell Lowell observes, not more wittily than truly, that the code of society is stronger with most persons than that of Sinai, and many a man who would not scruple to thrust his fingers in his neighbour's pocket, would forego green peas rather than use his knife as a shovel. Doubtless this state of things has its compensations. Nowhere else are men combined so easily for good purposes—nowhere built so easily into social structures, lasting or temporary, and thousands made to act as one man; yet is it not evident that we gain these advantages at a fearful cost —by too great sacrifices of individual power and individual character? Are we not too often chipped and chiselled into a dreary uniformity of thought and speech? Are we not apt to become like bricks in a wall, or marbles in a bag? In the watch-factories at Elgin and Waltham, watches are made interchangeably, so that a hundred may be taken into pieces and thrown into a heap, and the parts put together again at random. This is a good thing in watches, but who likes to see the same dull monotony in men and women?

We pity the Chinese who cramp their feet, and the Indians who flatten their heads, in obedience to custom; but are these checks upon physical growth half so contemptible as those put in civilized countries upon intellectual by the despotism of public opinion? Are we entitled to contemn the South-Sea Islander, who tattoos his face, while we bow slavishly to customs in dress that not only disfigure the person, but are destructive to health and comfort, and do every act with mental reference to "Mrs. Grundy," saying of her, as Cob did of Bobadil, "I do honour the very flea of her dog?" Mr. J. S. Mill, in his work on "Liberty," says, truly, that in this age the man who dares to think for himself and to act independently, does a service to the race. " Precisely because the tyranny of opinion is such as to make eccentricity a reproach, it is desirable, in order to break through that tyranny, that people should be eccentric. Eccentricity has always abounded when and where strength of character has abounded ; and the amount of eccentricity in a society has always been proportioned to the amount of genius, mental vigour, and moral courage which it contained. That so few now dare to be eccentric, marks the chief danger of the time."

CHAPTER VII.

ORIGINALITY IN AIMS AND METHODS.

"The powers of man have not been exhausted. Nothing has been done by him that cannot be better done. There is no effort of science or art that may not be exceeded ; no depth of philosophy that cannot be deeper sounded : no flight of imagination that may not be passed by strong and soaring wing."

Do that which is assigned you, and you cannot hope too much or dare too much. There is at this moment for you an utterance brave and grand as that of the colossal chisel of Phidias, or trowel of the Egyptians, or the pen of Moses or Dante, but different from all these.—R. W. EMERSON.

CLOSELY connected with self-reliance is another prerequisite to success, namely, originality in one's aims and methods, or the avoidance of imitation. For this purpose, it is well to cultivate some specialty. Find some new want of society—some fertile source of profit or honour—some *terra incognita* of business, whose virgin soil is yet unbroken, and there stick and grow. Specialties are the open sesame to wealth ; therefore whatever you deal in, whether groceries or speeches, bricks or law arguments, must be, or seem to be, phenomenal. Whether above or below mediocrity, they should be unique and exceptional. Byron satirizes certain namby-pamby rhymes as "so middling, bad were better;" and the sarcasm applies to all things that are "tolerable, and therefore not to be endured." That many-headed monster, the public, like the dervishes who replenished Aladdin's exchequer, requires, in this sensational age, to be forcibly *struck* before it will part with its silver. To get rid of your wares, whether material or immaterial—dry goods or professional advice—silks and calicoes, or "mouthfuls of spoken wind"—you must get your name into everybody's ears, and into everybody's mouth ; and to do this, there's nothing like a specialty.

Alexandre, of Paris, made "kid" gloves his specialty, and now his trade-mark imparts to manufactured ratskins a value incommunicable by any other talisman. William and Robert Chambers devoted their energies to the production of cheap books and periodicals, and their wealth is counted by millions. Faber has fabricated pencils till he has literally made his mark in every land, and proved the truth of the aphorism, " Quisque suæ fortunæ *faber.*" The genius of the great Dr. Brandreth ran to pills and internal improvements, and now his name and fame are as intimately and immortally connected with the alimentary canal as Clinton's with the Erie. Mason gave his whole soul to the invention of good blacking, and now his name shines like a pair of boots to which it has been applied. Herring has salamandered himself into celebrity, and Tobias has ticked his way to fame and fortune. Stewart has made bales of dry goods his stepping-stones to the proud position of a millionaire—becoming at once the Crœsus and the Colossus of the trade ; and Bonner, advertising by the acre, and tracking genius where *Ever-ett* goes, has discovered a new way of reaping golden harvests from the overworked soil of journalism.

The extent to which originality—a little thinking—may enable one who has a specialty to coin money in his business, was strikingly illustrated some years ago in the brass-clock business. One of the oldest and most noted manufacturers, wishing to keep his name perpetually before the public, contrived to do so by a succession of improvements—many of them exceedingly slight—which he invariably made known through the newspapers. Sometimes he added a new cog, or wheel or two, or altered the arrangement of the old ones ; sometimes the case was slightly remodelled. Now the face was painted in a very striking manner ; and, next, an added hammer was made to strike. This month his clocks were made to run eight days ; the next, fifteen ; then, thirty-one, or only four-and-twenty hours. No matter how trifling the change, it was invariably blazoned in all the leading public prints. By this artifice he created a ready market for all his manufactures, and became the most celebrated clock-maker in the land, though all the while scarcely a step was taken in the invention of a new principle or even in the improvement of an old one.

Mix brains, then, with your business, if you would succeed, as Opie, the painter, did with his colours. Throw open the windows of your mind to new ideas, and keep, at least, abreast of the times—if possible, ahead of them. Nothing is more fatal to self-advancement than a stupid conservatism, or servile imitation.   In these days of intense competition, if you would achieve a high success, you must think for yourself, and, above all, cultivate pliableness and versatility.   The days when a man could get rich by plodding on, without enterprise and without taxing his brains, have gone by.   Mere industry and economy are not enough; there must be intelligence and original thought. Quick-witted Jacks always get ahead of the slow-witted giants.

Whatever your calling, inventiveness, adaptability, promptness of decision must characterize and utilize your force; and if you cannot find markets, you must make them. In business, you need not know many books, but you must know your trade and men; you may be slow at logic, but you must dart at a chance like a robin at a worm.   You may stick to your groove in politics and religion; but in your business you must switch into new tracks, and shape yourself to every exigency.   We emphasize this matter, because in no country is the red-tapist so out of place as here.   Every calling is filled with bold, keen, subtle-witted men, fertile in expedients and devices, who are perpetually inventing new ways of buying cheaply, underselling, or attracting custom; and the man who sticks doggedly to the old-fashioned methods—who runs in a perpetual rut—will find himself outstripped in the race of life, if he is not stranded on the sands of popular indifference.   Keep, then, your eyes open and your wits about you, and you may distance all competitors; but ignore all new methods, and you will find yourself like a lugger contending with an ocean racer.

Although the Americans are famous the world over for their inventiveness, yet there is no people on whose cranium the organ of imitation is so prominent as on ours.   We are not the only people who "run everything into the ground;" but we certainly do it more generally, and with greater rapidity, than any other nation on the globe. No matter what branch of business is started,—from the manufacture of pills or matches to that of. sewing-machines or watches, from the ice-trade to the traffic in guano or Japanese goods,—the moment any business is discovered to be profitable, it is rushed into by thousands and tens of thousands, till a reaction follows, and it is ruined. How many times have we seen the lumbering business, both East and West, from a state of ordinary activity, which yielded a handsome profit to those engaged in it, swelled to enormous proportions,—prices raised,—lands changing owners at fast rising rates,—thousands plunging into it who hardly knew hemlock from pine,—new sawmills going up on every mill-site, and old ones running day and night,—the market glutted,—when suddenly the bubble burst, bankrupting all concerned! How many times have we seen the ship-building business swell and collapse with the same suddenness and disaster! Men who did not know halyards from shrouds, or a jibboom from a tiller, have again and again taken up their investments in stocks and mortgages, even borrowed money on accommodation paper, in their mad haste to share in the fabulous profits made by navigation. So with other branches of business; at one time the tide sets towards the raising of *morus multicaulis,*—at another the heads of the entire community are turned by reports of gold-mines,—and at another, by the fortunes made out of wool or oil. To-day, some shrewd Yankee starts a "gift" bookstore, and immediately all the newspapers in the land are flooded with advertisements of gift enterprises. To-morrow another sharp Yankee conceives the idea of a "dollar store," and, the hit proving a lucky one, there is instantly a stampede from all the other branches of trade to the "dollar store" business, till it is so overdone as to be worthless.

The same tendency to avail ourselves of other men's wits is seen in the names of our hotels, of which some, as Tremont, Revere, St. Nicholas, etc., are repeated *ad nauseam.* It is a poor kind of enterprise which thus depends upon the judgment of others, strikes out no new paths, and follows blindly every man who says, "I have made money." Nothing is more certain than that when a business pays very large profits its race is nearly run. Those who are already in it may get rich, but the late-comers, who strike in only after its profitableness has leaked out and become known to the whole community, will not only be ruined, but will cut down the profits to a point so fine as to render them merely nominal or worse. Let every man stick to the business he knows, constantly studying new plans to make it more productive, to lessen his expenses and to increase his profits. The man who knows all about a ship from the keel up will make a living profit, while the amateur, who only knows what others tell him, will lose. The foreign trader, who knows precisely the wants of the market to which he sends his goods, will get rich, while his neighbour, who gets his information at second-hand from prices current and general information accessible to everybody, will almost inevitably fail.

Above all, in literature it is imperatively essential to success that one should be phenomenal. To make a name which will live beyond the hour, you must do something or say something worth being done or said, and which has not been done or said before. Authors often speak feelingly of the difficulty of being original,—of saying anything worth saying which has not been said, and better said, by some one of their billions of predecessors ; and the dearth of books which are not a mere rehash of old ones—which are not got up as an apothecary prepares a prescription, by pouring out of many big bottles into a little one—proves the truth of the complaint. A proof yet more striking is afforded by the host of imitations which almost every successful book provokes. No sooner does a writer make a "hit," or produce a work which makes a decided sensation, than scores of other works upon similar themes and in a similar vein are forthwith extemporized, rushed through the press, and crowded in quick succession upon the public. The success of Mr. Butler's exquisite satire, "Nothing to Wear," provoked a flood of imitations ; "Ecce Homo" was followed by "Ecce Deus," "Ecce Deus Homo," and other pale and spiritless copies of the great original ; "The Gates Ajar" was followed by "The Gates Wide Open," and we had "Gates" of every kind slammed in our faces for months afterwards. Being imitations, all of these books that are written from no inward impulse or inspiration, but, like Pindar's razors, to sell, are of course inferior to their originals, as an echo is fainter than the sounds it mocks —for, as Quintilian pithily says, " he who follows must necessarily come after or behind another." When will our writers have done with this folly ? When will they abjure the jackdaw vanity of strutting in borrowed plumage ? When will they be content to " gang their ain gait," instead of mimicking the step and pace of another ? When will they learn that a good book is a cistern into which a man has poured the thoughts and feelings of years,—the net result of a lifetime of experiences,—and can no more be " rushed up" in a few weeks or months than a man can by taking thought add a cubit to his stature ? When will they leave a man who has electrified the community by an original work to enjoy the sensation he has created, instead of rushing in to steal his honours, and disgusting the public by a senseless imitation of his thoughts and style ?

The harshest verdict that can be pronounced upon any literary performance is to say that it is an imitation. It is wholly damnatory. Better to be able to say of your production, as Touchstone said of his wife, " It is an ill-favoured thing, but mine own," than that it is brilliant, but borrowed from or modelled after another. If you feel the gad-fly stinging you, as the Greeks used to say, and *must* write, choose a theme of your own, and handle it in your own way,—giving to the world the hived honey of your mind, your " thrice winnowed " ideas,— and never trouble yourself with the thought how this or that literary magnate or big-wig would treat the subject. Tell the world clearly what is passing within your own soul ; if it be a poor, needy, begging, borrowing soul, with no native ideas, such a process will, no doubt, annihilate you as an author ; but so much the better,—you will have ended at once, in an honest and courageous attempt, an abortive literary life, and restored to your country a useful cobbler, carpenter, or hatter. But if you have within you any native pith and substance, any of the stuff out of which authors are made, it is thus, and thus only, that you will bring your hidden ores, your gems of thought, to the light, and give them splendour and polish. It has been truly said that what are called *flashes of mind* in a writer are ignited by the rapid pen, and that one flash of a man's own mind is more profitable to himself, and will do him more credit with the public, than a myriad of second-hand ones. We do not, of course, advocate an impossible originality. Thorwalsden's Mercury was suggested by a lad whom he had seen sitting at rest ; but that does not lessen our admiration of the sculptor's genius. Hazlitt tells us that when Kean was so much praised for the action of Richard III., in his last struggle with his triumphant antagonist, where he stands, after his sword is wrested from him, with his hands stretched out, " as if his will could not be disarmed, and the very phantoms of his despair had a withering power," he said that he borrowed the idea from seeing the last effort of Painter in his fight with Oliver. But this, surely, does not detract from Kean's merit. No doubt the most original writer, like the bee, will have drawn his capital stock of ideas, his funded store, from a variety of sources; but as the bee, though it rifles all the flowers of the field of their sweets, lets not the honey betray the prevailing flavour of any single nectary, so will it be with him who makes the honey of Hymettus. He will lay all literature under contribution to supply his stores; but every foreign thought will be passed through the alembic of his own brain, and its elements recombined, before it is given again to the public. Like old coin, it will be melted and reminted, before it is again put in circulation. A writer who is worth reading cannot servilely imitate; he has that within him which not only places him above so doing, but which would render such a process the severest and most unnatural task to which he could subject his powers. His style, as well as his thoughts, is the natural outgrowth of himself, and he can no more ape another man's style than he can ape his gait or wear his clothes.

Let the writer, then, who pants for notoriety or covets true fame, follow Pat's advice to a bad orator,—come out from behind his nose, and speak in his own natural voice. The heaven of popular approbation is only to be taken by storm. Emerson has startled the world by his Emersonisms, and not by echoes of Carlyle, as many imagine, for he is like Carlyle only in being original. Edgar A. Poe, with all his personal faults, eternized his name on the scroll of American authors simply by being Edgar A. Poe; but who reads the legion parodies of *The Raven?* Cooper has won a great name as a novelist, though his writings are stuck as full of faults as the firmament with stars; while thousands of romancers of equal ability have gone to the "tomb of the Capulets," because they have tried to be unlike themselves. Who can forget how, when Sir Walter Scott first kindled the torch of his genius at the fires of feudal poesy, working out new scenes of interest from the warblings of scalds and troubadours and minnesingers, his thrilling cadences were mimicked by a whole forest of mocking-birds, who made the heavens vocal with the glories of moss-trooper and marauder, baron bold and gay ladye, hound in leash and hawk in hood, bastion huge and gray chapelle, henchmen and servitors, slashed sleeves and Spanish

boots, "guns, trumpets, blunderbusses, drums and thunder ¦
No sooner had the Wizard of the North gracefully resigned
his wand to a mightier Prospero, whose star of popularity had
shot with a burst to the zenith, than, *presto !* down went
Rhoderick Dhu and Wat of Buccleuch before Hassan and
Selim; the pæans to Rosabelle were exchanged for the praises
of Medora; the plaid and the bonnet for the white turban
and the baggy trousers; and over the whole realm of song
arose the Oriental dynasty under the prime viziership of Byron.
Ten thousand puny rhymsters called the moon "Phingari,"
daggers "Ataghans," drummers "Tambourgis," and women
"Houris;" became lovers of gin and haters of pork; dis-
carded their neck-cloths, and put on sack-cloth; strove perse-
veringly in turn-down collars to look Conrad-like and misan-
thropic; swore by the beard of the Prophet, and raved in
Spenserian stanzas about their "burning brows," or mourned
over their "dark imaginings;" dreamed by night of gazelle-
eyed beauties, by day of Giaours, Jereed-men, and Janizaries;
and, whether baker's, butcher's, or barber's apprentices, became
the oracles of impassioned wretchedness, and—when they
could raise money enough—adventured, in hacks hired by the
hour, imitations of Mazeppa at a hand-gallop along the highway. Where are they all now? Alas! the whole swarm of
romances in six cantos with historical notes, alike with the
ten thousand echoes of Byron, have long since gone to the
land of forgetfulness; or, if they live in an accommodated
sense of the term, owe it to the tender mercies of the pastry-
cook and the trunkmaker.

What can be more absurd than for a man to hope to rank as
a thundering Jupiter, when he borrows all his thunder? How
can you expect the world to honour you, when you despise
yourself? The great I is the first element of an Idol. Be true
to yourself, if you would have the world true to you. Your
own gift you can exhibit every moment with the cumulative
force of a whole life's cultivation, but of the borrowed talent of
another you have only a temporary half-possession. Do not be
frightened because your idiosyncrasies stick out, and provoke
criticism; it is only by these that you can be identified. If
you are knock-kneed and hump-backed; if you are squint-eyed,
and look two ways at once—so much the better; you can't

be confounded with the commonplace, stereotyped bipeds who make up that "numerous piece of monstrosity," the public. If your hair is red, let it be red; to be called red-headed Smith or Brown will distinguish you from other Smiths or Browns.

If a writer is conscious of inward emptiness, let him be dumb, remembering that "*ex nihilo nihil fit;*" but if he has any native pith and substance—any of the genuine stuff of thought—within him, he can hardly be too fearless in thrusting himself before the public. It is not your herd of imitators —the *servile pecus*, who are always looking abroad for models, who are for ever trying to catch the tone, air, gait, or periwig of this or that great original—that gain celebrity as authors. A man's nature can only *squeak out*, when subjected to such discipline. "Shakespeare," says Emerson, "never will be made by the study of Shakespeare. The Scipionism of Scipio is precisely that part he could not borrow." Let the young author be what Andrew Jackson Allen, the eccentric New York costumer, used to proclaim himself in his advertisement, "himself alone;" let him grapple firmly and fearlessly with his own ideas, and wreak his own thoughts upon expression in his own way, if he would win the praise of immortality. "To know his own aims," as Goethe recommends, "in the first place, and then manfully to follow them, looking neither to the right nor left, forward or backward," is the great secret of authorship.

Such a writer legislates from the independent throne of a separate existence, and his are the words to command the respect due to oracular authority, and to win the meed due to undisputed fame. Lady Mary Wortley Montagu said that in all her extended travels she had found but two classes of human beings—men and women; but strong as may be the generic resemblance between different minds, the fact is nevertheless obvious, that no man lives who has not his mental peculiarities and idiosyncrasies—who differs not in many respects, in soul as in body, from every other man; and if a writer fails to excite a sympathetic thrill in the public mind, it is because he lacks self-reliance—because, parrot-like, he repeats the sayings of others, instead of giving us the coinage of his own brain— because, in short, he does not stamp his writings with his own individuality.

CHAPTER VIII.

ATTENTION TO DETAILS.

My man who is to succeed must not only be industrious, but, to use an expression of a learned friend of mine, he must have "an almost ignominious love of details."—ARTHUR HELPS.

On the first publication of his (Wellington's) "Despatches," one of his friends said to him, on reading the records of his Indian campaigns : "It seems to me, Duke, that your chief business in India was to procure rice and bullocks." "And so it was," replied Wellington, "for if I had rice and bullocks, I had men ; and if I had men, I knew I could beat the enemy."—CHARACTER, BY SAMUEL SMILES.

ANOTHER indispensable element of success is attention to details. Some years ago an Eastern merchant, who had amassed a large fortune, was asked to what he attributed his success. Was it to mere chance ? No ; for other men had even better luck, yet did not get rich. Was it to industry ? Not wholly ; for many persons as indefatigable as himself had remained poor. Was it to energy ? Only in part ; for he had observed that even the most energetic men sometimes failed. But, if there was any one thing to which, more than to others, he could attribute his wealth, it was that he had made it a point never to neglect the details of his business. Many business men, he added, content themselves with planning ; regarding comprehensive views as incompatible with scrupulous attention to small matters, they leave the execution of their schemes to subordinates ; and the result is, that in the majority of cases, their plans fall through in consequence of the neglect of some clerk or other employee, and they remain for ever at the foot of the ladder.

Does not every day's experience prove the sagacity of these observations ? In the case of gifted men, especially, what cause of failure do we find more fruitful or frequent than that here indicated,—the contempt of details ? Their souls fire with lofty conceptions of some work to be achieved ; their minds warm with enthusiasm as they contemplate the object already attained;

but, when they begin to put the scheme into execution, they turn away in disgust from the dry minutiæ and vulgar drudgery which are required for its perfection. Hence the world is full of mute, inglorious Miltons, who languish, not from lack of talents, but because, in spite of their many brilliant parts, they lack something which the famous possess. Some little defect mars all their excellences, and they hang fire. They are like Swift's dancing-master, who had every qualification except that he was lame. The watch is nearly complete; it only lacks hands. The cannon is perfect, except it has no touch-hole. The mouse-trap is just the thing, but they have forgotten tho cheese. Such men bewail their fate, and so would addled eggs, if they could speak, which are so like the rest, but so dishonourably inferior. Failing to do the small tasks of life well, they have no calls to higher ones, and so they complain of neglect; as if the skipper of a schooner, on which every rope was sagging, and every sail rotting, through his negligence, should complain of the injustice done him in not making him commander of a seventy-four! The truth is, to be successful in any profession, one must have what has been called " an almost ignominious love of details." It is an element of effectiveness with which no reach of plan, no loftiness of design, no enthusiasm of purpose, can dispense. It is this which makes the difference between the practical man, who pushes his thought to a useful result, and the mere dreamer; between the Stephenson, who created a working locomotive-engine, and his predecessors, who conceived the idea of it, but could not put their thought into execution. In literature it is the conscientious and laborious attention to details—nicety in the selection and arrangement of words, even particles—that distinguishes a masterpiece of composition from a merely clever performance. So, too, in art. Whoever has looked over the collections of drawings of the old masters must have been most deeply impressed by the slow growth of their works, owing to their conscientious nicety about little things. In nothing do they differ more from common painters than in their almost endless dwelling upon some small detail,—a foot, or a hand, or a face,—fashioning and re-fashioning it, but never once losing sight of the original idea.

It has often been said that, if a man conceives the idea of becoming eminent in learning, and cannot toil through the million little drudgeries necessary to carry him on, his learning will soon be told. Or, if he undertakes to become rich, but despises the small and gradual advances by which wealth is ordinarily accumulated, his expectations will, of course, be the sum of his riches. Let a lawyer neglect the apparently petty circumstances of his case, and he will be almost sure to lose it; for some vital fact, perhaps the keystone of the whole, will be likely to escape his attention. Let the conveyancer omit the details of a deed—the little words that seem like surplusage— and he will continually involve his clients in litigation, and often subject them to the loss of their property. The difference between first and second class work in every department of labour lies chiefly in the degrees of care with which the minutiæ are executed.

All successful men have been remarkable, not only for general scope and vigour, but for their minute attention to details. Like the elephant, they can move colossal masses or pick up a pin. When Daniel Cady, the celebrated New York lawyer, had a case to argue, his labour on the details was enormous. He took it to his bed and board; had inspirations concerning it in his sleep; repeatedly arose at night to secure these by memoranda; and never ceased to mine and chamber in a great case, till it was actually called on the calendar. Then were to be seen the equipment and power of a great lawyer. When Brunelleschi elaborated the design of that cathedral in Florence which is one of the wonders of Italy, he did not content himself with leaving the execution of it to others, but personally superintended the laying of every brick of the dome, 'and even, it is thought, ascertained its specific gravity before laying it in its place.

It is said of Turner, the great English landscape painter, who sucked into the vortex of his own marvellous genius each past faculty of each past landscape painter, and re-created the art, that, though he began poor, and did a deal of drudgery for a small pittance, he never slighted even the humblest piece of work. Whether washing in skies in India ink upon other people's drawings at so much a night, or drawing cheap frontispieces for almanacs, he did everything conscientiously, never slobbering over his task, and making each day a step in advance upon his previous work. So in war. The general whose name rings in every ear, and thrills a nation with pride, does not become a hero by lofty conceptions alone, but by the patient acquisition of military details, and incessant, business-like care for the food, dress and health of his men. Ten thousand tedious trifles attended to—ten thousand orders given and disappointments borne—go to the making up of a triumph. "See, the conquering hero comes!" is an excellent tune; but before this he has had to march in the mud, pore over crumpled maps, and work vulgar sums after midnight, by a flickering lantern, in a gusty tent. While you were snoring in a feather bed, *he* has slept on the ground in wet clothes, stung by mosquitoes, *without* a supper, and *with* a headache. He has had to taste rations, economize hard tack, order executions, disarm jealousy, hire mules, eat mouldy biscuit, swallow chagrins, and digest opposition. He has brooded with ceaseless interest over military problems during the piping times of peace; he has read, like Havelock, every military memoir, and familiarized himself with every memorable battle and siege of ancient and modern times; he has kept his soul "up in arms," and his wits at his fingers' ends, year after year; and now, but not until now, has the steady fire of his life burned up into a national triumph, and the people split their throats with the name of Sherman or Grant.

Napoleon was a striking illustration of what we have stated. What was the secret of his brilliant victories? Was it not his habits of personal observation and minute attention to details? Two qualities he had in a pre-eminent degree—strict economy of time, and the habit of mastering the whole of every subject which he needed to be acquainted with. To a vivid imagination, which enabled him to look along extended lines of action, he united the ability to deal with the smallest matters essential to success with almost unerring judgment and rapidity. While other generals trusted to subordinates, he gave his personal attention to the marching of his troops, the commissariat, and other laborious and small affairs. His vast and daring plans, it has been truly said, would have been visionary in any other man; but out of his brain every vision flew a chariot of iron, because it was filled up in all the details of execution, to be a solid and compact framework in every part. No miserly merchant ever showed more exact attention to the pence and farthings, or exhibited a more thorough knowledge of the state of his ledger, than did the hero of Austerlitz concerning his men, horses, equipments, and the minute details, as well as the totality, of his force.

We find him directing where horses were to be obtained, arranging for an adequate supply of saddles, ordering shoes for the soldiers, and specifying the number of rations of bread, biscuit, and spirits that were to be brought to camp, or stored in magazines for the use of his troops. In one letter he asks Ney if he has received the muskets sent to him ; in another he gives directions to Jerome about the shirts, great-coats, clothes, shoes, shakos, and arms to be served out to the Wurtemberg regiments ; then he informs Daru that the army wants shirts, and that they don't come to hand. Again, to the Grand Duc de Berg he sends a complaint that the men want sabres ; " send an officer to obtain them at Posen. It is said that they also want helmets; order that they be made at Ebling." Again he writes : " The return which you sent me is not clear. I do not see the position of Gen. Gardanne's division, nor his force.... I see companies that do not properly belong to the army of Naples. This carelessness will at last derange the administration of the army and destroy its discipline. Send me perfectly accurate returns." " The returns of my armies," says he, in a letter written in 1806, " form the most agreeable portion of my library." Again, speaking of these monthly reports, which filled twenty thick volumes, he says : " When they are sent to me, I give up every occupation in order to read them in detail, and to observe the difference between one monthly return and another. No young girl enjoys her novel so much as I do these returns." Lord Brougham, in noticing this extraordinary attention to details, says : " The captain who conveyed Napoleon to Elba expressed to me his astonishment at his precise and, as it were, familiar knowledge of all the minute details connected with the ship. I heard from one connected with the great Helvetic mediation, in 1802, that, though the deputies soon found how hopeless they were of succeeding with the First Consul, yet they felt themselves defeated in the long discussion by one more thoroughly master of all the details of the complicated question than they could have believed it possible for any foreigner to become."

It was this practice which enabled him to concentrate his forces in so overwhelming numbers on a given point; for his close scrutiny into details—his almost preternatural knowledge of the place where a corps, or even a company, of his vast armies was to be found at any time—produced exactness and punctuality among his sub-officers, and hence the various detachments of his army were always where he wished at the very hour. His armies, in short, were, together, "only one great engine of desolation, of which he was the head or brain. Numbers, spaces, times, were all distinct in his eye. The wheeling of every legion, however remote, was mentally present to him; the tramp of every foot, the beat of every drum, the rumbling of every carriage-wheel sounded in his ear." The success of his plans, therefore, being left to no contingency, so far as contingencies could be guarded against, was as absolutely certain as human wit or wisdom could make it. A striking illustration of this is furnished by the campaign of 1805, as described by an English writer. In that year Napoleon broke up the great camp he had formed on the shores of the Channel, and gave orders for that mighty host to defile toward the Danube. Vast and various, however, as were the projects fermenting in his brain, he did not simply content himself with giving the orders, and leaving the elaboration of its details to his lieutenants. To details and minutiæ, which inferior captains would have deemed too microscopic for their notice, he gave such exhaustive attention, that, before the bugle had sounded for the march, he had planned the exact route which every regiment was to follow, the exact day it was to arrive at each station on the road, the exact day and hour it was to leave that station, as well as the precise moment when it was to reach its place of destination. These details, so thoroughly premeditated, were carried out to the letter, and the result— the fruit of that memorable march—was the victory of Austerlitz, which sealed for ten long years the fate of Europe.

It was to the same business qualities, not less than to his military genius, that Napoleon's great opponent, the Duke of Wellington, owed his successes. He left nothing to chance, but carefully provided for every contingency. He gave his attention, not only to the great matters, but to the pettiest details of the service; and was wont to concentrate all his energies, at times, on things apparently so ignominious as the manner in which the soldiers were to cook their provisions, their shoes, camp-kettles, biscuits, horse-fodder, and the exact speed at which bullocks were to be driven. It was owing in a large measure to this practical talent and constant watchful ness of small matters that he not only won brilliant victories amid the greatest discouragements, but had the rare distinction of never losing a battle.

So with our own generals, Sherman and Thomas. The correspondence of the former during the late war, published by the Government, shows that for months and months before his "great march" through the South, he was studying the country through which he was about to go, its resources, its power of sustaining armies, its populousness, the habits of the people—in short, everything that could throw light upon the probable success of his expedition. He had, in fact, literally gone over the entire country in advance. Of General Thomas, his comrade, General Steadman tells us that " he was *careful in all the details of a battle,* but once in the fight, was as furious and impetuous as Jackson. He lacked nothing to make a perfect man. No man ever imparted so much enthusiasm to his troops, and I never saw a commander who could hurl at any enemy the entire force of his army with such violence as General Thomas."

Is it not strange that, in the face of these facts, men will neglect details ? that many even consider them beneath their notice, and when they hear of the success of a business man who is, perhaps, more solid than brilliant, sneeringly say that he is "great in little things ? " Is it not the " little things " that, in the aggregate, make up whatever is great ? Is it not the countless grains of sand that make the beach ; the trees that form the forest ; the successive strata of rock that compose the mountains; the myriads of almost imperceptible stars that whiten the heavens with the milky-way ? And of what is human happiness made up, but of little things ? "One principal reason," says Jeremy Bentham, "why our existence has so much less of happiness crowded into it than is accessible to us, is that we neglect to gather up those minute particles of pleasure which every moment offers to our acceptance. In striving after a sum total, we forget the ciphers of which it is composed ; struggling against inevitable results, which he cannot control, too often man is heedless of those accessible pleasures whose amount is by no means inconsiderable when collected together. Stretching out his hand to catch the stars, man forgets the flowers at his feet, so beautiful, so fragrant, so multitudinous, and so various."

CHAPTER IX.

PRACTICAL TALENT.

" Every fish has its fly ; but even the right fly is not enough ; you must play it nicely at the right spot."

The man who sees too widely is nearly sure to be indecisive, or to appear so. Hence, also, comes an appearance, sometimes of *shuffling*, and sometimes of over-subtlety, which is very harmful to a man.—ARTHUR HELPS.

> And thus the native hue of resolution
> Is sicklied oe'r with a pale cast of thought.—SHAKESPEARE.

Ni Bacon, ni Shakespeare, ni Molière, ni Pascal, ni Tasse, ni Dante, n'auraient fait grande figure dans une revolution. Ils auraient trop vu, trop compris, trop douté, trop craint, trop souffert, trop pressenti, et trop dedaigné.—PHILERETE CHASLES.

" At a gathering in Australia, not long since, four persons met, three of whom were shepherds on a sheep-farm. One of these had taken a degree at Oxford, another at Cambridge, the third at a German university. The fourth was their employer, a squatter, rich in flocks and herds, but scarcely able to read and write, much less to keep accounts."

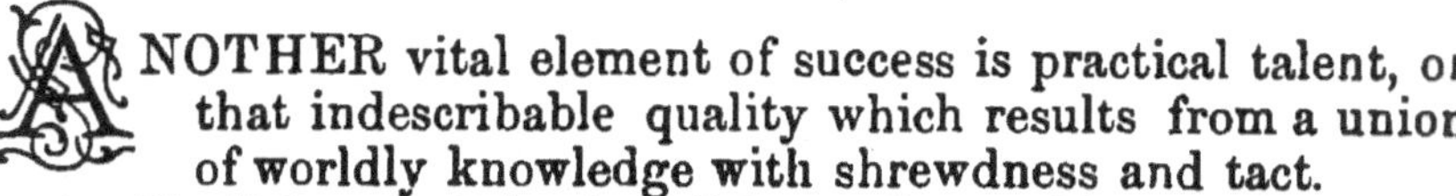

ANOTHER vital element of success is practical talent, or that indescribable quality which results from a union of worldly knowledge with shrewdness and tact.

An English writer, in describing a thoroughly practical man, says that " he knows the world as a mite knows cheese. The mite is born in cheese,—lives in cheese,—beholds cheese. If he thinks at all, his thoughts (which, of course, are *mitey* thoughts) are of cheese. The cheese-press, curds and whey, the frothy pail, the milkmaid, cow, and pasture, enter not the mite's imagination at all. If any one were to ask him, ' *Why* cheese ?' he would certainly answer, ' *Because* cheese ;' and when he is eaten by mistake, he tastes so thoroughly of the cheese that the event remains unnoticed, and his infinitesimal identity becomes absorbed in the general digestion of caseine matter, without comment of the consumer."

These remarks, though a seeming jest, only burlesque an important truth ; namely, the thorough identification with his business, and comparative indifference to all things else,

which are necessary to every man who would succeed in any
art, trade, or profession. Of all the causes of failure, there is
none more frequent or fruitful than the lack of practical talent.
The fact that to give good advice implies no capacity of following it, has often been illustrated in the world's history. The
mere theorist rarely evinces practical wisdom ; and, converse-
ly, the practical man rarely displays a high degree of speculative ability. The possession of brilliant intellectual qualities,
in ninety-nine cases out of a hundred, proves a bar rather than
a help to worldly advancement. If you try to cut a stone with
a razor, the razor will lose its edge, and the stone remain un-
cut. A very high education, again, unless it is practical as
well as classical and scientific, too often unfits a man for contest with his fellows. You have rifled the cannon till the strength
of the metal is gone. Intellectual culture, if carried beyond a
certain point, is too often purchased at the expense of moral
vigour. It gives edge and splendour to a man, but draws out
all his temper. There is reason to fear that in the case of not
a few persons the mind is so rounded and polished by education, so well balanced, as not to be energetic in any one faculty.
They become so symmetrical as to have no point ; while in other
men, not thus trained, the sense of deficiency and of the sharp,
jagged corners of their knowledge lead to efforts to fill up
the chasms, that render them at last far more learned and better educated men than the smooth, polished, easy-going gradu-
ate who has just knowledge enough to prevent the consciousness of his ignorance. In youth it is not desirable that the
mind should be too evenly balanced. While all its faculties
should be cultivated, it is yet desirable that it should have two
or three rough-hewn features of massive strength. Young men
who spend many years at a school are too apt to forget the
great end of life, which is to *be* and *do*, not to read and brood
over what other men have been and done. Emerson tells us
that England is filled with " a great, silent crowd of thorough-
bred Grecians," who prune the orations and point the pens of
its orators and writers, but who, " unless of impulsive nature,
are indisposed from writing or speaking by the fulness of their
minds and the severity of their tastes." Is such culture a
blessing ? Can any one doubt that a training which thus
paralyzes the energies, which converts the powers of the mind

that should be creative into qualities purely negative and critical, is a bar rather than a help to worldly success? Do we
not see daily, in all the walks of life, half-educated men rush
in with eagerness, and, by their daring, their outspoken sym-
pathies, their fulness and earnestness of utterance, sway mul-
titudes of their fellow-beings, while the over-educated, " silent
Greeks," with their doubts, their misgivings, their critical fas-
tidiousness, their half-utterances, and, above all, that spirit of
self-depreciation which comes from high culture, suffer their
native hue of resolution to be sicklied o'er with the pale cast
of thought ? " It has been justly said that the creative age in
every literature has preceded the critical, and that so must
it be in every man's life. A little blindness, a little self-confidence, a little ignorance of his own weaknesses and defects,
are imperatively necessary, if one would strive with hope and
pluck to win the world's prizes. Many a young man is so exquisitely cultivated as to be good for nothing but to be kept
in a show-case as a specimen of what the most approved system of education can do. With the exception of the few
comet-like geniuses that, at rare intervals, flash through the
firmament of humanity, it is the slow-headed, dull, unimagi-
native man, with colossal powers of labour, and the patience to
abide results, and to profit by the mistakes of his more gifted
fellow-mortals, that is most likely to come out ahead in the
race of life. At cricket playing it is hard hitting and quick
running that win the game. Good fielding, elegant wicket-
keeping, fast bowling, are all well in their way ; but only
notches score. So the game of life is won less by brilliant
strokes than by energetic, yet cautious play, and never missing
an easy hazard.

Do not misunderstand this. We do not decry culture. No
doubt intellectual training is to be prized. But practical
knowledge is necessary to make it available. The experience
gained from books, however valuable, is of the nature of learning ; but the experience gained from actual life is wisdom,
and an ounce of the latter is worth a pound of the former.
All history shows that the rough work of the world is not done
by men of fine culture. Courage is not developed by the study
of Greek accents. Creative power is not increased by logic.
Insight is an instinct,—not a product of education. The

greatest men in the world have not been elegant and polished scholars. There were wise men in Europe before there were printed books. The men who wrested Magna Charta could not write their own names. Bolingbroke, the scholar-statesman, fled an exile from England; while Walpole, who scorned literature, held power for thirty years. "In general," says his son, "he loved neither reading nor writing." Lord Mahon justly observes that Walpole's splendid success in life, notwithstanding his want of learning, may tend to show what is too commonly forgotten in modern plans of education, that it is of far more importance to have the mind well disciplined than richly stored,—strong rather than full. Brindley and Stephenson did not learn to read and write till they were twenty years old; yet the one gave Britain her railways and the other her canals. It has been remarked that Disraeli, whose speeches are often a literary luxury, has never laid down a single principle of policy, foreign or domestic, nor brought forward a great measure which was not ignominiously scouted. On the other hand, Sir Robert Peel, whose speeches were often the heaviest of platitudes, and whose quotations were usually from the Eton grammar, reversed his country's financial policy, regenerated Ireland, and died with the blessings of all Englishmen on his head. What practical good have the lettered politicians of France achieved for their country? or what nation is more misgoverned than that which makes literary culture the sole criterion of fitness for office,—the Chinese? Did not Napoleon complain of Laplace, that as Minister of the Interior he was always searching after subtleties, that all his ideas were problems, and that he carried the spirit of the infinitesimal calculus into the management of business? Where shall we find men of finer culture than the professors who filled the Frankfort Diet in 1848? Yet, with all their scholarship, they made themselves the laughing stock of Europe, and, with sixty millions of brave men at their back, were snuffed out without a struggle. Life teems with such illustrations. Every day we see men of high culture distanced in the race of life by the upstart who cannot spell —the practical dunce outstripping the theorizing genius. "Men have ruled well," says Sir Thomas Browne, "who could not perhaps define a commonwealth; and they who understood not the globe of the earth command a great part of it. Charlemagne could barely sign his own name ; Cromwell was "inarticulate ;" Macaulay's asthmatic hero scarcely possessed a book ; and Frederick the Great could not spell in any of the three languages which he habitually mispronounced. Many of our greatest men were born in the backwoods ; and the strongest hand that has held the helm of our government,—a hand that would have throttled Secession in its cradle,—belonged to one whom his biographer pronounces " the most ignorant man in the world."

All experience shows that for worldly success it is far more important to have the mind well trained than rich in the spoils of learning. Books, Bacon has well observed, can never teach the use of books. It is comparatively easy to be a good biographer, but very difficult to live a life worth writing. Some of the world's most useful work is done by men who cannot tell the chemical composition of the air they breathe or the water they drink, and who, like M. Jourdain, daily talk nouns, verbs, and adverbs without knowing it. They know nothing of agricultural chemistry, but they can produce sixty bushels of corn to the acre. They cannot give a philosophical account of the lever, but they know, as well as George Stephenson, that the shorter the " bite " of a crowbar the greater is the power gained. Like Sir John Hunter, they may be ignorant of the dead languages, but they may be able to teach those who sneer at their ignorance "that which they never knew in any language, dead or living." Like Andrea Ferrara, of Scotland, who, in the fourth century, turned out so delicately tempered blades from his dark cellar in the Highlands, they may lack all the tools and appliances of modern skilled labour, yet surpass in their manufactures all competitors. On the other hand, there are many persons in whose intellectual and moral character, as Macaulay says of the Duke of Monmouth, the natural son of Charles II., there is an abundance of those fine qualities which may be called luxuries, and a lamentable deficiency of those solid qualities which are of the first neces sity. "He had brilliant wit and ready invention without common-sense, and chivalrous generosity and delicacy without common honesty."

Even the highest genius will not enable a man to achieve worldly success without practical knowledge. It is, no doubt, the peculiar privilege of genius to anticipate the tardy conclusions of experience, and to see as by a flash what others learn by years of observation. The eagle swoops down upon the prey which the cat must cautiously approach, and secure after patient watching. But no genius, however exalted, can dispense with experience in the practical affairs of life. A mineralogist is not necessarily a good miner. Astronomy is not navigation, and even Bowditch or Bond must give place to a pilot in getting a ship out of the harbour of New York.

In short, the crown of all faculties is common sense. It is not the men of thought, but the men of action, who are best fitted to push their way to wealth and honour. The secret of all success lies in being alive to what is going on around one ; in adjusting one's self to his conditions ; in being sympathetic and receptive ; in knowing the wants of the time ; in saying to one's fellows what they want to hear, or what they need to hear, at the right moment ; in being the sum, the concretion, the result, of the influences of the present time. It is not enough to do the right thing *per se ;* it must be done at the right time and place. Frederick the Great said of Joseph II., Emperor of Germany, that he always wanted to take the second step before he had taken the first. The world is full of such unpractical people, who fail because they refuse to recognise the thousand conditions which fence a man in, and are impatient to reach the goal without passing over the intermediate ground. It is not so often talents which the unsuccessful man lacks as tact. " Talent," says a writer, " knows *what* to do, tact knows *how* to do it ; talent makes a man respectable, tact will make him respected ; talent is wealth, tact is ready money. For all the practical purposes of life, tact carries it against talent ten to one. Talent has many a compliment from the bench, but tact touches fees from attorneys and clients. Talent speaks learnedly and logically, tact triumphantly. Talent makes the world wonder that it gets on no faster, tact excites astonishment that it gets on so fast. And the secret is, that it has no weight to carry ; it makes no false steps ; it loses no time ; it takes all hints ; and by keeping its eye on the weathercock, is able to take advantage of every wind that blows."

As Emerson sings—

> " Tact clinches the bargain ;
>   Sails out of the bay ;
>   Gets the vote in the Senate,
>   Spite of Webster or Clay.'

There are some men who, with heads little better than a pin's, are apparently successful in everything they undertake. If wealth is their aim, they seem to stumble by mere good luck upon the philosopher's stone ; they have Midas's ears, but everything they touch turns to gold.   Men, on the other hand, who have shown the profoundest ability in their writings, have proved feeble and inefficient in active life—incapable of acting upon their own conclusions.   They are acute and sagacious enough as observers, but the moment they descend from their solitary elevation, and mingle with the crowd of their fellow-creatures, their wisdom evaporates in words. With broad views and a capacity for deep reasoning on human affairs, they feel themselves bewildered in every actual emergency ; keen and close observers of the talents and accomplishments, and even the weaknesses, of their fellow-men, they cannot actualize their own ideal of wise conduct.   Giants in the closet, they prove but children in the world.

Lord Bacon, who was one of the wisest of human beings, was a striking illustration of this truth.   He stood on the high vantage-ground of genius and learning; had an amazing insight into human nature ; and traced, " as in a map the voyager his course," the long, devious march of the human intellect, its elevations and depressions, its windings and its errors. Yet even this mighty genius, in whom reason worked as an instinct, though he was the most sagacious of men in his study, nevertheless, when he stepped from its " calm, still air " into the noisy arena of life, stooped sometimes to actions of which he could strikingly have shown the impropriety in a moral essay.   Addison, it is well known, rose by the force of his own genius to be Secretary of State ; but, though he had every opportunity for qualifying himself for his post, he found himself incompetent, and was forced to solicit his dismission with a pension of fifteen hundred pounds a year.   The fine intellect of Cowper could trace with subtlety and truth all the crooks and windings of human nature ; yet when he came to act for himself, he was a sorry bungler, and showed no tact in turning his sense and knowledge to practical account. Such were his timidity and shyness, that he declared any public exhibition of himself to be mortal poison to his feelings. Dean Swift, the pride of his master at school, was buried in a country parsonage at eight-score pounds a year; while Stafford, his school-mate, an impenetrable blockhead, acquired half a million of dollars. Dante, boiling with indignation against his enemies, could curse better than he could conspire. Machiavelli, consummate master of all the tricks and stratagems of politics, could not invent one to get his bread. Corneille did not reserve a crown for his old age, and was so miserably poor as to have his stockings mended at the street-corner. Beethoven was so ignorant of finance that he did not know enough to cut the coupon from a bond to raise a little money, instead of selling the entire instrument. He was so unpractical that, when thirty-seven years old, he sent a friend three hundred florins to buy him linen for some shirts and a half-dozen pocket-handkerchiefs; and about the same time, when he had a little more money than usual, he paid his tailor three hundred florins in advance. Often he was compelled to write music to meet his daily necessities; and one of the passages of his diary is entitled " Four Evil Days," during which he dined on a simple roll of bread and a glass of water. Need we add to all these the case of Adam Smith, who taught the nations economy, but could not manage the economy of his own house? or that of Goldsmith, whose essays teem with the shrewdest and most exquisite sense, but who never knew the value of a dollar; who, though receiving the largest sums for his writings, had always his daily bread to earn; who, when he sought to take orders, attempted to dazzle his bishop by a pair of scarlet breeches; and of whom Johnson said that no man was wiser when he had a pen in his hand, or more foolish when he had not ?

This tact, or worldly knowledge, the importance of which we have so emphasized, is rather a negative than a positive quality; why then, it may be asked, should it be deemed so vital ? We answer, simply because its influence, though negative, is felt at every turn and in every sphere of life. It is like the indispensable oil of machinery, which is a very small thing *per se*, but without which the engine ceases to work smoothly, if it works at all. Practical knowledge will not, of itself raise a man to the Presidency ; but, for want of it, many a man has failed of that and other elevations. Without it, the best runner, straining for the prize, finds himself suddenly tripped up, and lying on his back in the midst of the race. Without it, the shrewdest merchant will find his goods lying in unsold piles upon his shelves. Without it, the acutest theologian will live and die in an obscure village, and the subtlest legal acumen will never adorn the bench. The man who lacks it may be a great thinker, or a great worker. He may be an acute reasoner, and an eloquent speaker. He may be capable of writing a profound treatise on the origin of evil, and may be able in metaphysics to distinguish between the " me " and the " non-me " with more than Hermaic subtlety. He may be able to out-dive Heyne in Latin, and in Greek to excite to jealousy the shades of Porson and Parr. And yet, for all this, he fails to get on. " There is a hitch, a stand still, a mysterious want somewhere. Little impalpable trifles weave themselves into a web which holds him back. The fact is, he is not sufficiently in accord with his surroundings. He has never fairly broken the crust of individuality in which he is encased. He has never seen the importance of adjusting his scale of weights and measures to imperial standards. In a word, he is not a man of the world."

But, it may be asked, what is this practical wisdom, which is so vital to success—the want of which makes all other qualities, even the most brilliant, comparatively useless ? In what does it consist ? We answer, that it is more easy to describe it by negatives than by positives—to tell what it is not than to tell precisely what it is. An English writer* truly says that " at one end it runs up into the art of governing ; at the other it descends to that of merely pleasing. It is as indispensable to the Premier in Parliament as to the Foreign-office clerk in the salons. But between these poles—between aims the loftiest and most trivial—is the proper and legitimate sphere for the exercise of knowledge of the world. A man may be said to possess it when he exhibits practical wisdom in all the minor relations of social life. As a guest, as a host, as a national creditor, as an income-tax payer, as a railway passenger, as the vendor or purchaser of a horse, he has functions and duties

* The *Saturday Review*.

to perform. The way in which these are discharged makes the difference between the social simpleton and the worldling. The former will be perpetually coming to grief in one or the other of them. If he is entertaining, he will abuse the grandmother of the most influential man at his table. If he dines out, he will ask for fish twice in spite of the waning proportions of the cod and the indignant glances of the lady of the house. As a contributor to the revenue, he will be always in arrears and incurring the terrors of the Somerset House. At a railway station he will disturb the equanimity of the porters by a fussiness arising from a vague but awful regard of steam-power. In all dealings with horse-flesh he will be guided by the simple rule of buying in the dearest market, and selling in the cheapest. As a letter-writer he shows characteristic *naïveté*. There is a curious infelicity in his style. To a subordinate he will write with undue familiarity, or an air of ridiculous assumption—to an equal, with a smack of arrogance. The oddest rays of comfort will gleam across his letters of condolence, while his congratulations will partake of a somewhat funereal character. In addressing members of those world-wide families, he will not be particular as to the ' y ' in Smyth or the ' p ' in Thompson."

The sum of the matter is, that life is *action*. Thoughts and schemes, while they remain such, will avail you nothing, unless you are a Buddhist, bent on amalgamating yourself by meditation with the ineffable and divine essence. A Boston gentleman, who takes a business view of things, did not untruly characterize the whole race of poetic impracticables in a single felicitous sentence. Being asked the character of a certain transcendentalist,—" O," said he, " he is one of those men who have soarings after the infinite, and divings after the unfathomable, but who *never pay cash !* "

The want of practical talent in men of fine intellectual powers has often excited the wonder of the crowd. They are astonished that one whose genius has grasped, perhaps, the mightiest themes, and shed a flood of light on the path to be pursued by others, should be unable to manage his own affairs with dexterity. But this is not strange. Deep thinking and practical talents require habits of mind almost entirely dissimilar. A man who sees limitedly and clearly is both more sure

I

of himself, and is more direct in dealing with circumstances and with others, than a man with a large horizon of thought, whose many-sided capacity embraces an immense extent of objects and objections,—just as a horse with blinkers chooses his path more surely and is less likely to shy. Besides, it must be remembered that energy and self-possession alone, without superiority of intellect, suffice to give a man practical talent. There is no force in intellectual ability —mere intellectual ability, standing, to use a phrase of Burke, "in all the nakedness and solitude of metaphysical abstraction." It is passion which is the moving, vitalizing power; and a minimum of brains will often achieve more, when fired by a strong will, than a vastly larger portion with no energy to set it in motion. Practical men cut the knots which they cannot untie, and, overleaping all logical preliminaries, come at once to a conclusion. Men of genius, on the other hand, are tempted to waste time in meditating and comparing, when they should act instantaneously and with power. They are apt, too, to give unbridled license to their imaginations, and, desiring harmonious impossibilities, to foresee the difficulties so clearly that action is foregone. They have put microscopes to their eyes, and cannot drink for fear of the animalcules. In short, they theorize too much. A loaf baked is better than a harvest contemplated. An acre in Cook County is better than a principality in Utopia. Genius, to be practically useful, says the author of " Lacon," " must be endowed, not only with wings whereby to fly, but with legs whereon to stand." Both practical and speculative ability are, no doubt, modifications of mental power; but one, on that account, by no means implies the other, any more than dexterity in performing a juggler's feats involves the art of reefing a sail, though they are both instances of physical skill.

CHAPTER X.

DECISION.

" Lose this day loitering—'twill be the sam
Jo-morrow, and the next more dilatory ;
The indecision brings its own delays,
And days are lost lamenting over days.
Are you in earnest ? Seize this very minute—
What you can do, or dream you can, begin it.
Boldness has genius, power and magic in it.
Only engage, and then the mind grows heated,—
Begin, and then the work will be completed."

He (the upright student) keeps his purpose—and whatever he has resolved to do, that he does, were it only because he has resolved to do it.—
FICHTE.

But so it is with many men : " We long for the merchandise, yet would
fain keep the price," and so stand chaffering with fate in vexatious alterca-
jon till the night comes and our fair is over.—CARLYLE.

"There is nothing so imprudent as excessive prudence."

IT is but a truism to say that there can be no success in
life without decision of character. In spite of De Quincey's protest, we believe that John Foster, in his celebrated essay, did not exaggerate the importance of that quality,
though we admit that it is not strictly a moral power, and that
the most inexorable decision is much more closely connected
with physical differences of temperament than with any superiority of mind. Indeed, Foster himself expresses the opinion
that, could the histories of all the persons remarkable for decisive character be known, it would be found that the majority
of them have possessed great constitutional firmness. By this
is not meant an exemption from disease and pain, nor any certain measure of mechanical strength, but a tone of vigour, the
opposite to lassitude, and adapted to great exertion and endurance. Decision of mind, like vigour of body, is a gift of God.
It cannot be created by human effort. It can only be cultivated. It has been truly said that, as resolution, or strength of
will, is a primary power in man, there is no higher power which

can give birth to it, for this higher power would necessarily involve the existence of the lower that was to be produced. But every man has the germ of this quality, which can be cultivated by favourable circumstances and motives presented to the mind ; and, by method and order in the prosecution of his duties or tasks, he may by habit greatly augment his will-power, or beget a frame of mind so nearly resembling resolution that it would be difficult to distinguish between the two. Let no one despair because he has often broken his resolutions. Fichte has well observed that nothing is more destructive of character than for a man to lose all faith in his own resolutions, because he has so often determined, and again determined, to do that which, nevertheless, he has never done. Here, as elsewhere, " the stature of the perfect man " is attained only by slow gradations of travail, study, effort and patience. The whole armour cannot be put on at once. The first victory will render the succeeding one easier, until the very combat will be desired for the luxury of certain conquest. " The angel of martyrdom is brother to the angel of victory."

But, whether inborn or acquired, decision is a quality vitally important to him who would get on in the world. Even brains are secondary in importance to will. The intellect is but the half of a man ; the will is the driving-wheel, the spring of motive power. A vacillating man, no matter what his abilities is invariably pushed aside in the race of life by the man of determined will. It is he who resolves to succeed, and who at every fresh rebuff begins resolutely again, that reaches the goal. The shores of fortune are covered with the stranded wrecks of men of brilliant ability, but who have wanted courage faith and decision, and have therefore perished in sight of more resolute but less capable adventurers, who succeeded in making port. Hundreds of men go to their graves in obscurity, who have been obscure only because they lacked the pluck to make a first effort ; and who, could they only have resolved to begin would have astonished the world by their achievements and successes. The fact is, as Sydney Smith has well said, that " in order to do anything in this world that is worth doing, we must not stand shivering on the bank, and thinking of the cold and the danger, but jump in and scramble through as well as we can. It will not do to be perpetually calculating and adlusting nice chances; it did all very well before the Flood, when a man could consult his friends upon an intended publication for a hundred and fifty years, and then live to see its success for six or seven centuries afterwards; but at present a man waits, and doubts, and hesitates, and consults his brother, and his uncle, and his first-cousins, and his particular friends, till one day he finds that he is sixty-five years of age,—that he has lost so much time in consulting first-cousins and particular friends, that he has no more time left to follow their advice." The world was not made for slow, squeamish, fastidious men, but for those who act instantaneously and with power. Obstacles and perplexities every man must meet, and he must either promptly conquer them, or they will conquer *him.* It is rarely that the comparative good and evil of different modes of action are equally balanced; and he who would do anything to the purpose in this world should perceive the slightest inclination of the beam with an eagle's glance. It is better to decide wrong occasionally, than to be for ever wavering and hesitating, now veering to this side, and then to that, with all the misery and disaster that follow from continued doubt.

It has been truly said that the great moral victories and defeats of the world often turn on minutes. Fortune is proverbially a fickle jade, and there is nothing like promptness of action,—the timing of things at the lucky moment,—to force her to surrender her favours. Crises come, the seizing of which is triumph, the neglect of which is ruin. This is particularly true on the field of battle. Nearly every battle turns on one or two rapid movements executed amid the whirl of smoke and thunder of guns that jar the solid globe. It was at such moments that the genius of Napoleon shone forth with the highest lustre. His mind acted like the lightning, and never with more promptness and precision than in moments of the greatest confusion and danger. What confounded others only stimulated him. He used to say that one of the principal requisites of a general is an accurate calculation of time; for, if your adversary can bring a powerful force to attack a certain post ten minutes sooner than you can bring up a sufficient supporting force, you are beaten, even though all the rest of your plans be the most perfect that can be devised. At Arcola he saw that the battle was going against him, and at once called up twenty-

five horsemen, gave them each a trumpet, and made a dashing
charge that won the victory.   So at Montebello he computed
the distance of the Austrian cavalry, saw that it would require
a quarter of an hour for them to come up, and in those fifteen
minutes executed a manœuvre that saved the day.   The reason,
he said, why he beat the Austrians, was that they did not know
the value of five minutes.   At the celebrated battle of Rivoli
the day seemed on the point of being decided against him.
He saw the criticial state of affairs, and instantly formed his
resolution.   He despatched a flag to the Austrian headquarters,
with proposals for an armistice.   Napoleon seized the precious
moments, and, while amusing the enemy with mock negotia-
tions, rearranged his line of battle, changed his front, and in a
few moments was ready to renounce the farce of discussion for
the stern arbitrament of arms.   The splendid victory of Rivoli
was the result.

Another signal example of this promptness of decision occurs
at an earlier date in Napoleon's career.   He had made his wondrous burst into Northern Italy, and had driven the Austrian
troops before him like sheep.   Hardly anything was wanting
to the conquest of Lombardy but the taking of Mantua, to
which he devoted 10,000 of his troops.   At this juncture he
heard of the coming of a new Austrian army, consisting of
60,000 men, while he had in all but 40,000.   By marching
quickly along the banks of the Lake of Garda they cut off his
retreat to Milan, and thus greatly endangered his position ;
but, as the Austrians came on both sides of the lake, 20,000
on the one and 40,000 on the other, Napoleon determined to
take a position at the end of the lake, so as to be between the
two parties when they should attempt to unite.   " By rapidly
forming a main mass," says the historian, M. Thiers, " the
French might overpower the 20,000 who had turned the lake,
and immediately after return to the 40,000 who had defiled
between the lake and the Adige.   But, to occupy the extremity of the lake, it was necessary to call in all the troops from
the Lower Adige and the Lower Mincio ; Angerau must be
withdrawn from Legnago, and Serrurier from Mantua, for so
extensive a line was no longer tenable.   This involved a great
sacrifice, for Mantua had been besieged during two months, a
considerable battering-train had been transported before it, the

fortress was on the point of capitulating, and by allowing it to be revictualled, the fruits of these vigorous efforts, an almost assured prey, would escape his grasp. Napoleon, however, did not hesitate. Between two important objects he had the sagacity to seize the most important and sacrifice to it the other —a simple resolution in itself, but one which displays not only the great captain, but the great man. It is not in war merely it occurs in politics, and in all the situations of life, that men encounter two objects, and, aiming to compass both, fail in each. Bonaparte possessed that rare and decisive vigour which prompts at once the choice and the sacrifice. Had he persisted in guarding the whole course of the Mincio, from the extremity of the Lake of Garda to Mantua, he would have been pierced. By concentrating on Mantua to cover it, he would have had 70,000 men to cope with at the same time,—60,000 in front and 10,000 in the rear. He sacrificed Mantua, and concentrated at the point of the Lake of Garda." The results of this rapid decision was a brilliant reward of the masterly genius he had displayed. Meeting first the corps of 20,000 under Quasdanovich, he drove back its vanguard ; whereupon the Austrian general, surprised to find everywhere imposing masses of the French, was alarmed, and resolved to halt till he should hear of the other corps under his commander, Wurmser. Guessing what was passing in Quasdanovich's mind, Napoleon contented himself with having checked his march, and turned to meet the other body. Of this corps a large portion had passed on with Wurmser to Mantua, leaving 20,000 behind, under Bayalitsch. This army advanced with widespread wings to envelop the French ; but Napoleon pierced its weakened centre, and compelled it to retreat. The French pursued, greatly damaging it ; other battles followed ; and in six days from the beginning of hostilities the Austrian generals were again flying back to the Tyrol, having lost the kingdom of Lombardy and 20,000 men.

At the close of his career the hero of Austerlitz and Marengo was guilty of the same mistake of which he used to accuse the Austrians ; he ceased to recognise the value of minutes. Waterloo was lost to him, mainly because the swiftness of decision and promptness of action which had characterized his previous career were wanting—because he wasted precious hours before, on, and after the day of Ligny, and on the morning of Waterloo, when he should have fallen on the enemy like a thunderbolt. Wellington, on the other hand, who never lost a battle, manifested the same decisiveness and promptitude in the field to the very end of his military life. Just before the great battle in which he won his most brilliant laurels, Sir Sydney Smith being told that the Duke had decided to keep his position at all hazards, exclaimed, " O, if the Duke has said that, of course t'other fellow must give way." An amusing illustration of the Duke's characteristic qualities is the reply which he is said to have made when in danger of shipwreck. It was bed-time, when the captain of the vessel, in great affright, came to him and said, " It will soon be all over with us." " Very well," was the reply, " then I shall not take off my boots."

The superiority which decision combined with pluck gives to a few men over a great number was vividly illustrated by an incident that occurred a few years ago in the town of Lynn, Massachusetts. During a public disturbance, twenty of the Boston police cowed and kept in subjection a crowd of nearly three thousand persons. The mob was led by reckless men, who appeared determined to do violence, particularly to the policemen. With loud outcries, and armed with bricks, clubs and other weapons, the rioters advanced to the attack, expecting to overwhelm the little squad of their opponents at the first onset. Instead of making them quail, however, the only effect upon the latter was to make them more determined to maintain the public peace, which they had been sworn in and delegated to perform. They passed fearlessly into the heat and centre of the riotous demonstration, faced the thickest of the shower of missiles, and seized the ringleaders with a grip and valour that sent a shock of trepidation into the rebellious throng. The whole thing was accomplished in the briefest time, and for the reason that the police went straight to the point—took the citadel at the start. It was a triumph of promptness and pluck over numbers—of a few determined men over a half-hesitating rabble.

Of course there are occasions when caution and delay are necessary—when to act without long and anxious deliberation would be madness. All wisdom is a system of balances. It is well enough to be careful and wary up to a certain point, out beyond that a hesitating policy is as ruinous as downright rashness. Thousands of men owe their failures in life simply to procrastination. Brobdingnag in words and Lilliput in acts, they scrupulously follow Fox's advice, " Never do to-day what, by any possibility, can be put off till to-morrow." They never know their own minds, but, like Coleridge, debate with themselves the whole journey which side of the road they will take, and meanwhile keep winding from one to the other. Many a business man has made his fortune by promptly deciding at some nice juncture to expose himself to a considerable risk. To know when to sacrifice a little to win a great deal, when to abandon important minor objects to accomplish a great end, exacts the soundest judgment, and the decision has sometimes to be made in a moment's thought. There are two moments, says Browning, in a diver's life (and the same applies to every man's career) :—

> "One, when a beggar, he prepares to plunge ;
> One when, a prince, he rises with his pearl."

There are crises in almost every man's life, when the Rubicon must be passed, when the Wellington of the mart or forum must not wait for Blucher to come up, but must himself arise and charge. The battle of life is constantly presenting new phases, and he only can expect to be victorious who is ready to show a new front as often as the situation shows a new per. A sword that breaks in the very crisis of a duel, a horse killed by a flash of lightning in the moment of collision with the enemy, a bridge carried away by a freshet at the instant of a commencing retreat, are events which are paralleled in every man's business career, and call for instant decision. They confound and paralyze the feeble mind, but rouse a terrific reaction of haughty self-assertion in that order of spirits which matches and measures itself against difficulty and danger. It is told of Pellissier, the hero of the Crimea, that getting angry one morning with a sub-officer of a cavalry regiment, he cut him across the face with a whip. The man drew a pistol and attempted to explode it in the face of his chief ; but it missed fire. Uttering a fearful oath, but otherwise calm, " Fellow ! " said the grim chief of the Zouaves, " 1 order you a three days' arrest, for not having your arms in better order."

There is hardly any calling in which promptness, decision, o. presence of mind is not sometimes imperiously needed. A lawyer often needs to have all his wits about him; a sudden turn in a case, the introduction of unexpected testimony, an unlooked-for ruling by the judge, an unsuspected line of argument taken by the opposing counsel, may necessitate a complete "change of base," and demand an instant decision as to the policy to be adopted. The physician, too, must have his mind at his fingers' ends. He must get cooler in the degree that his patient gets scared. It matters not with how much medical learning his head is crammed; it is useless unless in a critical moment it is instantly available. Presence of mind is especially needed by all men who have occasion to face sudden danger. Dr. John Brown, in speaking of this quality, well observes : " It is a curious condition of mind that this requires. It is like sleeping with your pistol under your pillow, and the pistol on full cock ; a moment lost, and all may be lost. There is the very nick of time. Men, when they have done some signal feat of presence of mind, if asked how they did it, do not very well know,—they just *did it*. It was in fact done, and then thought of; not thought of and then done, in which case it would likely never have been done at all. It is one of the highest powers of mind thus to act ; it is done by an acquired instinct."

It is the lack of this promptness so characteristic of the gladiatorial intellect—of this readiness to meet every attack of ill-fortune with counter resources of evasion—which causes so many defeats in life. There is a race of narrow wits that never get rich for want of courage. Their understanding is of that halting, balancing kind, which gives a man just enough light to see difficulties and start doubts, but not enough to surmount the one or remove the other. They do not know what force of character means. They seem to have no back-bone, but only the mockery of a vertebral column, made of india-rubber, equally pliant in all directions. They come and go like shadows, speak like women, sandwich their sentences with apologies, are overtaken by events while still irresolute, and let the tide ebb before they feebly push off. Always brooding over their plans, but never executing them, they remind one of Voltaire's sarcasm upon La Harpe, whom he called an oven that was always heat ing up, but which never cooked anything. They never get ahead an inch, because they are always hugging some coward maxim, which they can only interpret literally. " Never change a certainty for an uncertainty."   " A bird in the hand is worth two in the bush," are their favourite saws ; and very good ones they are, too, but not to be followed too slavishly. Of what use is it " to be sawing about a set of maxims to which there is a complete set of antagonist maxims ? " Proverbs, it has been well said, should be sold in pairs, a single one being but a half-truth.

It is hardly possible to conceive of a more unhappy man than one afflicted with this infirmity. It has been remarked that there are persons who lack decision to such a degree that they seem never to have made up their minds which leg to stand upon—who deliberate in an agony of choice, when not a grain's weight depends on the decision, on the question what road to walk on, what chair to sit down upon, what bundle of hay to munch first. " A man without decision," says John Foster, " can never be said to belong to himself ; since, if he dared to assert that he did, the puny force of some cause, about as powerful, you would have supposed, as a spider, may make a seizure of the unhappy boaster the very next moment, and contemptuously exhibit the futility of the determinations, by which he was to have proved the independence of his understanding and will. He belongs to whatever can make capture of him ; and one thing after another vindicates its right to him, by arresting him while he is trying to go on ; as twigs and chips, floating near the edge of a river, are intercepted by every weed and whirled in every little eddy. Having concluded on a design, he may pledge himself to accomplish it—*if* the hundred diversities of feeling which may come within the week will let him. His character precluding all foresight of his conduct, he may sit and wonder what form and direction his views and actions are destined to take to-morrow ; as a farmer has often to acknowledge that next day's proceedings are at the disposal of its winds and clouds."

One of the greatest defects in the character of Charles V., Emperor of Germany, was his slowness of decision in the cabinet and in the field. Had he been prompt and decisive, he might have crushed the Reformation in the bud. Coligny, one of the champions of Protestantism in France, who perished in the massacre of St. Bartholomew, had a similar defect. A braver man never drew the sword ; but in critical moments he failed to reap the natural fruits of his valour by his hesitation and delay.

Literary men are more apt to lack decision than men who have to deal with practical matters. A melancholy example of this is furnished by the life of Sir James Mackintosh, whom Sir Henry Lytton Bulwer, in his "Historical Characters," terms "The Man of Promise." The career of Sir James was a perpetual struggle between that which he desired to be and that for which his talents fitted him. At the University of Aberdeen he was alike remarkable for his zeal in politics and his love for metaphysics, —that is, for his alternate coquetry between an active and a meditative life. At Edinburgh, also, where he went to study medicine, it was the same thing. Spending his mornings in poetical lucubrations, his evenings in making speeches at a "spouting" club, he gave little attention to the study of medicine till absolute necessity compelled him. He then applied himself with a start to that which he was obliged to know ; but his diligence was not of that resolute and steady kind which ensures success as the consequence of a certain period of application ; and, after rushing into the novelties of "The Brunonian System," which promised a knowledge of medicine with little labour, and then rushing back again, he tried to establish himself as a medical practitioner at Salisbury and at Weymouth in England, but, getting no patients, retired, disgusted and wearied, to Brussels. He next dabbled in politics ; wrote the famous pamphlet, " Vindiciæ Gallicæ," in reply to Burke ; delivered soon after at Lincoln's Inn a course of learned and eloquent lectures on Public Law, which were received with great enthusiasm ; defended M. Peltier in a speech at the bar, which was read with admiration not only in England, but on the Continent, and though he lost his cause, led him to be considered no less promising as a pleader than, after the "Vindiciæ Gallicæ," he had been considered as a pamphleteer ; became Recorder of Bombay ; returned to England, and, feeling that " it was time to be something decided," resolved " to exert himself to the utmost" if he could get a seat in Parliament ; entered the

House of Commons, and made several remarkable speeches ; accepted a professorship at the same time in Haileybury College, unable " either to commit himself to the great stream of public life, or to avoid lingering on its shores ;" planned a great historical work, which, like his projected work on Morals, was " always to be projected ;" and, at length, within a few yards of the grave, galled by the thought that the season for action was almost passed, and he had accomplished nothing worthy of his great powers, made a start, and crowded into the last few years of his life the most ambitious of his works—works all, however, of a third-rate character, neither worthy of his abilities nor justifying even in a moderate degree the expectations of his friends. The fatal defect in his character was lack of decision, of concentration, of power to choose some one object to be accomplished, and to sacrifice to its attainment all interfering inclinations. " No man," says Sir Henry L. Bulwer, " doing so little, ever went through a long life continually creating the belief that he would ultimately do so much." He passed from Burke to Fox in half an hour, and remained weeks in determining whether he should employ "usefulness" or "utility" in some particular composition. From the beginning of his life to its close he ever remained the *man of promise ;* until, amidst hopes which his vast and various information, his wonderful memory, his copious elocution, and his transitory fits of energy still nourished, he died in the sixty-seventh year of his age, universally admired and regretted, though without a high reputation for any one thing, or the ardent attachment of any particular set of persons.

Let every man who would avoid a life so abortive as this decide early what he wishes, and for what his talents fit him ; and having fixed upon an object to be attained, let him give his whole soul to its attainment, without swerving to the right or the left. " I respect the man," says Goethe, " who knows distinctly what he wishes. The greater part of all the mischief in the world arises from the fact that men do not sufficiently understand their own aims. They have undertaken to build a tower, and spend no more labour on the foundation than would be necessary to erect a hut."

Not only is decision necessary, but promptness also, without which decision loses half its value. " Is Philip at Paris ?"

asked Charles V., after his son, the King of Spain, had gained
the decisive victory over the French at Quentin.   He estimated
Philip's temper by his own.   When Ledyard was asked by the
African Association when he would be ready to start for Africa,
he replied, "To-morrow morning."   A similar answer was
made by Sir Colin Campbell, when asked when he would set
out to lead the British army to India.   It was the promptness
of Blucher that won for him the cognomen of "Marshal Forward" throughout the Prussian army.   Again, besides promptness, tenacity of decision is indispensable to him who would
make his mark in the world, or achieve any rare success.   All
the men whose names have been blazoned on the scroll of
fame have been distinguished by their firm adherence to their
purposes, by the *nescit vox missa reverti*, which has made their
spoken word like an oath.   When a certain commissary-general
complained to the Duke of Wellington that Sir Thomas Picton
had declared that he would hang him if the rations for that
general's division were not forthcoming at a certain hour, the
Duke replied, "Ah! did he go so far as that? Did he say he'd
hang you?"   "Yes, my lord."   "Well, if General Picton said
so, I have no doubt he will keep his word; you'd better get up
the rations in time."   When a man of iron will is thus known
to be so tenacious in his adherence to his resolution that, once
declared, it is like a decree of fate, there is no limit to the good
or bad results he may accomplish.   Such a will draws men and
things after it as a boat does the drift in its wake.   Men feel
that to oppose its possessor would be as futile as

> "To wound the light winds, or, with bemocked-at stabs,
>   To kill the still closing waters."

Some forty years ago murder was so rife in Havana that it
seemed literally to be cultivated as one of the fine arts, to use
De Quincey's phrase; and the city, if less libidinous, was
probably more blood-stained than Sodom or Gomorrah.   Yet,
in a short time, by the vigour and decision of one man, this
hideous state of things was entirely changed; and through
Havana then, as through England under Alfred, or through
Geneva now, the most gentle-nurtured woman could walk at
midnight with a female attendant, unscared and unharmed.
One night a murder was committed, and Tacon, the chief of

police, heard in the morning that the perpetrator was still at large. He summoned the prefect of the department in which the crime was committed. " How is this, sir ? a man murdered at midnight, and the murderer not yet arrested ?" " May it please your Excellency, it is impossible. We do not even know who it is." Tacon saw the officer was lying. " Hark you, sir. Bring me this murderer before night, or I'll garrote *you* to-morrow morning." The officer knew his man, and the assassin was forthcoming.

CHAPTER XI.

MANNER.

Manners makyth man.—WILLIAM OF WYKEHAM.

Prepare yourself for the world as the athletæ used to do for their exer·
cises; oil your mind and your manners to give them the necessary supple-
ness and flexibility ; strength alone will not do.—CHESTERFIELD.

> "The churl in spirit, howe'er the veil
> His want in forms, for fashion's sake,
> Will let his coltish nature break
> At seasons through the gilded pale."

The courtesies of a small and trivial character are the ones which strike
deepest to the grateful and appreciating heart. It is the picayune compliments which are the most appreciated ; far more than the double ones which
we sometimes pay.—HENRY CLAY.

AMONG the qualities of mind and heart which conduce
to worldly success, there is no one the importance of
which is more real, yet which is so generally underrated
at this day by the young, as courtesy—that feeling of kindness,
of love for our fellows, which expresses itself in pleasing manners. Owing to that spirit of self-reliance and self-assertion,
and that contempt for the forms and conventionalities of life,
which our young men are trained to cherish, they are too apt
to despise those delicate attentions, those nameless and exquisite tendernesses of thought and manner, that mark the true
gentleman. Yet history is crowded with examples showing
that, as in literature, it is the delicate, indefinable charm of
style, not the thought, which makes a work immortal—as a
dull actor makes Shakespeare's grandest passages flat and un-
profitable, while a Kean enables you to read them " by flashes
of lightning"—so it is the bearing of a man toward his fellows
which oftentimes, more than any other circumstance, promotes
or obstructs his advancement in life. We may complain, if
we will, that our fellow-men care more for form than substance,
for the superficies than the solid contents of a man ; but the

fact remains, and it is the clue to many of the seeming anomalies and freaks of fortune which surprise us in the matter of worldly prosperity.

No doubt there are a few men who can look beyond the husk or shell of a fellow-being—his angularities, awkwardness, or eccentricity—to the hidden qualities within ; who can discern the diamond, however incrusted ; but the majority are neither so sharp-eyed nor so tolerant, and judge a person by his appearance and demeanour more than by his substantial character. Daily experience shows that civility is not only one of the essentials of high success, but that it is almost a fortune of itself, and that he who has this quality in perfection, though a blockhead, is almost sure to get on where, without it, even men of high ability fail. " Give a boy address and accomplishments," says Emerson, " and you give him the mastery of palaces and fortunes wherever he goes ; he has not the trouble of earning or owning them ; they solicit him to enter and possess." Among strangers a good manner is the best letter of recommendation ; for a great deal depends upon first impressions, and these are favourable or unfavourable according to a man's bearing, as he is polite or awkward, shy or self-possessed. While coarseness and gruffness lock doors and close hearts, courtesy, refinement, and gentleness are an " open sesame" at which bolts fly back and doors swing open. The rude, boorish man, even though well meaning, is avoided by all. Even virtue itself is offensive when coupled with an offensive manner. Hawthorne, himself a shy man, used to say : " God may forgive sins, but awkwardness has no forgiveness in heaven or earth." Manners, in fact, are minor morals, and a rude man is generally assumed to be a bad man. " You had better," wrote Chesterfield to his son, " return a dropped fan genteelly than give a thousand pounds awkwardly ; and you had better refuse a favour gracefully than grant it clumsily....All your Greek can never advance you from secretary to envoy, or from envoy to ambassador ; but your address, your air, your manner, if good, may."

What a man says or does is often an uncertain test of what he is. It is the way in which he says or does it that furnishes the best index of his character. It is by the incidental expression given to his thoughts and feelings by his looks, tones, and gestures, rather than by his deeds or words, that we pre-

J

fer to judge him, for the simple reason that the former are invol-
untary. One may do certain deeds from design, or repeat certain professions by rote ; honeyed words may mask feelings of
hate, and kindly acts may be performed expressly to veil sinister
ends ; but the " manner of the man" is not so easily controlled.
The mode in which a kindness is done often affects us more
than the deed itself. The act itself may have been prompted
by one of many questionable motives, as vanity, pride, or interest ; the warmth or coldness with which the person who has
done it asks you how you do, or grasps your hand, is less likely
to deceive. The manner of doing anything, it has been truly
said, is " that which marks the degree and force of our internal
impression ; it emanates most directly from our immediate or
habitual feelings ; it is that which stamps its life and character
on any-action ; the rest may be performed by an automaton."
A favour may be conferred so grudgingly as to prevent any feeling of obligation, or it may be refused so courteously as to
awaken more kindly feelings than if it had been ungraciously
granted.

Hazlitt observes truly that an author's style is not less a criterion of his understanding than his sentiments. " The same
story told by two different persons shall, from the difference of
the manner, either set the table in a roar, or not relax a feature
in the whole company. . . . One of the most pleasant and least
tiresome of our acquaintance is a humourist, who has three or
four quaint witticisms and proverbial phrases, which he always
repeats over and over, so that you feel the same amusement
with less effort than if he had startled his hearers with a succession of original conceits. Another friend of ours, who never
fails to give vent to one or two real *jeux d'esprit* every time you
meet him, from the pain with which he is delivered of them,
and the uneasiness he seems to suffer all the rest of the time,
makes a much more interesting than comfortable companion.
If you see a person in pain for himself, it naturally puts you in
pain for him. The art of pleasing consists in being pleased.
To be amiable is to be satisfied with one's self and others."

The same principle is vividly illustrated by an anecdote told
by Henry Ward Beecher in a recent lecture. In the early
Abolition days two men went out preaching, one an old Quaker,
and another a young man full of fire. When the Quaker lec-

tured, everything ran along very smoothly, and he carried the audience with him. When the young man lectured, there was a row, and stones and eggs. It became so noticeable, that the young man spoke to the Quaker about it. He said, "Friend, you and I are on the same mission, and preach the same things ; and how is it that while you are received cordially, I get nothing but abuse?" The Quaker replied, "I will tell thee. Thee says, 'If you do so and so, you shall be punished,' and I say, ' My friends, if you will *not* do so and so, you shall not be punished.'" They both said the same thing, but there was a great deal of difference in the way they said it.

Politeness has been defined as benevolence in small things. A true gentleman is recognised by his regard for the rights and feelings of others, even in matters the most trivial. He respects the individuality of others, just as he wishes others to respect his own. In society he is quiet, easy, unobtrusive ; putting on no airs, nor hinting by word or manner that he deems himself better, wiser, or richer than any one about him. He is never "stuck up," nor looks down upon others because they have not titles, honours, or social position equal to his own. He never boasts of his achievements, or angles for compliments by affecting to underrate what he has done. He prefers to act, rather than to talk ; to be, rather than to seem ; and, above all things, is distinguished by his deep insight and sympathy, his quick perception of, and prompt attention to, those little and apparently insignificant things that may cause pleasure or pain to others. In giving his opinions he does not dogmatize ; he listens patiently and respectfully to other men, and, if compelled to dissent from their opinions, acknowledges his fallibility, and asserts his own views in such a manner as to command the respect of all who hear him. Frankness and cordiality mark all his intercourse with his fellows, and, however high his station, the humblest man feels instantly at ease in his presence.

Wordsworth has well expressed one of the cardinal laws of politeness in the admonition—

> " Never to blend our pleasure or our pride
> With sorrow to the meanest thing that feels."

One of the ways in which this rule is most frequently violated

is by saying witty things at others' expense. Many a man
sacrifices his worldly success to his love of jesting. There are
persons who would rather lose a life-long friend than their
joke. But friends are not so plentiful that any man can afford
to lose one for a moment's gratification, nor even for a whole
day of conversational triumphs. It has been wisely said that
spite and ill-nature are among the most expensive luxuries in
life. Dr. Johnson—who, unfortunately, violated his own precept, and to whom one is tempted to say, with Sir Thomas
Browne, "Since thou so hotly disclaimest the Devil, be not
thyself guilty of diabolism"—said on a certain occasion:
"Sir, a man has no more right to *say* an uncivil thing than to
act one; no more right to say a rude thing to another than
to knock him down." One of the redeeming points in Sheridan's character was that, though thriftless and intemperate,
he wounded no man's feelings by his jests :—

> "His wit in the combat, as gentle as bright,
>   Never carried a heart-stain away on its blade."

It is easy to depreciate these gentlemanly qualities as trifles ;
but trifles, it must be remembered, make up the aggregate of
human life. It is not so often the great acts of others that
we treasure up and remember, as the petty incivilities, slight
neglects, microscopic rudenesses, of which men are guilty
without thought, or from lack of insight or sympathy. "A
beautiful form," says the shrewdest of American essayists, " is
better than a beautiful face, and a beautiful behaviour is better
than a beautiful form ; it gives a higher pleasure than statues
or pictures; it is the finest of the fine arts." There is no
society where smiles, pleasant looks, animal spirits, are not
welcomed ; where they are not of more importance than sallies
of wit or refinements of understanding. The little courtesies
which form the small change of life may appear, separately, of
little moment, but, like the spare minutes, or the penny a day,
which amount to so enormous sums in a lifetime, they owe
their importance to repetition and accumulation. The man
who thrives in any calling is not always the shrewdest or most
laborious man, but he is almost invariably one who has shown
a willingness to please and to be pleased, who has responded
to the advances of others, not now and then, with conscious

effort, but heartily, through nature and habit, while his rival has sniffed and frowned and snubbed away every helping hand.

It is said of the Duke of Marlborough that his charming manners often changed an enemy into a friend, and that to be denied a favour by him was more pleasing than to receive one from another man. It was these personal graces that made him both rich and great, for, though he had nothing shining in his genius, and, according to Chesterfield, was eminently illiterate—"wrote bad English, and spelt it worse"—yet his figure was beautiful, and his manner irresistible by man or woman. It was this which, when he was Ensign of the Guards, charmed the Duchess of Cleveland, the favourite of Charles II., who gave him five thousand pounds, with which he laid the foundation of his subsequent fortune. His address was so exquisitely fascinating as to dissolve fierce jealousies and animosities, lull suspicion, and beguile the subtlest diplomacy of its arts. His fascinating smile and winning tongue, equally with his sharp sword, swayed the destinies of empires. Before the bland, soft-spoken commander, "grim-visaged war," in the person of Charles XII. of Sweden, "smoothed his wrinkled front;" and the fiery warrior-king, at his appeal, bade adieu to the grand and importunate suitor for his alliance, Louis XIV., whom it was his great mission to defeat and humble. It was by the same charm of manner that he was able so long to keep together the members of the grand alliance against France, and direct them, in spite of their clashing interests, their jealousies, and their perpetual dissensions, to the main objects of the war.

It is said that bees will not sting a person whose skin is smeared with honey. The gracious manner of Charles James Fox preserved him from personal dislike even when he had gambled away his last dollar, and, politically, was the most unpopular man in England. A charming manner not only enhances personal beauty, but hides ugliness and makes even plainness agreeable. There is hardly any career in which an ill-favoured countenance is not a stumbling-block at the outset that may never be surmounted. There are people called "unpresentable," who have giants to contend with at their first start in life. Yet who does not know how much a happy manner often does to neutralize the ill effects of forbidding looks ? The fascination of the demagogue Wilkes's manner triumphed over both physical and moral deformity, rendering even ugliness agreeable ; and he boasted to Lord Townsend, the handsomest man in Great Britain, that, with half an hour's start, he would get ahead of his lordship in the affections of any woman in the kingdom. The ugliest Frenchman, perhaps, that ever lived was Mirabeau ; yet such was the witchery of his manner that the belt of no gay Lothario of his day was hung with a greater number of bleeding female hearts than that of this thunderer of the Tribune, who shook from his locks " pestilence and war," and whose looks were so hideous that he was compared to " a tiger pitted by the small-pox." The success which Aaron Burr achieved, up to the hour when he betrayed his party in 1801, arose not more from his political skill and knowledge than from his inimitable address and his infinite tact in conversation.

Is any one ignorant of the charm which a fine manner gives to oratory ? Demosthenes, in reiterating the importance of " action," is supposed to have meant manner only. How many able discourses have been emasculated by a false or tasteless delivery ! How many shallow ones have passed for deep, how many commonplace ones for eloquent and original, on account of a charming intonation ! Chesterfield tells us that the Duke of Argyle, though the weakest reasoner, was the most impressive speaker he ever heard in his life. He ravished his audience, " not by his matter, but by his manner of delivering it. I was captivated, like others," continues Chesterfield ; " but when I went home and coolly considered what he had said, stripped of all those ornaments with which he had dressed it, I often found the manner flimsy, the argument weak, and I was convinced of the power of those adventitious concurring circumstances which it is ignorance of mankind to call trifling." D'Aguesseau says of Fénélon, that the charm of his manner, and a certain indescribable expression, made his hearers fancy that, instead of mastering the sciences he had discoursed upon, he had invented them. Lord Chatham was a wonderfully eloquent man, but his manner added to his eloquence. The delivery of Lord Mansfield, the silver-tongued Murray, had such ease, grace, and suavity that his bare narrative of a case was said to be worth any other man's argument. The student of English history, as he reads Wilberforce's speeches, wonders at his reputation; but, had he heard them from the lips of the orator, delivered in tones full, liquid, and penetrating, with the matchless accompaniments of attitude, gesture and expression, he would have found that a dramatic delivery can convert even commonplace into brilliant rhetoric. Napoleon thought so much of manner that he studied it under Talma, the actor, and thought, with the Romans, that youth should early be brought into contact with the posture-master and the orator.

Of the necromantic effects which manner may work in legislative bodies, Lord Chesterfield has given a striking account. Being asked to procure the adoption of the Gregorian Calendar by England, he introduced into Parliament a bill for that pur pose. "But then," he adds, " my difficulty began. I was to bring in this bill, which was necessarily composed of law jargon and astronomical calculations, to both of which I am an utter stranger. However, it was absolutely necessary to make the House of Lords think that I knew something of the matter, and also make them believe that *they* knew something of it themselves, which they did not. For my own part, I could just as soon have talked Celtic or Sclavonian to them as astronomy, and they would have understood me full as well; so I resolved to do better than speak to the purpose, and to please instead of informing them. . . . . I was particularly attentive to the choice of my words, to the harmony and roundness of my periods, to my elocution, to my action. This succeeded, and ever will succeed; they thought I informed, because I pleased them; and many of them said that I had made the whole very clear to them, when, God knows, I had not even attempted it. Lord Macclesfield, who had the greatest share in forming the bill, and who is one of the greatest mathematicians and astronomers in Europe, spoke afterwards with infinite knowledge and all the clearness that so intricate a matter would admit of; but as his words, his periods, and his utterances were not nearly so good as mine, the preference was most unanimously, though most unjustly, given to me."

Almost every man can recall scores of cases within his knowledge where pleasing manners have made the fortunes of lawyers, doctors, divines, merchants, and, in short, men in every walk of life. Raleigh, as we have already remarked, flung down his laced coat into the mud for Elizabeth to walk on, and got for his reward a proud queen's favour. The politician who has this advantage easily distances all rival candidates, for every voter he speaks with becomes instantly his friend. The very tones in which he asks for a pinch of snuff are often more potent than the logic of a Webster or a Clay. Polished manners have often made scoundrels successful, while the best of men by their hardness and coldness have done themselves incalculable injury,—the shell being so rough that the world could not believe there was a precious kernel within. Civility is to a man what beauty is to a woman. It creates an instantaneous impression in his behalf, while the opposite quality excites as quick a prejudice against him. It is a real ornament, —the most beautiful dress that man or woman can wear,—and worth more as a means of winning favour than the finest clothes and jewels ever worn. The gruffest man loves to be appreciated ; and it is oftener the sweet smile of a woman, which we think intended for us alone, than a pair of Juno-like eyes, or "lips that seem on roses fed," that bewitches our heart, and lays us low at the feet of her whom we afterwards marry.

It is a common mistake to suppose that persons who are distinguished by their sweetness and tenderness of disposition must lack force. Some of the examples of courtesy we have already given sufficiently refute this, and Faraday, the great English physicist, was another striking proof of the contrary. He was one of the gentlest of men, yet underneath his sweetness and gentleness was the heat of a volcano. Naturally he was excitable and fiery ; but "through high self-discipline," says Tyndall, "he has converted his fire *into a central glow and motive power of life,* instead of permitting it to waste itself in useless passion." It is such men that form the motive forces of the world,—persons who, though they quickly flame, and burn to a white heat when angry, yet rule their own spirits, and utilize all their fire by directing it into professional channels. On the other hand, satirical writers and talkers are not half so clever as they think themselves, or as they are thought to be. "They do winnow the corn, 'tis true, but 'tis to feed upon the chaff. It requires some talent and some generosity to find out talent and generosity in others ; though nothing but self-conceit and malice are needed to discover or to imagine faults."

One of the greatest foes to politeness is that shyness which is so characteristic of the Anglo-Saxon race. The Anglo-Saxon, wherever found, is naturally stiff, reserved and uncommunicative, and carries with him a stock of *fluide Britannique* which, as George Sand says, renders him impassive under all circumstances, and as impervious to the atmosphere of the regions he traverses as a mouse in the centre of an exhausted receiver. Dr. Guthrie, of Edinburgh, is reported to have observed in a recent address : " Ask a person at Rome to show you the road, and he will always give a civil and polite answer; but ask any person a question for that purpose in this country (Scotland), and he will say, 'Follow your nose, and you will find it.' But the blame in this country is not with the lower classes. The blame is with the upper classes ; and the reason why in this country the lower classes are not polite, is because the upper classes are not polite. I remember how astonished I was the first time I was in Paris. I spent the first night with a banker, who took me to a *pension*, or, as we call it, a boarding-house. When we got there, a servant-girl came to the door, and the banker took off his hat, and bowed to the servant-girl, and called her mademoiselle, as if she was a lady. Now, the reason why the lower classes there are so polite is because the upper classes are polite and civil to them."

Americans are not generally supposed to be timid or bashful, but Hawthorne, the essayist and novelist, who shunned so studiously the society of his fellow-beings, showed himself by his morbid shyness to be of genuine English descent. He makes record in his diary of a day when he resolved to speak to no human soul. He went to the village, got his mail at the post-office, returned and triumphantly records the fact that he spoke to no man. Is it strange that, with all his genius, the author of " The Marble Faun " was a melancholy and essentially an unhappy man ? Or is it strange that he lived so long in obscurity before his exquisite endowments were recognised by the public ?

It is true that it costs some men a much greater effort to be polite than others. It was said with bitter spleen of an English statesman, " Canning can never be a gentleman for more than three hours at a time." It is true, too, that there are times in every man's life when to be even coldly courteous makes an exhausting draught on one's patience ; but silently to devour the many chagrins of life, and to maintain a respectful bearing towards others, even under circumstances of vexation and trial, is not only a Christian duty, but worldly policy. Dr. Valentine Mott said wisely to a graduating class : "Young gentlemen, have two pockets made —a large one to hold the insults, and a small one to hold the fees." Hundreds of men have owed their start in life wholly to their winning address. " Thank you, my dear," said Lundyfoote to the little beggar-girl who bought a pennyworth of snuff. " Thank you, my dear, please call again," made Lundyfoote, a millionnaire. Some years ago a dry-goods salesman in a London shop had acquired such a reputation for courtesy and exhaustless patience that it was said to be impossible to provoke from him any expression of irritability or the smallest symptom of vexation. A lady of rank, hearing of his wondrous equanimity, determined to put it to the test by all the annoyances with which a veteran shop-visitor knows how to tease a shopman. She failed in the attempt, and thereupon set him up in business. He rose to eminence in the haberdashery trade, and the mainspring of his later as of his early career was politeness. It is related of the late Mr. Butler, of Providence, Rhode Island, that he was so obliging as to re-open his store one night solely to supply a little girl with a spool of thread which she wanted. The incident took wind, brought him a large run of custom, and he died a millionnaire, after subscribing $40,000 toward founding a hospital for the insane,—a sum which he was persuaded to give by Miss Dix, whom he was too polite to shake off, though almost as penurious as she was persevering.

Chesterfield does not exaggerate in saying that the art of pleasing is, in truth, the art of rising, of distinguishing one's self, of making a figure and a fortune in the world. It is said that some years ago in England a curate of narrow income but kindly disposition perceived two elderly spinsters in old-fashioned costume, beset with jeers and jibes by a mob of men and boys lounging round the church porch while the bell was ringing for service. Forcing his way through the crowd, he gave

one lady his right arm and the other his left, led them both
into church, and escorted them politely up the middle aisle to a
convenient pew, regardless of the stares and titters of the congregation. Some years afterwards the needy curate was agreeably surprised by the announcement that the two old ladies,
having lately died, had bequeathed him a handsome fortune in
recognition of his well-timed courtesy.

A striking illustration of the pecuniary value of obliging-
ness is found in the success of the late Mr. Ingram, publisher
of the *London Illustrated News*, who perished in Lake Mi-
chigan when the "Lady Elgin" was wrecked. He began life at
Nottingham, England, as printer and newsdealer; and, having
among his customers a gentleman who wanted his paper very
early, he was so anxious to save him from disappointment, that
one day he walked ten miles to supply a single paper. On
another occasion he rose from bed at two in the morning, and
travelled all the way to London to get some copies of a newspaper, because there was no post to bring them, being determined that his customers should have their journal. There is
no man so "hard shelled" that his soul cannot be reached by
kindness. It is said that the celebrated miser, Jack Elwes, to
save butchers' bills, made a point of eating his own sheep from
head to tail, even though the mutton almost crawled off the
plate before it was consumed. And yet the same sordid being
gave hundreds to advance the interests of an officer whose manners had pleased him in a few casual interviews; thus showing
that, when all else had failed, the oiled key of courtesy could
force back the rusty wards even of the miser's double-locked
heart.

It was through his civility to a couple of strangers, one of
them a foreigner, that Mr. Winans, of Philadelphia, is said to
have obtained, some years ago, his invitation to go to St. Petersburg and manufacture locomotives for the Russian Czar. The
gentleman had been shown with indifference through the larger
establishments of Philadelphia, but, on their coming to Mr.
Winan's, a third or fourth-rate factory, he took so much pains
to show all its parts and workings, and was so patient in his
explanations and answers to their enquiries, that, within a year,
he was surprised by an invitation to transfer his labours to
Russia. He went, accumulated a large fortune, and ultimately

received from his Russian workshops a hundred thousand dollars a year. Investing his money in real estate, he laid the foundation of one of the largest private fortunes in Philadelphia ; and all this was the result of civility to strangers.

Few men have influenced more powerfully the persons with whom they have come in contact than Bishop Fénélon. The secret of his sway over hearts was his uniform courtesy, a politeness springing from a profound love for his fellow-beings, of whatever rank or class. Lord Peterborough, the distinguished English general, said of him, that he was "a delicious man"—that " he had to run away from him to prevent his making him a Christian." Military men, as a class, are courteous the world over, attention to manner being a part of their training. Canon Kingsley observes that the love and admiration which that truly brave and loving man, Sir Sidney Smith, won from every one, rich and poor, with whom he came in contact, seems to have arisen from the one fact, that, without, perhaps, having any such conscious intention, he treated rich and poor, his own servants and the noblemen his guests, alike, and alike courteously, cheerfully, considerately, affectionately—so leaving a blessing and reaping a blessing wherever he went."

True courage and courtesy go hand in hand. The bravest men are the most forgiving, and the most anxious to avoid quarrels. It was said of Sir John Franklin that he was a man " who never turned his back upon a danger, yet of that tenderness that he would not brush away a mosquito." At a late period in life the Duke of Wellington wrote to a friend : "I am not in the habit of deciding upon such matters hastily or in anger ; and the proof of this is, that *I never had a quarrel with any man in my life !*" Considering the long and varied career, civil and military, of " The Iron Duke," and that too, in different parts of the globe ; the countless persons, of the most opposite qualities, with whom he had to deal ; his constant vexations in the Peninsula with Spanish pride and suspicion, and red-tapism at home ; the habits of his army at that time ; and his trials in political life—it is truly wonderful that the great captain, whose truthfulness was extreme, could at the age of sixty have thus spoken of himself. It is evident that he could never have said it, had he not learned, before commanding others, to command himself, watching and governing his own feelings with the same coolness and self-possession with which he handled his troops on the battle field.

If manner has such consequences, is it not folly to despise or neglect it? On the contrary, should not the cultivation of it be an important part of every man's education? We have dwelt at length upon it, because upon no other point are young men so apt to make a serious mistake as upon this. They think that if they only have the substance, the form is of little moment. But manners are more than mere form; they are "a compound of form and spirit—spirit acted into form." With business tact and energy, with learning and professional skill, the neophyte flatters himself he is sure to succeed. He can push his way through by main force. And no doubt a man may have abilities and a force of character so extraordinary as to compel all obstacles to give way before him. But advancement so gained is gained by a great waste of power. The same abilities accompanied with prepossessing manners would have achieved far more brilliant results. No doubt, by the use of mere brute force one may make a certain amount of impression; and so, too, may a soldier hew down his foes with an old-fashioned battle-axe or with a scythe, but would he be wise in preferring such a weapon to the keen Damascus blade?

Even Christian men sometimes fail in courtesy, deeming it a mark of weakness and effeminacy, or neglecting it from mere thoughtlessness. Yet, if we note the men who by their forceful qualities have most powerfully influenced their fellows, we shall find them to have added this to their other virtues, and that it was by this that they got access to the hearts they moved. An old English poet reverently styles our Saviour "the first true gentleman that ever breathed." Nobody will accuse Paul or Peter of effeminacy; yet, though they never hesitated to declare "the whole counsel of God," and often thundered into unwilling ears the most disagreeable truths, their epistles are as full of gentleness and graceful courtesy as of logic and invective. A great many good men would double their influence if they could contrive to be less stiff and inelastic—if they would but put a hinge into their necks and keep it well oiled. Gentleness in society, it has been truly said, " is like the silent influence of light, which gives colour to all nature ; it is far more powerful than loudness or force, and far more fruitful.　It pushes its way silently and persistently, like the tiniest daffodil in spring, which raises the clod, and thrusts it aside by the simple persistence of growing."

It is sometimes said that civility costs nothing ; and it is true, if by it is meant a mere external varnish, a thin wash, made up of grimaces and bows.　But the civility we mean is not a mere superficial, skin-deep politeness, "a candy'd deal of courtesy," the indiscriminate fawning of a spaniel, the grimaces of an unctuous impostor, but a hearty wish to make others happy at our own cost; a manly deference, without hypocrisy or obtrusion.　The first law of good manners, which epitomizes all the rest, is, "Thou shalt love thy neighbour as thyself."　True courtesy is simply the application of this golden rule to all our social conduct ; or, as Dr. Witherspoon so happily defined it, "it is real kindness, kindly expressed." It may be met in the hut of the Arab, in the court-yard of the Turk, in the hovel of the freedman, in the cottage of the Irishman, but is very rare in the houses of the *nouveaux riches* or in ball-rooms.　That neither morality, nor genius, nor both combined, will ensure its manifestation, is evident from the examples of Dr. Johnson and Carlyle.　The former, the despot of the "Literary Club," was so rude and gruff in manner as to acquire the nickname of "Ursa Major ;" and though Goldsmith pleaded with truth in his behalf, "No man alive has a more tender heart ; he has nothing of the bear about him but his skin," yet we cannot call a man polite who ate like an Esquimau, and with whom "You don't understand the question, sir," and "You lie, sir," were the extremes of his method in arguing with scholars on his own level.

Johnson had an abundance of nobleness, courage, and kindness of heart ; but neither of these without kindness of manner is politeness.　Nor can Carlyle, with his many noble qualities, be deemed polite, if, as a leading London journal asserts, his supreme contempt for the persons who disagree with him exasperates even those who have the highest respect for his integrity and insight.　Washington, on the other hand, was polite when he promptly returned the salute of a coloured man ; Arnold was polite when the poor woman felt that he treated her as if she were a lady; Chalmers was polite when every old woman in Morningside was elated and delighted with his courteous salute; and so was Robert Burns when he recognised an honest farmer in the street of Edinburgh, declaring to one who rebuked him that it was "not the great-coat, the scone bonnet, and the Saunders boot-hose" that he spoke to, "but the man that was in them."

Such politeness can never be acquired by studying artificial rules in books of "Etiquette." The effect of all such efforts is to make one think of himself rather than of others; whereas thinking of others, rather than of one's self, is the very essence of all courtesy. "Few young people," it has been truthfully said, "can lay themselves out to please after the Chesterfieldian method, without making themselves offensive or ridiculous to persons of any discernment; but a frank committal of one's self into benevolent hands, a trust in good intentions, a graceful self-adaptation, some remains of that confiding temper of infancy which opens its mouth and shuts its eyes, confident that something sweet, some untried good, will reward the trust—such a disposition, allied to ordinary talent and discretion, is a fortune in itself. Society does not, in fact, want the abstract best man—which means somebody who would be best if many things in him were different from and opposite to what they are—but the man who can work best with others, who can bring out and be brought out, and with whom it can most pleasantly get along."

It has been well remarked that whoever imagines legitimate manners can be taken up and laid aside, put on and off for the moment, has missed their deepest law. "A noble and attractive every-day bearing comes of goodness, of sincerity, of refinement. And these are bred in years, not moments. The principle that rules your life is the sure posture-master. Sir Philip Sidney was the pattern to all England of a perfect gentleman; but then he was the hero that, on the field of Zutphen, pushed away the cup of cold water from his own fevered and parching lips, and held it out to the dying soldier at his side!"* Such civility implied self-sacrifice, and it has reached maturity after many struggles and conflicts. It is an

* Rev. F. D. Huntington, D.D.

art and a tact, rather than an instinct or an inspiration. It is the last touch, the crowning perfection, of a noble character ; it has been truly described as the gold on the spire, the sunlight on the cornfield, the smile on the lip of the noble knight lowering his sword-point to his lady-love ; and it results only from the truest balance and harmony of soul.

CHAPTER XII.

BUSINESS HABITS.

Usus efficacissimus rerum omnium magister.—PLINY.

> "Habit at first is but a silken thread,
> Fine as the light-winged gossamers that sway
> In the warm sunbeams of a summer's day;
> A shallow streamlet, rippling o'er its bed;
> A tiny sapling, ere its roots are spread;
> A yet unhardened thorn upon the spray;
> A lion's whelp that hath not scented prey;
> A little smiling child obedient led.
> Beware! that thread may bind thee as a chain;
> That streamlet gather to a fatal sea;
> That sapling spread into a gnarled tree;
> That thorn, grown hard, may wound and give thee pain;
> That playful whelp his murderous fangs reveal;
> That child, a giant, crush thee neath his heel."

"A man is not physically perfect who has lost his little finger. It is no answer to say that such a man can do many things as well as before his mutilation. Can he do *every* thing as well? So every bad habit cripples in kind, though not in degree."

Custom is a violent and treacherous schoolmistress. She, by little and little, slyly and unperceived, slips in the foot of her authority, but having by this gentle and humble beginning, with the aid of time, fixed and established it, she then unmasks a furious and tyrannic countenance, against which we have no more the courage nor the power so much as to lift up our eyes.—MONTAIGNE.

IN some of our large mechanical establishments may be seen a machine invented to operate upon cold iron. With all the ease and quiet of a common printing-press, it exerts a force equal to a thousand tons, whilst at every pressure of the "cam" large cubes are pressed out of the solid bar as easily as one can break earthenware or mould clay. It will push its hard steel finger through iron two inches thick, without the slightest jarring or failure in the regularity of its action. What is the secret of this prodigious and constant power? It is found in the accumulated force of the balance-wheel, which, revolving one hundred and thirty times a minute, bears with over-

K

whelming force upon the steel punch, and must either break the whole machine into fragments, or pierce through every obstacle.

In this ingenious piece of mechanism we have a striking illustration of the power of habit. Who has not seen, in hundreds of instances, a moral force accumulated by it as resistless as that of the balance-wheel? There are times of pressure in every man's life when he would utterly fail but for the help thus afforded; but, fortunately, at the crisis, by the force of principles that have gathered energy by long and persevering habit, he is carried over the dead-point, and then is able to rally his strength for new trials. The vast reserve power that lies in habit has often been noticed by moralists. Man, says Paley, is a bundle of habits; and habit, according to the proverb, is a second nature, which, we all know, is sometimes so powerful as to exterminate the first. Metastasio held so strong an opinion as to the power of repetition in thought and act, that he said, "All is habit in mankind, even virtue itself." Beginning with single acts, habit is formed slowly at first, and it is not till its spider's threads are woven into a thick cable that its existence is suspected. Then it is found that, beginning with cobwebs, it ends in chains. Gulliver was bound as fast by the Lilliputians with multiplied threads as if they had used ropes. "Like flakes of snow that fall unperceived upon the earth," says Jeremy Bentham, "the seemingly unimportant events of life succeed one another. As the snow gathers together, so are our habits formed; no single flake that is added to the pile produces a sensible change; no single action creates, however it may exhibit, a man's character; but as the tempest hurls the avalanche down the mountain, and overwhelms the inhabitant and his habitation, so passion, acting upon the elements of mischief which pernicious habits have brought together by imperceptible accumulation, may overthrow the edifice of truth and virtue."

The force of this principle is strikingly illustrated in the fact that it renders pleasant things which at first were intensely disagreeable or even painful. Walking upon the quarter-deck of a vessel, though felt at first to be intolerably confined, becomes by custom so agreeable to a sailor, that in his walk on shore he often hems himself within the same bounds. Lord Kames tells of a man who, having relinquished the sea for a country life, reared in the corner of his garden an artificial mount, with a level summit, resembling most accurately a quarter-deck, not only in shape, but in size, where he generally walked. When Franklin was superintending the erection of some forts on the frontier, as a defence against the Indians, he slept at night in a blanket on the hard floor, and, on his first return to civilized life, could hardly sleep in a bed. Captain Ross and his crew, having been accustomed during their polar wanderings to lie on the frozen snow or the bare rock, afterwards found the accommodations of a whaler too luxurious for them, and he was obliged to exchange his hammock for a chair. The same principle, in another form, is illustrated in the case of persons born blind, or deprived of sight, who, acquiring a habit of nice observation through the sense of feeling, astonish us by their accurate descriptions of things which they have examined by means of their exquisitely delicate touch. So powerful is this effect of the constant repetition of actions, that men whose habits are fixed may be almost said to have lost their free agency. Their acts become of the nature of fate, and they are so bound by the chains which they have woven for themselves, that they do that which they have been accustomed to do, even when they know it can yield neither pleasure nor profit. Fielding has strikingly illustrated this in a scene in the "Life of Jonathan Wild," where that person is represented as playing at cards with the Count, a professed gambler : " Such was the power of habit over the minds of these illustrious persons, that Mr. Wild could not keep his hands out of the Count's pocket, though he knew they were empty ; nor could the Count abstain from palming a card, though he was well aware Mr. Wild had no money to pay him."

It has been truly said that even happiness itself may become habitual. One may acquire the habit of looking upon the sunny side of things, and he may also acquire the habit of looking upon the gloomy side. He may accustom himself by a happy alchemy to transmute the darkest events into materials for hope, or he may indulge in the practice of croaking till like the malevolent being of the poet,

Vix tenet lacrymas quia nil lacrymabile cernit,

Hume, the historian, said that the habit of looking at the bright side of things was better than an income of a thousand a year. It was said of Cromwell that hope shone like a fiery pillar in him when it had gone out in all others.

Such being the power of habit, can any one doubt that upon the early formation of good habits hinges the question of success in life? Above all, can we doubt that habits of patient and accurate observation, such as we have said the blind man evinces, would be of incalculable value, if brought to bear upon the thousand and one details of business life? Or is there a question that the opposite habits of negligence and inattention must lead to disaster or ruin?

Hazlitt seems to have regarded a business life as so much a matter of habit, of mere routine, as to be adapted only to plodders. In one of his brilliant essays he represents business men as mere machines. They are put in a go-cart, and are harnessed to a profession,—yoked to fortune's wheel. All they have to do, he says, is to let things take their course, and not go out of the beaten road. "The great requisite for the prosperous management of business is the want of imagination, or of any ideas but those of custom and interest on the narrowest scale." Take what you can get, he adds, and keep what you have got ; seize eagerly every opportunity that offers for promoting your own interest, and make the most of the advantages you have already obtained, and by plodding, persevering industry, you will become a first-class merchant.

This is a favourite doctrine of some literary men, but nothing can be more untrue. No doubt there are narrow-minded men of business, who measure everything by yard or tape-measure; who believe in nothing which, as Burke says, " they cannot measure with a two-foot rule,—which they cannot count with their ten fingers ;" and whose lives run in a groove from which they never escape. But are there no lawyers, doctors, or theologians who were plodders ; and do literary men never echo the old commonplaces, instead of delighting us by their breadth and originality of thought? Great men in every profession must necessarily be few. The legal boasts but few Marshalls, Pinckneys, and Websters ; the medical but few Coopers, Brodies, Velpeaus, and Warrens ; the clerical but few Barrows, Edwardses, Masons, and Channings. The names of our great

statesmen may almost be counted on the fingers.   A small business demands but a small mind ; but, that business when conducted on a large scale, does not give scope for the display of
the very highest powers of the mind, it is not easy to believe.
In past ages, before the invention of the steam-engine and the
electric telegraph, when commerce had a narrow range, but few
faculties of the mind were called into play by business ; but
to-day when submarine cables are making of the whole world
a whispering gallery, and the fluctuations of one market are
felt in every other, when so varied a knowledge and so constant a watchfulness are necessary to success, it cannot be
doubted that application to work, absorption in affairs, contact
with men, and all the stress which business imposes, give a
most efficient training to the intellect, and the highest scope for
the discipline of character.   When we consider what mental
powers are demanded to conduct a colossal trade, or to push
through any great commercial scheme,—that it demands sound
judgment, precise adaptation of means to ends, great energy,
promptness of decision and action in emergencies, skill in or-
ganizing and tact in managing men in large numbers, as well as
many minor qualities,—we shall conclude that consummate
men of business are as rare almost as great poets, orators, or
painters.

A writer in the London *Pall Mall Gazette* says, justly, that
"it is an utterly low view of business which regards it as only
a means of getting a living.   A man's business is his part of
the world's work, his share of the great activities which render
society possible.   He may like it or dislike it, but it is work,
and as such requires application, self-denial, discipline.   It is
his drill, and he cannot be thorough in his occupation without
putting himself into it, checking his fancies, restraining his impulses, and holding himself to the perpetual round of small details—without, in fact, submitting to his drill.   But the perpetual call on a man's readiness, self-control, and vigour, which
business makes, the constant appeal to the intellect, the stress
upon the will, the necessity for rapid and responsible exercise
of judgment—all these constitute a high culture, though not the
highest.   It is a culture which strengthens and invigorates, if
it does not refine ; which gives force, if not polish—the *fortiter
in re*, if not the *suaviter in modo*.   It makes strong men, and

ready men, and men of vast capacity for affairs, though it does not necessarily make refined men or gentlemen."

Among the habits required for the efficient prosecution of business of any kind, the most important are those of application, observation, method, accuracy, punctuality, and despatch. There are persons who will sneer at these virtues as little things, trifles unworthy of their notice. But it must be remembered that human life is made up of trifles ; and that, as the pence make the pounds and the minutes the hours, so it is the repetition of things severally insignificant that make up human character. In nine cases out of ten where men have failed of success, it has been owing to the neglect of little things deemed too microscopic to need attention.

Upon the importance of assiduity, or unremitting *application* to business, it is needless to dwell. All the men who have made their own fortunes have been pre-eminently distinguished for their intense and steady industry, the habit of which was early formed. If you would succeed, you must give your whole mind, heart, and soul to your work. To do this, you must *love* your work ; in no other way can you be diligent ; the very word, in its etymology, implies it. It is not talents or acquirements, but enthusiasm and energy, that win the battle of life. It is ardour and earnestness that make a man's blows tell ; a sharp stroke from a whip will do more execution than a deliberate swing of a bar of iron. It was well remarked by a Wall Street capitalist, that a bank never becomes very successful until it has a president who takes it to bed with him. Next to the youth who has no calling, he is most to be pitied who toils without heart, and is therefore forever *dawdling*—loitering and lingering, instead of striking with all his might. Laziness, fickleness, impatience, may be cured ; but the habit of dawdling, once formed, is ineradicable. Its consequences are the more disastrous because it is never found alone, but always in company with other bad habits, such as procrastination, fickleness, lack of punctuality, and often with untruthfulness. One of the qualities which early distinguished John C. Calhoun was his *power of attention*. A gentleman who, in his youth, was wont to accompany Mr. Calhoun in his strolls states that the latter endeavoured to impress upon his friends the importance of cultivating this faculty ;

"and to encourage me in my efforts," says the writer, "he stated that to this end he had early subjected *his* mind to such a rigid course of discipline, and had persisted without faltering until he had early acquired a perfect control over it ; that he could now confine it to any subject as long as he pleased, without wandering even for a moment ; that it was his uniform habit, when he set out alone to walk or ride, to select a subject for reflection, and that he never suffered his attention to wander from it until he was satisfied with its examination."

It has been remarked by Sir William Hamilton that " the difference between an ordinary mind and the mind of Newton consists principally in this, that the one is capable of a more continuous attention than the other,—that a Newton is able, without fatigue, to connect inference with inference in one long series towards a determined end ; while the man of inferior capacity is soon obliged to break or let fall the thread which he has begun to spin. . . . . . Nay, genius itself has been analyzed by the shrewdest observers into a higher capacity of attention. ' Genius,' says Helvetius, ' is nothing but a continued attention.' ' Genius,' says Buffon, ' is only a protracted patience.' ' In the exact science, at least,' says Cuvier, ' it is the patience of sound intellect, when invincible, which truly constitutes genius.' And Chesterfield has also observed that ' the power of applying an attention, steady and undissipated, to a single object, is the sure mark of superior genius.' "

Cultivate, then, this habit, if you would succeed in business. Make it a second nature. Have a work for every moment, and mind the moment's work. Whatever your calling, master all its bearings and details, all its principles, instruments, and applications. Let nothing about it escape your notice ; sound it " from its lowest note to the top of its compass."

The habit of *method* is essential to all who have much work to do, if they would get through it easily and with economy of time. Fuller, the old divine, says to those who would remember what they read : " Marshal thy notions into a handsome method. One will carry twice more weight trussed and packed up in bundles, than when it lies untowardly flapping and hanging about his shoulders." Cecil, who was a prodigious worker, has a similar hint. " Method," he says, " is like packing things in a box ; a good packer will get in half as much again as a bad one." The biographer of Noah Webster tells us that "method was the presiding principle of his life ;" and it is evident that without it he never could have got through with the herculean task of compiling his great dictionary. Coleridge, though himself one of the most immethodical of men, yet thought so highly of method that he wrote a treatise on it for the Encyclopædia Metropolitana. It is said that Whitefield could not go to sleep at night, if, after retiring, he remembered that his gloves and riding-whip were not in their usual place, where he could lay his hand upon them in the dark or any emergency. Napoleon, who astonished the sovereigns of Europe at the Congress of Erfurt by the minuteness of his knowledge of historic dates, was an eminently systematic man. He used to say that his knowledge was all deposited in drawers, and he had only to open a particular drawer, and all that he had learned on a subject was ready to hand.

There is no business which does not demand system. The meanest trade exacts it, and will go to ruin without it. But in a complicated business it is indispensable. It is this that binds all its parts together, and gives unity to all its details. Without it the vast energies of the great merchant who gathers and distributes the products of every clime, linking the four quarters of the globe by his far-reaching agencies, would be an impossibility. Commissioners of insolvency say that the books of nine bankrupts out of ten are found to be in a muddle,—kept without plan or method. Let every young man, therefore, see to it that his work is systematized,—arranged according to a carefully studied method, which takes up everything at the right time and applies to it adequate resources. It is easy, of course, to sneer at "red tape." In the sense of a mere dead and meaningless routine, it merits all the contempt poured upon it. The mere formalist, with his cast-iron rules that never bend to circumstances, is a poor creature. Method without flexibility, which ceases to be a means, and becomes an end, proves a hindrance rather than a help ; and he who, forgetting its inner meaning, becomes its slave, shows a narrowness of mind which is unfitted for great and comprehensive enterprises. But an intelligent method, which surveys the whole work before it, and assigns the several parts to distinct times and agents, which adapts itself to exigencies, and keeps ever in its eye the object to be attained, is one of the most powerful instruments of human labour. The professional or business man who despises it ,will never do any thing well. It matters not how clever or brilliant he is, or how fertile in expedients, if he work without system, catching up whatever is nearest at hand, or trying to do half a dozen things at once, he will sooner or later come to grief. Not only in the less intellectual callings, but in the learned professions, the mere plodder who " pegs away" with steady, methodical industry, will outstrip him in the end.

The importance of system in the discharge of daily duties was strikingly illustrated in the experience of Dr. Kane when he was locked up among the icebergs of the Arctic Circle, with the prospect of months of weary imprisonment. With his men enfeebled by disease and privations, and when all but eight of his company had left him to search for a way of escape, he sustained the drooping spirits of the handful who clung to him, and kept up their energies by systematic performance of duties and moral discipline. " It is," he observes, " the experience of every man who has either combated difficulties himself or attempted to guide others through them, that the controlling law shall be systematic action. Nothing depresses and demoralizes so much as a surrender of the approved and habitual forms of life. I resolved that everything should go on as it had done. The arrangement of hours, the distribution and details of duty, the religious exercises, the ceremonials of the table, the fires, the lights, the watch, the labours of the observatory, and the notation of the tides and the sky,— nothing should be intermitted that had contributed to make up the day."

The necessity of *accuracy* to success in any calling is so obvious as hardly to need remark. Vital in scholarship, of the utmost importance to the professional man, it is scarcely less indispensable to success in trade or the mechanical callings. Whatever is worth doing at all is worth doing well. It is better to do a few things carefully, precisely as they should be done, than to do ten times as many in a loose, slovenly way. Evident as all this is, yet hardly any quality is more rare than that of which we speak. Lawyers, in questioning witnesses, have painful experience of this fact. They find nothing harder than to get the exact truth without substraction or addition, colouring or qualification. Always there is a more or less, and this, too, when the witness is conscientious, and anxious " a round, unvarnished tale" to deliver. Scientific men, also, have complained bitterly of the difficulty of getting men to define a fact accurately. "I do not know that there is anything, except it be humility," says Arthur Helps, "which is so valuable as an incident of education as accuracy. And accuracy can be taught. Direct lies told to the world are as dust in the balance when weighed against the falsehoods of inaccuracy. These are the fatal things ; and they are all-pervading. I scarcely care what is taught to the young, if it will but implant in them the habit of accuracy."

It matters little what virtues a man has, if he is habitually inexact. Be he a lawyer, an architect, an accountant, or an artisan, his work is done so poorly that it has to be done over again, causing infinite trouble and perplexity. The author of Self-Help observes that it was one of the characteristic qualities of Charles James Fox, that he was thorougly pains-taking in all that he did. " When appointed Secretary of State, being piqued at some observation as to his bad writing, he actually took a writing-master, and wrote copies like a school-boy, until he had sufficiently improved himself. Though a corpulent man, he was wonderfully active in picking up cut tennis balls, and when asked how he contrived to do so, he playfully replied, ' Because I am a very pains-taking man.' The same accuracy in trifling matters was displayed by him in things of greater importance ; and he acquired his reputation like the painter, by ' neglecting nothing.' "

Punctuality is another virtue which must be cultivated by all who would succeed in any calling, whether lofty or humble. It is emphatically the virtue of a mercantile and busy community. Nothing inspires confidence in a man sooner than this quality, nor is there any habit which sooner saps his reputation than that of being always behind time. Thousands have failed in life from this cause alone. Unpunctuality is not only a serious vice in itself, but it is also the parent of a large progeny of other vices, so that he who becomes its victim becomes involved in toils from which it is almost impossible to escape. He who needlessly breaks his appointment shows that he is as reckless of the waste of others' time as of his own. His acquaintances readily conclude that the man who is not conscientious about his appointments will be equally careless about his other engagements, and they will refuse to trust him with matters of importance. To the busy man time is money, and he who robs him of it does him as great an injury, so far as loss of property is concerned, as if he had picked his pocket, or paid him with a forged check or counterfeit bills.

Whether a man steals from me a dollar, or the half-hour in which I can earn that sum, is to me a matter of indifference. The former crime may be the more demoralizing to the offender ; but my loss is as great in the one case as in the other. It has been justly said that there is as much injustice and cruelty in destroying a man's comfort during the five minutes you keep him waiting, as in giving him an actual blow. But suppose ten or twenty men are kept waiting for one man, and that, too, in the business part of the day, when every moment is precious; what shall we say of such conduct ? The robbery is as great as that of a quarter or half of a day to one man. By an utterly inexcusable negligence he causes an utter perdition of capital and labour to that amount—more, perhaps, than by his own industry he can replace in a month—to say nothing of the vexation he has caused, unfitting twenty men for their duties for all the rest of the day.

It is a familiar truth that punctuality is the life of the universe. The planets keep exact time in their revolutions, each, as it circles round the sun, coming to its place yearly at the very moment when it is due. So in business, punctuality is the soul of industry, without which all its wheels come to a dead stand, If the time of a business man is properly occupied, every hour will have its appropriate work. If the work of one hour is postponed to another, it mnst encroach upon the time of some other duty, or remain undone ; and thus the whole business of the day is thrown into' disorder. " When a regiment is under march," writes Sir Walter Scott to a yonng man who had asked his advice, " the rear is often thrown into confusion because the front do not move steadily and without interruption. It is the same thing with business. If that which is first in hand, be not instantly, steadily, and regularly despatched, other things accumulate behind, till affairs begin to press all at once, and no human brain can stand the confusion."

Let every business man then, keep a watch, and let him carefully regulate it, so that it may never be ahead or behind the stroke of the bell.   Captain Cuttle had a watch of which he said that "if he could only remember to set it ahead half an hour in the forenoon, and back a quarter of an hour in the afternoon, it would keep time with anybody's watch"   Too many business men have similar timekeepers, which they forget to set ahead; the resuit of which is that they are late at the counting-room, late at the office, or late on 'change.   True, they are often tardy but five or ten minutes, but it is just enough to break their engagement, damage their reputation, and lose a bargain.   Punctuality should be made not only a point of courtesy, but a point of conscience.   The beginner in business should make this virtue one of the first objects of professional acquisition.   Let him not delude himself with the idea that it is easy of attainment, or that he can practise it by and by, when the necessity of it shall be more cogent.   It is not easy to be punctual, no, not even in youth; but in after-life, when the character is fixed, when the mental and moral faculties have acquired a cast-iron rigidity, to unlearn the habit of tardiness is almost an impossibility.   It sticks to the man, though the reason be fully convinced of its criminality and inconvenience.

The successful men in every calling have had a keen sense of the value of time.   They have been misers of minutes.   Nelson attributed all his success in life to having been a quarter of an hour before his time.   Napoleon studied his watch as closely as he studied the maps of the battle-field.   His victories were not won by consummate strategy merely, but by impressing his subordinates with the necessity of punctuality to the minute. Manœuvring over large spaces of country, so that the enemy was puzzled to decide where the blow would fall, he would suddenly concentrate his force and fall with resistless might on some weak point in the extended lines of the foe—a plan the successful execution of which demanded that every division of his army should be at the place named at the very hour. It is related that on one occasion his marshals, who had been invited to dine with him, were ten minutes late.   Rising to meet them, the Emperor, who began his dinner as tle clock struck and had finished, said : "Gentlemen, it is now past dinner, and we will immediately proceed to business ;" whereupon the marshals were obliged to spend the afternoon in planning a campaign on an empty stomach. Later in life Napoleon was less prompt ; and it was his loss of precious hours on the morning of Ligny, and his inexplicable dawdling on the day after the defeat of Blucher, which contributed more than any other cause to the fatal overthrow at Waterloo. On the other hand, it was the promptness and punctuality of "Marshal Forward" (as Blucher was nicknamed by his troops) which enabled Wellington to convert what otherwise would have probably been a drawn battle into a brilliant victory. The Napoleon of Austerlitz and Jena would have made history tell a different story. It is said that Colonel Rahl, the Hessian commander who in the American Revolution was routed and taken prisoner at Trenton, lost the battle through procrastination. Engrossed in a game of cards, he postponed the reading of a letter which reached him, informing him that Washington was about to cross the Delaware, and thus lost the opportunity of thwarting the design of the American general, and perhaps giving a different direction to the War of Independence. Washington, on the other hand, was so rigidly punctual, that when Hamilton, his secretary, pleaded a slow watch as an excuse for being five minutes tardy, he replied : "Then, sir, either you must get a new watch, or I must get a new secretary."

In the business world punctuality is as important as in the military. "Take care of the pence, and the pounds will take care of themselves," is the secret of getting rich ; and so in the time-currency, minutes are the precious pence that, saved or lost, make the millionnaire or the bankrupt. How many persons have been ruined by neglecting for a day, or even an hour, to renew an insurance policy ! How many merchants are made bankrupts by delays of their customers in paying their notes or accounts ! Often the failure of one man to meet his obligations promptly causes the ruin of a score of other men, just as in a line of bricks the toppling down of the master brick necessitates the fall of all the rest.

John Quincy Adams, who filled a greater number of important offices, political and civil, than has any other American, was pre-eminently punctual. He was an economist of moments, and was never known to be behind time. His reputation in this respect was such that when in his old age he was a member of the House of Representatives at Washington, and a gentleman observed that it was time to call the House to order, another replied, "No, Mr. Adams is not in his seat." The clock, it was found, was actually three minutes too fast; and, before three minutes had elapsed, Mr. Adams was at his post.

While the business man should be especially punctual to his express engagements with other persons, he should also keep all his implied engagements, and therefore should be always at his shop or office at the regular hour. There are some kinds of work which men are comparatively excusable for doing irregularly. Literary labour, which depends so much upon the condition of the mind and body, is of this kind. Milton was in the vein only in the springtime; and many lesser writers can realize their ideals only when they are inspired by circumstances beyond their control. Yet not a few writers have schooled themselves to write at set hours; and Dr. Johnson went so far as to say that a man could write at any hour and in any mood, if he would but set himself doggedly about it. But mercantile men and business men generally have no excuse for irregularity. They have not to wait for moods and impulses,—for the afflatus or inspiration which is so capricious with men whose business is all of the brain and none of the hand. They are therefore expected, and justly expected, to be promptly at their posts, ready always to attend to the business of buying and selling, giving professional advice, or whatever other duties belong to their calling; and it is evident that of two such men of equal talents, the one who is always at his desk or shop at the striking of the clock cannot fail to secure the greater number of customers.

To all the habits we have named should be added, lastly, that of *despatch*. The other qualities upon which we have insisted are of more vital importance; but when this is added, it puts the keystone to the arch of a business character. Many professional men, traders, and artisans do their work thoroughly, accurately, and punctually, who fail just here. They have

never caught the knack of doing it quickly. Hardly anything
is more characteristic of a first-class workman than the brisk,
expeditious way in which he executes any job intrusted to him.
Of course, quickness should always be secondary to thorough-
ness. Nothing can atone for the lack of completeness and accuracy. True despatch is not a smart and facile activity, which
skims over a subject lightly, or dashes off a job perfunctorily,
satisfied with imperfect work, provided it is done speedily. It
is a quickness which follows from thorough knowledge and the
highest skill,—from the perfection of a method which takes
everything at the right time, and applies to it the needed resources. It is the triumph of experience and system. To the
energetic, systematic man it matters not how complex a business is. The more it tasks his faculties, the more does it
evoke his latent powers, so that to do increases the capacity of
doing, and a large amount of work is done with greater ease
than a small amount by a slow man.

It is an inestimable advantage when to a habit of despatch
is added the gift of *readiness*,—the ability to use all one's resources instantly and at the right moment. We say " gift,"
because the ready man is born, not made. No amount of cultivation will enable a man to say and do the best things on the
spur of the moment, to dash off a masterly newspaper or review
article on some memorable event immediately after it occurs, or
to take instant advantage of an enemy's blunder, like Napoleon
or Marlborough. Readiness is a natural tact or intuition, an
inspiration, a kind of presence of mind which enables one to
meet a crisis, parry a thrust, strike a blow, or say the right
word, in the very " nick of time," without reflection or delay.
In war, politics, journalism, at the bar and in the Senate, in
social intercourse, it is a great power. In all kinds of tongue-
fence— the close hand-to-hand encounter of intellects, where the
home thrust is often so suddenly given—it is indispensable.
It is not the amount of knowledge, the number of facts or statistics which a man has in his cranium, that makes him a dangerous antagonist, but his ability to marshal them and bring
them to bear instantly upon any point. So, too, in business
pursuits, the ready man, other things being equal, is pre-eminently the successful man.

The Americans, as a people, have no lack of readiness. Collectively considered we do not want dash and *élan*. Our intellectual resources such as they are, are usually at our command, and we can concentrate them with wonderful quickness in any exigency. Still there are not a few of us who find ourselves at times in the condition of Artemus Ward in respect to oratory : "I have the gift of oratory," said the Maine Yankee, "but I haven't it about me." How often an opportunity occurs to a young lawyer, or other professional man to make a reputation by a single speech or other intellectual effort, if he were only ready ! If he could have a little time for preparation,—a day or a few .hours only,—he would acquit himself brilliantly. But time never is given ; and because he cannot act now at the very crisis, he loses the golden opportunity forever. To achieve any rare success in this world we must be *semper parati*, with our wits always about us. We must think and act as quickly and wisely in an emergency as did Baron Munchausen, who, being once threatened at the same moment by a crocodile and a tiger, disposed of both his assailants by stepping aside and allowing the tiger to jump down the crocodile's throat. It is not enough, after the game has flown, that we *might* have brought it down, *if* our guns had been cocked and loaded. " 'What a scathing reply I could have made to Smith about Darwinism !' is the regretful reflection of Jones as he retires heated and discomfited from a contest with Smith on the subject of natural selection. What capital things we might say and don't ! . . . . When we are alone we invent the happiest of retorts ; the most unanswerable arguments flash upon us without an effort on our part ; we feel that we have more weapons in our mental armoury than Brown ever dreamed of ; yet, somehow, when Brown attacks us suddenly, we cannot bring our twelve-pounder to bear upon him before he has shot us through and through with his ready little revolver. We of the superior metal find ourselves spiked, so to speak. The fact is, we lack readiness."

It was so, if we may credit Fuller, with Ben Jonson in his "wit-combats" with Shakespeare. The two were "like a Spanish great galleon and an English man-of-war. Master Jonson, like the former, was built far higher in learning; solid, but slow in his performances. Shakespeare, with the English man-of-war, lesser in bulk but lighter in sailing, could turn with all tides, tack about and take advantage of all winds, by the quickness of his wit and invention."

A powerful encouragement to the formation of business habits is found in the fact that once formed they operate spontaneously. The wonderful accuracy of the forest-bred Indian in detecting and describing the number and character of a party who have preceded him through the woods, and the certainty with which he will determine the time since they left any particular spot, have often astonished white men, who could perceive no signs upon which to found an opinion. Yet the red man rarely blunders, for he has schooled his senses into unerring habits of nice and accurate observation. But, because it is a habit, he is not obliged to *force* his mind ; it is his pleasure, and forms one of the charms of forest life, to watch every indented leaf, every faint footprint, every minute and barely perceptible sign that some one has gone before him. So when a merchant has acquired the habit of watching the markets, studying the laws of demand and supply, ascertaining the probability of a financial crisis, and looking after all the other details of his business, it becomes a pleasurable excitement instead of a wearisome effort. Indeed, the very habits of nice order and observation which require the most painstaking care to form them, often become a hobby, at last, which one delights to ride as much as a child his rocking-horse. It is notorious that those persons who have reached the highest eminence in the law were disgusted with it at first. Lord Somers told Addison that, having been obliged to search among old musty records, the task which was inexpressibly irksome at first became at last so very pleasant that he preferred it to reading Virgil or Cicero, though classical literature had been his constant delight.

To sum up all, what is business but habit, the soul of which is regularity ? Like the fly-wheel upon a steam-engine, it is this principle which keeps the motion of life steady and unbroken, distributing the force equally over all the work to be performed, such habits as we have commended are not to be formed in a day, nor by a few faint resolutions. Not by accident, not by fits and starts,—being one moment in a paroxysm of attention, and the next falling into the sleep of indifference,—are they to be attained, but by steady, persistent effort. Above all, it is

L

necessary that they should be acquired in youth ; for then do they cost the least effort. Like letters cut in the bark of a tree, they grow and widen with age. Once attained, they are a fortune of themselves ; for their possessor has disposed thereby of the heavy end of the load of life ; all that remains he can carry easily and pleasantly. On the other hand, bad habits, once formed, will hang forever on the wheels of enterprise, and in the end will assert their supremacy, to the ruin and shame of their victim.

CHAPTER XIII.

SELF-ADVERTISING.

The pious and just honouring of ourselves may be thought the radical moisture and fountain-head from whence every laudable and worthy enterprise issues forth.—MILTON.

I know that I am censured of some conceit of my ability or worth; but I pray your Majesty impute it to my desire—*possunt quia posse videntur.*—LORD BACON to JAMES I.

Although men are accused for not knowing their own weaknesses, yet perhaps as few know their own strength. It is in men as in soils, where sometimes there is a vein of gold which the owner knows not of.—SWIFT.

On ne vaut que ce qu'on veut valoir.—LA BRUYERE.

SHALL a man be his own trumpeter? or, relying on his merits, shall he aim *to be* rather than *to seem* qualified for his business, and leave the world to find out the fact for itself? This is a question which confronts every man at the outset of his career. How the world has answered it we need not say. The mythologists tell us that Minerva threw away the flute when she found that it puffed up her cheeks; but if in this age men cast away the flute, it is to use a more potent instrument of puffing, by blowing their own trumpets. This instrument, it is almost universally agreed, should be of brass. Not only in trade, but in all the professions, self-trumpeting is now acknowledged to be the great talisman of success, and the man who can blow his horn the longest and loudest is regarded as the most likely to reach the pinnacle of riches and respectability, if not of honour.

The old-fashioned modes of securing patronage or custom, by strict integrity and quiet attention to one's business, are scouted on all hands. Merit is voted "a slow coach," and modesty a humbug. A writer in one of our most popular magazines goes so far as to assert that a tinge of charlatanism seems, indeed, almost necessary to a career, whether in business, literature, art or science. " A little unscrupulousness," he adds, "generally flavours the finest achievements. Nature insists, apparently, that the best of us shall use some contrivance, and will permit nobody to neglect it entirely, without suffering penalties." Acting under this doctrine, an enterprising tradesman, whose business chances to be hat-making, never dreams of setting himself diligently to make better hats than another, that so the heads of the human race may be more honourably covered ; but he sets up an enormous lath-and-plaster hat on wheels, and sends it circulating through the streets with the speculative hope of persuading us into a conviction of his superiority, and thereby gaining an influx of custom. He outbids the world for its patronage by the boldness of his proclamations, and expects to succeed by the very extravagance of his pretensions. A man who has music neither in his soul nor in his larynx, and whose voice, when he attempts to sing, reminds you of Milton's infernal gates, "grating harsh thunder," would have you believe him a fine vocalist ; and so, instead of ravishing your ears with

> " Many a winding bout
> Of linked sweetness long drawn out."

he resorts to the "dodge" of paying six hundred dollars for a seat at Jenny Lind's first concert in America. Gullibility, in short, is deemed the surest avenue to success, and hence human ingenuity is evermore racked and tortured for new means of attracting and securing attention, the results of which everywhere confront us,—on the walls of buildings, in endless circulars, in newspaper advertisements, in boys at street corners thrusting mysterious slips of paper into our hands, in huge placards borne on men's shoulders, and in the lumbering caravans with ear-stunning bands of music which obstruct the thoroughfares of our large cities. Blow your own trumpet is the advice of every one, if you do not wish to be trampled under foot in the rush of competitive strife, and die in obscurity. Sound your charge, and ride over somebody, or somebody will sound *his* charge, and ride over you.

Now and then you meet with a simple-minded man who gives all his soul to doing his work well. But this, the worldly wise will tell you, is an egregious mistake. Such a mode of procedure might do in Mars or Saturn, but is totally out of place in this puffing, advertising, bill-sticking part of creation. The art of self-advancement is not so much to do a thing well, as to get a thing which has been moderately well done largely talked about. The works of a De Quincey, without newspaper puffing, would find purchasers only among pastry-cooks and barbers; while the sensational novel of the Monk Lewis or Ainsworth school, whose name stares out upon you in Gothic capitals from newspapers and posters, sells as well as Jayne's Expectorant, and the platitudes of Martin F. Tupper are as popular as Mustang Liniment.

Now that this policy, however sharply it may be censured by the moralist, is more conducive to success than its opposite, cannot, we think, be doubted. Travellers in Oriental countries tell us that to him who would be respected there a certain air of conscious importance is indispensable. The Orientals, they say, have no notion that it can "pay" to respect a man who does not respect himself; and therefore if a Pacha of two tails does you the honour of a visit, you must demean yourself as if you were a Pacha of three. But does not the same rule hold good all the world over?

How often do we see families taking a high rank in the social scale, without any adventitious circumstances to back their pretensions, simply because they set a high value upon themselves, and discourage all intimacies except from aristocratic quarters! How often, too, do we see the reverse exemplified in families that have every factitious advantage, but which never rise in the social scale, because they never stickle on the score of dignity, and are ready to receive advances from all persons, even the humblest and most plebeian! So the modest maiden links herself to some shallow coxcomb, who is every way unworthy of her, but whose whole demeanour and conversation show that he deems her honoured by his addresses. Indeed, it has been a standing complaint against the sex that they yield too readily to brazen-faced assurance, recognising those virtues only that are played off like the ring on the finger; that "are written as a scroll on the bold front, or triumph in the laughing eye." So do we often determine our position in less important relations, —at the festive board, or in the social intercourse of man with man. What is more common than to see the different jests of a professed wag echoed with loud laughter, because his own lungs have begun to crow like chanticleer before he has uttered them, while the timid, self-distrusting, nervous humourist stammers out the wittiest conceits that are damned in the doubtful delivery, and excite more pity than merriment ? Does not the empty, noisy debater, who puts forth the weakest arguments "with a confident blow, and a throng of words that come with more than impudent sauciness from him," too often carry off the palm with the multitude in preference to the logical reasoner, who, by his less positive and assured manner, his qualifications and hair-splittings, awakens a doubt of the strength of his con-victions ?

Look, again, at the literary world ; is it not true here also, that, as La Bruyère says, *on ne vaut que ce qu'on veut valoir ?* For a respectable niche in the temple of fame, it is not enough to have real abilities alone ; one must add that self-assurance which will lead him to aim at high ends, and to assert his claims before the public. "If you wish to pass for a great author," says Hazlitt, "you ought not to look as if you were ignorant that you had ever written a sentence or discovered a single truth. If you keep your own secret, be assured the world will keep it for you." The same writer tells an amusing story of a literary man, who, after having written upwards of sixty co-lums of original matter for a leading London paper on politics, criticism, belle-lettres, etc., was told, at the end of six months, on applying to the editor for a renewal of his engagement, that "he might give in a *specimen* of what he could do !" The trouble was, says Hazlitt, he had, while thinking of his literary matter, neglected "to point the toe," to hold up his head higher than usual (having acquired a habit of poring over books when young), and to get a new velvet collar to an old-fashioned great-coat. These are the graceful ornaments to the columns of a newspaper, the Corinthian capitals of a polished style ! "Don't you remember," says Gray, in one of his letters, "Lord C——— and Lord M———, who are now great statesmen, little dirty boys playing at cricket ? For my own part, I don't feel myself a bit taller or older or wiser than I did then." It is no wonder that a poet who thought in this manner of himself was hunted from college to college ; that he left so few precious specimens of his fine powers, and shrunk from his reputation into a silent grave.

Take, again, the learned professions. Paul Louis Courier tells us that the greatest Greek scholar of his time, from his lack

of worldly tact, failed to obtain any of the appointments destined for scholars ; while his successful rival—Greek professor,
Greek librarian, Greek academician—saw that study led to
nothing, and preferred having ten scholars' situations to qualifying himself for one that he had not. The time and toil which
the one student devoted to books, the other devoted to ingra-
tiating himself with the dispensers of patronage, and in rendering them good offices which had no connection with the Greek
tongue. Such is too often the result; the scholar gets learning,
the office-seeker position and patronage. Those of our readers
who are familiar with the brilliant comedies of Sheridan will not
forget his great statesman who gained his honours simply by a
shake of the head. The gentleman passed through life universally feared and respected simply on the strength of this ominous speech : "Ah! I *could* say something ; but I won't." This
thunderbolt he kept always in reserve ; he walked through life
with a loaded pistol in his hand, which he never discharged.
At length, on his death-bed, he was entreated by his mourning
friends not to leave the world without disclosing to them the
true nature of the terrible sarcasm which he had so long kept in
store. Vainly striving to shake his head for the last time, as the
pallor of death was stealing over his countenance, he feebly
murmured, "Ah! I could say it, but I won't," and the oracle
was forever dumb. Is not success sometimes achieved by this
oracular demeanour ?

Again there are two rival doctors in town, equal in learning
and skill, and who have just begun their professional careers.
Dr. Easy puts his card on his door and in the newspapers, and
then sits down in his office and waits patiently for patients. If,
fortunately, somebody is good enough to break a leg or to be
seized with the cholera at his very door, he secures a customer ;
otherwise he may spend years in putting knowledge into his
head by study before he will put any money into his purse.
Not so with Dr. Push. He has a mean opinion of the passive
system, and not only puts up a stunning brass plate on his
door, but gets himself puffed in the newspapers, salaams to all
the "big-wigs" of the town, dresses in the height of the fashion, talks learnedly of borborygmus and asphyxia, looks wise
as an owl, keeps a splendid turnout, or "two-forty" horse
and carriage, before he has a visit to make. He hires persons

to startle his neighbours at midnight with the peals of his bell ; is continually called out of church ; and, more than once, has had his name shouted, as being instantly wanted, while attending a concert or lecture at the Academy of Music.　Instead of sitting down in his office and dozing over Brodie and Magendie, he scours the streets and the whole adjoining country with his carriage, driving from morning till night at a killing pace, as if life and death hung on his steps ; and, neglecting no form of advertisement, is probably charging two thousand dollars a year before Dr. Easy has heard the rap of his first patient. Now, of the two men, Dr. Push may be the humbug ; but he certainly is not the fool.

Let us not be misunderstood.　While we would say to the aspirant, " Be not too fastidious or over-sensitive," we do *not* mean, " Be unscrupulous.　Better sink into the abyssmal depths of failure than give your conscience a single pang.　But is there no medium between the two extremes—between the noisy, blatant pretension, that is forever stunning us with proclamations of its own ability, and the excessive humility which " strips itself to a buff-jerkin, to the doublet and hose " of its real merits, and shrinks into a corner, frightened at the smallest shadow of its own fame ?　Assuredly, such a medium there is, difficult to describe exactly in words, but not impossible to realize in practice ; and at this every one who would succeed in life by honourable means should aim.　Because there is danger of invoicing yourself above your real value, it does not always follow that you should underrate your own worth.　Because to be successful, conspicuous, known, you should not retire upon the centre of your conscious resources, you need not necessarily be always at the circumference of appearances.　But, of the two, an excess of modesty is worse than an excess of pride ; for it is in fact, an excess of pride in another form, only it is more hurtful to the individual, and less advantageous to society, than the grossest and most unblushing vanity.

It is true we all patronize humility in the abstract, or, when enshrined in another, it worships ourselves.　We have to meet a lowly man, who never piques our vanity, or thrusts himself between us and the object of our pretensions.　There is no one who, if questioned, would not be found in the depths of his heart secretly to prefer tho modest man, proportionately despising one swaggerer who "goes unbidden to the head of the feast." But, while such is our deliberate verdict when taken to task in the matter, it is not the one we practically give. The man who entertains a stout good opinion of himself always contrives, somehow, to cheat us out of a corresponding one, to a considerable extent ; and we are too apt to acquiesce in his assumptions, even though they may strike us unpleasantly. Nor is there anything strange in this. It is but natural that we should yield more readily to an *active* than to a *passive* claim upon us. "Admiration," it has been said, " like mocking, is catching, and the good opinion which gets abroad of us begins *e'* home." The great mass of men have no time to examine the merits of others. They are busy about their own affairs, which claim all their attention. They cannot go about hunting for modest worth in every nook and corner ; those who would get their good opinion must come forward with their claims, and at least show their own confidence in them by backing them with vigorous assertion. If, therefore, a man of tolerably fair talents arrays his pretensions before us, if he duns and pesters us for an admission of his merits, obtruding them upon us incessantly, we are forced, at last, to notice them ; and, unless he fairly disgusts us by the extravagance of his claims, shocking all sense of decency, we are inclined to admit them, even in preference to superior merits which their possessor, by never pressing them upon our notice, seems to undervalue.

From all this, it will not appear strange that a degree of assurance is so essential to success in the world. The difficulty is not that we do not decide fairly between the modest and the pretending, when we actually weigh their claims ; but we are constantly apt to forget the true merits, from their unobtrusiveness. Unless something peculiar rouses us, we fail to notice them, and they are in as bad a predicament as if they had never existed. The self-esteeming, on the contrary, are always on the alert, pushing their claims wherever and whenever they can obtain an advantage. Believing that, as lawyers say, " continual claims keep alive the title to an estate," they omit no opportunity to enforce their pretensions, but keep them ever before us. By dint of continual assertion they worry the arbiters of fame or favour out of that which their cool, unbiassed judgment would assign to the more humble. Besides, one hates to be always setting a high value upon those who set no value upon themselves, and who sneak away into the obscurest seats on all occasions. Great deeds they *may* have done, possibly, evincing brilliant abilities, but who can believe the fact, while they themselves never speak of them, except perhaps to underrate them? It is the opinion we appear to cherish of ourselves, from which (deeming we must be the best judges of our own merits) others take, in a great measure, their opinion of us on trust. It is taken for granted, in an age like the present, that every man pretends to the utmost he can do, and he who pretends to little is apt to be thought capable of nothing.

In short, lowliness and " unobtrusive worth " are very pretty in theory, and pleasant to read of in moral disquisitions: but he who relies on them; who is always crouching in a corner, and cannot ask for his due; and who goes about, as Robert Hall said, " with an air of perpetual apology for the unpardonable presumption of being in the world;" who never puts himself forward, or, if he does, does so with the forlorn hope with which Snug, the joiner, begs the audience to take him for a lion; who cannot *say* that he wants anything, or cannot say it with sufficient loudness and pertinacity; who cannot make himself prominent at the right time, though he knows it *to be* the right time,—may be a beautiful object of creation, very loveable, and very much to be admired, but must expect to be not only outstripped, but knocked, crushed, and trampled underfoot, in the rush and roar of this nineteenth century.

It is a common trick of persons who have failed to get on in the world to put on an air of injured innocence, and to complain of the world's injustice in conferring its honours and patronage on merely pushing men, while they, whose claims are solid, are neglected. Indeed, no old saw is oftener repeated than the threadbare one about modest merit being neglected, while pretentious demerit is loaded with riches and applause. Of this stereotyped talk Washington Irving justly says that " It is too often a cant by which indolent and irresolute men seek to lay their want of success at the door of the public. Modest merit, however, *is too apt to be inactive or negligent or uninstructed merit.* Well-matured and well-disciplined talent is always sure of a market, provided it exerts itself; but it must not cower at home and expect to be sought for. There is a good deal of cant, too, about the success of forward and impudent men, while men of retiring worth are passed over with neglect. But it usually happens that those forward men have that valuable quality of promptness and activity without which worth is a mere inoperative property. A barking dog is more useful than a sleeping lion.

The last sentence contains the whole truth in a nutshell. Wisely did Pythagoras enjoin his pupil to "reverence himself." To think meanly of one's self, it has been truly said, "is to sink in one's own estimation as well as in that of others. As the thoughts are, so will the acts be. Man cannot aspire, if he look down; if he will rise, he must look up." The poor Scotch weaver was therefore not very far out of his way, in praying daily that he might have a better opinion of himself. The sum of the whole matter is, self-reliance makes ability available. More than this, it frequently leads to the very possession of the qualities only at first assumed. A man of the most ordinary powers, inspired and strengthened by this principle, will often perform a giant's labours, while without it the noblest intellect will expend itself in the triflings of a dwarf, and be eclipsed by inferior talent, endowed with little merit beyond that of mere assurance. Do not, then, expect the world's attention or patronage while you sit in solemn dignity, with folded arms, in the chimney-corner. As well might you wait, like the rustic, for the stream to run by. In the closet you should undoubtedly act on the assumption that your intellectual attainments fall far short of what is required by the necessities of your station. But in the world's busy hum, an unshaken confidence in your own resources should be the firm conviction of the understanding, and the genuine feeling of the heart. Put yourself forward, then, if you would be known. Blow some kind of a trumpet, or at least a penny whistle, to draw the world's eye upon you; but be sure that you *are* what you pretend to be, before you blow; then, having entered the arena, if you fail in the athletic games—if, to use Webster's language to Hayne, "the vigour and spirit of the attack fall short of the lofty and sounding phrase of the manifesto"—woe be unto you! But if you triumph, your fortune is made.

CHAPTER XIV.

THE WILL AND THE WAY.

"There are men whose cant is simply can't."

Nous avons plus de force que de volonté; et c'est souvent pour nous ex-
cuser à nous-mêmes que nous nous imaginons que les choses sont impos-
sibles.—ROCHEFOUCAULD.

Success in most things depends on knowing how long it takes to succeed.—MONTESQUIEU.

Our greatest glory is not in never falling, but in rising every time we fall.
—CONFUCIUS.

Valour is stability, not of legs and arms, but of courage and the soul. He
that falls obstinate in his courage, *si succederit de genu pugnat;* if his legs
fail him, fights upon his knees.—MONTAIGNE.

AMONG the oft-quoted maxims in our language there is
none finer, or more replete with sterling truth, than
that which often falls so lightly from men's lips:
Where there is a will, there is a way. No doubt there are limits
to human capability in all human affairs; in every sphere of
activity men may meet with obstacles which even the utmost
energy cannot overcome. Almost every man is more or less the
victim of circumstances, which sometimes operate so powerfully
that it is impossible to crush his way through them. But the
frequency with which such occasions occur, is greatly over-
estimated; and the fact that mountains so often dwindle into
molehills when we once resolutely determine to cross them,
shows that, after every allowance for extraordinary cases, the
old Saxon saw is still true generally, and that he who intensely
wills to do a thing will find a way. An intense desire itself
transforms possibility into reality. Our wishes are but pro-
phecies of the things we are capable of performing; while, on
the other hand, the timid, feeble-willed man finds everything
impossible because he believes it to be so. As Virgil says of
his boatmen, men are able because they think they are able—
possunt quia posse videntur; to resolve upon attainment is

often attainment itself. We are all aware of the fact that the roads which we incline not to travel are all sadly beset by specimens of the feline tribe ; and, when a gentleman is asked for money by a neighbour often in need of it, he is extremely apt to have a large and exhausting payment to make at the end of the week. But when one is really determined to push his way along the road, opposing lions have usually little terror for him ; and, if he is anxious to oblige his friend, he will almost certainly be able to do so without breaking any of his own engagements.

It is, indeed, wonderful, at times, to see what marvels are accomplished by men acting under the impulse of a powerful will. A remarkable example of this is furnished by the captured Texans of the Santa Fé Expedition, who, after having marched until they were nearly dead with fatigue and exhaustion, yet, being told that any who should prove unable to walk would be shot, contrived to pluck up, and set off at a round pace, which they kept up all day. So Quintin Matsys, the famous Dutch painter, in his youth, despaired of being ever able to paint, till his master told him that only by producing a picture of merit within six months could he have his daughter's hand ; and then he set vigorously to work and brought forth "The Misers," a masterpiece of art, which connoisseurs have admired for ages. It is related of a young French officer that he used to walk about his apartment exclaiming, " I *will* be marshal of France and a great general ;" and his burning desire proved a presentiment of his success. Smiles, in his " Self-Help," tells of an English carpenter who was observed one day planing a magistrate's bench, which he was repairing, with more than usual carefulness ; and, when asked the reason, replied, ' Because I wish to make it easy against the time when I come to sit upon it myself." Singularly enough, the man actually lived to sit upon that very bench as a magistrate.

Nearly all great men—those who have towered high above their fellows—have been remarkable above all things else for their energy of will. Of Julius Cæsar it was said by a contemporary, " *Quicquid vult, valde vult ;*" it was his activity and giant determination, rather than his military skill, that won his victories. A glance at Hannibal's life will show that a resolute will was the leading quality of that commander, though less conspicuous, perhaps, in him than in others, because of the exact proportion in which all the military qualities were united in him, rendering him, by the common consent of soldiers as well as historians, the greatest captain the world has seen. His resolution to brave the whole power of Rome by provoking a war, the invasion of Italy by a route which was a march of discovery as much as a military operation ; his passage of the Rhone and the Alps ; his long continuance in Italy, though unsupported by Carthage ; and, when at last defeated and driven from the country, the zeal with which he sought throughout the world to raise up enemies against Rome, at an age when time and toil would have chilled most men's ardour,—are examples of the rarest determination. His stubbornness of will is only rivalled by that of his enemies, the Romans, of whom he learned, by a captive,—after he had defeated every army they had sent against him, and arrived within three miles of the city, and was momentarily expecting an offer of a surrender,—that the very ground on which his army was encamped had just been sold in the Forum at as high a price as in times of peace.

So with the great captains of modern times ; the strength of Suwarrow's character lay in his power of willing, and he "preached it up as a system." "You can only half will," he would say to persons who failed. It was one of Napoleon's principal characteristics to regard nothing as impossible. His marvellous successes were due not more to his vast military genius than to his almost superhuman strength of will. He toiled terribly, half killing his secretaries, and threw his whole force of brain and hand upon his work. "Impossible," said he, " is a word only to be found in the dictionaries of fools." When told that the Alps stood in the way of his armies, "There shall be no Alps," he replied, and the road across the Simplon was the result. His great adversary, Wellington, was distinguished by a similar inflexibility of purpose. The entire Peninsular campaign was but one long-continued display of an iron will, resolute to conquer difficulties by wearing them out. In the life-and-death struggle between England and France, of which that campaign was a part, and which lasted nearly a quarter of a century, it was the stubborn will of the former which triumphed in the end ; for though Napoleon defeated the British coalitions again and again, yet new ones were constantly formed, until at last the French people, if not their Emperor, were completely worn out. And, finally, the battle of Waterloo, which was the climax of this stupendous struggle, was another illustration of the enormous energy, the exhaustless patience, the bull-dog will of the English. In that fearful contest, French impetuosity and prowess proved an unequal match for English pluck and resolution. For eight long hours the British army stood up against the murderous fire of the enemy ; column after column fell, and the entire side of one square was literally blown away by a volley of grape. One sullen word of command ran along the line as thousands fell, "File up ! file up ! " and the troops silently obeyed. At length the crisis came ; the order to charge was given ; and the men who had stood like statues before the "iron hail" of the French artillery swept like a whirlwind upon the foe.

Among the many causes of failure in life, none is more frequent than that feebleness of the will which is indicated by. spasmodic action,—by fitful effort, or lack of persistence. Dr. Arnold, whose long experience with youth at Rugby gave weight to his opinion, declared that " the difference between one boy and another consists not so much in talent as in energy." "The longer I live," says another competent judge, Sir Thomas Fowell Buxton, "the more I am certain that the great difference between men, between the great and the insignificant, is energy, invincible determination, an honest purpose once fixed, and then death or victory. This quality will do anything in the world ; and no talents, no circumstances, will make a two-legged creature a man without it." The very reputation of being strong-willed, plucky, and indefatigable, is of priceless value. It often cows enemies and dispels at the start opposition to one's undertakings which would otherwise be formidable. The world sometimes yields to a man a coveted prize from pure admiration of his persistence in contending for it. Marcus Morton ran sixteen times in vain for Governor of Massachusetts, when some of his opponents, admiring his pluck, voted for him in 1840, and he was chosen by one majority. Men feel that it is useless to struggle against one who will never yield. If such a one does encounter opposition, it becomes a help, rather than a hindrance, to his general success. The diffi culties he conquers are his stimulus and aliment ; they are his gymnasium and palæstra, by which his muscles are strengthened.

It has been justly said of the poet Wordsworth, who was scoffed at by the critics on his first appearance, and seemingly was born too soon. that he came not a day too early. He had the difficult task of shaping the culture of a nation. and creating his audience among those who ridiculed him; but he conquered recognition at last, and it was the very struggle with a world reluctant to hear him that gave him power and renown. When William Lloyd Garrison commenced the publication of the "Liberator," he began with these memorable words, " I am in earnest,—I will not equivocate,—I will not excuse,—I will not retreat a single inch,—and *I will be heard.*" He *has* been heard,—with what result the country knows. It has been said that you may put a Yankee on a desolate island in the Pacific, and only have with him a jack-knife, and he will get home as soon as, if not sooner than. the ship that left him there. " Put him in anywhere, and he will get out if he wants to . put him out anywhere, and he will get in, if he wishes to." This is the spirit that guarantees success in every calling and profession. Men moan over difficulties; but the earnest, manly spirit looks upon them as opportunities for distinction. There is no obstacle that may not be converted into a stepping-stone to success by an heroic spirit. An almost total blindness compelled Euler to work those calculations in his mind which others put upon paper, and to retain in his brain these *formulæ* for which others trust chiefly to books. What was the result? The extent, the readiness, and exactness of his mathematical memory grew by this means to be so prodigious, that D'Alembert declared that even when one had witnessed it, it almost staggered belief. It has been well observed by a writer in the "Quarterly Review," that the instances in which there is a strong motive to attain an end show the unsuspected triumphs of which the understanding is capable. The reason why they are so rare is, that men ordinarly relax their efforts when the imperative demands of life have been satisfied. There would be hardly any limit to improvement, if the same pains which they were compelled to take to gain their resting-place *were afterwards employed in rising to fresh heights.*

It is difficult to see any advantage in mere stupidity ; yet, according to Sergeant Talfourd, it is no inconsiderable power in a lawyer. If accompanied, as it usually is, with fluency, it enables its possessor to protract a contest long after he is beaten, because he neither understands his own case nor the arguments by which he has been answered. Even physical defects may have their compensating advantages. During the late civil war, a Wisconsin newspaper advertised for a journeyman printer; "a cripple," said the editor, "will be preferred, as he won't go off to the war." A volunteer from the same State, writing to his father from the field, expressed his thankfulness that he had bow-legs; for, on the day before, he had narrowly escaped losing both of these limbs, a cannon-ball having passed harmlessly through the space occasioned by "the natural crook." A popular essayist observes that a squinting eye is a treasure to a boxer; a left-handed batter is a prize in a cricket-ing eleven; and one of the best gymnasts in Chicago is a per-son with a wooden leg, which he takes off at the beginning of operations, thus economizing weight and stowage, and perform-ing feats impossible except to unipeds. It was the lameness of Scott and Talleyrand that made the one a poet and novelist, and the other a statesman and diplomatist; and no one can doubt that the bitterness and morbid irritability caused by Byron's club-foot drove him into verse.

It is remarkable how many of the world's great men have been little men. It would be a curious inquiry how far the distinctions attained by celebrated men have been owing to personal disadvantages, to an uneasy sense of personal in-significance. It is remarked by greyhound fanciers that a well-formed, compact-shaped puppy never makes a fleet dog; and it is certain that many a loose-jointed, awkward, and clumsy man, as well as many a humpbacked and ugly-looking one, has found in his deformity, as Bacon long ago remarked, "a per-petual spur to rescue and deliver him from scorn." History is full of examples of pygmies, who, tormented by a mortifying consciousness of their physical inferiority, have been provoked thereby to show that their lack of flesh and blood has been more than made up to them in brains. Many a Liliputian in body has proved himself a Brobdingnagian in intellect. When Lord Nelson was passing over the quay at Yarmouth to take possession of the ship to which he had been appointed, the

M

people exclaimed, " Why make that little fellow a captain ?" The sneer of disparagement was but a " foregone conclusion" in his own mind, and he thought of it when he fought the battles of the Nile and Trafalgar. Had Bonaparte been six inches higher, says Hazlitt, it is doubtful whether he would have gone on that disastrous Russian expedition, or whether he would even have been First Consul or Emperor. It was the nickname of " Little Corporal " that probably first pricked the sides of his ambition, and stung him into that terrible activity which made all Europe tremble.

Nearly all of the poets, and many of the greatest prose writers of ancient and modern times have been little men. One of the great poets of Athens was so small that his friends fastened lead to his sandals to prevent his being toppled over or blown away. Aristotle, as we have already remarked, was a pygmy in person, though a giant in intellect. Of Pope, who was so small and crooked as to be compared to an interrogation point, Hazlitt asks, " Do we owe nothing to his deformity ?　He doubtless soliloquized, " Though my person be crooked, my verses shall be straight.'"　It was owing, doubtless, in some degree, to the fact that he could boast of but four feet and six inches in stature, that phenomenon of the eighteenth century, the Abbé Galiani, owed the vast and solid erudition which Grimm says he joined to a luminous and profound *coup d'œil.* Personally, says Marmontel, the Abbé was the prettiest little harlequin that Italy ever produced ; but upon the shoulders of that harlequin was the head of Machiavelli. Moore, the Irish poet, was so small that George IV. once threatened to clap him into a wine-cooler.

It is true that many persons have to begin the voyage of life against both wind and tide ; and it seems at times as if they were doomed to " wage with fortune an eternal war." But who ever heard of a man's failing to succeed at last in any business which he had stuck to faithfully for ten years together? Look at Bulwer. His whole life has been a series of temporary failures, crowned with ultimate triumphs. His first novel was a failure ; his first drama was a failure ; his first poems were failures ; and so were his first speeches. But he *fought* his way to eminence,—fought it through defeat and ridicule, till now he has his own enchanted circle, where " none durst walk but he," and stands on one of the summits of the three-peaked hill, the compeer of Dickens and Thackeray. Look at Disraeli. From his birth the odds were against him. The child of a hated and branded race, he made himself a power in the most conventional country in the world. Without a liberal education, he won the honours of literary skill and scholarship; without aristocratic connections, he became a star of fashion in the most exclusive society in Europe. Coughed and hissed down on his first essay in Parliament, he told the House that the time would come when they would hear him, and he persevered until they, under whose laughter he had writhed, were made to writhe in their turn under his terrible sarcasm. Look at Brougham. Ranging during sixty years over the fields, not only of law and politics, but of science and literature, he triumphed in all; and such was his love of excellence, so indefatigable his perseverance, that it has been said that, if he had begun life as a shoeblack, he would never have rested content till he had become the best shoeblack in England.

In further illustration of the same point, we might cite the case of Savonarola, who broke down in his first sermon, and was humiliated beyond expression. Resolved, however, to succeed, he kept on, preaching to peasants and children, and in the solitude of his own chamber, till at last he acquired a facility of utterance and a command of striking language which made him the prophet of his age and the first orator in Italy. Robespierre, contending with the disadvantages of a harsh voice, an ugly face, and hesitating tongue, failed in his first essays at speaking so egregiously that not one man in a thousand, under the circumstances, could have helped being disheartened; yet by ceaseless effort he succeeded in leading the National Assembly of France. Mr. Cobden's first speech was a humiliating failure. He was nervous, confused, and finally broke down; yet he did not retire to a corner, and mope and whine, but persevered, till at last he became one of the most powerful speakers of the Anti-Corn-Law League, and extorted the praise of the accomplished Sir Robert Peel.

When Daniel Webster attended an academy in his boyhood, though he was proficient in the other branches of education, there was one thing, he tells us, he could not do,—he could not

declaim before the school. "The kind and excellent Buckmin-
ster especially sought to persuade me to perform the exercise
of declamation like the other boys, but I could not do it. Many
a piece did I commit to memory, and rehearse it in my own
room over and over again ; but when the day came, when the
school collected, when my name was called, and I saw all eyes
turned upon my seat, I could not raise myself from it. Sometimes the masters frowned, sometimes they smiled. Mr. Buck-
minster always pressed and entreated with the most winning
kindness that I would only venture *once ;* but I could not command sufficient resolution, and when the occasion was over I
went home and wept bitter tears of mortification."

Francis Wayland began his ministerial career under many
discouragements. They would have crushed a feeble man, but
only stimulated him to greater efforts. Son of an English
currier, who had abandoned a profitable trade to become a
Baptist preacher, he gave up the profession for which he
had partially prepared himself, and followed the example of
his father. A single year at Andover, where he was so poor
that he had once to choose between a coat and a copy of
Schleusner's lexicon, summed up his study of theology ; yet
he had so faithfully improved this slender opportunity, that he
was called to the pastorate of the First Baptist Church in
Boston. On a cold, rainy night in October, 1823, he preached
before the Baptist Foreign Missionary Society a sermon on
Missions. There were about fifty persons present ; the discourse kindled no enthusiasm ; and with keen chagrin the
preacher next morning flung himself upon a lounge in the study
of a friend, exclaiming, " It was a complete failure ; it fell perfectly dead." Luckily, among the hearers was a shrewd printer,
a deacon in the church, who insisted that the sermon should be
published. Against his own will, the author consented. The
discourse—the memorable one on " The Moral Dignity of the
Missionary Enterprise "—ran through several editions both in
this country and in England, called forth the warmest encomi-
iums of the press without distinction of sect, and kindled a new
enthusiasm in behalf of missions throughout the Christian
world. Robert Hall, on reading it, predicted a still greater
distinction for the preacher ; and only three years later the

author, hitherto an obscure man, was elected to the Presidency of Brown University almost by acclamation.

To these examples might be added those of Talma, the greatest of French actors ; Sheridan, the orator, who broke down in his first speech ; and many others who failed at first as public speakers, and who finally succeeded only because they knew the eloquence was in them, and determined that it "should come out." Thomas Erskine, whom Lord Campbell pronounces the greatest advocate and most consummate forensic orator that ever lived, began his legal career under many discouragements. Though he had a sublime self-confidence, which was itself almost a sure prophecy of success, yet he fought the battle of life for many years up hill and against many obstacles. His father's means having been exhausted in educating his two elder brothers, he was obliged to start in life with but little training and a scanty stock of classical learning. While pursuing his law studies he found it hard, even with the strictest economy, to keep the wolf from the door. For several years he lived on cow beef, because he could not afford to buy better, and was declared by Jeremy Bentham to be " so shabbily dressed as was quite remarkable." Conscious, all the time, of powers that fitted him to adorn a larger sphere, he chafed against the iron circumstances that hemmed him in, like an eagle against the bars of his cage. A chance conversation led to his being employed as counsel in an important case. The effect produced was prodigious. He won a verdict for his client, and by a single giant bound, overleaping all barriers, passed from want to abundance, from the castle of Giant Despair to the Delectable Mountains. Entering Westminster Hall that morning a pauper, he left it a rich man. As he marched along the hall after the judges had risen, the attorneys flocked around him with their briefs, and retainer fees rained upon him. From this time his business rapidly increased, until his annual income amounted to £12,000.

Even the most successful poets, who are born, not made, have failed more or less in their early productions. Byron's first effort was severely censured by the critics. Keat's first poem was a failure ; but, though damned by the critics, he did not feel disheartened, for he felt that the genius of poetry must work out its own salvation, and that by leaping headlong into

the sea, as he did in Endymion, he had become better acquainted with the soundings, the rocks, and the quicksands, than if
he had stayed upon the green shore, and piped a silly pipe, and
took tea and comfortable advice. " I was never afraid of failure," said he, " for I would sooner fail than not be among the
greatest."

It is this pluck, this bull-dog tenacity of purpose and stubbornness of perseverance, that wins the battles of life, whether
fought in the field, or in the mart, or in the forum. " It is
the half a neck nearer that shows the blood and wins
the race ; the one march more that wins the campaign ; the
five minutes more of unyielding courage that wins the fight."
History abounds with instances of doubtful battles or unexpected reverses transformed by one man's stubbornness into
eleventh-hour triumphs. It is opinion, as De Maistre truly
says, that wins battles, and it is opinion that loses them.
The battle of Marengo went against the French during the first
half of the day, and they were expecting an order to retreat,
when Dessaix, consulted by Napoleon, looked at his watch,
and said, " The battle is completely lost; but it is only two
o'clock, and we shall have time to gain another." He then
made his famous cavalry charge, and won the field. Blucher,
the famous Prussian general, was by no means a lucky leader.
He was beaten in nine battles out of ten ; but in a marvel-
lously brief time he had rallied his routed army, and was as
formidable as ever. He had his disappointments, but turned
them, as the oyster does the sand which annoys it, into a
pearl.

Washington lost more battles than he won, but he organized
victory out of defeat, and triumphed in the end. It was because they appreciated this quality of pluck, that, when the
battle of Cannæ was lost, and Hannibal was measuring by
bushels the rings of Roman knights who had perished in the
strife, the Senate of Rome voted thanks to the defeated general, Consul Terentius Varro, for not having despaired of the
republic. In the vocabulary of such men there is no such word
as " fail." Impossibilities, so called, they laugh to scorn.
" Impossible !" exclaimed Mirabeau on a certain occasion ;
" talk not to me of that blockhead of a word !" " Impossible !"
echoed the elder Pitt, afterwards Lord Chatham, in reply to a

colleague in office who told him that a certain thing could not be done; "I trample upon impossibilities!" Before such men mountains dwindle into molehills, and obstacles that seem unconquerable are not only triumphed over, but converted into helps and instruments of success by their overwhelming will.

There was never, probably, a time in the world's history when high success in any profession demanded harder or more incessant labour than now. Men can no longer go at one leap into eminent position. The world, as Emerson says, is no longer clay, but rather iron, in the hands of its workers, and men have got to hammer out a place for themselves by steady and rugged blows. Above all, a deep and burning enthusiasm is wanted in every one who would achieve great ends. No great thing is, or can be, done without it. It is a quality that is seen wherever there are earnest and determined workers,—in the silence of the study, and amid the roar of cannon; in the painting of a picture, and in the carving of a statue. Ability, learning, accomplishment, opportunity, are all well; but they do not, of themselves, insure success. Thousands have all these, and live and die without benefiting themselves or others. Men, on the other hand, of mediocre talents, often scale the dizzy steps of excellence and fame because they have firm faith and high resolve. It is this solid faith in one's mission,—the rooted belief that it is the one thing to which he has been called,—this enthusiasm, attracting an Agassiz to the Alps or the Amazon, impelling a Pliny to explore the volcano in which he is to lose his life, and nerving a Vernet, when tossing in a fierce tempest, to sketch the waste of waters, and even the wave that is leaping up to devour him,—that marks the heroic spirit; and, wherever it is found, success, sooner or later, is almost inevitable.

The lack of this stimulating and ennobling quality will explain a large proportion of the bankruptcies and breakdowns in every calling of life. Men do not succeed because they do not put *heart* into their work. Too many novices are disheartened by their first failure, and are impatient to run before they have learned to walk. What the elder Kean said of the stage is applicable to every profession and art in life: "Acting does not, like Dogberry's reading and writing, 'come by nature;'

with all the high qualities which go to the formation of a great exponent of the book of life (for so the stage may justly be called), it is imposible, totally impossible, to leap at once to fame. ' What wound did ever heal but by slow degrees ? ' says our immortal author ; and what man, say I, ever became an 'actor' without a long and sedulous apprenticeship ? I know that many think to step from behind a counter or jump from the high stool of an office to the boards, and take the town by storm in Richard or Othello, is ' as easy as lying.' O the born idiots ? they remind me of the halfpenny candles stuck in the windows on illumination nights ; they flicker and flutter their brief minute, and go out unheeded. Barn-storming, my lads, barn-storming—that's the touchstone ; by that I won my spurs ; so did Garrick, Henderson, and Kemble ; and so, on the other side of the water, did my almost namesake, Lekain, and Talma."

It cannot be too often repeated that it is not the so-called blessings of life, its sunshine and calm and pleasant experiences that make men, but its rugged experiences, its storms, tempests, and trials. Early adversity, especially, is often a blessing in disguise. It has been observed that perhaps Madame de Maintenon would never have mounted a throne had not her cradle been rocked in a prison. It is the rough Atlantic seas, the cold, dark, winter nights, and the fierce " northers," that make the British and the American sailors the toughest and most skilful in the world. The school of adversity graduates the ablest pupils, and the hill of difficulty is the best of all " constitutionals " for the strengthening of mental backbones.

" C'est des difficultés que naissent les miracles."

It is the misfortune of many young persons to day that they begin life with too many advantages. Every possible want of their many-sided nature is supplied before it is consciously felt. Books, teachers, mental and religious training, lectures, amusements, clothes and food, all of the best quality and without stint in quantity—in short the pick of the world's good things, and helps of every kind—are lavished upon them, till satiety results, and all ambition is extinguished. What motive has a young man, for whom life is thus "thrice winnowed," to exert himself ?   Having supped full of life's sweets, he finds them palling on his taste ; having done nothing to earn its good things, he cannot appreciate their value.   "Like a hot-house plant, grown weak and spindling through too much shelter and watching, he needs nothing so much as to be set in the open air of the world, and to grow strong with struggling for existence,"

Mere hardship, of course, will not make a man strong, but it is an important aid in the development of greatness.   Want, confinement, opposition, roughness alternating with smoothness, difficulty with ease, storm with sunshine, sorrow with joy,—these constitute the discipline of life, the education which makes a man of a being who would otherwise be little better than an animal.   It has been justly said that in deprivation alone there is untold might.   Imprison a gill of water in a solid rock, and deprive it of heat, and it will burst its flinty bonds as did Sampson the cords of the Philistines.   Apply a match to a pound of powder in the open air, and it explodes with a harmless flash ; but confine it in a rifle-barrel, and tease it with the minutest spark, and it carries doom to a distant life. Great men can no more be made without trials, than bricks can be made without fire.   Indeed, the *freightage* of a great mind can be estimated only by the amount of displacement it creates. Thousands of men are bemoaning their poverty or obscurity, who might have won riches or honour, had they only been compelled by early hardships to cry, with Burns,

> " Come, firm Resolve, take thou the van,
> Thou stalk of earle-hemp in man !

and to task to the uttermost all their faculties.

In past ages men believed in the existence of ghosts—a belief which has disappeared before the light of intelligence ; but the truth is, they really exist, only in a different form from that with which the popular imagination has invested them. A ghost is popularly supposed to be a soul without a body, fond of darkness and graveyards, and wearing a thin white drapery, which you can see, but not touch.   Tom Hyer might strike through it without hitting or hurting it.   A character in one of Dickens's novels knew a ghost "because he could see straight through the body to the buttons on the back of the coat."   But the real ghost is the man who has no pluck ; no perseverance, firmness, or energy ; no backbone of determination ; in short, the pigeon-liveried *thing*, for it is not worthy to be called a *man*, that has a body without a soul. Well has Shakespeare said that—

> " In the reproof of chance
> Lies the true proof of men. The sea being smooth,
> How many shallow bawble boats dare sail
> Upon her patient breast, making their way
> With those of nobler bulk !
> But let the ruffian Boreas once engage
> The gentle Thetis, and, anon, behold
> The strong-ribbed bark through liquid mountains cut,
> Bounding between the two moist elements,
> Like Perseus's horse ; where's then the saucy boat,
> Whose weak, untimber'd sides but even now
> Co-rival'd greatness ?"

After all, there is but one true way in which to meet the troubles and trials of life, and that is to encounter them un-flinchingly. It is doubtless very pleasant to sit in some snug loophole of retreat, and now and then, oyster-like, cautiously open one's bivalves, and thank God he is not buffeting the billows like his fellows. Those who risk nothing can, of course, lose nothing ; sowing no hopes, they cannot suffer from the blight of disappointment. But let him who is enlisted for the *war* expect to meet the foe. Either accept the advice of the tawny Philip to his hesitating warrior—"Go away with the children and the squaws,"—or be prepared, not only for the contest, but for its consequences. Fortunately, adversity is often like a panther ; look it boldly in the face, and it turns cowering away from you. It is with life's troubles as with the risks of the battle-field ; there is always less of aggregate danger to the party that stands firm than to that which gives way—the cowards being always cut down ingloriously in the fight.

No doubt it is easier to moralize on " the uses of adversity" than to bear it. We are aware that it is hard to begin life without a dollar, hard to be poor, and harder to seem poor in the eyes of others. No young man, especially no-young man in our cities, likes to make his *entrée* in life with his boots patched ; to wear an antediluvian hat, and clean gloves smelling of camphene and economy ; nor to carry a cotton umbrella ;

nor to ask a girl to marry him and live in the " sky-parlour " of a cheap boarding-house. We all like to drive along smoothly, to have a fine turnout, to have the hinges of life oiled, the backs padded, and the seats cushioned. But such is not the road to success in any profession or calling ; and if you are poor, and feel that you cannot climb the steeps of life unassisted — that you must be carried in a vehicle, instead of trudging on foot along the dusty highway—then confess your weakness, and seek your Hercules in the first heiress who is as wanting in judgment as you in nerve and resolution. Marry $5,000 a year, if you can, and be a stall-fed ox for the remainder of your days. But do not, while thus "boosted" into, boast of your success. Do not, while rising in the world like a balloon, by pressure from without instead of from within, fancy you have any claim to triumph. The world will touch its hat to you, and give you plenty of ceremonious respect ; but its real regard, its loftiest esteem, it will reserve for the moral hero who has the nerve to throw his hat into the ring, and fight out the battle of life in a manly and creditable way.

There are some persons who deny that men owe their positions in life mainly to themselves. They explain all the differences in worldly success by the magic word " fortune." Others attribute all great or rare success to that indefinable quality which they call genius; and, no doubt, there are native differences in the intellectual stature of men, but not to the extremes imagined. There are no giants like those of Brobdingnag, nor pygmies like those of Liliput. It matters not what are a man's natural gifts ; he can never attain in any profession to high success, without going through with a vast deal of work which, taken by itself, would rightly be called drudgery; and hence some one has defined genius as " an immense capacity for taking trouble,"

What is the difference that distinguishes the musician or the painter from the mere amateur ? What is it, as one has wisely said, " but the long-continued discipline of hand, of ear, or eye, which has made all the faculties of body and mind subservient to the purposes of the art ? The man who has no such training may have, to begin with, the same natural faculties, the same genius. the same inspiration ; but they are not cultivated, and they have no command over the only means by which their fine conceptions can be express d. And what is the cultivation which such genius always needs ? It needs unwearied labour at what to another man would seem the drudgery of the art ; what only ceases to be drudgery because the light of genius is always present in every trifling act. Nothing can be a greater mistake than to suppose that genius dispenses with labour. What genius does is to inspire the soul with a power to persevere in the labour that is needed ; but the greatest geniuses in every art invariably labour at their art far more than all others, because their genius shows them the value of such patient labour, and aids them to persist in it. . . . . It is the loving labour at his own tasks which makes a man a thorough scholar. It is incessant practice which makes a man skilful at a game. And why is all this ? Apparently because our nature is so framed that in this way only can any knowledge or skill or art or faculty or whatever else you may call that which enables us to do what we wish to do so really well, be *so worked into us* as to be completely ours. To see how to do a thing is not enough. The power of really doing it implies that the needful science or skill have penetrated us through and through until we do instinctively, almost mechanically all that is needed for the purpose ; until the little trifles which are so hard always to attend to, and which are so absolutely necessary to true success, cease to demand attention, because, indeed, it would require an effort not to do them ; until in all trivial matters we do the right thing as unconsciously, as instantaneously as we put out our hands to break our fall whenever our foot slips under us as we walk." *

It is almost impossible to exaggerate the wonders that may be wrought in a brief life-time by intense and persistent labour urged on by an iron will. The enormous labour and preparatory training which men undergo for comparatively low and trivial accomplishments should shame the indolent and the supine who are engaged in noble pursuits. You will see one man toiling for years to draw sweet strains from a fiddle-string, or to bring down a pigeon on the wing ; another tasking his inventive powers, and torturing verbs and substantives

* Dr. Temple's Rugby Sermons. Third Series.

like a Spanish inquisitor, to become a punster ; a third devoting half his life to acquiring the art of balancing himself on a rope, or of standing on his head on the top of a pole ; a fourth spending time enough in getting the mastery of chess to go through the entire circle of the sciences, and learn half a dozen languages. A Taglioni, to insure the agility and bounds of the evening, rehearses her pirouettes again and again, for hours together, till she falls down exhausted, and has to be undressed, sponged, and resuscitated ere she is conscious. You listen to a Jaell, a Strakosch, or other great pianist, whose touch seems miraculous, and whose fingers glide rapidly over the keys, you almost imagine that they are instinct with thought and feeling oozing from the tips, as if the soul had left its inner seat to descend into the hands. But, on inquiry, you learn that from the age of six or eight to manhood he sat on the piano-stool from morning till night, practising almost without interruption, except for meals and elementary instruction, and that incessant toil was the price of the skill which affects us like magic.

Handel, the composer, had a harpsichord, every key of which, by incessant practice, was hollowed like the bowl of a spoon. When an East-Indian is learning archery, he is compelled by his master to exercise the attitude and drawing the string to his ear, *secundum artem*, for three months together, before he is suffered to set an arrow. Half the intellectual and physical efforts which, put forth by some persons for petty or worthless, perhaps shameful, objects, would suffice, in many cases, if directed to noble ends, to place them on a level with the great lights of the age,—the superior intelligences of art, literature, and science,—and to lay the foundation of a glory which might vie hereafter with that of " the mighty dead." And yet the cry of most dullards, and of many who are not, is, " I am too low in the scale ; it is of no use for *me* to try to rise ; I am not, and never shall be, anybody." But does a prisoner cling to his captivity and hug his fetters because his dungeon is low and dark and noisome ? No ; he pants for the " upper air " all the more aspiringly. The very consciousness of his prostration should be a spur stimulating one to raise himself by all possible efforts.

No man should be discouraged because he does not get on

rapidly in his calling from the start. In the more intellectual professions especially, it should be remembered that a solid character is not the growth of a day, that the mental faculties are not matured except by long and laborious culture. To refine the taste, to fortify the reasoning faculty with its appropriate discipline, to store the cells of the memory with varied and useful learning, to train all the powers of the mind symmetrically, is the work of calm and studious years. A young man's education has been of little use to him if it has not taught him to check the fretful impatience, the eager haste to drink the cup of life, the desire to exhaust the intoxicating draughts of ambition, which is characteristic of Young America. The motto of Gideon's fatigued but determined troop—*Faint, yet pursuing*—should be that of every earnest man when baffled by hindrances and discouragements. Let him patiently bide his time, steadily and conscientiously doing his daily work, that, when a great occasion comes, he may be equal to it. "To know how *to wait*," said De Maistre, "is the great secret of success.

It is now well known that the Duke of Wellington, when a subaltern, was anxious to retire from the army, where he despaired of advancement, and actually applied to the Lord Lieutenant of Ireland for a commissionership of customs. Yet he conquered success at last, as did the immortal Havelock, who lived in comparative obscurity till he was far advanced in life, and, who, ten years before his death, could not have anticipated that he would ever gain a name in history. But when the auspicious moment came, a few months only sufficed to build up that edifice of success and fame for which his whole previous life had been a training. Ten years ago Moltke was unknown to the world, though he had already reached the mature age of sixty-one. Yet he had no less genius then than when by his masterly combinations he was humbling Austria, or winning more brilliant triumphs in the late campaign against France.

Some of the most successful lawyers have passed many years in obscurity before their abilities were recognised. When the late Mr. Chitty was consulted by an anxious father about the qualifications of the bar, he asked, "Can your son eat sawdust without butter?" Sir Samuel Romilly, one of the most distinguished Chancery lawyers of England, had made no progress in his legal career at the end of his sixth or seventh circuit. "When a man first makes his appearance in court," says he, "no attorney is disposed to try the experiment whether he has any talents ; and when a man's face has become familiar by his long having been a silent spectator of the business done by others, his not being employed is supposed to proceed from his incapacity, and is alone considered as sufficient evidence that he must have been tried and rejected." In spite of this inauspicious beginning, Romilly attained at last to a success which his wildest and most sanguine dreams had never painted to him, gaining an income of £8,000 or £9,000 a year.

John Scott, afterwards Lord Eldon, rose at first slowly to distinction. While studying law at London, he rose at four every morning and studied till late at night, binding a wet towel round his head to keep himself awake. Too poor to study under a special pleader, he copied out three folio volumes from a manuscript collection of precedents. When finally called to the bar, he hung long about the courts without employment. His prospects were so gloomy that he meditated leaving the metropolis and settling down as a provincial barrister in New-castle, where a comfortable house in High Street was his castle in air. It was agreed between him and his wife that whatever he got during the first eleven months should be his, and whatever he got in the twelfth month should be hers. "What a stingy dog," he says, "I must have been to have made such a bargain ! I would not have done so afterwards. But, however, so it was ; and how do you think it turned out? In the twelfth month I received half a guinea ; eighteen pence went for fees, and Bessy got nine shillings ; in the other eleven months I got not one shilling."

In the second year of his profession, "business," wrote the eldest brother, William, to the second, Henry, "is very dull with poor Jack,—very dull indeed ; and, of consequence, he is not very lively. I heartily wish that business may brisken a little, or he will be heartily sick of his profession. I do all I can to keep up his spirits, but he is very gloomy." Early in the third year occurred a case which laid the foundation of his fame. As he left Westminster Hall, a respectable solicitor touched him on the shoulder, and said, "Young man, your bread and butter is cut for life." In about eight years from his call to the bar he was on the high road to its highest honours. During the six years he was Attorney-General, his annual emoluments varied from £10,000 to £12,000.

After he had become Lord Chancellor, an application was made to him one day for an order to allow a young man an income of two hundred a year out of an estate in dispute. "Young gentleman," said Lord Eldon, seeing the applicant in court, "I hope that you will reflect that this is a very critical order I am making in your favour. This sum may furnish opportunity to talent, or it may paralyze all exertions. If I had had a certain two hundred a year at your age, I should not now be sitting where I am." When Wilberforce asked the Chancellor's advice about the best mode of study for the young Grants, to fit them for the bar,—"I have no rule to give them," was the reply, "but that they must make up their minds to live like a hermit and work like a horse." Happily, it has been said, the hermit-and-horse life need not be long, or it would be better to turn galley-slave.

Lord Kenyon and Lord Thurlow began their legal careers under circumstances similar to those of Eldon. The two used to dine together, in vacation, at a small eating-house near Chancery Lane, London, where their meal was supplied co them at sevenpence-halfpenny a head. Lord Camden, though a judge's son, went the Western Circuit for ten or twelve years without success, and at last resolved on trying one circuit more, and then retiring upon his fellowship. A legal friend, hearing of this resolution, contrived to get him retained as his own junior in a cause of some importance, and then absented himself on the plea of illness. Camden won the cause, and thenceforth was on the high road to prosperity and fame.

Lord Ellenborough's early experience at the bar was yet more painful than that of any of the great men we have named. The son of a bishop, and a wrangler at Cambridge, he was an eminently proud man, perfectly conscious of his superiority ; yet, as a student, he resolutely submitted to all that drudgery without which no man can become a great lawyer, however he may distinguish himself as an advocate. Writing from the Inner Temple at this time to a college friend, Archdeacon

Coxe, he says : " Let us cheerfully push our way in our different lines: the path of neither of us is strewed with roses, but they will terminate in happiness and honour. I cannot, however, now and then help sighing, when I think how inglorious an apprenticeship we both of us serve to ambition, while you teach a child his rudiments, and I drudge the pen for attorneys. But if knowledge and a respectable situation are to be purchased only on these terms, I, for my part, can readily say, *Hac mercede placet.* Do not commend my industry too soon; application wears for me, at present, the charm of novelty ; upon a longer acquaintance, I may grow tired of it." He did not tire of it, however, for he possessed, to a degree that is rarely exhibited even by the resolute, an indomitable will ; and when distaste, disinclination, or weariness crept over him, as they will, at times, over the most determined men, he would write and set before his aching eyes, " Read or starve ! " three monosyllables which have achieved as many miracles as even the magic word " Failure ! " For many years he found little to do as a legal practitioner, till, through a family connection, he was employed in the defence of Warren Hastings, when he was repaid for years of toil and privation by rising at once to distinction.

Lord Campbell, late Lord Chancellor of England, rose slowly and after many struggles to his high position, having been compelled by poverty to report for the press while qualifying himself for the practice of the law. At the beginning of his career, he used to walk from county town to county town when on circuit, being unable to afford the luxury of riding. Lord Mansfield came to the bar with a brilliant reputation for scholarship and eloquence, yet even he did not scale the rugged steeps of fame and honour at once. He used to say that he knew no interval between no income and three thousand pounds a year. Not a few years had elapsed since his call to the bar, and he had found no opportunity of displaying his abilities, when his senior in a case, Sergeant Eyre, as the tradition goes, was seized with a fit, and the conduct of the case devolved on Murray. Obtaining, by the favour of the presiding judge, a short adjournment, he made so admirable speech that clients rushed to him in crowds.

The experience of medical practitioners is not unlike that of lawyers. Men of the highest ability have read and observed for years in poverty and obscurity before they have gained a respectable practice. In 1788 a medical student at Edinburgh University lived in the third story of a house in Bristol Street, in a room which cost him six shillings and sixpence a week. In after life, when swaying the surgical sceptre of England as Sir Astley Cooper, his professional income in a single year amounted to £23,000 ; and yet, during the first twelve months after he had settled down in London, his private practice yielded but five guineas. It is much the same in all professions and callings. It costs many a hard struggle to earn one's bare expenses, at first; but when the tide is turned, the dollars come rolling in like an avalanche, "not in single files, but in battalions." Nothing, said Talleyrand, is so successful as success.

Nearly all of the world's great scholars, artists, authors and philosophers, as well as the men who have become famous by the invention of new processes, or the improvement of old sciences, have forced their way to distinction against many trials and discouragements. Dr. Adam Clarke, the well-known Wesleyan commentator, was the son of a poor Irish schoolmaster. When at the age of twenty he sought in England employment as a preacher, his slender pecuniary outfit was soon reduced to three halfpence ; yet, with this sum in his pocket, he was able to say to Wesley, "I wish to do and be what God pleases," and was sent at once to his work. The labour he did for many years was of the humblest and most laborious kind ; yet he adhered resolutely to the advice given him by Wesley, " to cultivate his mind so far as his circumstances would allow, and never to forget anything he had ever learned." Having acquired some knowledge of Oriental tongues, he began to wish earnestly for a polyglot Bible ; but three pounds per quarter and his food, which was the whole of his income as a preacher, could ill supply any sum for the purchase of books. Unexpectedly he received a bank-note for ten pounds from a friend, and exclaiming, " Here is the polyglot," wrote to London for a copy, which he obtained for exactly ten pounds, from which time his progress in his favourite studies was extremely rapid. He denied the possibility of having too many irons in the fire, and writing to a friend, playfully said : " I think it strange that you are of the opinion that we cannot carry on consentaneously two or three languages at a time. If I could not do so, I think I should be tempted to run out into the street, and dash the place where the brains *should be* against the first post I met."

It is related of Dr. Adam, the distinguished rector of the High School of Edinburgh, that when at college he had to be content with a penny roll for his dinner. Similar to those of Dr. Adam and Dr. Clarke, though more severe, were the early trials of Samuel Drew. At the age of ten he was apprenticed to a shoemaker, a calling which he continued to follow long after he had become celebrated as an author. For days and days together, in his early life he was too poor to spend even a penny for his dinner ; and he was accustomed, when dinner-time came, to tie his apron-strings tighter to lessen the pang of hunger, and go on with his work till evening. Through years of hardship and drudgery his courage never forsook him ; amidst ceaseless labour he strove unremittingly to improve his mind, studying astronomy, history, and metaphysics ; and finally, from the humblest circumstances, he rose to occupy a conspicuous place in England as an author, a philosopher, and a metaphysician. The notice of a metaphysician brings to mind the history of the late Sir William Hamilton, who, notwithstanding his great ability and encyclopædic erudition, did not find, till his forty-eighth year, the position for which he was so pre-eminently qualified, and to which he may be said to have had a natural right, namely, a university chair. For six and twenty years he competed unsuccessfully for poorly paid chairs in Scotland, and though at forty recognised as the most learned scholar of his day in the history of philosophy, was elected finally only by a majority of four votes over a competitor far inferior.

The history of authorship is a history of struggles, privations, and trials rarely equalled in any other calling. Many of the books which have sold most rapidly, or won the highest reputation for their authors, went a long time begging for publishers. The life of Balzac, the French author whose brilliant abilities won for him at last such wealth, fame, and influence in France, is a type of many a literary career. At the age of twenty his wealthy parents wished to make him a notary. He announced his determination to become an author. "But," urged the father, "do you not know to what state the occupation of a writer will lead you ? In literature a man must be either a king or a hodman." "Very well," replied Balzac, "*I will be king !*" The family left town ; the youth was left to his fate in a garret, with the magnificent allowance of twenty-five francs a month. The first ten years he fought with poverty and all its evils ; the second decade made him his own master. These ten years, says a writer in a British magazine from which we gather these facts, were years of glory, wealth, and luxury. He had really won the literary crown, as in youth he predicted. But it was won by dint of labour such as ordinary men can scarcely conceive ; and, in his passage to his goal of success, he went through all the terrible vicissitudes of poverty, debt, and contention. His later residences were palaces, richly decorated with the choicest furniture that could be procured ; full of beautiful and rare pictures, statuary, and valuable curiosities. During his career he had seven different residences. The first was the bare garret in the Rue Lesdiguières, where in silence, in hunger, and in the deepest poverty, his genius consolidated itself.

The most successful men in America, both in early and in later times, have nearly all fought their way to wealth or dis-tinction against formidable obstacles. Rumford, Franklin, Rit-tenhouse, Patrick Henry, Bowditch, Clay, Webster, Jackson, Douglas, Lincoln, Grant, were all the sons of poor parents. Senator Wilson, who was for a long time a shoemaker, said recently, in addressing the people of Great Falls, N. H. : " I was born here in your county. I was born in poverty. Want sat by my cradle. I know what it is to ask a mother for bread when she has none to give. I left my home at ten years of age, and served an apprenticeship of eleven years, receiving a month's schooling each year, and, at the end of eleven years' hard work, a yoke of oxen and six sheep, which brought me eighty-four dollars. A dollar would cover every penny I spent from the time I was born until I was twenty-one years of age. I know what it is to travel weary miles and ask my fellow-men to give me leave to toil. I remember that in September, 1833, I walked into your village from my native town, and went through your mills seeking employment. If anybody had offered me eight or nine dollars a month, I should have accepted it gladly. I went down to Salmon Falls, I went to Dover, I went to Newmarket, and tried to get work, without success ; and I returned home weary, but not discouraged, and put my pack on my back, and walked to the town where I now live, and learned a mechanic's trade. The first month I worked after I was twenty-one years of age, I went into the woods, drove team, cut mill-logs, and chopped wood ; and though I rose in the morning before day-light, and worked hard until after dark at night, I received for it the magnificent sum of two dollars. And when I got the money, those dollars looked to me as large as the moon looks to-night."

Thurlow Weed, for a long time one of the most influential editors and politicians of the country, published recently a sketch of his early life, in which he thus speaks of his efforts at self-culture. "Many a farmer's son has found the best opportunities for mental improvement in his intervals of leisure while tending 'sap bush.' Such, at any rate, was my own experience. At nights you had only to feed the kettles and keep up the fires, the sap having been gathered and the wood cut 'before dark.' During the day we would always lay in a good stock of 'fat pine,' by the light of which, blazing bright before the sugar-house, in the posture the serpent was con-demned to assume as a penalty for tempting our great first grandmother, I passed many and many a delightful night in reading. I remember in this way to have read a history of the French Revolution, and to have obtained from it a better and more enduring knowledge of its events and horrors, and of the actors in that great national tragedy, than I have re-ceived from all subsequent reading. I remember also how happy I was in being able to borrow the book of a Mr. Keyes, after a two-mile tramp through the snow. shoeless, my feet swaddled in remnants of a rag-carpet."

Henry Ward Beecher, the most eloquent and popular preacher in the world, began preaching in an obscure town in Indiana to a church of nineteen members. The building in which he delivered his sermons would not hold over a hundred and fifty people ; it had no lamps, and no hymn-books ; and the whole congregation could hardly raise from two hundred to two hundred and fifty dollars salary. "There was nobody in the church to light the lamps," he says in a late lecture at New Haven, "and they could not afford to get a sexton. Such a thing was unknown in the primitive simplicity of that Hoosier time. Well, I unanimously elected myself to be the sexton. I swept out the church, trimmed the lamps and lighted them. I was, literally, the light of that church. I didn't stop to groan about it, or moan about it, but I did it."

The most successful editors in this country have graduated, not from a college, but from a printing-office. The history of Horace Greeley, the editor-in-chief of the most powerful and widely circulated political journal in America, is familiar to all. He began life at the bottom of the ladder, and reached the top by his own efforts, without asking help from friends or relatives. The early life of James Brooks, the editor and proprietor of the New York *Daily Express*, as detailed by a leading religious journal,* is a type of the triumphant contention with obstacles by which many a poor boy has found his way to the editorial chair or to a seat in Congress. Mr. Brooks began his career as a clerk in the Village of Androscoggin, Me., where he was to remain till twenty-one years of age, when, by contract, he was to receive as capital from his employer a hogshead of New England rum. Unfortunately for his employer and the hogshead of rum, the town library was kept in the "store," of which the clerk made a liberal use. His first venture in business enabled him to save money enough to pay one dollar a week for his board, while a kind gentleman assisted him to go to school. As soon as he knew enough to teach school, he began as a pedagogue on the liberal salary of ten dollars per month and his board. In a year he was rich enough to enter Waterville College. Studying and teaching by turns, he graduated at the end of two years, carrying his trunk to the stage-office, as he did when he entered, to save a few of his hard-earned and scanty shillings. From this hour he provided a home for his mother and her two younger children, his father having died in his childhood.

Mr. Brooks next studied law with the noted John Neal, of Portland, taught school, and at the same time wrote a series of anonymous letters for the Portland *Advertiser*, a daily Whig paper, which were so popular that its proprietor made him an offer of five hundred dollars per year to write constantly for his journal. At this time, though only twenty years old, he

---

* The New York *Independent.*

had become one of the most popular and eloquent orators of his State. After serving in the Legislature of Maine, in connection with his editorial duties on the Portland *Advertiser* he went to Washington in 1832, and began the series of letters which for the first time caught up and reflected in clear and brilliant light the multiform life of the American capital. The letters became immediately popular, and were copied by the press from Maine to Louisiana. One of the most signal proofs of their brilliancy and power is to be found in the words of Senator Wilson: "I shall never forget what those letters were to me. The first I had ever read, they came to me in my obscurity and poverty as the revelation of an unknown and wonderful life. They made me want to go to Washington. They made me feel that I must go there, and see the men and witness the national scenes which I read about in these letters."

Subsequently Mr. Brooks wrote a series of letters from the Southern States; then visited Europe, and, travelling on foot through the principal countries, sent home to the Portland *Advertiser* letters depicting almost every phase of life, from that seen in the palace of the nobleman to the cottage of the peasant. Next he started the New York *Express*, carrying it alone for years under a heavy load of debt and discouragement —acting as leading editor, reporter, day editor, night editor, and even type-setter,—and in 1849 was elected to Congress as a representative of New York City, a place which, with the exception of a single term, he has held ever since. In that place he has distinguished himself by his eloquence and high legislative qualities, representing in the House, it is said, the type of culture and oratory of which Mr. Sumner is the exemplar in the Senate.

Even those sucessful men who have begun their professional careers in America under favourable circumstances have not gone through the battle of life unscathed. They all bear in their faces and bodies the scars of the fighting-man,—the signs of desperate conflict. Such was emphatically the case with Rufus Choate, as his haggard face and trembling, nervous frame too plainly showed; and such, if we may trust a reporter of a New York paper, is the case with one of the most brilliant lawyers of that city: "In that pale and almost emaciated face," says the writer, "that fragile enwrapment of body which seems

shaken with the earnestness of its own talk under the picture
of Humboldt at the mantel-piece, is packed that library of
knowledge and that fiery concentration of eloquent speech
which, collectively, make up the product among men called
William M. Evarts. He looks like a man whom his soul has
burned up with its own intensity till all that was inflammable
has exhaled,—leaving a thin asbestos body, and a face lit up
with great, weird, far-seeing eyes. He seldom laughs, but he
is not ungenial,—only so immeasurably in earnest that he has
no time to laugh."

It is true that, in every calling, one meets sometimes with
obstacles that seem utterly insurmountable,—obstacles which
baffle for a time the sagacity and energy of the most determined
men, and almost compel them to give up in despair. But *nil*
desperandum ; do not give up, reader, while you have health
and strength, however dark your present prospects. The circumstances which now obstruct and hem you in (circumstances
are made of india-rubber for strong men, of iron for weak men,)
may give way, if you keep on. " Go ahead,"—keep pushing,
—and a passage will by and by open, as if by magic, before
you, and your little bark of hope and adventure will pass
through unharmed, as did Dr. Kane's boats more than once
through horrible cliffs of ice on either side, which threatened to
crush them in a moment. It has been observed that in going
through the Notch of the White Mountains the road seems frequently to the traveller to be shut in by frowning precipices,
so as to render further progress impossible ; but, as he nears
the obstacles, he finds the path curving gracefully and safely
along the terrace cut for it through the gorge. So the fearful
obstructions that bid defiance to our progress in life are generally only apparent, and will vanish as soon as we confront them.

Even if battling with inward disease, as well as with outward
foes, you may, with a heroic spirit, triumph in the end. Men
have cured themselves of painful diseases by a herculean effort of
the volition, and physicians always count upon a cheerful, hopeful frame of mind in their patients as one of the most important
agencies in effecting a restoration to health. Aaron Burr laid
aside a wasting fever like a garment, to join the expedition
against Quebec. One of the greatest generals of the Thirty Years'
War was Torstenson. On account of his sufierings from the

gout, he was usually carried about in a litter ; yet the rapidity of his movements was the astonishment of the world. When Douglas Jerrold, being very sick, was told by his physician that he must die, "What!" he said, "and leave a family of helpless children ?   I *won't* die !" and die he did not for several years. When were the prospects of any man gloomier than those of Wolfe just before he captured Quebec ? From his early youth he had suffered severely from a fatal disease, and the seeds of others were deep laid in his constitution.   He had been severely repulsed in an attack on Montcalm's intrenchments south of Quebec; his troops were dispirited ; the promised auxiliaries under Amherst and Johnson had failed to arrive ; and he himself, through the fatigue and anxiety preying on his delicate frame, fell violently ill of a fever. Partially recovering his health, he writes to the Government at home, as if to prepare the public mind in England for his failure or retreat, a letter full of gloom, concluding thus : "I am so far recovered as to do business, but my constitution is entirely ruined, without the consolation of having done any considerable service to the State or without the prospect of it." Within five days only from the date of that letter, the Heights of Abraham had been scaled, Montcalm defeated, the seemingly impregnable fortress surrendered and the name of Wolfe had become immortal to all ages!

CHAPTER XV.

THE WILL AND THE WAY (*continued*).

Pitch thy behaviour low, thy projects high,
  So shalt thou humble and magnanimous be.
Sink not in spirit; who aimeth at the sky
  Shoots higher much than he that means a tree,
                              —GEORGE HERBERT

Kites rise against, not with the wind.......No man ever worked his passage anywhere in a dead calm.—JOHN NEAL.

No man can end with being superior, who will not begin with being inferior.—SYDNEY SMITH.

" Les existences foibles vivent dans les douleurs au lieu de les changer en apothègmes d'expérience. Elles s'en saturent et s'usent en retrogradant chaque jour dans les malheurs consommés. Oublier, c'est le grand secret des existences fortes et créatrices—oublier à la manière de la Nature, qui ne se connait point de passé, qui recommence à toute heure les mystères de ses indefatigables enfantements."

A politician weakly and amiably in the right is no match for a politician tenaciously and pugnaciously in the wrong.—E. P. WHIPPLE.

NOT only perseverance is necessary to worldly success, but patience also, or a willingness to bide one's time. Indeed, of all the lessons that humanity has to learn in this school of the world, the hardest is *to wait*. Not to wait with folded hands that claim life's prizes without previous effort, but, having toiled and struggled, and crowded the slow years with trial, to see then no results, or perhaps disastrous results, and yet to stand firm, to preserve one's poise, and relax no effort—this, it has been truly said, *is* greatness, whether achieved by man or woman. The world cannot be circumnavigated by one wind. The grandest results cannot be achieved in a day ; the fruits that are best worth plucking usually ripen the most slowly ; and therefore every one who would gain a solid success must learn "to labour, and to wait." It is said that a transcendentalist, after years of profound speculation, came to the conclusion "to accept the universe,"—an example which common natures would do well to imitate.

As "temper is nine-tenths of Christianity," so cheerfulness and steady labour are nine-tenths of practical wisdom. A sunny disposition is the very soul of success, enabling a man to do double the labour that he could without it, and to do it with half the physical and mental exhaustion. Yet nothing is more common than for men to be dissatisfied with their callings, and grumble because they are chained to them by the necessity of getting a living. Losing all interest in their work, they go shifting about from this business to that, following nothing long enough to make it pay, but just long enough to see that *it*, too, has its thorns, perplexities, and vexations, and finally landing in the grave or the poor-house. While it is true, that the round man sometimes gets into the square hole, yet, after having spent years in getting used to it, it is often better to remain there than to try to better himself. Generally there cannot be a greater error than to be constantly changing one's calling or business. As capital tends always to an equilibrium in profits, one kind of business pays in the long run just as well as another.

Look around you, reader, among your acquaintances, and you will find that nearly all the successful men have stuck resolutely to one pursuit. Two lawyers, for example, begin to practise at the same time. One gives all his energies to his profession, lays in day by day a stock of legal learning, labours conscientiously upon the few cases he has, and waits patiently for years before he finds an opportunity to demonstrate his skill and erudition. The other, impatient of neglect and despairing of clients, plunges into politics, becomes an insurance agent, or engages in speculation. At the end of twenty years the latter will be without property and in debt, while the former will have a profitable and growing practice, and will count his thousands in bank stocks, government bonds, or mortgages. So in the mechanical professions. The same restless uneasy discontented spirit which sends a mechanic from the East to the South, the Rocky Mountains, or California, renders continuous application anywhere irksome to him ; and so he goes wandering about the world, a half-civilized Arab, getting the confidence of nobody, and almost sure to die insolvent.

Every man who would get on should try to put heart into everything that he does. Macaulay tells us that the political

party to which Halifax belonged was the party which at that
moment he liked least, because it was the party of which at
that moment he had the nearest view; and so every calling
has its peculiar cares, anxieties, and vexations, which seem
more numerous and trying than those of any other. To fly
from them is only to exchange them for a different and perhaps
more teasing class. Troubles in some form are incident to
man's imperfection. It is therefore the very wantonness of
folly to search them out, and brood over and magnify them.
" Worry kills more men than work." The petty trials of life,
if suffered to wear upon a man, often weaken more than great
afflictions, as the ship that will survive a hard thump may be
sunk by tiny insects boring through her timbers. There is
nothing, it has been well said, like heart-varnish to cover up
the innumerable evils and defects of life. Cultivate cheerfulness, then; the spectres of neglect, unkindness, and despair
will fly before it as fogs before the sun. Is your situation un-
congenial ? Do as Sydney Smith did when labouring as a poor
parish priest at Foston-le-Clay, in Yorkshire. "I am resolved,"
he said, " to like it, and reconcile myself to it, which is more
manly than to feign myself above it, and to send up complaints
by the post of being thrown away, and such like trash." There
is no profession so forbidding, no work so crabbed, that a man
who strives to extract the utmost happiness from it may not
twine about it the roses of fancy, and hide the most of its
thorns. "There is always hope," says Carlyle, " in a man that
actually and earnestly works. In idleness alone is there perpetual despair."

History and biography abound with examples of signal
patience shown by great men under trying circumstances.
The Chinese tell of one of their countrymen, a student, who,
disheartened by the difficulties in his way, threw down his book
in despair; when, seeing a woman rubbing a crowbar on a
stone, he inquired the reason, and was told that she wanted a
needle, and thought that she would rub down the crowbar till
she got it small enough. Provoked by this example of patience
to "try again," he resumed his studies, and became one of the
three foremost scholars in the empire. The gentle word
Sir Isaac Newton to his dog Diamond, when it upset a lighted
taper on his desk, by which the laborious calculations of years

were destroyed, are familiar to all. A like mischance befell Thomas Carlyle, when he had finished the first volume of his French Revolution. He lent the manuscript to a friend for perusal, and it having been left, by some carelessness, on the parlour floor, the maid-of-all-work, finding what she supposed to be a bundle of waste paper, used it to light the kitchen and parlour fires. The first composition of the book had been a labour of love ; the drudgery of rewriting it, with no help but memory, was contemplated by the author with a degree of anguish which it is not easy to conceive. Yet, without wasting time in plaints, he set resolutely to work, and at last triumphantly reproduced the book in the form in which it now appears. A similar anecdote is told of Robert Ainsworth, a celebrated writer and antiquary of the eighteenth century. He had toiled for years in compiling a voluminous dictionary of the Latin language, during which time he gave so little of his society to his wife, that, before he had quite completed the work, she committed it to the flames. Instead of abandoning himself to despair, he began at once to rewrite the book, which, with almost incredible labour, he finally accomplished.

The patience of two of our own countrymen was put to an equally severe test. When Edward Livingston had finished his great code of Louisianian law, he had the anguish of beholding the labour of long years perish instantly in the flames ; yet he was not disheartened, but patiently recommenced and reperformed his herculean task. After Audubon had wandered and toiled for years to get accurate representations of American birds, he found that two Norwegian rats had in a night destroyed two hundred of his original drawings, containing the forms of more than a thousand of the inhabitants of the air. All were gone but a few bits of gnawed paper, upon which the thieving rascals had reared a family of their young. "The burning heat," says the noble-hearted sufferer, "which instantly rushed through my brain was too great to be endured without affecting the whole of my nervous system. I slept not for several nights, and the days passed like the days of oblivion, until the animal powers being called into action, through the strength of my constitution, I took up my gun, my note-book, and my pencils, and went forward to the woods as gayly as if nothing had happened." He set to work again, pleased that he might now make better drawings than before, and in three years, by his indomitable energy, his portfolio was refilled.

There are some professions and some places in which patience is peculiarly requisite to success. It is said that in London the faculty of sitting still on a chair is largely rewarded. Men obtain great emoluments because they are forty years of age and upwards. Medical men, we know, get trusted, simply because their names have appeared for twenty years on the same brass plates on the same weather-beaten doors. A young attorney's most brilliant speech stands but little chance by the side of a graybeard's prosy argument. Even this faculty of sitting still, however,—often the hardest thing to do,—can be educed only by culture ; and, in general, the old adage is true, that there is no excellence or rare success without great labour. "Pigeons ready roasted," said the author of that exquisite musical composition, Midsummer Night's Dream, to a friend, "do not fly into the mouths of the most talented artists. As a rule, you must first catch, pluck, and roast them." Even the gold of Colorado exacts hard work. It cannot be picked up like the stones in the street, nor is it to be coaxed out with kid gloves. Men of genius have seldom revealed to us how much of their fame was due to hard digging. There were many headaches before the polished verses that fall so harmoniously on your ear were tortured into shape ; many a trial before Michael Angelo hewed out in marble or personated in fresco the awful conceptions of Dante. "Not even the Sybarite was at ease on his rosebed. Even *he* had some labour to perform ; no hand save his own could uncrumple the rose-leaf that chafed him."

Ninety per cent of what men call genius is a talent for hard work ; only the remaining tenth is the fancied ability of doing things without work. The mere drudgery which some men are said to have gone through with in executing their plans almost staggers belief. To acquire a polished style, Lord Chesterfield for many years wrote down every brilliant passage he met with in his reading, and either translated it into French, or, if it was in foreign language, into English. A certain eloquence became at last, he says, habitual to him, and it would have given him more trouble to express himself inelegantly than ever he had taken to avoid the defect. To gain a mastery of language, Lord Chatham not only used to translate Demosthenes into English, but also read Bailey's folio dictionary twice through with discriminating attention. For the same purpose, his son, William Pitt, before he was twenty years old, had read the works of nearly all the ancient classic authors, many of them aloud, dwelling sometimes for hours on striking passages of an orator or historian, noticing their turns of expression, and trying to discover the secret of their charm or power. "The silver-tongued" Mansfield not only translated all of Cicero's orations into English, but also retranslated the English orations into Latin. Butler, who exhibits in his Hudibras an amount of wit, comic illustration, and curious and out-of-the-way learning that is absolutely portentous, kept a commonplace-book, in which, according to Dr. Johnson, he had deposited for many years, not such events or precepts as are gathered by reading, but such remarks, similitudes, allusions, assemblages, or inferences, as occasion prompted or incliuation produced—those thoughts which were generated in his own mind, and might be usefully applied to some future purpose. "Such," adds Johnson, "is the labour of those who write for immortality." Before the great essayist himself began the "Rambler," he had collected in a common-place book a great variety of hints for essays on different subjects. Addisou amassed three folios of manuscript materials before he began the "Spectator." The papers in that periodical, like most essays which have survived the changes of time and the caprice of fashion, were simply the form which their author chose to impart to the world thoughts which, for the most part, had long been shaping and clothing themselves with words in his own mind.

Jean Paul Richter did the same thing. For years he went on reading, studying, and observing, making great books of extracts for future use, which he called his *quarries*. These note-books contained a kind of repertory of all the sciences; and he also carefully noted down his daily observatiens of living nature. The great Catholic writer, De Maistre, for more than thirty years noted down whatever he met with of striking interest in his reading, accompanying his extracts with comments; and he also placed in the same "immense volumes" those "thoughts of the moment, those sudden illuminations, which are extinguished- without result, if the flash is not made permanent by writing." Hume toiled thirteen hours a day while preparing his " History of England." Lord Bacon, notwithstanding the fertility of his mind, economized his thoughts, as the many manuscripts he left, entitled " Sudden Thoughts set down for Use," abundantly testify. Erskine made numerous extracts from Burke, of whom he was an intense admirer; and Lord Eldon copied " Coke upon Littleton" twice, re-reading that crabbed work till his whole mind was saturated with its lore and spirit. Southey was unwearied in his efforts to prepare himself to write. Not content with a mere reference in a table-book, whenever he met anything available in his reading he marked the passage with his pencil, and it was transcribed, docketed, and deposited in an array of pigeon-holes. Nothing short of this exhausting industry could have produced the " Commonplace Book " or " The Doctor."

When we look at the prodigious acquisitions of some men and the colossal performances of others, we are apt to think that such persons enjoy an immunity from the general law,— that the former class know intuitively without the trouble of learning, and that the latter execute great works without any real toil. We are apt to fancy that men of transcendent abilities are endowed with some special faculty,—with one sense more than belong to common men. In contemplating the wondrous creations of Shakespeare or the masterpieces of Milton and Dante, in thinking of Newton discovering the mechanism of the heavens, of Watt constructing the steam-engine, or of Morse inventing the electric telegraph, we are so utterly baffled in attempting to trace the process by which they reach these results, that we are tempted to ascribe them to a species of second-sight, rather than to the normal workings of the human mind. Even such histories as those of Gibbon, Guizot, and Buckle imply a capacity of acquiring knowledge and a tenacity of memory so immeasurably beyond those of common men, that we are apt to think these faculties in them to be different in kind as well as in degree. But a peep into the biographies of these and other great men dissipates these illusions. We find that, almost without exception, the men of brilliant genius, whether poets, orators, statesmen, historians, generals, or teachers, have been the hardest kind of workers, toiling more laboriously than smiths or carpenters ; and that the reason why they have surpassed other men is simply that they have taken more pains than other men.

Few of the great works of genius have been thrown off amid luxuries and abundant leisure. Generally they have been elaborated in the intervals of less congenial toils, amidst neglect, anxiety, and privation. The men who have spread light through the world, it has been truly said, had often scarcely oil for the lamp by which they worked; they that have left imperishable records of their minds had often little to support the body, and gave forth the incense in which their knowledge is embalmed "in self-consuming flames." But poor or independent in circumstances, the great men of the world have worked. Heyne, the great German classicist, shelled the peas for his dinner with one hand, while he annotated Tibullus with the other. Matthew Hale, while a student at law, studied sixteen hours a day. Sir Thomas More, and Bishops Jewell and Burnett, began studying every morning at four o'clock. Paley rose at five; Gibbon was hard at work, the year round, at six. Burke was the most laborious and indefatigable of human beings; Pascal killed himself by study, or rather by study without exercise; Cicero narrowly escaped death from the same cause; Hooker, Barrow, and Jeremy Taylor were industrious scholars; Milton kept to his books as regularly as a merchant or an attorney. "My morning haunts," proudly says the latter, in one of the few passages in which he gives us a peep into his private life, "are where they should be, at home; not sleeping or concocting the surfeits of an irregular feast, but up and stirring; in winter, often ere the sound of any bell awakens men to labour or devotion; in summer, as oft with the bird that first rouses, or not much tardier, to read good authors, or cause them to be read, till attention be weary or memory have its full freight; then with useful and generous labours preserving the body's health and hardiness."

The old idea of a genius, once so popular with lazy men, as one who never studies, or who studies nobody can tell when— at midnight, or at odd times and intervals, when the fit chances to be upon him—and who scorns to be shackled by methods or rules, is now pretty nearly exploded. It is acknowledged by all sensible men, that, as Dr. Dewy says, "genius *will study*; it is that in the mind that *does* study; that is the very nature

o

of it."   "There is but one method of attaining to excellence," says Sydney Smith, "and that is hard labour; and a man who will not pay that price for distinction had better at once dedicate himself to the pursuits of the fox, or sport with the tangles of Neæra's hair, or talk of bullocks, and glory in the goad! There are many modes of being frivolous, and not a few of being useful; there is but one mode of being intellectually great."

We hear a great deal about the extempore productions of men of genius—great works dashed off at a heat; but could we learn the secrets of the literary workshop, we should find that most of these marvellous improvisations, like the cut-and-dry, elaborate impromptus of conversations, which have been kept in pickle for weeks, have been the result of years of anxious thought and care. Sheridan is said to have written "Pizarro" at Drury Lane Theatre, over port wine and sandwiches; but every one familiar with his life knows that he was a literary trickster, who polished and repolished the brilliant off-hand sayings with which he used to dazzle the House of Commons with the greatest care—that they were, in fact, the results of previous reflection, kept ready for use in a memorandum-book. The brunt of the labour upon "Pizarro" had probably been done before he set pen to paper.

No man appears to write with more ease than Dickens; yet a published letter of his shows that when he was brooding over a new book his whole soul was "possessed," haunted, spirit-driven by one idea; and he used to go wandering about at night into the strangest places, seeking rest, and finding none till he was delivered. When that little Christmas book, "The Chimes," was about to rise from the ocean depths of his thought, he shut himself up for a month close and tight, till all his affections and passions got twined and knotted up in it, and, long ere he reached the end, he became "haggard as a murderer." It is said that on being requested to read at his public recitations a new selection from his writings, he replied that he had not the time to prepare himself, as he was in the habit of reading a piece once a day for six months before reciting it in public. That the author of "David Copperfield" had little faith in improvisations is evident from the following golden words: "The one serviceable, safe, certain, remunerative, attainable quality in every study and every pursuit is the quality of attention. My own invention or imagination, such as it is, I can most truthfully assure you, would never have served me as it has but for the habit of commonplace, humble, patient, daily, toiling, drudging attention." This is the way the most fertile, imaginative, vivacious writer of modern fiction does his work.

Rousseau, who wrote with so seeming ease, as he cast

> " O'er erring thoughts and sentences a hue
> Of words, like sunbeams, dazzling while they past
> The eyes that o'er them shed tears feelingly and fast,"

tells us that it was only "by ceaseless inquietude," by endless blotches and erasures, that he attained the magic beauty of his style. Molière, whose verse has all the easy flow of conversation, would pass whole days in fixing upon the freest and most vernacular mode of turning his couplets. Petrarch, in writing his impassioned amatory sonnets to Laura,—

> " Watering the tree which bears his lady's name
> With his melodious tears,—"

seems to have suffered more keenly from the pangs of rhyming than from the loss of his mistress, if we may judge by the operose corrections in his manuscripts. No one would dream that Beranger's light chirping verse, which seems as spontaneous as the twittering of a sparrow, is the result of intense labour; yet the author bestowed weeks and months even upon a single song, in order to give it that appearance of ease and simplicity at which he constantly aimed. Cardinal Bembo had a desk with thirty divisions, or pigeon-holes; and whenever he completed a sonnet, he put it into the first of them, whence he took it after a certain interval, and, having read and corrected it, put it into the next department. In a little time he would take it out, give it some more touches here and there, and promote it to another pigeon-hole. In this way he used to make his sonnet run the gauntlet through all the crypts, till he took it from the last of them, a pure and perfect chrysolite, —as complete a piece of literature as his persevering taste could make it. Buffon, who used to say of style that it was, in fact, the man, was slow with the pen, and asserted that genius was nothing but patience.   Rochefoucauld sc castigated his "Maxims" by revision, that he left them the hard literary muscle which we find them.

Addison wore out the patience of his printer.   He would often stop the press to insert a new preposition.   Gibbon wrote out his autobiography, a model of its kind, nine times before he could satisfy himself.   Haslitt tells us that he was assured by one who knew, that Burke's Letter to a Noble Lord, the most rapid, impetuous, glancing, and sportive of all his works, was returned to the printing-office so completely blotted over with alterations that the compositors refused to correct it as it was, took the whole matter to pieces, and reset the copy. Hazlitt himself spent so many weary years before he could wreak his thoughts upon expression, that he almost despaired of ever succeeding as an author.   John Foster was a most painfully laborious writer.   He tells us that in revising one of his essays, his principle was to treat no page, sentence, or word with the smallest ceremony, but " to hack, split, twist, prune, pull up by the roots, or practise any other severity on whatever he did not like."   The consequence was "alterations to the amount, very likely, of several thousands."   When Chalmers, after a visit to London, was asked what Foster was about, he replied, " Hard at it, at the rate of a line a week."

Even the light, facile verse of Tom Moore was the efflorescence of deep strata of erudition ; a quaint piece of learning often blossomed into a song, and knowledge gathered out of scores of folios bloomed into whole wilderness of beauty. Washington Irving tells us that Moore used to compose his poetry while walking up and down a gravel walk in his garden, and when he had a line, a couplet, or a stanza polished to his mind, he would go to a little summer-house near by, and write it down.   Ten lines a day he thought good work, and would keep the little poem by him for weeks, waiting for a single word.   Some of his broadest squibs cost him whole weeks of inquiry.

The ductility of language, in the hands of Hawthorne, sur-prises and delights every cultivated reader.   But for his lately published " Note-Books " which betray the secret of his art— reveal the laws by which his genius wrought,—we might fancy him an exception to the rule that intense labour is the price of all high excellence. We find him in these not trusting to inspirations, but day by day, through every month and every year, patiently jotting down every random thought that chanced to stray into his mind, pinioning every hint in ink, securing every fact or fancy that may possibly serve as material for or adornment of some future work. Not one of his books was flung off from the top of his mind in a white heat. We find on the contrary, that it was by condensing into a chapter, and sometimes into a sentence, the fruits of months of waiting and watching hints by the wayside and stray suggestions followed up and wrought out, moonlight meditations, and flashes of illumination, from electric converse with congenial minds, that he wove his spells, so weird, so dark, and so potent.

It is said that a rival playwright once jeered at Euripides, because he had taken three days to compose five lines whilst *he* had dashed off five hundred in the same time. " Yes," was the just retort, " but your five hundred lines in three days will be dead and forgotten whilst my five will live forever." The number of hours spent in the manual labour of writing a book is no measure of the brain-labour expended in composing it. Thoughts to flow easily must overflow from a full mind. Alonzo Cano, the Spanish Sculptor, completed a beautiful statue in twenty-five days. When the sordid merchant who had employed him wished to pay him by the day, he cried out, indignantly, " Wretch ! I have been at work twenty-five years, learning to make this statue in twenty-five days." So, as an English reviewer thoughtfully suggests, great painters may finish off great pictures with wonderful speed, as if hurried along by a whirlwind of inspiration ; so also great writers, like Sir Walter Scott (though even in his case with very doubtful advantage), may be able to dictate works of enduring interest and give them to the world without revising or retouching them at all ; but the reason in all these cases is the same. Long years of study and practice and meditation have so arranged and fitted, and as it were lubricated, the delicate mental instruments which the matter in hand requires, that when the motive power is applied, when the steam is up, they work with the precision and regularity of a machine.

As in literature, so in art,—the works that have challenged the world's admiration for ages have been the result of unwearied toil.   Michael Angelo, who, if any man, had a right to rely on genius only, said of himself that all was due to study.   He went sometimes a week without taking off his clothes. " During the nine years that I was his wife," said the widow of the great painter Opie, " I never say him satisfied with one of his productions ; and often, very often have I seen him enter my sitting-room, and throwing himself in an agony of despondence on the sofa, exclaim, 'I never, never shall be a painter as long as I live ! ' " It was this noble despair, which is never felt by vulgar artists, this pursuit of an ideal which, like the horizon, ever flew before him, that spurred on Opie to higher and yet higher efforts, till he filled one of the highest niches in the artistic temple of his country. When a lady once asked Turner what his secret was, he replied, " I have no secret, madam, but hard work.   This is a secret that many never learn and they don't succeed because they don't learn it. Labour is the genius that changes the world from ugliness to beauty, and the great curse to a great blessing."

Of oratory it has been said that there never was a good speaker who did not acquire his proficiency at the expense of his hearers.   If ever any man was born an orator, it was Charles James Fox who, as Wilberforce said, could begin at full speed, and roll on for hours without fatiguing himself or his audience ; yet even *his* talents were gradually developed by practice, for he made a point of speaking as often as he could—once every night if an opportunity offered—expressly with a view to his own improvement. Sir Robert Peel began when a boy to cultivate those abilities which, though only mediocre, made him one of the weightiest speakers in the House of Commons. When he was quite a child his father used frequently to set him upon a table, and say, " Now, Robin, make a speech, and I will give you this cherry." What few words the little fellow produced were applauded, and applause, stimulating exertion, produced such effects that before he was ten years old he could really address the company with some degree of eloquence. As he grew up his father constantly took him every Sunday into his private room, and made him repeat as much as he could of the sermon he had heard. Little progress was made at first; but by steady per-severance the habit of attention grew powerful, and the sermon was repeated at last almost verbatim. When many years after-wards he replied in succession to the arguments of his parlia-mentary opponents, stating each with extraordinary fulness and accuracy, it was little suspected that the power to do so had been acquired under his father's training, in Drayton Church.

America has probably produced no greater orator than Henry Clay. Though endowed with great natural gifts, he was no exception to the rule that *orator fit*. He attributed his success to the one single fact that at the age of twenty-seven he began, and continued for years, the practice of daily reading and speak-ing upon the contents of some historical and scientific book. "These off-hand efforts," he says, "were made sometimes in a cornfield, at others in the forest, and not unfrequently in some distant barn, with the horse and ox for my auditors. It is to this early practice in the great art of all arts that I am indebted for the primary and leading impulses that stimulated me for-ward, and shaped and moulded my subsequent entire destiny. Improve, then, young gentlemen, the superior advantages you here enjoy. Let not a day pass without exercising your powers of speech. There is no power like that of oratory. Cæsar controlled men by exciting their fears; Cicero, by captivating their affections and swaying-their passions. The influence of the one perished with its author; that of the other continues to this day." Henry Ward Beecher, when a theological student, was drilled incessantly by a skilful elocutionist in posturing, gesture, and voice-culture. There was a large grove between the seminary and his father's house, and it was the habit, he tells us, of his brother Charles and himself, and one or two others, to make the night, and even the day, hideous with their voices, as they passed backward and forward through the wood, exploding all the vowels from the bottom to the very top of their voices. It is said that the greatest sermon ever preached by Dr. Lyman Beecher, the father of Henry,—one of the most powerful pulpit orators in America,—was one on "The Gov-ernment of God." When asked, as he descended the pulpit steps, how long it took him to prepare that sermon, he replied. "About forty years, sir."

It cannot be too often repeated that all extraordinary skill is the result of vast preparatory training.   Facility of every kind comes by labour.   Nothing is easy, not even walking or reading, that was not difficult at first.   Emerson tersely says : "All the great speakers were bad speakers at first.   Stumping it through England for seven years made Cobden a consummate debater. Stumping it through New England for twice seven years trained Wendell Phillips.   The way to learn German is to read the same dozen pages over and over a hundred times, till you know every word and particlo in them, and can pronouuce and repeat them by heart.   No genius can recite a ballad at first reading so well as mediocrity can at the fifteenth or twentieth reading. The rule for hospitality and Irish 'help' is, to have the same dinner every day throughout the year. At last Mrs. O'Shaughnessy learns to cook it to a nicety, the host learns to carve it, and the guests are well served.   A humorous friend of mine thinks that the reason why nature is so perfect in her art, and gets up such inconceivably fine sunsets, is that she has learned how, at last, by dint of doing the same thing so very often. Cannot one converse better on a topic in which he has experience than on one which is new ?   Men whose opinion is valued on 'Change are only such as have a special experience, and off that ground their opinion is not valuable."

But little reflection is needed to satisfy us that it is for wise purposes that Providence has established the inexorable decree that intense toil shall be the price of all rare excellence or success.   Men are so constituted as to think lightly of, and even despise, that which it has cost them but a slight effort to win. When the maiden is too forward, her lover deems it time to draw back.   Besides, there would be no exclusiveness in excellence, nothing to distinguish it, or make it peculiarly desir able, if it could be too cheaply purchased.   It is told of two highwaymen, that, chancing once to pass a gibbet, one of them, with an ill-boding sign, exclaimed, "What a fine profession ours would be if there were no gibbets!"   "Tut! you blockhead," replied the other, "gibbets are the making of us ; for, *if there were no gibbets, every one would be a highwayman."* Just so with every art, trade, or pursuit ; it is the difficulties that scare and keep out unworthy competitors.   What Jean Paul Richter said of poverty, writing to a friend at the very time when he was in the clutches of a remorseless creditor, is true of many a trial in life. "What is poverty," said he, "that a man should whine under it ? It is but the pain of piercing the ears of the maiden, and you hang precious jewels in the wound." Even the dreariest tasks, like the ugly toad with the jewel in its head, have some redeeming circumstances that cheat them of their repulsiveness. "The ugliest trades," says Douglas Jerrold, "have their moments of pleasure. Now if I were a grave-digger, or a hangman, there are some people I could work for with a great deal of enjoyment."

In conclusion, we would say to every man who wishes to get on in the world, in the words of the poet Holmes,—

> Be firm ; one constant element of luck
> Is genuine, solid, old Teutonic pluck.
> Stick to your aim : the mongrel's hold will slip,
> But only crowbars loose the bull-dog's grip ,
> Small though he looks, the jaw that never yields
> Drags down the bellowing monarch of the fields !

CHAPTER XVI.

RESERVED POWER.

A man so trained in youth that his body is the ready servant of his will. and does with ease and pleasure all the work that as a mechanism it is capable of,—whose intellect is a clear, cold logic-engine, with all its parts of equal strength and in smooth working order, ready like a steam-engine to be turned to any kind of work, and spin the gossamers as well as forge the anchors of the mind.—HUXLEY.

Every person represents something, stands for something. At least he represents a value antecedently created in his own character. As was said of Bias, the wise Greek, himself is the treasure that a whole life has gathered. He stands for the wealth of being that a thousand struggles have contributed to form.—REV. F. D. HUNTINGTON, D.D.

It is told of Hercules, god of real force, that " whether he stood, or walked, or sat, or whatever thing he did, he conquered."—IB.

IN the great international boat-race which occurred some years ago on the Thames between the clubs of Harvard and Oxford, the boat manned by the former took the lead almost from the start. Rowing forty-six strokes to the minute, while their adversaries rowed but forty-two, the Harvard men were soon half a length, next a whole length ahead, and to a superficial observer, seemed likely to win the race. But presently the pace sinks to forty and thirty-nine ; foot by foot, and inch by inch, the men of the dark-blue colours, with the slow, steady, ponderous swing of their oars, creep up on their adversaries ; the men of the crimson colours strain every sinew to its tension, fighting every inch of the way ; but lo ! suddenly their stroke, hitherto so impetuous, begins to slacken and look distressed ; their opponents are steadily pulling forty strokes a minute to their thirty-nine or less ; a few minutes more, and Oxford moves victoriously ahead, and, in spite of the last desperate "spurts" of Harvard, maintains her superiority to the goal, and the race is won.

A great many explanations have been given of Harvard's defeat, but is it not evident that the main cause was a lack of that vital element in all contests and struggles, that element

which Americans are so apt to despise or neglect, namely,
reserved power? Is it not true that, not only in boat-races, but
everywhere,—in all the intellectual and moral contests of life,
—in the commercial mart, in the senate, in the pulpit, and in
the forum,—men fail of success from early exhaustion, from
a lack of that accumulated force, whether physical, mental, or
spiritual, which only can qualify them to meet any unexpected
draught upon their powers? In the composition of an army,
one of the first essentials of effective action is a well-constituted,
powerful reserved force. It consists of picked men, trained
veterans, with a cool, sagacious commander, who can be thrown
at any moment into the very thick of the fight, to sustain a
faltering legion, or to turn a doubtful combat into a decisive
victory. The lack of such a force, or its lack of numbers and
discipline, has often made the difference between a battle won
and a battle lost. Who that is familiar with the campaigns of
Napoleon does not remember how often the trembling scale was
turned, and the exultant legions of the enemy were rolled back,
just as victory was about " to sit eagle-winged on their crests,"
by the resistless charge of the Imperial Guard? And at Waterloo, when his star went down in darkness, to what mainly was
the disaster owing, but to the fact that this reserved force had
been diminished and enfeebled by the necessity of repelling
the attack on his right flank, so that when he partially broke
the British line at La Haye Sainte, he could not follow up his
success with a deadly blow?

Life is a warfare : it, too, has its decisive moments, when
success or failure, victory or defeat, must hinge upon our reserved power. At the bar, in the senate, in the pulpit, in the
fields of business, in every sphere of human activity, he only
organizes victory and commands success behind whose van and
corps of battle is heard the steady tramp of the army of the
reserve. Is it not enough that the rank and file of our forces
will suffice for ordinary occasions ; that, if the campaign takes
just the direction which we had expected, and there are no unforseen obstacles to surmount, no attacks by the enemy in
overwhelming numbers, no strategy for which we had not
provided, we shall *then* be victorious. We must be prepared for
unexpected crises,—for incredible emergencies, remembering
that, as the French proverb has it, nothing is sure to happen

but the unforseen.   Above all we must not cheat ourselves
with the delusion that, if we had failed to organize a sufficient force at the outset, we can impress men on the line of
march, or forage for supplies as we go along.   Much less can
we extemporize in the battle-field evolutions which we have
never practised on the parade ground.

Do we appreciate this truth? Is it one which "Young
America " emphasizes and acts upon ? Do we, as professional
men, in planning life's campaign, see to it that our spiritual
forces are made up of picked men, sound in wind and limb, all
the maimed, halt and blind being rigorously excluded from our
muster-rolls ; and, above all, do we keep our recruiting-offices
constantly open, remembering that the war ends only with life ?
Do our young men, in preparing for this war, spend years in patient and severe training, drilling and exercising their intellectual forces by all the approved, and some non-approved methods
of discipline ; testing them by mock fights, concentrating them
now upon this point and now upon that, now bidding them
storm some fortress of error, and anon to sap and mine, till
every raw recruit is a prompt and obedient soldier, so loyal, so
trained to action, that he will rally and form into line at the
first tap of the drum ?   Or, on the contrary, is it not a melancholy fact that nine-tenths of our professional men despise, or
at least underrate the necessity of, thorough training ; and with
raw levies, troops hastily conscripted, not for a life campaign,
but for each particular battle, rush forward confidently to meet
the enemy, only to encounter a Bull Run rout and overthrow ?
In other words, do we as professional men lay in abundant
stores of knowledge before we begin our professional life, adding daily to their sum, or do we intellectually live from hand
to mouth ? Do we not, at least too many of us, cram for each
occasion, like a turkey stuffed for Thanksgiving and starved all
the rest of the year? Do we not invest all our physical, mental and moral capital in our business, instead of keeping a part
in bank ? While economizing our gold and greenbacks, while
" alting down " our hard cash for a rainy day,—accumulating
for future use lands, houses, mortgages, and stocks,—do we
cultivate *intellectual* thrift ?

Not that the material stores are unnecessary ; by no means.
No army can do without a base of supplies. Our late civil

war has taught us that other things are necessary to victory besides men, discipline, and valour. We have learned that the long purse tells more powerfully upon the issue of a contest than long-ranged cannon ; that often, as Louis XIV. said of his struggle with the allies, it is the last crown that wins ; that a base of supplies is just as essential to military success as well-armed battalions ; that often it is not so much the regiments thrown forward into the field as the reserved forces intrenched in productive industry at home, and supporting the advancing column by their contributions and moral influence, that decide a campaign. Wellington won Waterloo, indeed, by his veterans ; but, back of this, it was the steam-engine, giving to England a working-power equal to fifty millions of men, —of men who fed upon coal and water, instead of on meat and bread,—that overturned the First Empire, and set down Napoleon in mid-ocean to meditate upon the might and majesty of that reserved force which he had not calculated upon in his scheme of personal aggrandizement. Granting all this, however, it is nevertheless true that our chief lack is that of spiritual force and discipline ; and that as here lies our weakness, this fact should furnish a hint as to where we should direct our efforts.

Let us now proceed to consider some of the reasons why we should collect and train this reserved force.

We answer, first, because it is the easiest and most economical way of carrying on, not only a military campaign, but the campaign of life. To serve a long and weary apprenticeship to any calling, to spend years in gymnazing and training the faculties till one has become an athlete, costs, we know, patience and self-denial ; but we appeal to every wrestler in the world's arena if it is not the cheapest in the end ? Does not all experience show that in the long run it is easier *to be* than *to seem*,—to acquire power than to hide the lack of it ? Was there ever a lazy boy at school, or student in college, who did not take infinitely more pains to dodge recitations and to mask his ignorance than would have been necessary to master his lessons, however dry or crabbed ? Is there a mechanic who scrimps his work, that does not cheat himself in the end ? Depend upon it, reader, nothing is more exhausting than the shifts to cover up ignorance, the endless contrivances to make nothing pass for something, tinsel for gold, shallowness for depth, emptiness for fulness, cunning for wisdom, sham for reality. Add to this the perpetual fear of detection,—the constant trembling lest some blunder should expose one's emptiness, lest some shaft should penetrate a weak joint in the harness, lest a protruding ear should reveal the ass in the lion's skin,—and it will be seen that no other possible procedure is half so labour-saving as thorough knowledge, exact training, profound and varied culture, the careful composition and constant renewal of our spiritual reserves. The true way to treat a difficulty is to face it boldly, and cut through or remove it. Go round it, and unlike Mr. Micawber's "something," it will be forever "turning up again," growing more and more formidable every time you dodge it.

It is true that this is not the popular doctrine. We live in an age of "fast" men,—of steam and electricity,—and now that people travel by "lightning lines," going from New York to Chicago in twenty-nine hours, the cry on all sides is for " short cuts " to the professions, and science-made-easy methods of intellectual culture. Instead of toiling painfully on foot up the rugged steeps of learning, the student of to-day flies with lightning-like speed along a railway track, finding every cliff cut through, every valley bridged. Even the Mt. Washingtons have railways leading to their tops, and every Hoosac is tunnelled. Perhaps the new methods of intellectual culture are best, but there are some " old fogies " left who will doubt it. They will doubt the value of royal roads. They will question the expediency of making education very easy, if it is to prepare one for a world where labour is the eternal condition on which the rich man gains an appetite for his dinner, and the poor man a dinner for his appetite. They will inquire whether to simplify every study, to lead the mind along a planked road or railway to knowledge, so that no efforts on its own part, no long, distressing discipline of thought and research, no grappling with difficulties, is required, be not to defeat the chief end of study. If you wish to toughen the body, do you make the exercises of the gymnasium—the climbing of ladders, the jerking of dumb-bells, the swinging on parallel bars—light and unfatiguing? Is it not in the very hardness of the thing done that its value consists? The savage believes that every time he slays an enemy the spirit of that enemy enters into him, and becomes added to his own, accumulating a warrior's strength for the day of battle. So, when you conquer a difficulty, the spirit of that difficulty passes into you, transformed into power ; it adds to the mind's *reserved* force, just as the resisting of one temptation tends to disarm the next of its power. Every intricate problem solved by the pupil unaided is a true victory over himself, and inspires confidence for new conquests. On the other hand, the student of cyclopædias and notes and handbooks and keys never knows anything positively, and, thrown upon his own resources, is utterly helpless. He can never go without his crutches.

The lack of reserved power will explain many failures which otherwise would seem unaccountable. Why is an author's second book so often unreadable ? Is it not because, instead of drawing from a living spring, he exhausts himself, pumps himself dry, in his first effort ? For years he has dreamed over one projected composition to which all his experience has stood re-. lated, all his thought has converged. It is the net result of his experience up to a certain time ; it is the cistern into which he has poured his accumulated life. Elated by success, he mistakes the cistern for a fountain, taps his brain again, and the result is, we get but the dregs and lees of his thought. The first book he wrote because he had something to say, the second because he wanted to say something ; and the one is but the echo of the other.

Secondly, reserved power gives yet greater force and effect to power in action. Indeed, power exerted, however great, never impresses us in the profoundest degree, unless we feel that behind it there is a power greater than itself, by which it can be at any moment augmented. The force that is exhausted in a single jet inspires but a limited degree of admiration or awe. For its highest effect we must feel that it is a Niagara fed by vast inland seas, the vanguard of a coming host, the shower that foreruns the coming tempest,

The baby finger
Of the giant mass of things to come
At large.

Nobody is thrilled to his being's core by an exhibition of power that is evidently draining itself to the very dregs. The race-horse that, panting and gasping, just reaches the goal ; the loco-motive that tugs at its load ; the bank that is drained by a day's run ; the philosopher with one idea ; the hen cackling over its one egg; the student who just escapes " plucking ;" the " Single-speech Hamilton," who never opens his mouth a second time in Parliament ; the Sir Egerton Brydges, who writes but one fine sonnet, though it rivals Milton's ; the governor elected by one vote,—provokes our sympathy rather than our respect. Our last term of contempt is " played out." Who are the men that impress us most in history ? Are they not those that are felt to be greater than their deeds,—who by their acts only beget an expectation that outruns all their performance ? The large part of their power is latent, a reserved force which acts directly by presence, and without means. Their victories are won by demonstration of superiority, not by crossing of bayonets. It has been often remarked that a speech never seems truly great unless there is a man behind it who is greater than the speech. A brilliant but shallow, heartless orator never yet stole the secret of a sincere conviction. As it was not the Prussian needle-gun, destructive as it is, which won the late Prussian victories, but the intelligence and discipline of the Prussian soldier,—the man behind the gun, educated in the best common schools in the world,—so it is the latent heat of character, the man behind the words, that gives *them* momen-tum and projectile force. It was this which gave so prodigious a power to the words of Chatham, and made them smite his adversaries like an electric battery. Men who listened to his oratory felt that he " put forth not half his strength,"—that the man was far greater than anything he said. It was the magnetism of his person, the haughty assumption of superi-ority, the scowl of his imperial brow, the ominous growl of his voice, " like thunder heard remote," and, above all, the evidence which these furnished of an imperious and overwhelming will, that abashed the proudest peers in the House of Lords, and made his words perform the office of stabs and blows.

The impression which every speaker, whether on the plat-form or in conversation, makes on his fellows, is the moral re-sultant, not of what he *says*, but of all that he has grown up to *be ;* of his manhood, weak or strong, sterling or counterfeit ;

of a funded but unreckoned influence, accumulated unconsciously, and spending itself, as the man is deep or shallow, like a reservoir, or like a spout or an April shower.

In reading the great masters of English thought, we are constantly impressed by this reserved force. We feel, as we slake our thirst at these "wells of English undefiled," that we can never drain them dry; that they are not cisterns, but living fountains, whose depths are fathomless. Read a page of Macaulay, and you exhaust the thought of a single perusal. Read a page of Bacon twenty times, and at each reading you will discover new meanings unobserved before. That haze which the naked eye could not penetrate, is found by the telescope to be a nebula, composed of innumerable distinct stars. The one writer informs, the other stimulates, the mind. The one enlightens, the other inspires. The first communicates facts and opinions ; the second floods and surcharges you with mental life. So in Barrow,—of whom Charles I. said that he was an unfair preacher, because he left nothing for others to say,—it is not the Amazonian fulness of the thought that impresses you so much as the air of conscious facility with which he discusses every theme. Be the subject mathematical, metaphysical, or moral, he brings always to it a mind superior to the occasion, and holds it with a giant grasp. He handles the most ponderous problems of theology with an heroic ease, like that of Homer's champions, . hurling stones which nine degenerate men of modern times would have failed to lift.

And so with him whom we call "oceanic," "the myriad-minded," "the thousand-souled,"—the great master of the human heart, who swept all its strings, or rather, whose soul was a mighty organ through which Nature gave utterance to the full diapason of her notes,—the dramatist whose exhaustless fertility of thought is such that in the whole range of his characters he never once repeats himself, the "suggestive sorcery" of whose language affects us like the spell of a mighty enchanter,—what is the distinguishing characteristic of his genius but that reserved power which makes his greatest efforts seem "like the play, the sport of his mighty spirit, waves borne to our feet from a deep sea which oar has never vexed nor plummet sounded ? "

The biographer of the German metaphysician, Fitche, contrasting his wealth of thought with the formalism of a contemporary, observes that " all the truth that the latter has written is not worth a tithe of the false which Fitche may have written. The one gives me a small number of known truths ; the other gives me perhaps one truth, but, in so doing, opens before me the prospect of an infinity of unknown truths." Who does not recognise here the portraits of two classes of thinkers that are to be found in every department of philosophy, science, and literature,—the one consisting of poverty-stricken thinkers, who instruct but do not rouse, who enlighten but do not electrify ; the other, of those mighty and sustained spirits that open up new paths with every step they take ; that wrestle with their subjects only to grind them to powder ; that struggle with language in order to wrest from it words enough for their wealth of thought ; that do not so much lead as seize and hurry us along ; who seem to say all that they do say only that we may conjecture how much more they *could* say ; and who move about in the intellectual world with an ease and confidence which proclaim that they not only dwell but rule there ?

It has been truly said that the great orator is not he who exhausts his subject and himself at every effort, but he whose expressions suggest a region of thought, a dim vista of imagery, an oceanic depth of feeling, beyond what is compassed by his sentences. He affects you hardly less by what he leaves out than by what he puts in. The thoughts he so eloquently utters only apprise you of the nearness of a world whose thoughts are more eloquently *unuttered*.

Nature has her reserved forces, the knowledge of which impresses us more than her grandest displays of material power. Her mightiest operations are performed in silence, and the effect is deepened and intensified by the sense of a greater power behind that which we see or feel. Art, too, touches us by its reserved power. There are paintings whose meaning lies on the surface and is exhausted by a single look ; and there are others which disappoint at first, yet, reverently studied, gradually glow with beauty, disclosing new marvels of skill, hidden depths of meaning, at each examination, till at last the genius of the artist stands confessed, and you gaze transfixed by a mighty enchanter.

Perhaps the highest proof of this reserved power in the artist is the ease with which, however hard he may have laboured, he will seem to perform his marvels. When Michael Angelo proposed to fortify his native city, Florence, and was desired to keep to his painting and sculpture, he observed that these were his recreations,—what he really understood was architecture. This is what Sir Joshua Reynolds considered as the praise of Rubens, that he seemed to make a plaything of the art. "A picture must not only be done well," he said, "it must seem to have been done easily." Northcote, the painter, speaking of the laboured and timid productions of the modern French and Italian schools, remarks that "they are the result of such a tedious, petty, mechanical process, that it is as difficult for you to admire as it was for the artist to execute them; whereas, when a work seems stamped on the canvas by a blow, you are taken by surprise, and your admiration is as instantaneous and electrical as the impulse of genius which has caused it. I have seen pictures with such a power that it thrilled through your whole frame, and you felt as if you could take up your brush and do anything."

Another advantage of reserved power is that, when it cannot prevent defeat, it will at least save us from rout and despair. The military leader who brings all his troops to the front has no resource when beaten; every defeat is a Waterloo. Not so with the man who has always battalions in reserve; he fights more and more valiantly after each overthrow. Like Blucher at Ligny, he may be forced back from his position; but he will retreat in good order, and in two days more the thunder of his guns will be heard at Waterloo, sending death and dismay into the ranks of his late victors. Like Washington, he may lose more battles than he wins; but he will organize victory out of defeat, and triumph in the end. Napoleon said of Massena that he was not himself until the battle began to go against him; then—when the dead began to fall in windrows around him— awoke his marvellous powers of combination, and he put on terror and victory as a robe.

We all remember the conduct of Phil. Sheridan on a certain occasion when he found his army retreating before the victorious Early. "O sir," said the general in command, "we are beaten!" "No, sir," was the reply; "*you* are beaten, but this army is *not* beaten;" and then, seizing his army as Jupiter, his thunderbolt, he hurled it upon the enemy. We all remember too, the case of Curran. He had a defect in his speech, from which he was nicknamed "stuttering Jack Curran;" and when he essayed his first speech, the features of his audience swam before his eyes, the candles seemed to glare unmercifully upon him, his words stuck in his throat, and he sank into his seat filled with mortification and shame. But he knew his reserved strength, and when on a second trial he was ridiculed as *Orator Mum*, the very sarcasm stung him into eloquence; he replied with a triumphant speech, and was able at last to charm the fastidious ear of the House of Commons, and to make a corrupt bench tremble.

Disraeli's first effort was a failure. It would have killed an ordinary man. All the wiseacres shook their double chins at him; but he simply replied, "The day will come when you will be glad to hear me," a prophecy which his sneering critics have seen abundantly fulfilled. Robert Hall failed even more ignominiously. In his first sermon he "stuck" almost at the beginning. Covering his face with his hands, he sobbed aloud, "O, I have lost all my ideas!" and burst into a flood of tears. A second trial ended in a more agonizing failure; but the man who at the age of eight had made Butler's "Analogy" and "Edwards on the Will," his intellectual recreations was not to be silenced by two failures. A third trial was made, and from that hour he took rank as the most brilliant pulpit orator of England. When Thoreau published that unrivalled New England pastoral, "A Week on the Concord and Merrimack Rivers," only three hundred copies were sold or given away, and the other seven hundred were returned to him by the publisher. How does he notice the fact in his diary? "I have now," he writes in grim triumph, "a library of some nine hundred volumes, *seven hundred of which I wrote myself.* Nevertheless, in spite of this result, sitting beside the inert mass of my works, I take up my pen to record what thought or experience I may have had with as much satisfaction as ever."

A striking illustration of the advantage which a reserved power gives to the man of letters, especially when contending on the battle-fields of thought, is furnished by the famous Phalaris controversy which raged in England about two centuries ago. The dispute had its origin in France, where Fontenelle and Perrault claimed for the moderns a general superiority over the writings of antiquity. A reply to these arguments was published by Sir William Temple, who, in his Essay on "Ancient and Modern Learning," declaring for the ancients, maintained with more elegance of manner than weight of matter that the oldest books extant were still the best of their kind, and, in proof of this assertion, cited the "Fables" of Æsop, and the "Epistles of Phalaris." This led to the publication of a new edition of the "Epistles" by the scholars of Christ Church, Oxford, the nominal editor being Hon. Charles Boyle. Meanwhile William Wotton, a Cambridge scholar of marvellous precocity, who had taken his degree at the age of thirteen, had published a very able and impartial estimate of the controversy in his Reflections upon Ancient and Modern Learning ; and at his earnest request, Richard Bentley, the Master of Trinity College, and the greatest Hellenist of his age, had added to the second edition of that work a dissertation in the form of letters to his friend, in which he proved that the author of the " Epistles of Phalaris " was not the tyrant of Sicily, but some sophist of a later day.

Sir William Temple was greatly incensed at this publication, in which his own quackery and sciolism, as well as that of the Oxford wits, had been so mercilessly exposed ; and, at his request, Dean Swift entered the lists, and made an onslaught upon Bentley in " The Battle of the Books ;" but the rage of the knight was mild to that of the Christ Church men, who considered Bentley's attack an affront to the whole college, and resolved by joining their forces to crush the audacious assailant at once and forever. In a brilliant and skilfully written work, to which half a dozen of their best scholars contributed, and into which they poured all the stores of wit, sarcasm, acumen, and erudition which they could muster, they attacked Bentley in turn, and, in the estimation of the public, gained a complete victory. A shout of triumph went up from their ranks, which was echoed by all the spectators of the combat ; a second edition of the book, which was deemed absolutely unanswerable, was called for ; and Bentley was supposed, even by his own friends, to be silenced for ever. Nobody dreamed that he would even dare to reply, still less that he could ever again hold up his head in the republic of learning ; the cup of his adversaries' joy was full, and their exultation knew no bounds.   At Cambridge a caricature was exhibited of Phalaris putting the unfortunate critic into his brazen bull ; and as it was thought that a member of St. John's College, where Bentley was educated, could not properly make his exit without a pun, he was represented as saying, "I had rather be roasted than *Boyled.*"

Now was to be seen the signal advantage of reserved power. In the midst of all this outcry the literary lion remained unmoved.   "Hushed in grim repose," he lay couchant, and, with his eyes upon the gambols of his victims, was settling himself at leisure for his fatal spring.   Conscious of his own learning, compared with whose boundless stores the entire joint-stock of the confederacy was but that of school-boys—all that he had previously disclosed in the controversy being but the *sprinklings* of his treasures—Bentley resolved to prepare an answer which should not only annihilate his opponents at one fell swoop, but establish his reputation as one of the profoundest scholars the world had seen.   At length, when Achilles was armed for the field, the signal was given ; and with the fullest benefit of final revision, which left no room for friend or foe to point out a flaw, "that immortal dissertation," as Porson calls it, which was to make an epoch, not only in the life of the great Grecian, but in the history of literature, descended like a thunderbolt upon the enemy—

> " And in one night
> The trumpet silenced, and the plumes laid low."

Never was there a more crushing defeat.   Every position of the enemy was carried ; they were routed, horse, foot, and dragoons.   After this Waterloo, they never took the field again ; it was felt to be madness.   The victory over his adversaries, immortal as it was, forms but a small part of Bentley's achievement.   So profound is his learning, and such is his skill, that, while every page is controversial, he has embodied a mass of accurate information relative to history, chronology, antiquities, philology, and criticism, which has never, perhaps, been matched in any other volume ; while all is so luminously arranged and presented that the elementary student of classical literature may read with profit and pleasure, and the most veteran scholar find the circle of his knowledge enlarged.

A yet more memorable illustration of the value of reserved power is furnished by the debate in the United States Senate in 1830, concerning the sale of the public lands. "The occasion," says a thoughtful writer, "was not a great one ; the debate upon it for some days dragged heavily. The vast reserve power of one man made it the event of our history for a generation. The second speech of Mr. Hayne, to which Mr. Webster was called upon to reply, was able and brilliant, its constitutional argument specious, its attack upon New England and upon Mr. Webster sharp even to bitterness. But Mr. Hayne did not understand this matter of reserved power. He had seen Mr. Webster's van and corps of battle, but had *not* heard the firm and measured tread behind. It was a decisive moment in Mr. Webster's career. He had no time to impress new forces, scarcely time to burnish his armour. All eyes were turned to him. Some of his best friends were depressed and anxious. *He* was as calm as a summer's morning ; calm, his friends thought, even to indifference. But his calmness was the repose of conscious power, the hush of nature before the storm. He had measured his strength. He was in possession of himself. He knew the composition of his 'army of the reserve.' He had the eye of a great commander, and he took in the whole field at a glance. He had the prophetic eye of logic, and he saw the end from the beginning. The exordium itself was the prophecy, the assurance of victory. Men saw the sun of Austerlitz, and felt that the Imperial Guard was moving on to the conflict. He came out of the conflict with the immortal name of the Defender of the Constitution. Of this speech, and of the mode of its delivery, one of the greatest of our orators has said, 'It has been my fortune to hear some of the ablest speeches of the greatest living orators on both sides of the water ; but I must confess I never heard of anything which so completely realized my conception of what Demosthenes was when he delivered the Oration for the Crown.' I venture to add that, taking into view the circumstances under which the speech was delivered, and especially the brief time for preparation, the importance of the subject, the breadth of its views, the strength and clearness of its reasoning, the force and beauty of its style, its keen wit, its repressed but subduing passion, its lofty strains of eloquence, the audience to which it was addressed (a more than Roman audience), its effect upon that audience and the larger audience of a grateful and admiring country, history has no nobler example of reserved power brought at once and effectively into action. The wretched sophistries of nullification and secession were swept before his burning eloquence as the dry grass is swept by the fire of the prairies."*

Here, did space permit, we might speak of the self-confidence, the dignity of manner, which reserved power gives to him who knows that he is equal, and more than equal, to the occasion. In describing his feelings while making the speech we have just noticed, Mr. Webster is reported to have said to a friend : " I felt as if everything I had ever seen or read or heard was floating before me in one grand panorama, and I had little else to do than to reach up and cull a thunderbolt and hurl it at him ! "

But the reader may ask, How is this reserved force to be got ? How is it to be gathered and trained ?

We answer, first, by hard study. Capital, in whatever shape it may be accumulated, pecuniary or intellectual, is hoarded labour. If we wish our drafts to be honoured in a crisis, there must be daily deposits in the savings bank. Tell me how much has been your patient toil in obscurity, and I will tell you how far you will triumph in an emergency. It has been well said that the mental balance never lets us overdraw. In life's school-room " each day recites a lesson for which all preceding days were a preparation. Our real rank is determined, not by lucky answers or some brilliant impromptu, but by the uniform diligence. For the exhibition-days of Providence there is no preconcerted colloquy,—no hasty retrieving of a wasted term by a stealthy study on the eve of the examination. Bonnivard, Huss, Wyckliffe, Alfred, Washington, Madame Roland, Catherine of Genoa,—these valiant souls were not inoculated for their apostleship *ex tempore.* The roots of all their towering greatness, so brave to the top, ran back under the soil of years."

<hr>

* Hon. B. F. Thomas, LL.D.

The best extempore efforts, the most brilliant impromptus, come from those who have acquired the ability to make them by years of toil. Chief Justice Parsons, when an attorney, once astonished Alexander Hamilton, his opponent, by the promptness with which he demolished one of his strongest points. But when beginning practice he had access to the best law-library in New England, and had literally mastered it, making briefs of the most important cases, among which were several involving the very point in question. The truth is, the ready man—the man full of resources, armed *cap-à-pie* for every emergency—is the man who has toiled long and hard *to be* ready, and to acquire that strength and flexibility which will prepare him for whatever he may have to do.

It is true there are men at the bar, in the pulpit, and in the senate, whose instantaneous and imperial command of ideas and words seems like an instinct. They have all their faculties and knowledges so completely at call,—they are able to bring all their powers to bear at once with such energy and earnestness on any given point, and to keep them so fastened on that point, that we ascribe the result, not to training, but to that mysterious something which we call genius. And geniuses, no doubt, there are in the world ; but, depend upon it, there are no geniuses in this nineteenth century that reap without sowing ; none that are idlers till the moment a demand is made upon their mind, and then answer it by intuition. All such have disappeared from the world with ghosts. The geniuses of our day are distinguished by their power of intense application, —application not always spread over a great lapse of time, but which hits the nail on the head, which has a fine aim for the heart of a subject or the hinge of a difficulty. If in professional life they astonish us by their readiness and fertility, it is because we forget that their minds have been previously so exercised on similar subjects, that not only the necessary words, but the necessary arguments and combinations of thought, have become by long practice as intuitive as those motions of the body by which we walk, talk, or do any habitual act.

If one man scowls and agonizes over a difficulty in theology, law, or medicine, straining his brain almost to lesion, and another sees at a glance where lies the difficulty and what is the solution, does this prove inevitably that the latter has more natural ability than the other? By no means. It simply shows that his faculties have been edged and sharpened by years of familiarity with such topics; and the ease with which he now does his work, so far from proving that he has always worked with ease, is, on the contrary, but the measure of the labour by which he has prepared himself to do it. The thorough mastery of even one subject can be the fruit only of hard thinking. It demands the element of time. It can be won by no power of cramming. "How easily he writes!" exclaimed a young lady as she laid down one of Irving's charming volumes. Had she said, "How easy it is to *read* his books!" they who know something of the agonies of "easy writing" might readily sympathize with her. The locomotive slips easily along the railway track; but ten thousand men toiled in quarries of iron and coal, in the bowels of mountains, in forests, and in machine and cabinet shops, before you could fly on the wings of steam at the rate of forty miles an hour. The steamboat, to use an illustration we have somewhere seen, glides gracefully and swiftly over the waters; but it is no *easy* power that gives to the water-traveller her steady and rapid motion. It is true she is tastefully decorated and gilded; her cabins are luxurious, and her prow is decorated with specimens of the sculptor's art. But descend with us to the engineer's fiery domain, and swelter there in the burning pit; see the sweating firemen, and listen to the bursting steam; behold the tremendous power of fire and water combined, until the strained and groaning boiler threatens to burst asunder and deluge her decks with the imprisoned fluid,—and you will confess that Ease, though a mild and pleasant damsel, has a terribly rough old father. It is slow and hard thinking that makes rapid and easy reading. The freedom and facility of the writer and speaker spring from the same source as the painter's, which, Sir Joshua Reynolds tells us, "are attained only by intense study and industry at first, though the pictures thus wrought with such pains now appear like the effect of enchantment, and as if some mighty genius had struck them off at a blow."

And here let us add that this labour must not be confined to the period of youth, but continued through life. The nucleus of the reserve force must be gathered and trained in the beginning of the war, but it must be enlarged and strengthened by

fresh recruits through the entire campaign. Professional culture must begin at the Law, Medical, or Divinity School, but
it must not end there. A public speaker is inexhaustible only
in proportion as he nourishes his mind by study ; and in mind,
as in body, when nourishment ceases vitality ends. The preacher
who shuts his books when he puts on his white choker, the
lawyer who tosses aside his "Coke upon Littleton" the moment
he is in the full tide of practice, does so at his peril. We
know the excuses that may be given for this. We know the
ten thousand distractions to which each is exposed—the moths
that eat into his time—especially when the one is pastor of a
city congregation, and the other is beset by a swarm of clients.
But we know that the world cares nothing about these excuses, and that the lawyer whose plea is shallow, the preacher
who, instead of pruning off all divergent activities, fritters his
time into shreds by making and receiving calls, going to
pic-nics, talking up reading-rooms and art-institutes, acting as
secretary of a dozen societies, serving on committees, delivering temperance lectures, listening to the twaddle of bores and
the complaints of grumblers, and neglects severe and continuous study, will speak, the one to yawning juries and the other
to empty pews.

Do you say that the writing of two sermons a week consumes
so much time that the young preacher has none left for general
culture ? We answer that it is the very absence of this culture
that makes sermon-writing so laborious and so consumptive of
time. *Ex nihilo nihil fit*—it *is* hard, and always will be hard,
to draw water from an empty cistern, even by means of a force-
pump. The fatal flaw in nine-tenths of the sermons one hears
is that they lack body of thought, vitalized knowledge, intellectual power. The preacher who would permanently and
powerfully impress his hearers should have large reserves of
knowledge; he must be like Bishop Brownrig, of whom
Fuller tells us that he not only "carried learning enough *in
numerato* about him in his pockets for any discourse," but
"had much more at home in his chests for any serious dispute." It has been well observed by the editor of one of our
ablest religious journals,* that "the merchant is in a danger-

<hr>

* Rev. W. W. Patton, D.D., in the *Advance*.

ous position whose means are in goods trusted out all over the country on long credits, and who in an emergency has no moneys in bank upon which to draw. A heavy deposit, subject to a sight-draft, is the only position of strength. And he only is intellectually strong, who has made heavy deposits in the bank of memory, and can draw upon his faculties at any time, according to the necessity of the case." Give two of the three days which you now spend in grinding out sermons to hard study, reading the ablest books, even some that are called heretical, mastering the greatest themes, and filling the cells of the brain with the fruits of the most varied culture, and you need not trouble yourself about the sermon; it will write itself, as the water from the lake gushes up in the fountain. The combustibles will be gathered; you will have only to apply the match.

Again, we must reserve time for meditation. We live in an age of bustle and excitement; the click of the telegraph, the whistle of the locomotive, the whir of machinery, is ever in our ears. The tendency of the times is to force every man of ability into great outward activity, and thereby in many cases to dam up and divert to the turning of this mill or that the stream which, if left unbroken, would have gathered volume enough to fertilize a vast tract of thought. Besides this, in our large towns every cultivated man is beset with a multiplicity of social enjoyments and excitements, the very waste-pipes of spiritual power; and the energies of the brain, instead of forming a fund that is continually deepening by influx from secret sources, are diffused and wasted on trivialities. Add to this the fact that the Americans are the most impatient people under the sun—that we are not content to wait through long and weary years for the fruits of our toil, but, in the stock-jobber's phrase, are anxious "to realize" at once—and can we wonder that so few of us accumulate the reserve power which is indispensable if we would do anything worthy of our faculties? Is it strange that our intellectual work is so poor, when our lives are so full of disquiet, and we have hardly a grain of that patience of nature which slowly and with the forethought of a century of growth builds up and elaborates a forest tree? Need we to be told that while knowledge is acquired by labour, wisdom cometh by opportunity of leisure," and that the ripest thought comes from a mind which is not always on the stretch, but fed at times "by a wise passiveness?"

The literary worker, above all men, should remember that leisure, and oftentimes protracted leisure is an absolute necessity of his intellectual life. The electric eel cannot be always giving off shocks. No field, however rich its soil, will bear continual cropping. It has been justly said that Aaron's beard would not have come down to us in history, if he had but shown the Israelites what he could shave from his chin day by day; and even an Emerson would be unrecognisably diluted, if he were trickled though a daily editorial. There is no mental reservoir of such capacity that it will not be empty at last, if we perpetually draw from it and never pour into it. Besides, we must remember that, as the Country Parson has told us, the mind can be emptied in much shorter time than it is possible to fill it. "It fills through an infinity of little tubes, many so small as to act by capillary attraction; but in writing a book, an article, or a sermon, it empties itself through a twelve-inch pipe." When old Dr. Bellamy was asked by a young clergyman for advice about the composition of his sermons, he replied: "Fill up the cask! fill up the cask! fill up the cask! and then if you tap it anywhere you will get a good stream. But if you put in but little, it will dribble, dribble, dribble, and you must tap, tap, tap, and then you get but a small stream, after all."

Thirdly, to acquire reserved power, we must concentrate our energies upon some one thing, yet be careful at the same time to avoid mental narrowness.

The mind, as well as the body, demands variety of discipline as well as generosity of diet. It will not grow to its full stature, nor be rounded into just proportions, nor acquire that blended litheness, toughness, and elasticity which it needs, if fed upon one aliment. There is no profession or calling which, if exclusively followed, will not warp and contract the mind. Just as in the body, if I resolve to be a rower and only a rower, the chances are that I shall have, indeed, strong arms, but weak legs, and perhaps lose my eyesight by the glare of the water; or as, if I become a pugilist, I shall be all muscle, with no brains,—so, in the mind, if I exercise but one set of faculties, and neglect the rest, I may become a subtle theologian, able to discriminate between the *Homoousion* and the *Homoiousian*, or between " efficacious " and " sufficient " grace, with more than Aquinas's subtlety ; or a sharp, hair-splitting lawyer, with the eye of a lynx and the scent of a hound to detect a legal flaw or like a profound classical scholar who, like Hudibras,

> " Can speak Greek
> As easily as pigs squeak,"

and **to** whom Latin

> " Is no more difficile
> Than to a blackbird 'tis to whistle,"—

but, as a *man* I may be below contempt.   The clergyman, es·pecially, is apt, without broad and generous culture, to get a mental twist, a narrowness and one-sidedness, which greatly lessens his power.   Reading and thinking of nothing but theology, he gets into a rut,—a rut which deepens every year, but never widens.   Travel with him in his narrow groove a twelve-month and you cease ever afterwards to see or hear anything new.   He may not literally turn the barrel over, but he preaches substantially the same sermons.   The texts may be new, but you recognise the same old thunder.   There is a continual iteration of old thoughts, the thrashing of the same straw without wheat, the same barrel-organ tunes, the turning of the wheel upon its own axis, the jogging on the same old roads with the "one-hoss shay."

For these reasons we would say to every man, strive for excellence in your calling, but, as subsidiary to this, do not fail to enrich your whole capital as *man*.   To be a giant, and not a dwarf, in your profession you must be always growing.   A town that is finished has already begun to decay.   The man that has ceased to go up intellectually has begun to go down. The more various your mental diet, the more inexhaustible will be your mental resources ; the wider your range of thought, the greater will be your chance of original combinations. Read the best non-professional works in science, history, and literature, and select for friends and associates some whose pursuits are unlike your own, and you will be astonished, when you write or speak, at the freshness of your thoughts and the multitude and variety of illustrations that will come trooping to the tip of your tongue or pen. Nothing conduces more to breadth of intellect than intercourse with various minds. "The commerce of intellect," it has been well said, "loves distant shores. The small retail trader deals only with his neighbour; when the great merchant trades he links the four quarters of the globe."

Upon the importance of concentration we need not dwell. While avoiding narrowness, we must remember that it will be impossible to accumulate much reserved power if we dissipate our strength upon many objects, instead of using it with economy and directing it to one grand end. But how shall we use it economically, when so many things are clamouring for our attention ? We answer, by concentrating our efforts upon the vitally essential part of our work, and neglecting the less important : in other words, by striking where the blows will be most effective. We must do as William Pitt did, when overwhelmed by official duties. He divided his work into three parts,—that which was not worth doing, that which would do itself, and that which was quiet enough for any man to attempt.

A vivid illustration of the advantage with which this may be done is furnished by an incident related some years ago in an Eastern magazine. "We once happened," says the writer, "into a country church on a Sunday forenoon in a strange place, and were seated in a pew in the broad aisle. The clergyman, a weakly seeming man, with a whisper of a voice, rose to his duties, and feebly went through the various services antecedent to the sermon. We wished ourselves out of it, but retreat was impossible ; we looked about, the church was full. What could people come to meeting for ? to see and hear such a dead-and-alive performance as that ? We settled ourselves down in desperate resignation, hoping that at least the sermon would be short. The sermon began, and the very first sentence of it was like the blast of a bugle. The pallid parson seemed all of a sudden to have had a quart of blood poured into his veins, a gallon of lungs put into his thorax, and the strength of a drover stowed away in his body and arms. For a half-hour he held us almost spell-bound with the most animated delivery, powerful argumentation, and vivid original illustration, rendered with vigour of voice, and with every appearance of abundant physical power. So we learned the secret of the great congregation, and the toleration of his opening dulness or stupidity. So we learned, too, how a man really feeble, by husbanding his force against ineffective expenditures, and exerting it all when the greatest number of minds could be influenced at once, and by reason of the surroundings most powerfully influenced, could do a great work weekly, and sustain himself in the high estimation and valuation of society. Now, if this minister had attempted to conduct the whole service with as much vigour as he preached, his strength would have given out just as the sermon was commencing, and the effect of his whole week's labour and study would have been measurably lost." *

Robert Hall was wont to husband his physical strength in the same way. Though athletic in frame, he often announced his text and for some minutes spoke, in a tone so low as to be barely audible. During even the first twenty minutes there was nothing in his discourse indicating to his hearers that a giant stood before them ; but as his voice swelled from an almost unintelligible whisper to a trumpet peal, they were spell-bound by the enchantment of his oratory ; and when he was concluding the effect upon the nervous system of the listener was like the shock of artillery.

Lastly, we must avoid overwork. As we shall consider this subject in a subsequent chapter, we shall barely glance at it here. It is well known that the body or brain that is overtasked will soon lose its power, if it be not even smitten with paralysis or death. Yet aside from the victims of necessity, who must work at all hours, as and when they can, there is hardly any calling in which men are not overtasking themselves, toiling too long and too hard, to win a success which, when it comes, they will be too enfeebled to enjoy. The blow which struck down the Vice-President of the United States in his chair, and sent him staggering from the Senate Chamber, is one which at this moment is threatening hundreds of our leading men in all the professions,—the blow that is sure, sooner or later, to avenge overwork. His case is but one more added to the martyrology of the nineteenth century, the martyr-

* Walter Wells, in " Lippincott's Magazine."

ology, not of the stake or the scaffold, but of toil. The one thing which the great man of to-day cannot do, is—*to rest.* As did Peel, Canning, Cobden, Sir George C. Lewis, Sir William Hamilton, Macaulay, Choate, Stanton, Governor Andrew, and Raymond, so Gladstone, Bright, Bismarck, Sum·ner and Colfax are now doing,—killing themselves by inches, exhausting their vitality by excessive brain-work.

Now, can anything be more unwise than this? When shall we learn that play is as necessary as labour, that frequent respites from toil are the very safety-valves of professional men? Even if we can endure the strain, it is not prudent to work constantly up to the very highest rate of which we are capable. If an engineer on a railway were to keep the speed of his train constantly up to the maximum of which the locomotive is capable, his engine would soon be used up. Drive a horse day after day at the top of his speed, and you soon wind him. All machinists construct their machines so that there shall be a reserve force. If the power required is four-horse, they make a six-horse power, so that the machine may not only work easily, but last long. Our bodies and brains are engines, only more complex and delicate in structure, which should be used with even greater care and economy. The man who has strength to do ten hours' work a day, physical or intellectual, should do but seven or eight; and then he may hope to accumulate a reserve fund of energy which will not only round out his frame to fair proportions, and enable him to toil with ease, cheerfulness, and alacrity, but furnish a capital, a fund in bank, upon which he can draw heavily in any emergency, when called on to do two days' work in one. Without this capital, he will not only do his work painfully, forever tugging at the oar, but he will be incapable of increasing the strain upon his powers, however urgent the necessity ; he cannot put a pound more of pressure upon the engine without an explosion.

We emphasize this point, because there is no class of persons that need more to husband their strength than professional men. There are some of so dull and phlegmatic a temperament —"slow coaches," that jog on at so lazy a pace—that they need no note of alarm. They need the whip, not the rein ; and the utmost speed you can get out of them will only call their muscles into healthful activity. But there is another class,—

Q

the fiery, earnest, zealous men, the nervous men, tremulous as the aspen, enthusiastic in their callings,—who need to economise their nerve-force, unless they would prematurely exhaust themselves and sink into an early grave. Such men need to be reminded that they have but a limited fund of strength, upon which they are making draughts with every breath they draw and every word they utter, and that therefore they cannot guard too jealously against any waste of their nerve-power. Any needless expenditure of strength, however slight, whether by physical or mental effort, in conversation or study, in excitement, in worry or fidgeting of any kind, is just so much detracted from that which they need for their life-work. Throw your energy upon the effective point, whatever that may be; but don't waste your lightning upon things of no account.

Are you a preacher? Don't spend your strength on little week-day meetings and social and side matters, so that when Sunday comes, and every word you speak should tell upon a thousand, you will be as lifeless as a mouse in an exhausted receiver. It is better, one has well said, to lose a pint of blood from your veins than to have a nerve tapped. Do not make the mistake of one of New England's most brilliant lawyers,— we refer to Mr. Choate,—concerning whom a brother advocate laments that he not only worked too much, but had no just economy of labour. You remember his answer when blamed for thus endangering his constitution: "Good heavens, my dear fellow! my *constitution* was all gone years ago, and I'm living on the by-laws." No wonder his constitutional strength was exhausted, considering with what an utter lack of economy he laboured. "He did a thousand things," says Judge Thomas in the admirable address from which we have already quoted; "which men of narrower capacity might have done as well, or well enough. He expended upon his work a vast amount of superfluous strength. He brought the whole army of the reserve into action, when the victory might have been easily and gracefully won by the van and corps of battle." Avoid, we pray you, this mistake. Do not assail pygmies with eighty-four-pounders. Do not iminate Dr. Johnson, of whom Peter Pindar tells us that he

> " Uplifts the club of Hercules,—for what?
> To crush a butterfly, or to brain a gnat

> Creates a whirlwind, from the earth to draw
> A goose's feather or exalt a straw;
> Bids ocean labour with tremendous roar
> To heave a cockle-shell upon the shore.'

Here we may remark that the great secret of husbanding one's strength, so as to accumulate a fund, is to work *intensely*, not many hours. On this point we have the authority of one who was himself a prodigious worker, and accomplished the highest results, yet never worked with jaded or flagging powers, never strained the bow till it was bent, never weakened his brain by overtasking it. We refer to Daniel Webster. Some years ago Mr. Whipple, of Rhode Island, had occasion to consult him touching an important law-case,—a case in which were presented many cross-questions of law and equity, and so involved that it required days and weeks of hard labour to discover a channel-way over its shoals and amid its rocks. Meeting Mr. Whipple early in the morning, Mr. Webster by dinner time had threaded all the avenues and cross-paths of the labyrinth, and gave an opinion so clear and comprehensive that Mr. Whipple was constrained to ask him what had been his system of mental culture. In reply Mr. Webster observed, that it is a law of our natures that the body or the mind that labours constantly must necessarily labour moderately. He instanced the race-horse, which, by occasional efforts in which all its power is exerted, followed by periods of entire rest, would in time add very largely to its speed ; and the great walkers or runners of our race, who from small beginnings, when fifteen miles a day fatigued them, would in the end walk off fifty miles at the rate of five or six miles an hour. He also mentioned the London porter, who, at first staggering under the load of one hundred and fifty or two hundreds pounds, would in time walk off with six or eight hundred pounds with apparent ease. The same law governs the mind. When employed at all, its powers should be exerted to the utmost. Its fatigue should be followed by its entire rest. Mr. Webster added that, whatever mental occupation employed him, he put forth all his power, and when his mental vision began to be obscure, he ceased entirely, and resorted to some amusement or light business as a relaxation.

The last hint we would give to him who would increase his

reserved power is, get plenty of sleep. The harder we work during the day, the more sleep do we require to repair the waste of nervous energy. Americans not only work too hard, but sleep too little. The rapid development of the country, its intense industrial activities, the fiery ambition of the people, our dry, electric atmosphere, and our sunny climate, all tend to make us prematurely wakeful. American students, we fear, sit up too late and get up too early. A great many are killed by alarm-clocks. The best wakeners are sunlight and the twittering of birds. The anecdotes told of Brougham, Napoleon, and others, who are said to have slept but four or five hours out of the twenty-four, but who, we suspect, took a good many cat-naps in the day-time, have done much harm. The time taken out of eight hours' daily sleep is not time gained, but time worse than wasted. We may cheat ourselves, but we cannot cheat Nature. Because she lets us overdraw our accounts for many years, we fancy the accounts are not kept. But, depend upon it, she is a jealous creditor, who is sure in the end to exact with compound interest every loan she makes to us ; and if we continue borrowing for work the hours that are due to sleep, though we may postpone a settlement for years, the final and inevitable result will be physical and mental bankruptcy.

CHAPTER XVII.

ECONOMY OF TIME.

Dost thou love life ? Then do not squander time, for that is the stuff life is made of.—FRANKLIN.

> Think naught a trifle, though it small appear ;
> Small sands the mountain, moments make the year,
> And trifles, lite.—YOUNG.

Believe me when I tell you that thrift of time will repay you in after-life with a usury of profit beyond your most sanguine dreams, and that the waste of it will make you dwindle, alike in intellectual and in moral stature, beyond your darkest reckonings.—W. E GLADSTONE.

Lost, yesterday, somewhere between sunrise and sunset, two golden hours, each set with sixty diamond minutes. No reward is offered for they are gone forever.—HORACE MANN.

ONE of the most important lessons to be learned by every man who would get on in his calling is in the art of economizing his time. A celebrated Italian was wont to call his time his estate ; and it is true of this as of other estates of which the young come into possession, that it is rarely prized till it is nearly squandered ; and then, when life is fast waning, they begin to think of spending the hours wisely, and even of husbanding the moments. Unfortunately, habits of indolence, listlessness, and procrastination, once firmly fixed, cannot be suddenly thrown off, and the man who has wasted the precious hours of life's seed-time finds that he cannot reap a harvest in life's autumn. It is a truism which cannot be too often repeated, that lost wealth may be replaced by industry, lost knowledge by study, lost health by temperance or medicine, but lost time is gone forever.

In the long catalogue of stereotyped excuses for the neglect of duty, there is none which drops oftener from men's lips, or which is founded on more of self-delusion, than the want of leisure. Persons are always cheating themselves with the idea that they would like to do this or that desirable thing, "if they only had time." Hundreds of young men burn with an intense desire to cultivate their minds; they realize how essential, in this age of intelligence, are mental training and knowledge to success; they see the superficial, half-instructed men everywhere distanced in the race of life; but, alas! every moment of their waking hours is taken up by the pressing calls of business, and they have no leisure for reading or study. Hundreds there are who feel the profoundest sympathy for the poor, and who would out-Howard Howard in "carrying broth and blankets to beggars," and in distributing the bread of life in the form of Bibles and tracts; but their own affairs usurp all their time and attention, and they can do nothing for their fellow-men.

Such are the pleas by which the lazy and the selfish excuse themselves from a thousand things which conscience dictates to be done. Now, the truth is, there is no condition in which the chance of doing any good is *less* than in that of leisure. Life, it has been truly said, is composed of an elastic material, and wherever a solid piece of business is removed, there the surrounding atmosphere of trifles rushes in as certainly as the air into a bottle when you pour out its contents. If you would exhaust the air from a given spot, you must enclose it in a vessel of texture as firm and as carefully secured as would be required to protect the most precious and delicate substance; and so an hour's leisure, if one would not have it frittered away on "trifles light as air," needs to be guarded by barriers of resolution and precaution as strong as are needed for hours of study and business. Go hunt out the men in any community who have done the most for their own and the general good, and you will find that they are—who? Wealthy, leisurely people, with extensive stomachs and highly polished shoes, who have oceans of time to themselves, and nothing to do but to eat, sleep, and vegetate? No; they are almost uniformly the overworked class,—the toil-and-moil, almost-driven-to-death men, who seemed well-nigh swamped with cares, and are in a ceaseless paroxysm of activity from January to December. It is these men who find time to preside at philanthropic meetings, to serve on Tract or Missionary Society committees, to visit the poor, to attend noon prayer-meetings, and to attend to self-culture by reading not only the best old books, but the pick of the ever-multiplying new publications of the day; while a

ousy male trifler, who spends his time in laboriously doing
nothing, or a lady who lies upon her sofa, and has no creature
dependent upon her, will tell you that he or she has waited week
after week for leisure to answer a note.   Persons of the former
class, however crowded with business, are always found capable
of doing a *little more*, and you may rely upon them in their
busiest seasons with ten times more assurance than upon the
idle man.

It is common in every community to run with business to
lawyers and doctors who are already fully employed.   This is
not wholly from a senseless veneration for a name; it is because there is an instinct that tells us that the man who does
much is most likely to do more, and to do it in the best manner.   The reason is, that to do increases the power of doing ;
and it is far easier for one who is always exerting himself to
exert himself a little more for an extra purpose, than for him
who does nothing to "get up steam" preparatory to the same
end.   Give a busy man ten minutes to write a letter, and he
will dash it off at once; give an idle man a day, and he will
postpone it till to-morrow or next week.   There is a momen-
tum in the active man which of itself almost carries him to the
mark, just as a very light stroke will keep a hoop agoing, when
a smart one was required to set it in motion.   While others
are yawning and stretching themselves to overcome the *vis
inertiæ*, he has his eyes wide open, his faculties keyed up for
action, and is thoroughly alive in every fibre.   He walks through
the world with his hands unmuffled and ready by his side, and
so can sometimes do more by a single touch in passing than a
vacant man is likely to do by strenuous effort.

The men who do the greatest things achieved on this globe
do them not so much by prodigious but fitful efforts, as by
steady, unremitting toil,—by turning even the moments to account.   They have the genius for hard work, the most desirable
kind of genius.   A continual dropping wears the stone.   A
little done this hour and a little the next hour, day by day,
and year by year, brings much to pass.   The largest houses are
built by laying one brick upon another.   How have the men
who have died millionnaires acquired their wealth ?   Not generally by huge windfalls, but by minute and gradual accumulations.   It is not by large sums bequeathed to them one after

another, or gained by gigantic schemes of speculation, but by economizing the petty sums which so many thoughtlessly squander, by saving the cents and dimes and single dollars, adding them together year after year, that they have reared their pyramid of fortune. So with self-culture, the acquisition of knowledge, and the doing of good deeds; the time men often waste in needless slumber, in lounging, or in idle visits, would enable them, were it redeemed, to execute undertakings which seem in their hurried and worried life to be impossible.

Complain not, then, reader, of your want of leisure to do anything. Rather thank God that you are not cursed with leisure; for a curse it is, in nine cases out of ten. What if, to achieve some good work which you have deeply at heart, you can never command an entire month, a week, or even a day? Shall you therefore bid it an eternal adieu, and fold your arms in despair? No; the thought should only the more keenly "prick the sides of your intent," and goad and stimulate and urge you on to do what you can do in this swiftly passing life of ours. Try what you can build up from the broken fragments of your time, rendered more precious by their brevity. It is said that in the United States Mint at Philadelphia, when the visitor reaches the gold-working room, the guide tells him that the singular floor is a net-work of wooden bars to catch all the falling particles of the precious metal. When the day's labour is done, the floor, which is in sections or parts, is removed, and the golden dust is swept up, to be melted and coined. Learn from this the nobler economy of time. Glean up its golden dust; economize with tenfold care those raspings and parings of existence, those leavings of days and "wee bits" of hours,— so valueless singly, so inestimable in the aggregate,—which most persons sweep out into the waste of life, and you will be rich in leisure. Rely upon it, if you are a miser of moments, if you hoard up and turn to account odd minutes and half-hours and unexpected holidays,—the five-minute gaps while the table is spreading, the chasms while you are waiting for unpunctual persons,—your careful gleanings at the end of life will have formed a colossal and solid block of time, and you will die at last wealthier in intellectual acquisition, wealthier in good deeds harvested, than thousands whose time is all their own.

There are some men who must do what they do without interruption. They cannot read or think to advantage except in sacred silence. No wave from the wild sea of life must beat against their calm retreat. In some quiet, snug loophole they must think and toil. Interruptions, distractions of any kind, break their threads of thought, and they cannot rejoin them. Such persons find it hard to utilize the odds and ends of time. There are others who are so constituted that it is almost impossible for them to be systematic and continuously diligent. They can work only by spasms, when the fit is upon them; compensating in these paroxysms of activity, by the fine frenzy with which they labour, for the seasons in which they loaf or lounge. Such "heaven-born geniuses" are a law unto themselves, and are daily becoming more and more rare. Most persons, to achieve anything, need to be always busy; and for them it is better never to have any idle moments, but always to have some work on the anvil to which they can turn their hand.

It is wonderful what results have been achieved by those with whom the clock has never "clicked lazily behind the door," who have let none of their moments fall idly to the ground. It is related of a German critic that he could repeat the entire "Iliad" in Greek with scarcely an error. How many years, think you, of his brief threescore and ten, or less, did he spend in imprinting the immortal poem on his brain? Years he had not, nor even months, nor weeks, for he was a physician with large practice; but he contrived to master the old bard of Scio during the brief, hurried snatches of time when passing from one patient to another. Dr. Mason Good, the celebrated English physician, performed a similar feat, having translated into English verse the whole of Lucretius during his long walks in London to visit his patients. Dr. Darwin composed many of his works in the same way. While driving about in his sulky from house to house, he jotted down his thoughts on little scraps of paper which he carried with him for the purpose. Matthew Hale's "Contemplations" were composed while he was travelling as judge on circuit. Locke carried a note-book in his pocket, to catch the scintillations of even common conversation. Pope improved the wakeful hours of the night. Dr. Rush studied in his carriage while visiting his patients, and thus prepared himself to write, not only upon professional but other themes, works which are still almost as useful as when first published. Cuvier, the father of Comparative Anatomy, also studied while passing in his carriage from place to place, and by his ceaseless industry did perhaps more for the physical sciences than any other man that ever lived.

The biographer of George Stephenson tells us that the smallest fragments of his time were regarded by him as precious, and that "he was never so happy as when improving them." Franklin stole his hours of study from meals and sleep, and for years, with inflexible resolution, strove to save for his own instruction every minute that could be won. Henry Kirke White learnt Greek while walking to and from a lawyer's office. Hugh Miller found time while pursuing his trade as a stonemason, not only to read, but to write, cultivating his style till he became one of the most facile and brilliant authors of the day. Elihu Burritt acquired a mastery of eighteen languages and twenty-two dialects, not by rare genius, which he disclaimed, but by improving the bits and fragments of time which he could steal from his occupation as a blacksmith. Mr. Grote, the historian of Greece, whose work is by far the fullest and most trustworthy on the subject, and who also snatched time from business to write two large volumes upon Plato, was a banker. Sir John Lubbock, the highest English authority on prehistoric archæology, has made himself such by stealing the time from mercantile pursuits. John Quincy Adams, to the last day of his life, was an economist of moments. To redeem the time, he rose early. "I feel nothing like *ennui*," he said. "Time is too short for me, rather than too long. If the day were forty-eight hours long, instead of twenty-four, I could employ them all, if I had but eyes and hands to read and write." While at St. Petersburg, he complained bitterly of the great loss of his time from the civilities and visits of his friends and associates. "I have been engaged," he wrote, "the whole forenoon, and though I rise at six o'clock, I am sometimes able to write only a part of a private letter in the course of the day."

Let the young man who complains that he has "no leisure" for self-culture or for doing good to others, contrast if he can, without a blush, his plea with the resolution of a Roman Emperor[*] who was burdened with the responsibilities of a world-wide empire—" not frequently, nor without necessity, to say to any one, or to write in a letter, that I have no leisure ; nor continually to excuse the neglect of duties required by our relation to those with whom we live, by alleging urgent occupations." All the busy workers we have named felt that life, though short, is yet long enough, when its moments are economized, for every necessary labour. They felt as did Arnault, when he replied to the objection of Nicole, on a new work being proposed. " We are now old," said Nicole ; " is it not time we should rest ?" " Rest ! " exclaimed Arnault, " have we not all eternity to rest in ?"

There are few persons so engrossed by the cares and labours of their calling that they cannot give thirty minutes a day to self-culture ; and even that time, wisely spent, will tell at the end of a year. The affections, it is well known, sometimes crowd years into moments, and the intellect has something of the same power. Volumes have not only been read, but written, in flying journeys. Dr. Channing knew a man of vigorous intellect, who had enjoyed few advantages of early education, and whose mind was almost engrossed by the details of an extensive business, who yet composed a book of much original thought in steamboats and on horseback, while visiting distant customers. These examples are enough, and more than enough, to show that the moments commonly wasted during a long life by the busiest men would suffice, if avariciously improved, for the execution of even colossal undertakings, which seemingly demand a lifetime of uninterrupted leisure. We say, therefore, in the language of that prodigy of industry, Goethe, " Do not wait for extraordinary opportunities for good actions, but make use of common situations. A long-continued walk is better than a short flight." The small stones that fill up the crevices are almost as essential to the firm wall as the great stones ; and so the wise use of spare time contributes not a little to the building up in good proportions, and with strength, a man's mind. If you really prize mental culture, or are deeply anxious to do any good thing, you *will* find time or *make* time for it, sooner or later, however engrossed with other employ-

* Marcus Aurelius.

ments. A failure to accomplish it can only demonstrate the fee
bleness of your will, not that you lacked time for its execution.

" Old-fashioned economists," says the eloquent Wirt, " will
tell you never to pass an old nail, or an old horseshoe, or
buckle, or even a pin, without taking it up ; because, although
you may not want it now, you will find a use for it some
time or other. I say the same thing to you with regard to
knowledge. However useless it may appear to you at the
moment, seize upon all that is fairly within your reach. For
there is not a fact within the whole circle of human observation, nor even a fugitive anecdote that you read in a newspaper, that will not come into play at some time or other ; and
occasions will arise when they involuntarily present their dim
shadows in the train of your thinking and reasoning, as be-
longing to that train, and you will regret that you cannot recall them more distinctly." Daniel Webster once repeated with
effect an anecdote which he had treasured in his memory for
fourteen years.

While we thus urge upon the young man who is beginning
life the necessity of economizing his time, let us not be misunderstood. We advise no such saving of time as will rob him
of necessary recreation or sleep. Nor do we regard every
moment in which a man is seemingly idle as really wasted.
Especially is this true of intellectual pursuits. There are some
writers who appear to think that every hour in which a man is
not grinding away, " with malice prepense and aforethought,"
at some set task,—when the mind is left to itself, instead of
doing compulsory work,—is misspent. John Wesley took this
view of life, and therefore, as might be expected, denounced
all stop-gaps in passing one's time. " Never be unemployed,"
says he, " never be triflingly employed, *never while away time.*"
All this looks very plausible, and the last advice is just what
might have been expected from one of whom Dr. Johnson has
left this opinion : " John Wesley's conversation is good, but
he is never at leisure. He is *always obliged to go at a certain
hour.* This is very disagreeable to a man who loves to fold his
legs and have out his talk, as I do." Again that great naval
hero and sterling man, Lord Collingwood, gives the following
advice touching the education of his daughters : " They should

not only read, but it requires a careful selection of books ; nor should they ever have access to two at the same time ; but when a subject is begun, it should be finished before anything else is undertaken." This looks even more plausible; but all history and all experience refute the doctrine. The cat at our fireside refutes it ; for she got tired of lying in the same corner, cosey and snug and warm though it was, and so went over to the opposite, though no whit more agreeable, because she wanted a change. Read on but one subject at a time! As well might one eat but one thing at a time. Must one devour an entire ox before he is allowed to change his diet ? Such dietetics can end only in physical or mental scrofula.

But what *is* " whiling away time" ? When a man is roaming about his library, taking down this book and then that, pacing the floor, scribbling on a bit of paper, glancing at a magazine or newspaper, whistling a tune, musing by the window, looking into the fire,—or when he is sauntering in the woods and listening to the melody of the birds, or lolling under an old oak and drinking in the music of a babbling brook,—is he, though seemingly idle, necessarily " whiling away time" ? By no means. Where there is a vigorous, sleepless, inquiring mind, idleness is impossible. There is no hour in the day when the brain is not at work. When not browsing in books, it is ruminating; when not gathering the raw material of knowledge, it is elaborating that which has been gathered. The mind, if it is not a mere plodding, mechanical mind, is capricious in its workings, and will not be tyrannized over. Its methods are saltatory and impulsive. It thrives by casualties; it is powerful obliquely, and not by the direct stroke. It loves dearly to assert its independence, and will be consulted as to whether it will do this or that. It is not a mere machine, and cannot be used as if it were one. It must often " gang its ain gait," and sometimes must be left alone, even when it stoops to trifles. Many of its processes go on unbidden, without our control. In its very highest efforts it abhors task-work, and utterly refuses to be a drudge. The happiest thoughts, the most brilliant fancies, the aptest similitudes, are those sudden illuminations, those flashes, which comes to us in hours of relaxation, of play, when we throw the reins upon the neck of our winged steed and let it roam where it will.

" Every kind of knowledge," observes a thoughtful writer,
" comes into play some time or other; not only that which is
systematic and methodized, but that which is fragmentary, even
the odds and ends, the merest rag or tag of information. Single
facts, anecdotes, expressions, recur to the mind, and, by the
power of association, just in the right place. Many of these
are laid in during what we think our idlest days. All that
fund of matter which is used allusively in similitudes or illustrations is collected in diversions from the path of hard study.
He will do best in this line whose range has been the widest
and the freest. A man may study so much by rule as to lose
all this, just as one may ride so much on the highway as to
know nothing that is off the road."

It has been truly said that he who sets one great truth afloat
in the world serves his generation. " To utter one such truth
is more than to gain a field at Granicus or Waterloo. To attain
such truths is one of the great objects of living." But they
are not always obtained by deliberate search or thought. He
who is apparently whiling away his time may be discovering
some new principle of philosophy or law in science, which may
become a lever to move the world. When Watt sat in the
chimney-corner, watching the cover of the tea-kettle as the
steam forced it up, he only excited the indignation of his relative,
as he would, doubtless, that of Wesley; but he was designing
the steam-engine. Millions had seen the phenomenon before,
without their curiosity being piqued, and without the ability
to trace its cause. So with specific gravity and gravitation.
Thousands and tens of thousands before Archimedes had seen
water run over the side of a vessel when another substance
was immersed in it. It needed no ghost or ghostly philosopher
to tell the world of the fact; but it was the quantity of the
water and the depth of the immersion together which struck
Archimedes. Newton, sauntering through an orchard, does
not seem to be economizing his time; but the falling apple leads
to the discovery of gravitation. Tournefort forsook his college
class, that he might search for plants in the neighbouring fields;
and Smeaton in petticoats was discovered on the top of his
father's barn, fixing the model of a windmill which he had constructed. The one became the celebrated naturalist who enriched science by his discoveries, the other the engineer who

built the Eddystone Lighthouse ; yet Wesley would have said that Tournefort and Smeaton, as well as Watt and Archimedes, were triflingly employed, whiling away time.

Scores of illustrations might be cited to show that the amuse ments to which the young have resorted to while away time have coloured an intellectual life. Cowley beautifully com pares these boyish fancies to letters cut in the bark of a young tree, which grow and widen with it. Cowley himself might never have been a poet, had he not found the "Faerie Queen" in his mother's parlour ; Opie might have died in obscurity, had he not looked "idly" over the shoulder of his young companion, Mark Otes, while he was drawing a butterfly. "Only reading Robin, only Robin" (Robinson Crusoe), was the constant excuse for absence or idleness of a boy whose friends little dreamed that he would also be distinguished as a *man* of one book, and do more than any other to correct, illustrate, and restore the text of Skakespeare. The "Arabian Nights" used to lie under the parlour window of the old vicarage where the father of Coleridge resided ; and he has recorded the strange mixture of desire and apprehension with which, in his early boyhood, he was accustomed to look at the volume, and watch till the morning sun had reached and nearly covered it, when, seizing the treasure, he hastened to some corner of the playground, and soon lost his own identity in the magnificent capital of Ali Raschid. Who does not see, says an English essayist, that the temperament of the poet was influenced by his first love ? It often fares with other men as it did once with Johnson, that their very idleness—when occasional, not chronic—leads to advantage. In his youth, believing that his brother had concealed some apples beneath a large folio upon an upper shelf in his father's shop, he climbed up to make the capture, and, finding no apples, attacked the folio, which proved to be the works of Petrarch ; and thus "his very idleness instructed him, and the apples led him to literature."

CHAPTER XVIII.

MONEY,—ITS USE AND ABUSE.

The learned pate
Ducks to the golden fool.—SHAKESPEARE.

Whoever has sixpence is sovereign over all men to the extent of that sixpence; commands cooks to feed him, philosophers to teach him, kings to
mount guard over him,—to the extent of that sixpence.—CARLYLE.

Seek not proud riches, but such as thou mayest get justly, use soberly,
distribute cheerfully, and leave contentedly; yet have no abstract or friarly
contempt of them.—BACON.

Economy is of itself a great revenue.—CICERO.

No man is rich whose expenditures exceed his means; and no man is poor
whose incomings exceed his outgoings.—HALIBURTON.

Les dettes abrègent la vie.—JOUBERT.

THAT Providence has endowed man with the organ of
acquisitiveness, as phrenologists term it, for wise and
beneficent purposes, and that the civilization, refinement, virtue, wisdom, and happiness of every community are
largely dependent on its exercise, is a proposition which few
persons will controvert. It is true there are declaimers on the
incompatibility of wealth and virtue; but they are mere declaimers and nothing more. In the same breath in which they
decry the pursuit of pelf they will applaud or denounce an in-
stitution or measure according to its tendency to increase or to
diminish the public wealth. To cry out against the universal
craving and struggling for the good things of this world,—for
which money is a synonyme,—is to waste one's breath upon the
air. Men will not listen to abstract arguments against the
pursuit of gold or greenbacks while they fear the "wolf at the
door," and the most eloquent sermon in praise of poverty provokes but a smile. "Believe not much them that seem to despise riches," says Bacon; "for they despise them that despair
of them; and none worse when they come to them." Rarely
is their Spartan scorn proof against a fat legacy or other pecu-

niary windfall ; and in nine cases out of ten their policy is that of Virgil's harpies, that sought to excite disgust at the banquet which they themselves were eager to devour.

There is no sacrifice which men will not make for money. They will face belching cannon, clog their lungs with the dust of coal-mines or with the impalpable powder inhaled in the grinding of steel, become workers in arsenic, lead, phosphorus, or any of the other substances so fatal to life, blast with gun-powder, live amid malaria, and risk their soul's peace in this world and the next, for gold. No toil is so exhausting, no danger so appalling, that men will not confront the one and undergo the other, if the stakes are only sufficiently high. "A certain ten per cent.," says an English political economist, "will insure the employment of capital anywhere. Twenty per cent. certain will produce eagerness. Fifty per cent. positive, auda-city. One hundred per cent. will make it ready to trample on all human laws. Three hundred per cent., and there is not a crime at which it will scruple, nor a risk it will not run, even to the chance of its owner being hanged." Even the preacher's call swells from " the still small voice " to a trumpet peal when it comes with the offer of a double salary. Harassing doubts and indecision vanish like dew before the logic of five thousand a year and a parsonage. The parish that is made up of rich merchants, brokers, and capitalists, is seen to be " a larger field of labour " when viewed through gold spectacles.

It is easy, of course, to point out the dangers resulting from a too intense devotion to money-getting. Bacon calls riches " the baggage of virtue"; and we all know how the Romans, in their heroic days, when they annihilated their foes, expressed their contempt by a similar word, *impedimenta;* and that when they grew weak and degraded they clung to their gold, with which they bought off the barbarians who invaded them. But whatever may be said of the dangers of riches, the dangers of poverty are tenfold greater. A condition in which one is ex-posed to continual want, not only of the luxuries but of the veriest necessaries of life, as well as to disease and discourage-ment, is exceedingly unfavourable to the exercise of the higher functions of the mind and soul. The poor man is hourly beset by troops of temptations which the rich man never knows. Doubtless the highest virtues are sometimes found to flourish

R

even in the cold clime and sterile soil of poverty. Not only industry, honesty, frugality, perseverance amid hardships and ever baffling discouragements, but much more miraculous attributes, as meek contentment, severe self-sacrifice, tender affections, unwavering trust in Providence, all are found blooming in the hearts of the poorest poor,—even in the sunless regions of absolute destitution, where honesty might be expected to wear an everlasting scowl of churlishness, and a bitter disbelief in the love of God to accompany obedience to the laws of man. But it is the most insufferable of all cants to hear these qualities spoken of as if they were indigenous to poverty, when we know that they flourish in spite of it.

We have had enough of that silly sentimentalism which would canonize the poor because they are such ; which, because Jerrold has finely said, " Many a man who now lacks shoe-leather would wear golden spurs if knighthood were the reward of worth," sees a hero in every chimney-sweep, and Wordsworth's pedler in peripatetics who probably much more resemble Canning's knife-grinder. Poverty is a condition which no man should accept, unless it is forced upon him as an inexorable necessity or as the alternative of dishonour. No person has a right voluntarily to place himself in a position where he will be assailed hourly by the fiercest temptations, where he will be able to preserve his uprightness only by a strength little short of angelic, and where he will be liable at any moment to become by sickness a burden to his friends. Every man, too, should make some provision for old age ; for an old man in the poor-house, or begging alms, is a sorry sight, and suggests the suspicion, however ill-founded, that his life has been foolishly, if not viciously, spent. It is true we should not be over anxious about the morrow ; but they strangely misunderstand the spirit of our Saviour's teachings, who think that words spoken with reference to the genial climate and the simple modes of living in Judea have a *literal* application in the high latitudes and amid the desperate competitions in which so many millions live in this country and in this nineteenth century.

We say, therefore, that the philosophy which affects to teach us a contempt of money does not run very deep. Indeed, it ought to be clearer to philosophers than to other men that money is of high importance, and that its importance increases

with every generation. So manifold are its bearings upon the
lives and characters of mankind, that, as Henry Taylor observes, in his "Notes on Life," an insight which should search
out the life of man in his pecuniary relations would penetrate
into almost every cranny of his nature. "He who knows, like
St. Paul, how to spare and how to abound, has a great know·
ledge : for, if we take account of all the virtues with which
money is mixed up—honesty, justice, generosity, charity, frugality, forethought, self-sacrifice—and of their correlative vices,
it is a knowledge which goes near to cover the length and
breadth of humanity; and a right measure and manner in
getting, saving, spending, giving, taking, lending, borrowing,
and bequeathing would almost argue a perfect man."
It is money, or rather the want of it, which makes men
workers. It is the appetizing provocative that teases the business nerve of more than half the world; while most of the
results of ingenuity, skill, intellect, tact, address, and competition, depend upon its unremitting pursuit. Want of money
is the great principle of moral gravitation, the only power that
is strong enough to keep things in their places. It is this
scantiness of means, this continual deficiency, this constant
hitch, this perpetual struggle to keep the head above water and
the wolf from the door, that keeps society from falling to pieces.
Let every man in the community have, as a rule, a few dollars
more than he wants, and anarchy would follow. All labour,
whether of the hand or brain, would become spasmodic and
fitful, if, indeed, the great wheel of industry did not come to
a stand-still. The very labour a man has to undergo, the self-
denial he has to cultivate, in acquiring money, are of themselves
an education. They compel him to put forth intelligence, skill,
energy, vigilance, zeal, bring out his practical qualities, and
gradually train his moral and intellectual powers. Mental discipline may be got from money-getting as real as that which is
obtained from mathematics ; "the soul is trained by the ledger
as much as by the calculus, and can get exercise in the account
of sales, as much as in the account of stars." The provident
man must of necessity be a thoughtful man, living, as he does,
not for the present, but for the future; and he must also
practise self-denial, that virtue which is one of the chief elements in a strong and well-formed character. As with the

acquisition, so with the use of money ; the way in which a man spends it is often one of the surest tests of character. As Bulwer says in one of the most thoughtful essays in Caxtoniana —"Money is a terrible blab ; she will betray the secrets of her owner, whatever he do to gag her. His virtues will creep out in her whisper ; his vices she will cry aloud at the top of her tongue."

Again, money is not only character, but it is power. It is not merely for the comforts, but for the *influence* they bring, that riches are so intensely desired, so long and painfully sought, by any sensible man. It is wealth that, above all other things, gives character, standing, and respectability in this country. With it, the pygmy in intellect becomes a giant in influence ; without it, the best informed man is but a dwarf in power. Now, as in Shakespeare's time, " the learned pate ducks to the golden fool." Who does not know what weight and significance are imparted to a truism, what raciness to a dull jest, if they are backed up by ten thousand a year, by bank shares, mortgages and stocks ? Rank, talents, eloquence, learning and moral worth, all challenge a certain degree of respect ; but, unconnected with property, have comparatively little influence in commanding the services of other men. Admiration they may attract, but it is property that gives power. Detached from this their influence is as evanescent as the fragrance of the flowers detached from the soil. The soil itself may not claim our respect, but it is only by the virtues which they extract from the soil that the flowers maintain their beauty, fragrance and strength. Even the ancient Carthaginians, who were republicans, and had no hereditary aristocracy, would allow no man to hold office in the State unless he was more or less wealthy. It has been truly said that the heraldry of America is based on greenbacks. The social standing is indicated by the bank-book. The railway conductor accents his call, the hotel clerk assigns rooms, the dry-goods merchant graduates the angle of his bows by it. Even the seat to which the sexton bows you in church is chosen with nice reference to your exchequer.

Again, as civilization advances, human life is becoming more and more significant, richer in opportunities and enjoyments. Science is multiplying with amazing rapidity the comforts and

luxuries of life and the means of self culture, and money is
the necromancer by which they are placed at our disposal.
Money means a tight house, the warmest clothing, the most
nutritious food, the best medical attendance, books, music,
pictures ; a good seat in the concert or lecture room, in the
cars, and even in the church ; the ability to rest when weary
in body or brain, and, above all, independence of thought. It
is said that in England no man can afford to have an opinion
who has not an income of two thousand a year ; and even in
this land of broad acres there are already many men who think
themselves too poor to indulge in " the luxury of a conscience."
Every step in life is conditional on " the root of all evil." You
must pay to eat and drink, to sleep, to house and to clothe
yourself, and even to breathe. Every breath is a consumption
of carbon, which must be paid for as inevitably as the coal in
your grate. The creditor is at every man's heels, dogs him in
his last moments, and hardly stops short at the graveyard gate.
Not only is money thus indispensable, but the value of this representative of values was never before so great as now. With
this talisman, a man can surround himself with richer means
of enjoyment, secure a more varied and harmonious culture,
and set in motion grander schemes of philanthropy in this last
half of the nineteenth century than at any previous period in
the world's history. And precisely because it means so much,
because with it life is so rich in possibilities, the want of money
was never before so keenly felt as now. Though the poor to-
day have luxuries which a Crœsus could not have commanded
three centuries ago, though " the world must be compassed
that a washerwoman may have her tea," yet never was poverty
so hard to bear as to-day. Its pinch is far severer than in Dr.
Johnson's time ; yet he, with all his philosophy, did not hesitate to pronounce it a great evil. " When I was running about
this town a very poor fellow," said he, " I was a great arguer for
the advantages of poverty. Sir, all the arguments which are
brought to represent poverty as no evil show it to be evidently
a great evil. You never find people labouring to convince you
that you may live very happily upon a plentiful fortune."

Want of money is the almost universal disease, which alone
will explain the weight and sadness which one so often finds
in the social atmosphere. " Even passing through the streets,

how many wrinkled brows and careworn physiognomies we meet which we learn to trace to this one source ! The poor have no skill at disguising their anxieties. These are written in large characters on their whole bearing, and the very title we give them reveals the source of their anxieties; but others who have learnt the graceful art of concealment, who wear a social smile as part of a liberal education, how often we catch their faces betraying, as it were, some process of mental arithmetic, as though some sum were being cast up within which will not give the wished-for answer ! . . . . How many young spirits we see prematurely depressed by this want—it may be the consequence of their own folly ! How many manners, tempers, peculiarities, may be interpreted by it ! How many people are dull or proud or unsociable from the secret irritation of want of money ! How many bright intelligences are diverted from their highest development from the same cause ! ”

Again, there are men born with a genius for money-making. They have the instinct of accumulation. The talent and the inclination to convert dollars into doubloons by bargains or shrewd investments, are in them, just as strongly marked and as uncontrollable as were the ability and the inclination of Shakespeare to produce a Hamlet and an Othello, of Raphael to paint his cartoons, of Beethoven to compose his symphonies, or Morse to invent an electric telegraph. As it would have been a gross dereliction of duty, a shameful perversion of gifts, had these latter disregarded the instincts of their genius and engaged in the scramble for wealth, so would a Rothschild, an Astor, and a Peabody, have sinned had they done violence to their natures, and thrown their energies into channels where they would have proved dwarfs, and not giants. The mission of a Lawrence or a Cornell, equally with that of an Agassiz, a Bier-stadt, or a Powers, is defined in the faculties God has given him ; and no one of them has a right to turn aside from the paths to which His finger so plainly points. Academies, colleges, hospitals, museums, libraries, railroads,—none of which could have been possible without their accumulations,—are the proofs of their usefulness ; and though the millionnaire too often converts his brain into a ledger and his heart into a mill-stone, yet this starvation of his spiritual nature is no more necessary in his pursuit than in that of the doctor or the lawyer. Agassiz is reported to have said, half scornfully, that he had "no time to make money," having given himself to science. But how could he get leisure to study the secrets of nature, if others had not made money for him?

Let us, then, abandon the affectation of despising money, and frankly own its value. Let us even admit that more persons are ruined by under-estimation of the value than by greed of gold; that even in our great cities, where life is at white heat, and men stake body and soul on the prizes of the stock-board, there are twenty men who need incitements to industry and frugality where there is one who needs to be chocked in the fierce pursuit of riches. But let us remember, at the same time, the danger of forgetting the end in the means, and attaching more importance to gold itself than to the things which it will purchase. Let us remember the warning of "holy George Herbert:"—

> "Wealth is the Conjurer's Devil,
> Whom, when he thinks he hath, the Devil hath him.
> Gold thou mayst safely touch; but *if it stick
> Unto thy hands, it woundeth to the quick.*"

Especially should the business man, who is tempted to sacrifice everything to the golden calf, be cautioned against the common fallacy that happiness will increase in proportion to his gains. Dr. Johnson, indeed, once argued to the contrary. "If six hundred pounds a year," he said, "procure a man more consequence, and of course more happiness, than six pounds a year, the same proportion will hold as to six thousand, and so on as far as opulence can be carried." The facts do not sustain this theory. It may be doubted whether laige possessions do not bring as many pains as pleasures. After one has enough to satisfy every reasonable want, to give free play to all his tastes in art, literature, or science, it may be questioned whether any addition to his wealth does not bring more anxiety and responsibility than enjoyment. Bacon wisely remarks that a large fortune is of no solid use to the owner, except increase his means of giving; "the rest is but conceit; the personal fruition in any man *cannot reach to feel great riches.*"

The owner of capital really reaps the smallest portion of the advantages which flow from its possession, he being, in fact, but a kind of head bookkeeper, or chief clerk, to the business community. Though rich as Rothschild, he can neither eat, drink, nor wear more than one man's portion of the good things of life. As Astors and Stewarts, whose wealth is counted by tens of millions, are, after all, only the stewards of the nation, and however selfish, grasping, or miserly they may be, are compelled, even when they least desire to do so, to use their accumulations for the public good. Their money-making talents enable them to employ their capital, which would soon melt away in the hands of a spendthrift or bad financier, to promote the common welfare and to increase the general prosperity. The rich man in this country, who is ambitious to increase his riches, does not waste his money in luxuries or foolish schemes, but as one has well said, he invests it in all sorts of enterprises, to the selection of which he brings enormous natural shrewdness, strengthened by the experience of a lifetime, and in every one of which it is devoted wholly to the employment of labour. "If he puts it in unproductive real estate even, as he doubtless does sometimes, he releases some one else's money, which goes into production. If he builds houses to let, he employs labour and helps to lower rents ; if he makes railroads, he employs miners, ironfounders, machinists, and helps to transport commodities ; if he goes into spinning and weaving, or gardening, the result is still the same,—labour is employed, and employed with such sagacity that it is sure to return the capital and something more. If he loaded himself with diamonds, filled himself every day to the chin with French dishes and wines, and wore cloth of gold, and lived in a palace, it would be found that his salary was low. If we dismissed him, that is, took his property from him, and employed a philanthropist or editor or lyceum-lecturer to manage it in the interest of 'humanity' the probabilities are that there would not be a cent of it left at the end of five years. It would have been put into the production of goods that nobody wanted, of roads on which nobody would travel, or stolen by knaves and wasted by visionaries."

These truths are well illustrated in the anecdote told some years ago of two men who were conversing about John Jacob Astor's property. Some one was asked if he would be willing to take care of all the millionaire's property—ten or fifteen millions of dollars—merely for his board and clothing. "No !"

was the indignant answer; "do you take me for a fool?"
"Well," rejoins the other, "that is all Mr. Astor himself gets for
taking care of it; he's *found*, and that's all. The houses, the
warehouses, the ships, the farms, which he counts by the hundred, and is often obliged to take care of, are for the accommodation of others." "But then he has the income, the rents of
all this large property, five or six hundred thousand dollars per
annum." "Yes, but he can do nothing with his income but
build *more* houses and warehouses and ships, or loan money on
mortgages for the convenience of others. He's *found*, and you
can make nothing else out of it."

If a rich man wishes to be healthy, says Sir William Temple,
he must live like a poor one. Izaak Walton tells us that there
are as many troubles on the other side of riches as on this, and
that the cares which are the keys of riches hang heavily at the
rich man's girdle. How many men, on reaching the pinnacle
of wealth, find, as they look down upon their money-bags, that
they have only purchased one set of enjoyments by the loss of
another equally desirable! "Do you remember, Bridget,"
writes Charles Lamb, with a tender retrospect to his poverty,
"when you and I laughed at the play from the shilling gallery?
There are no good plays to laugh at now from the boxes."
Many a Sir Epicure Mammon, as he sits down with jaded appetite to his lobster salad and champagne, thinks with keen regret of the simple repasts which titillated his palate when he
was poor. The great railway king, Hudson, and his wife, feasting with dukes and duchesses in their big house at Albert
Gate, looked back with many a sigh to the days when they ate
sausages for supper in the little parlour behind their paltry
shop in the city of York.

Nothing, in the abstract seems easier than to get pleasure
out of money; yet to many persons nothing is apparently more
difficult. It seems delightful to be able to buy everything you
wish, without a thought of the cost; yet he who does not see
that the pleasure must pall in the degree that there is no difficulty? Did the earl to whom Robins knocked down the rare
Boccaccio feel in his conquest a tithe of the pride and joy which
Lamb felt when he bore home that black-letter folio, to procure which "the old brown suit was made to hang on six weeks
longer."

Even the most specious and plausible reason for seeking riches, namely, to be above the necessity of rigid economy, or the pressure of debt, Archbishop Whately shows to be unsound and deceptive.   " It is worth remarking he observes, as a curious circumstance, and the reverse of what many would expect, that the expenses called for by a real or *imagined* necessity of those who have large incomes are greater than those of persons with slenderer means ; and that, consequently, a larger portion of what is called the rich are in embarrassed circumstances than of the poorer.   This is often overlooked, because the *absolute number* of those with larger incomes is so much less, that, of course, the absolute number of persons under pecuniary difficulties in the poorer classes must form a very large majority.   But if you look to the proportions, it is quite the reverse.   Take the number of persons of each amount of income, divided into classes from $500 per annum up to $500,000 per annum, and you will find the *percentage* of those who are under pecuniary difficulties *continually augmenting* as you go upwards.   And when you come to sovereign States, whose revenue is reckoned by millions, you will hardly find *one* that is not deeply involved in debt ; so that it would appear, the larger the income, the harder it is to live within it. In other words, the tendency to spend increases in a greater ratio than the wealth ; and hence competence has been wittily defined as three hundred a year more than you possess.

The insufficiency of mere wealth alone to confer happiness was strikingly illustrated in the life of Nathan Myers Rothschild, the great Jew banker, who died in London some years ago, "one of the most devoted worshippers that ever laid a withered soul on the altar of Mammon." For years he wielded the purse of the world, opening and closing it to kings and emperors as he listed ; and upon certain occasions was supposed to have had more influence in Great Britain than the proudest and wealthiest of its nobles, perhaps more than the two houses of Parliament taken together. He once purchased bills of the Government in a single day to the amount of £4,000,000 and also the gold which he knew the Government must have to pay them ; and with the profits of a single loan purchased an estate which cost him £150,000.   Yet with the clearest and widest comprehension in money matters, with the most piercing insight into all possible causes affecting the money market, and with ingenuity to effect the profoundest, most subtle, and most unsuspected combinations—an ingenuity before which all the other prodigies which have from time to time appeared sink into nothing—he was, withal, a little soul. He exercised his talents and powers of calculation not only for the accumulation of millions and the management of national creditors, but for the determination of the smallest possible pittance on which a clerk's soul could be retained in connection with his body. To part with a shilling in the way of charity cut him to the heart. One of his grand rules, "never to have anything to do with an unlucky man or place," —which was also a principle of John Jacob Astor—however shrewd in a worldly point of view, was the very quintessence of selfishness and mammon-worship. "I have seen many clever men, very clever men," he used to say, "who had not shoes to their feet. I never act with them." He was, in short, a thorough-going mammon worshipper, whose soul had been converted into a machine for coining guineas, and every noble emotion, every immortal longing, died within him. Guineas he did coin to a sum that seems almost fabulous ; but, with all his colossal wealth, he was profoundly unhappy, and with sorrowful earnestness exclaimed to one congratulating him on the gorgeous magnificence of his palatial mansion, and thence inferring that he was happy : "*Happy !* ME *happy !*"

Those who think Rothschild's experience singular may be still further enlightened by that of Stephen Girard. When surrounded with riches and supposed to be taking supreme delight in the accumulation of wealth, he thus wrote to a friend : "As to myself, I live like a galley slave, constantly occupied, and often passing the night without sleeping. I am wrapped up in a labyrinth of affairs, and worn out with cares. I do not value a fortune. The love of labour is my highest motive. When I rise in the morning, my only effort is to labour so hard during the day that, when night comes, I may be enabled to sleep soundly."

To conclude : money is a good thing, of which every man should try to secure enough to avoid dependence upon others, either for his bread or his opinions ; but it is not so good a thing that, to win it, one should crawl in the dust, stoop to a mean or dishonourable action, or give his conscience a single pang. Money-getting is unhealthy when it impoverishes the mind, or dries up the sources of the spiritual life ; when it extinguishes the sense of beauty, and makes one indifferent to the wonders of nature and art ; when it blunts the moral sense, and confuses the distinction between right and wrong, virtue and vice ; when it stifles religious impulse, and blots all thought of God from the soul. Money-getting is unhealthy, again, when it engrosses all one's thought, leads a man to live meanly and coarsely, to do without books, pictures, music, travel, for the sake of greater gains, and causes him to find his deepest and most soul-satisfying joy, not in the culture of his heart or mind, nor in doing good to himself or others, but in the adding of eagle to eagle, in the knowledge that the money in his chest is piled up higher and higher every year, that his account at the bank is constantly growing, that he is adding bonds to bonds, mortgages to mortgages, stocks to stocks, and may say to himself, " Soul, thou hast much goods laid up for many years."

There is, indeed, no more pitiable wretch than the man who has mortgaged himself, soul and body, to Mammon,—in whom the one giant passion for gold has starved every other affection; no more painful spectacle than to see a man dragging his manhood at the heels of his employment, losing life for the sake of the means of living, disregarding the celestial crown held over his head, and raking to himself the straws, the small sticks, and dust of the earth. The poorest of all human beings is the man who is rich in gold, but intellectually and spiritually bankrupt,—*magnas inter opes inops.* As Cowley says, " the poor rich man's emphatically poor." Grant the utmost that can be said of the necessity and the value of money, it will still remain forever true that life is more than the means by which it is sustained, more than dwellings, lands, merchandise, stocks, bonds, and dividends, more even than food and raiment. All things are for the mind, the soul, the divine part within us ; and if this, our true self, is dwarfed and starved, the most royal worldly possessions only serve to set forth by contrast its deep poverty and servitude.

Let every one, then, who wishes to get on in the world, justly estimate the value of money. Let him neither, on the one hand, make it the only gauge and object of success, nor, on the other, affect for it a philosophic contempt which the necessities of life will compel him to unlearn. Let him neither strive for a mere living, nor (unless he has a rare genius for money-making) for a great fortune, but gather gear, as Burns says—

> " By every wile
> That's justified by honour;
> Not for to hide it in a hedge,
> Nor for a train attendant,
> But for the glorious privilege
> Of being independent."

A great deal has been written on the art of money-getting; but, though comparatively few become rich, there is no real secret about it. The pith of the world's wisdom on it is condensed into a few proverbs. To work hard, to improve small opportunities, to economize, to avoid debt, are the general rules in which is summed up the hoarded experience of centuries, and the most sagacious writers have added little to them. Of all the objects which a man can propose to himself, that of money-making is the simplest and most attainable, provided he will take the proper steps. To become an artist, a statesman, an orator, a poet, or a scholar, of high ability, is what few persons can expect. In some callings not even the most indefatigable effort and the most exhaustless patience are sure to win success. The man, on the contrary, who strives to gain money, knows that he is following no chimera, no phantom or will-o'-the-wisp, which will for ever beckon him on, yet for ever baffle him, or which, if attained, will only mock his expectations. He toils for a definite end, and there is no sense of incongruity between his toil and his hope. Money-getting is a pursuit in which almost any diligent, earnest, prudent man may hope to get on, without brilliant talents or genius. Any beginner in life who has mastered the three R's, " Reading, 'Ritin', and 'Rithmetic," may hope to become independent, if not rich, if he will but work persistently, be temperate, and save a part of his earnings. Mediocre abilities will suffice for this end, nay, may prove more advantageous than the most dazzling mental gifts.

There is no workingman in good health who may not be-

come independent, if he will but carefully husband his receipts,
and guard jealously against the little leaks of useless expenditure. But, to become independent, one must be willing to pay
the price. He must be industrious, and he must be prudent.
Perhaps the hardest of these rules to follow is the latter.
There are a hundred persons who can work hard, to every ten
who can properly husband their earnings. The classes that toil
the hardest squander most recklessly the money they earn.
Instead of hoarding their receipts, so as to provide against sickness or want of employment, they eat and drink up their earnings as they go, and thus in the first financial crisis, when mills
and factories stop, and capitalists lock up their cash instead of
using it in great enterprises, they are ruined. Men who thus
live "from hand to mouth," never keeping more than a day's
march ahead of actual want, are little better off than slaves.
They are not their own masters, but may have at any moment
to choose between the alternatives of bondage or starvation.
They cannot help being servile, for they know they can neither
command their time, nor choose how and where they shall live.

To one who has seen much of the miseries of the poor, it is
hard to account for this short-sightedness of conduct; but
doubtless the main cause is the contempt with which they are
wont to look upon petty savings. Ask those who spend all as
they go why they do not put by a fraction of their daily earnings, and they will reply, " That's of no use ; what good can the
saving of a few cents a day, or an occasional dollar, do ?   If I
could lay by four or five dollars a week, that would ultimately
amount to something." It is by this thoughtless reasoning that
thousands are kept steeped to the lips in poverty, who by a
moderate degree of self-denial might place themselves in a
state of comfort and independence, if not of affluence.   They
do not consider to what enormous sums little savings and little
spendings swell at last, when continued through a long series
of years.

What labourer is there in good health who may not save
from his earnings fifty dollars a year ? Yet this paltry sum,
compounded at six per cent. interest, amounts to $650 in ten
years, $1,860 in twenty ; $3,950 in thirty years ; and $7,700 in
forty years ; thus securing a snug provision for old age by the
saving of less than fourteen cents per day ! How impercep-

tibly may this last sum, or one twice as great, slip through one's fingers in the gratification of habits worse than useless, without a thought of the vast aggregate to which it finally amounts! What clerk or workingman, that spends twenty cents a day for a couple of cigars, dreams that by this expenditure, with the accumulated interest, he will in fifty years have smoked away twenty thousand dollars? Yet a man who by a life of industry had laid by such a sum would, in most country towns, be deemed rich. It is a hard thing to begin the world without a dollar, and yet hundreds of men, by petty savings at the outset of their career, have amassed large fortunes from a single shilling. Among the capitalists in one of our large cities some years ago was a builder, worth probably some hundreds of thousands, who began life as a bricklayer's labourer at a dollar a day. Out of that small sum he contrived to save fifty cents a day, and at the end of the first year had laid up $182, from which moment his fortune was made. Like a hound upon the right scent, he was on the track of riches, and the game, sooner or later won was sure to be his own. Of a leading firm in New York city, which some years ago had accumulated an immense property, it is stated that both members came to that city without a cent, and swept the very shop wherein they afterwards made their fortunes. Like the builder, they had an indomitable spirit of industry, perseverance and frugality, and so the first dollar became the foundation of a million.

The persons who despise small savings as unworthy of their care are ignorant of the main object of making them in early life, which looks not chiefly to the saving itself, but to *the formation of a habit of economy.* It is true, the saving of a few cents is in itself of little moment; but if the habit of saving a penny or two, whether in money or any other kind of property, once becomes fixed, and the thoughts be turned in the direction of advancement, the accumulation will go on and be ultimately successful. Hence it has been wisely said that there is no revolution in the history of a man so important in its consequences as that which takes place at the moment of the first saving. As it is the minutes that make the hours, so it is the pennies that make the pounds, the cents that make the dollars; and he who scrupulously economizes the former need give himself no concern about the latter, for the habit of look-ing sharply after them will have insensibly formed itself.　It is for this reason that the beginning of a deposit, however small, in a savings-bank, may be regarded as the crisis of many a moral destiny ; for from that moment the person ceases to be a slavish dependent, without manliness or self-respect, and be-comes a free, independent, self-relying man, who is under no bondage but that of kindness to his fellows, of which he now has the means.

" Whatever your means be," says Sir Edward Lytton Bul-wer, in an excellent essay upon " The Management of Money," "so apportion your wants that your means may exceed them. Every man who earns but ten shillings a week can do this if he please, whatever he may say to the contrary ; for, if he can live upon ten shillings a week, he can live upon nine and elevenpence.　In this rule mark the emphatic distinction be-tween poverty and neediness.　Poverty is relative and there-fore not ignoble.　Neediness is a positive degradation.　If I have only £100 a year, I am rich as compared with the major-ity of my countrymen.　If I have £5,000 a year, I may be poor compared with the majority of my associates, and very poor compared with my next-door neighbour.　With either of these incomes I am relatively poor or rich ; but with either of these incomes I may be positively needy or positively free from need-iness.　With the £100 a year I may need no man's help ; I may at least have ' my crust of bread and liberty.'　But with £5,000 a year I may dread a ring at my bell ; I may have my tyrannical masters in servants whose wages I cannot pay ; my exile may be at the fiat of the first long-suffering man who enters a judg-ment against me ; for the flesh that lies nearest my heart some Shylock may be dusting his scales and whetting his knife. Nor is this an exaggeration.　Some of the neediest men I ever knew have a nominal £5,000 a year.　Every man is needy who spends more than he has ; no man is needy who spends less.　I may so ill manage my money, that, with £5,000 a year, I purchase the worst evils of poverty,—terror and shame ; I may so well manage my money, that, with £100 a year, I purchase the best blessings of wealth,—safety and respect."

One of the reasons why many persons refuse to practise econ-omy is that it is associated in their minds with meanness. They look upon it as degrading to a man of spirit and lofty impulses ; as the virtue of little contracted minds. No doubt the practice of saving may be carried too far. It is said that the Earl of Westminster, who owns a park ten miles long and has an income of four millions of dollars a year, once dismounted from his horse, when riding out, on missing a button from his coat. and retraced his steps for some distance till he found it. The expediency of such savings may be questioned. Dr. Johnson once said, that " he who drinks beer, thinks beer "; and it is equally true that those who occupy themselves with endless cares for small savings get " to think candle-ends " as their reward. It has been justly doubted whether, among the classes of men who, whether they are economical or not, are sure never to go to bed hungry, there is anything in the accumulation of money to compensate for the deterioration of mind and feeling which is almost sure to accompany the pursuit of so trumpery an end as screwing fourpence a week out of the butter bill. But economy is a wholly different thing from penuriousness ; so different, indeed, that it is only the economical man who can afford to be liberal, or even to live with ease and magnanimity.

Wellington kept an exact account of all the moneys he received or paid ; and Washington, who was not a small man, did not disdain to watch his expenditures and to scrutinize the little items in the outgoings of his household. Not only the independence of individuals, but that of states, depends upon the practice of this virtue. What is the secret of England's greatness ? Is it not her savings ? Is it not evident that public wealth, in the long run, can only flow from private prosperity ! that it cannot increase when individual expenditure exceeds private income ? Surely, the system that is grand for a state cannot be mean for the individual. The truth is, no amount of means or earnings can justify waste or profusion, either by a nation or private person. God himself cannot afford to be extravagant. · Even when displaying His infinite power to the multitude, he teaches the needful lesson of economy. The miracle of the loaves and fishes ends with the command " to gather up the fragments that remain, that nothing may be lost." The autumn leaves are saved to manure the next year's crops, and the bodies of the dead fatten Sadowa's soil for the future seed-time. Nature knows no waste ; she

S

utilizes the smallest atoms; then why should man deem it degrading to husband his means for future wants and necessities?

Again, every man who would get on in the world should, as far as possible, avoid debt. From the very outset of his career he should sternly resolve to live within his income, however paltry it may be. The art of living easily as to money is very simple; it is, as Bulwer advises in the passage already quoted, to pitch your scale of living one degree below your means. All of the world's wisdom on the subject is most tersely epitomized in the words of Dicken's Micawber: "Annual income twenty pounds, annual expenditure nineteen nineteen six, result happiness. Annual income twenty pounds, annual expenditure twenty pounds ought and six, result misery." Mr. Micawber's experience, so vividly depicted by Dickens, is that of thousands whose whole lives are made miserable by the folly of living beyond their means. In this country, especially since the late war, there has been a growing tendency in all classes of society to overspend. In every town and village there is a fearful ambition abroad for being "genteel." One half of our families are engaged in a perpetual and desperate struggle to keep up appearances,—to pass for that which they are not. They have neither patience nor courage to go on in the paths to which God has appointed them, but must needs force themselves into some fashionable state to which they have called themselves, and where they may bask in the smiles of Mrs. Grundy. Everywhere "there is a constant struggle and pressure for front seats in the social amphitheatre, in the midst of which all noble, self-denying resolve is trodden down, and many fine natures are inevitably crushed to death." Marrying early, the young lawyer, merchant, or mechanic is not content to begin life in the simple style in which his father began, increasing his comforts as his earnings increase; but he must live from the very start as the veterans of his calling live after years of toil and economy. The rents he pays, the furniture and ornaments of his house, the luxuries of his table, the number of his servants, the clothes of himself and family, his expenditure for opera-tickets, concerts, lectures, hackney coaches,—not to include the cost of what Charles Lamb would call his "virtuous vices," such as smoking, etc., or dinners at Delmonico's are all far above his means. The result is, he gets into debt, then more deeply into debt, falls into the clutches of Shylock, is fleeced of large sums for interest, struggles vainly in the toils in which he is involved, becomes desperate, and mismanages his business or half does his work, and at last, after floundering and stumbling on for a few months, or years, with inevitable bankruptcy staring him in the face, succumbs under the heavy load of debts, duns, and anxiety, when the curtain falls, and the wretched play of "Keeping up Appearances" is ended.

When will this wretched state of things cease? Never till beginners in life have learned to feel a horror for debt; till those who are ambitious of display learn that it is dishonest to spend what they have not earned,—that, as Sir Charles Napier once said to some of his officers, " to drink unpaid-for champagne and unpaid-for beer, and to ride unpaid-for horses, is to be a cheat, and not a gentleman." Of all the foes to human prosperity and happiness, there is none more deadly than debt. Dr. Johnson held it not only to be an inconvenience, but a calamity. " Let it be your first care," he says, "not to be in any man's debt. Resolve not to be poor ; whatever you have, spend less. Poverty is a great enemy to human happiness ; it certainly destroys liberty, and it makes some virtues impracticable and others extremely difficult. It lowers a man in self-respect, places him at the mercy of the tradesman and his servant, and renders him a slave in many respects ; for he can no longer call himself his own master, nor boldly look the world in the face." It is also difficult for a man who is constantly in debt to be truthful ; hence it is said that " lying rides on debt's back."

> " An unthrift was a liar from all time ;
> Never was a debtor that was not deceiver."

Many a ruined man dates his downfall from the day when he began borrowing money. It is easy to avoid the first obligation ; but, that incurred, others speedily follow, one necessitating the other; every day the poor victim gets more and more inextricably entangled ; then follow pretexts, excuses, lies, till all sense of shame is lost, the whole life becomes a makeshift, and the debtor, despairing of deliverance from his embarrassments, deliberately resolves to live by indirect robbery and falsehood. "I am astonished," says Sir Richard Steele, "that men can be so insensible of the danger of running into debt. One would think it impossible that a man who is given to contract debts should not know that his debtor has, from that moment in which he trangresses payment, so much as that demand comes to in his debtor's honesty, liberty, and fortune. . . . Can there be a more low and servile condition than to be afraid or ashamed to see any man breathing? Yet he that is in debt is in that condition with relation to twenty different people. The debtor is the creditor's criminal, and all the officers of power and state, whom we behold make so poor a figure, are no other than so many persons in authority to make good his charge against him. Human society depends on his having the vengeance the law allots him; and the debtor owes his liberty to his neighbour as much as the murderer does his life to the prince." Yet the author of these remarks, who could so vividly depict the miseries of indebtedness, was perpetually struggling with them, and presents in his whole career one of the most melancholy examples which biography affords of the moral sacrifices which are so often occasioned by a disproportion between wants and the means of gratifying them. When reproached by Mr. Whiston, for having in the House of Commons given some votes in flagrant contradiction to his formerly professed opinions, he replied, "Mr. Whiston, you can walk on foot, but I cannot." A coach had become so essential to Steele, that, rather than do without it, he was willing to abandon his most cherished political principles and do violence to his conscience.

Let every young man who is shocked by the conduct of this inconsistent writer avoid the rock on which he split. Let him resolve early that he will at all times look his affairs squarely in the face, that he will know his exact financial condition, and that he will do any work that is honourable, and submit to the most pinching privation, rather than plunge into debt. Eloquently has Douglas Jerrold said : "Be sure of it, he who dines out of debt, though his meal be biscuit and an onion, dines in the 'Apollo.' And then for raiment; what warmth in a threadbare coat, if the tailor's receipt be in the pocket ! what Tyrian purple in the faded waistcoat, the vest not owed for !

how glossy the well-worn hat, if it covers not the aching head of a debtor! . . . . Debt, however courteously it be offered, is the cup of a siren, and the wine, spiced and delicious though it be, an eating poison. The man out of debt, though with a flaw in his jerkin, a crack in his shoe-leather, and a hole in his hat, is still the son of liberty, free as the singing lark above him ; but the debtor, though clothed in the utmost bravery, what is he but a serf out upon a holiday,—a slave to be re-claimed at any instant by his owner, the creditor? My son, if poor, see wine in the running spring ; let thy mouth water at a last week's roll ; think a threadbare coat the ' only wear' ; and acknowledge a whitewashed garret the fittest housing place for a gentleman ; do this and flee debt. So shall thy heart be at peace and the sheriff be confounded."*

* Heads for the People.

CHAPTER XIX.

MERCANTILE FAILURES.

To succeed, one must sometimes be very bold and sometimes very prudent —NAPOLEON.

I venture to point out to you what is the best temperament, namely, a combination of the desponding and resolute, or, as I had better express it, of the apprehensive and the resolute.   Such is the temperament of great commanders.   Secretly, they rely upon nothing and upon nobody.   There is such a powerful element of failure in all human affairs, that a shrewd man is always saying to himself, "What shall I do, if that which I count upon does not come out as I expect?"   This foresight dwarfs and crushes all but men of great resolution.—ARTHUR HELPS.

Let your first efforts be, not for wealth, but independence.   Whatever be your talents, whatever your prospects, never be tempted to speculate away, on the chance of a palace, that which you need as a provision against the workhouse.—E. L. BULWER.

A failure establishes only this, that our determination to succeed was not strong enough.—BOVEE.

ONE of the bad features of our American life is the growing disposition of our young men to get their living by their wits, and to leave manual labour, agricultural or mechanical, to be monopolised by foreigners.   Bodily toil, except of the lightest kind, is becoming to Young America more and more distasteful.   The sons of our farmers, shoemakers, blacksmiths, and carpenters no sooner become their own masters than they straightway throw down the scythe, the awl, and the hammer, and rush to the city to engage in the nobler work of weighing sugar, selling tape, hawking books, soliciting insurance, or posting ledgers.   And yet, if any fact has been demonstrated beyond the shadow of a doubt, it is the deceitfulness of the apparent facilities for getting rich in cities. The fact that while in other careers the mass of men are successful, ninety-five at least out of every hundred who embark in commerce either make shipwreck or retire sooner or later in disgust, without having secured a competence, has not only been verified again and again by statistics, but is a stereotyped observation which drops from the lips of business men daily.

Some years ago General A. H. S. Dearborn, of Boston, who had long been acquainted with the leading business men of that city, gave it as his opinion that only three men out of every hundred doing business there were successful. A gentleman who doubted the truth of this startling statement consulted an antiquarian friend who had known all the merchants doing business on Long Wharf from 1798 to 1840, and was informed that in the latter year only five out of a hundred remained. More striking still was the statement of a director of the Union Bank, which began its operations in 1798, that, of one thousand persons doing business with it, only *six* at the end of forty years remained; all the rest had failed or lost their property. "Bankruptcy," said the director, " is like death, and almost as certain ; *they fall single and alone, and are thus forgotten ;* but there is no escape from it, and he is a fortunate man who fails young.". A person who looked through the Probate Office in the same city found that ninety per cent of all the estates settled there were insolvent. Yet more discouraging to the commercial adventurer were the conclusions of Governor Briggs and Secretary Calhoun who a few years ago gave it as their deliberate opinion, after diligent inquiry, that, out of every hundred young men who come from the country to seek their fortunes in the city, ninety-nine fail of success. To all these statements may be added the opinions of some of the shrewdest and most experienced business men of New York and Philadelphia, that not more than one per cent of the best class of merchants succeed without failing in the former city, and that not more than two per cent of the merchants of the latter retire on an independence, " after having submitted to the usual ordeal of failure." After the crash in 1858 it was stated by high authority that there had been annually, for some years previous, twenty-seven thousand failures in the United States, for the gross sum of $50,000,000, of which enormous indebtedness only $10,000,000 was ever recovered by the creditors,—an estimate probably below the truth. In short, for every man who thrives in trade, counting his acquisitions by thousands of dollars, we can find scores of men with whom each day is but a desperate struggle to keep their heads above water ; and to every one who, after again and again trembling on the verge of bankruptcy, retires at last with money enough to pass his closing days in ease and affluence, a hundred might be named who wind up the vicissitudes of a long life of toil in utter failure, and spend their last days in trying to keep the wolf from the door.

The facts we have stated will seem incredible to those who have never weighed or investigated the subject ; and yet the proofs are open to every man who has his eyes upon and witnesses the changes going on around him. Go into any city or large town with which you were acquainted ten years ago, and you will be startled to see how many signs that once greeted the eye on stores and warehouses have been exchanged for new ones; how many names, once familiar as "household words," have been blotted from the Business Directory. Indeed, so few are the prizes and so numerous the blanks in this seeming lottery, that some persons have been inclined to regard luck as everything in trade,—experience, sagacity, energy, and enterprise as nothing, if linked to an unlucky star. As we have already observed in the chapter on "Good and Bad Luck," some of the shrewdest men, with indefatigable industry and the closest economy, fail to make money ; others, with apparently none of the qualities that insure success, are continually blundering into profitable speculations, and, Midas-like, touch nothing but to turn to gold. The great Chicago fire, which beggared hundreds of merchants, mechanics and professional men, and made a hundred thousand men, women, and children homeless, doubled and trebled the fortunes of other men, who were never insured and never burnt out. But while it must be admitted that there is such a thing as luck, meaning by it the occasional operations of causes over which one has no control, it would be absurd to ascribe to it the mass of failures. Bitterly as the broken merchant may bemoan some mishap that has blasted all his schemes and hopes, it is evident that, if there are nine shipwrecks to one safe voyage over the sea of business, there is some higher law than chance governing the matter ; and what this law is—in other words, what are the chief causes of bankruptcy—we shall now try to show.

What, then, are the causes of those failures of business men which are so numerous as to make success seem like the drawing of a prize in a lottery ? We answer—the first and most obvious cause is the *lack of business talents*. If there is any act demonstrated by experience, it is that no man can succeed in a calling for which Providence did not intend him. Of course, it is easy to exaggerate this doctrine. There are some men who, though they succeed best in a particular sphere, yet have a marvellous flexibility, versatility, and power of adaptation, which enables them to thrive in almost any pursuit they may choose. It has been even said that "the most unhandy person is a sort of Robinson Crusoe; plant him in a desolate island, and he would sprout a twenty-bladed penknife." But, in spite of exceptional cases, it may be affirmed that there is a work to which each person is fitted, to which he is called by his talents and endowments. As Emerson says: "He is like a ship in a river; he runs against obstructions on every side but one; on that side all obstruction is taken away, and he sweeps serenely over a deepening channel into an infinite sea." This easy thing with some men is making money in trade; but there are others to whom it is as difficult as for a man with no mathematical talent to calculate an eclipse, or a person with no eye for colour to paint "The Descent from the Cross." Who can wonder that such weaklings soon go to the wall; that in the sharp competitions of modern trade they are outwitted and overreached by men born for the business, and who have learned its crooks and turns by a long apprenticeship; and that, after stumbling on a few years, committing blunder after blunder through ignorance and lack of sagacity, they are shipwrecked by the first financial hurricane that sweeps over the land?

But it is needless to dwell on this topic, as we have already discussed it at length in the chapter on "The Choice of a Profession."

The next cause of bankruptcies which we shall mention, and a very prolific one, is *an excessive haste to get rich.* Americans are always in a hurry when they have an object to accomplish; but if there is any vocation or pursuit in which gradual, slow-coach processes are scouted with peculiar detestation, it is that of acquiring riches. Especially is this true at the present day, when fortunes are continually changing hands, and men are so often, by a lucky turn of the wheel, lifted from the lowest depths of poverty to the loftiest pinnacle of wealth and affluence. Exceptional persons there are, who are content with slow gains—willing to accumulate riches by adding penny to penny, dollar to dollar ; but the mass of business men are too apt to despise such a tedious, laborious ascent of the steep of fortune, and to rush headlong into schemes for the sudden acquisition of wealth. Hence honourable labour is too often despised ; a man of parts is expected to be above hard work ; and he is considered the shrewdest fellow who can throw double-sixes oftenest in the lottery of speculation. Thus we go, racing on like a high-pressure Mississippi steamer in the pursuit of fortune, pitching rosin into the furnace to get along faster, and piling weights upon the safety valves, until finally the boilers burst, hundreds are killed or crippled, and we are compelled to stop for a while, until we can get over the fright of the explosion. Pretty soon the repairs are made, the steam is up again, we are buoyant with confidence, " Hope enchanting smiles, and waves her golden hair," again we are " going it " at a fearful pace, and in due time another crash occurs. The warnings of the past are lost upon us ; cautious men are voted old fogies, and their advice and admonitions clogs on the wheels of enterprise. Americans must be Americans, and blow up as a necessity of their existence.

Hardly anything is more fatal to success in business than this all-absorbing, grasping anxiety for wealth, which is so characteristic of the times we live in. The very ambition to be rich, to accumulate what is called a " big pile," and to reckon one's property by hundreds of thousands, is self-defeating, and leads to ruin. It blinds the judgment of its victim, and lures him into visionary schemes and dangerous speculations, till at , last he loses all taste for slow and sure gains and all capacity for calm and logical reasoning. One of the worst consequences to which it leads is overtrading. Instead of aiming to do a snug, easily managed, and therefore safe business, which will yield a reasonable, but not colossal profit, many merchants buy and try to sell double the quantity of goods which their capital will justify. Instead of spreading an amount of canvas proportioned to the tonnage of their craft, the mass of those who embark on the treacherous ocean of trade crowd on all sail, and are only ambitious to make the utmost possible number of knots an hour. For a while,

" Fair laughs the morn, and soft the zephyr blows,"

and to all appearance they will reach the haven of wealth in half the time of the slow sailers ; but suddenly, at a moment and from a quarter least expected, a squall springs up, and they are swept, in spite of every effort, towards a lee shore, and speedily go to the bottom. The great fault of many who start in the race for riches is, that they are not willing to creep before they can walk, to walk before they run, to run before they attempt to fly. A man who has a capital of five thousand dollars does a business of twenty thousand ; a trader with twenty-five thousand is content to do nothing less than a business of a hundred or a hundred and fifty thousand ; and the possessor of the last-mentioned sum aims at a gigantic traffic, which would be justified only by a capital of half a million. As in education, dissipation, and all things else, the " fast " system prevails among our merchants, and, rushing along as they do at a race-horse pace, a crash, when it comes, produces an amount of disaster and misery which is incalculable.

Another fruitful cause of bankruptcies is *speculation*. In every community there are men who are determined not to work if work can be shirked. Without avowing this determination to themselves, or reflecting that they are fighting against a law of nature, they begin life with a resolution to enjoy all the good things that are accumulated by the labour of man, without contributing their own share of labour to the common stock. Hence the endless schemes for getting rich in a day,— for reaching the goal of wealth by a few gigantic bounds, instead of by slow and plodding steps. It matters not in what such men deal, whether in oroide watches or in watered stock ; whether they make " corners " in wheat or in gold ; whether they gamble in oats or at roulette ; whether they steal a railway or a man's money by " gift-concerts,"—the principle is in all cases the same, namely, to obtain something for nothing, to get values without parting with anything in exchange. Everybody knows the history of such men, the vicissitudes they experience,—vicissitudes rendering the millionnaire of to-day a beggar to-morrow, and which have been thus briefly epitomized :—

> " Lundi, j'achetais des actions ;
> Mardi, j'avais des millions ;
> Mercredi, j'établis mon ménage ;
> Jeudi, je fis mon equipage ;

> Le Vendredi, je fus au bal,
> Et Samedi à l'hôpital";

which, briefly translated, means

> " Monday, I dabbled in stock operations,
> Tuesday, owned millions, by all calculations;
> Wednesday, my Fifth Avenue palace began;
> Thursday, I drove out a spanking bay span;
> Friday, I gave a magnificent ball;
> And Saturday, ' *smashed* ' with nothing at all."

Such is the career of thousands in this country. Beginning business on Monday, they are reeking and rioting in riches on Tuesday, live gorgeously during the week. Saturday morning their paper goes to protest, and by Saturday night they are vibrating between the sheriff and starvation. " The darkest day," says Horace Greeley, " in any man's earthly career is that wherein he first fancies that there is some easier way of gaining a dollar than by squarely earning it. . . . . He has lost the clue to his way through this mortal labyrinth, and must henceforth wander as chance may dictate."

Even of those merchants who start in their careers with a determination to avoid all gambling operations, how few persevere to the end! How many, after having accumulated a snug sum by years of toil and economy, are tempted by the example of some lucky neighbour to hazard their laboriously acquired fortune in some big speculation,—some attempt to monopolize a commodity,—breaking down in which, they are stripped of the earnings of years! How many lock up their ready cash in wild lands or corner lots, which, proving dull of sale, or falling in value, are knocked off by the auctioneer's hammer at half the cost! Or perhaps they hire a part of the purchase-money, project unwise improvements on the property, cover themselves with bonds and mortgages, and finally incur " a street debt " of some thousands, which swiftly rolls up to double the amount, and crushes the life right out of them. There are many such who are literally owned by brokers,— who work for them, live for them, and even die for them,— die literally of a street debt upon which they have weekly exhausted their strength in a frenzied effort to roll it ahead from one day to seven. To justify a merchant in the bold attempt to monopolize a commodity which is largely produced, he should have, not only plenty of cash or credit, but a profound and exact knowledge of the markets, and of the causes of excess and scarcity, which is possessed only by the sagacious and discerning few. Nearly all the most successful merchants in this country have won their fortunes, not by sudden gains, by bold and masterly yet hazardous strokes of speculation, but by the slow but sure accumulations of commercial industry. Peter C. Brooks, of Boston, who died worth two millions, never once in his life indulged in speculation, and however brilliant the prospect of gain, shunned every transaction which required the use of borrowed means. Mr. Lorillard, who died immensely rich in New York, pursued a similar course, and used often to remark that his prosperity arose from not having been in haste to get rich. He launched into no wild and uncertain schemes, which risk the earnings of a life on the chances of a day, but was content with the regular proceeds of his legitimate business.

Perhaps there is no way in which merchants are oftener involved in inextricable embarrassments than by an unwise investment of their surplus profits. Many are tempted by dazzling bargains to go beyond their depth. Buying when money is abundant, they are called on to pay in a time of great stringency, and are suddenly ruined. Let the merchant who has a surplus capital invest it, not in dead property, but in good floating securities, easily convertible into money ; and especially let him use it in discounting his own four or six months' bills, and his paper will be pronounced "gilt-edged" and " fire-proof." Cash and property, in merchandising, it has been well observed, are two different things, as the business of the trader and that of the capitalist are two different pursuits. Of all the dividend-paying investments, stocks, owing to their flexibility and to the probability of their yielding cost, or nearly cost, in any exigency when the money is needed, are the best for the business man ; yet the temptation to speculate even in this kind of security should be sternly resisted by all who are engaged in trade. A business man has no time to watch the stock-market, and when he loses by gambling in these securities, he gets little sympathy from those who suffer by his failure. On the other hand, a man who is overtaken by a sudden and unavoidable calamity does not lose his credit, even if he is able to pay but a small percentage of his debts. If his capacity and integrity have never been challenged, he will be promptly aided in his attempts to retrieve his fortunes, and none will extend a readier hand than those who have suffered most severely by his losses.

Another cause of failures is *frequent changes of business.* Every business has its peculiarities and mysteries, its crooks and turns, a knowledge of which cannot be acquired by intuition. Years are required to master the details . of any branch of trade ; and there are some departments of commerce in which one may go on learning for a lifetime. The shrewd-est business men will admit, after twenty years' experience in a certain trade, that, though they thought themselves wise when they embarked in it, they were really very ignorant, and that they have not yet exhausted all the facts relating to it. Yet, obvious as are these truths, hundreds of men are perpetu-ally changing from one business to another, sticking to no one long enough to make it profitable. In every occupation they encounter a new set of trials and perplexities, are baffled by fresh obstacles ; yet they are lured on by new will-o'-the wisps, enticed from their callings by stories of fortunes made in other pursuits, and thus spend their lives in changing their plans, getting a smattering of many kinds of business, but a profound knowledge of none. Hardly anything is more fatal to success in business than this impatience for immediate re-sults. All those kinds of business which are surest in the end, which pay best in the long run, are slowest in beginning to yield a return. The truest success in every profession is often like the growth of the American aloe, for many years slow and imperceptible. Then, all at once, when the time comes, there is a crisis. The plant shoots up a stalk ten or fifteen feet high, hung with innumerable flowers. To change one's occupation, therefore, because he does not start off with a grand dash, is an egregious mistake. It is to throw away all the progress he has made, all the knowledge he has acquired, in the one al-ready begun. "It is," as another has said, "to go back to the beginning of the course for a fresh start. The different professions and kinds of business in this respect are not so much parallel tracks, where you can be switched from one into another without loss of progress, but rather tracks radiating from a common centre.   To pass from one to another, you must in each case go back to the original station.   You must begin your career anew.   The comparison, of course, cannot be applied with rigour.   Yet it has substantial truth."

A good illustration of these truths is found in the following facts stated by an American journalist: "An acquaintance, a seed-dealer, stated that for the first five years he could not ascertain that he made anything.   But he was learning.   Before ten years he was clearing five thousand dollars per year.   Another was doing well in manufacturing ropes.   But he was unstable in mind, and although his friends advised him to 'hang to the ropes,' he was not getting rich fast enough ; but he meddled with business he had not learned sufficiently, bought a mill, bought grain, and then broke a bank by his large failure.   Some farmers come to the conclusion that cows are the most profitable ; purchase animals, erect buildings, and begin well.   But, it being a new business, they do not succeed as they expected ; they might, if they would stick to it.   The next year they sell their dairy, and buy sheep.   The price of wool is low that year ; and they hear that much money has been made by raising tobacco.   Thus they go on, changing from one thing to another, and never succeeding in any.   Stick to your business."

Another prolific source of bankruptcies is *extravagance of living*, indulgence in luxury beyond their means by the middle classes.   An English assignee in bankruptcy stated some years ago, after examining the books and documents of seventy-six bankrupts, that *forty-nine* had been ruined by expending more than they could reasonably hope their profits would be, although their business yielded a fair return.   Another assignee found, after a similar investigation, that, out of fifty-two failures, thirty-two had arisen from the same cause, and the rest from imprudent expenditure combined with speculations or bad luck. The proportion of men in our own country who are ruined by spendthrift habits is probably greater than in Europe.   The credit system, together with the insane anxiety of merchants to "get off" their goods, enables and tempts thousands of men and women to gratify their appetites for superfluities beyond their means, and they rush on in the race of extravagance at a "killing pace."   Especially do the women in our large cities,

in these high-pressure times, keep up a "two-forty" pace on the
Fashion race-course. To live in a lofty marble palace, as dreary
and comfortless-as it is stately; to load the person with gorgeous jewellery and apparel, the cost of which would be sufficient to
set up a retail trader; to outshine all rivals in the giddy circles
of Newport, Niagara, and Saratoga,—is the height of many a
woman's ambition, whose husband, instead of discouraging, ex-
ults in her extravagance, and squanders in sustaining it sums
which he bitterly regrets when he sees the abyss of bankruptcy
staring him in the face, and knows not how to steer clear of it.
The hoop-skirts now in vogue typify the swelling conceit, the
empty pride and vanity, which, beginning with the upper
circles, is mimicked and caricatured by all the orders of society,
from the family of the millionnaire down to that of the humble
grocer and fruit-dealer. Few persons estimate the enormous
sums to which the money needlessly wasted in personal and
household expenses would accumulate, if saved and put at
interest. It is said that the merchant who half a century ago
would have lived upon five hundred dollars a year, now spends
four thousand. The difference between these two sums for fifty
years, with the accumulation of compound interest, is over a
million of dollars.

Another fruitful cause of bankruptcies is the credit system,
which is often pushed beyond all reasonable bounds. A merchant who has heavy notes to lift, on investigating his resources finds, instead of cash in his safe or at his banker's, a thick
pile of "promises to pay" by A., B., and C., doing business from
a mile to two thousand miles distant, and not one half of whom
can be relied on in a crisis, when the gulf of bankruptcy yawns
before him. Formerly men scrupled to take credit, if they
doubted their ability to pay for goods. That scruple was by no
means overcome by the thought that in case of failure they
might obtain a *legal* discharge. Just because they were in earnest, and meant to fulfil their promises to the letter—if necessary, by hard work and stern self-denial—they were cautious
about imposing such tasks upon themselves. Not so in these
days of overtrading and swiftly made fortunes. Credit is no
longer what it once was, the result of many successes and hard-
fought battles with the world, the smallest stain upon which
is regarded with horror. It has ceased to be regarded as a

vase of rare and costly workmanship, which years of skill and labour only can bring to the highest perfection, but which an unlucky blow may shiver into fragments ; as something which should not only be kept spotless, but, like Cæsar's wife, above suspicion. Debts, as now created, are often the frailest of things to lean upon when one's liabilities thicken. They are too frequently a mere stake played for in a game of law by the debtor and creditor, until the courts and attorneys "rake down the pile."

To such a pitch has the evil sometimes reached, that some writers have seriously advocated as a remedy the repeal of all laws for the collection of debts. But while banks, the grand embodiment and exponent of credit, are allowed to flood the country with its symbols, often stimulating speculation, interrupting the regular course of trade, and seducing merchants to their ruin, it is ridiculous to talk of abolishing a system created and authorized by law ; not to mention that such violent, Sangrado-like remedies are too much like cutting off one's head to cure the toothache. There is no doubt that our country has been largely indebted to this system for the rapid and marvellous development of her productive powers ; and, therefore, though it is now admitted by all our economists that long credit, with all its attendant abuses, was the grand cause of the financial hurricane that swept over the country in 1858—though this is proved by the fact that the crash came when gold was pouring by millions into the land, when we were vexed neither by war nor famine, but were exulting in a large harvest, and suffering from no external drain—yet we need not expect that the practice of selling goods on time will ever be abandoned. The most that can be expected is, that the system will be subject to certain limitations which may prevent the frightful consequences that flow from its present abuse.

When a vessel is sent on a whaling expedition, or despatched to China for a cargo of tea, long credit is not unreasonable, for a year or more may roll by before the merchant can get a return. So with the East India and the California trades, where goods have to be shipped round Cape Horn. The same principle holds good regarding any business where a long cycle of time must revolve between the venture and the return. New avenues of communication, however, like the

T

Pacific Railroad, are shortening these cycles, and, by the revolutions they are causing, are rendering long credits less and less necessary even here. But is there any analogy between these cases and that of a country merchant who buys in the city goods which can be brought by steamboat or railroad in a few days to his door, and which he can turn into cash in a few months? To sell goods on four or six months to A., B., C., and so on throughout the alphabet all over the Northwest or South, or any other section of the country,—goods that can be bought, shipped from New York to Minnesota or Kansas, opened and exposed for sale in a fortnight's time,—is a wretched abuse of credit, which nothing but the fiercest competition among wholesale dealers could ever have led them to tolerate. It is an abuse the more intolerable, as it damages both debtor and creditor. Goods bought on six months are often speedily converted into cash, and the money, lying idle in the trader's hands, is invested in wild lands or "Peter Funk" railroad speculations; meanwhile, at the end of four months, before a dollar is paid for the former stock, a fresh one is bought with a new "promise to pay;" and when the first note has matured, the promissor has become bankrupt, his bubbles of speculation have bursted, and his estate does not pay twenty-five cents on the dollar.

Abuses like this show that the short credit system is the only safe one; and hence after every great crash, like that of 1858, it is generally adopted, and for a while rigidly adhered to, but the pressure of competition soon breaks it down. Desirable as it may be, we cannot shut our eyes to the fact that it has many obstacles to overcome which are not generally counted upon. In order that the country storekeeper may pay cash, or do with short credit from the city trader, he must either have a large capital, or must himself sell for cash or on short credit to customers who will pay *him* promptly. All reform in this matter, to be thorough and lasting, must begin with the consumer. The sin of the credit system does not lie entirely on the shoulders of the jobbers and country traders. The farmer, the mechanic, the day labourer, the lawyer, doctor, and clergyman, all who run in debt instead of paying cash for the necessaries and the luxuries of life, are equally responsible for its existence. So long have all these classes of persons

been accustomed to pay their bills semi-annually, which practically means about once a year, that years would be required to revolutionise the present system. There is no bad
habit to which men cling with such obstinacy as to that of
getting and keeping in debt. Cigars, tobacco, "old Bourbon,"
may be exorcised with a far less struggle. No one trader in a
village can make any headway towards a cash or short credit
system, except by selling much cheaper than his rivals ; and it
is doubtful whether this is a sufficiently powerful temptation
to the mass of purchasers to buy for cash.

Another cause of failure is the prevalent indisposition to
look resolutely and squarely *at the real state of one's affairs.*
Instead of taking an account of stock every year, carefully
weighing and measuring all his goods, allowing for their deterioration or depreciation, and also for his bad debts—working
night and day, if need be, to ascertain his real position—the
hopeful man is only anxious to increase his business ; or, if he
stops to make an inventory and to see what his balance-sheet
will show, he refuses to classify his bills payable, counts them
all good, and values his merchandise at more than it will yield.
The changes in styles, and the fluctuations in the markets;
the overstock of goods not durable in quality ; the loss of interest, which is certain to accrue before the whole stock is sold ;
the worthlessness of some of his debtors, and the "shaky"
condition of others,—are circumstances which are carefully
noted by the shrewd and cautious trader, but which the over-
sanguine merchant never looks in the face. The result is, that
his profits, like those of the shopkeeper who made a thousand
dollars one night by simply marking up his goods to ten per
cent., are always on paper, never in greenbacks or gold. It is
a well-ascertained fact that insolvency is almost invariably accompanied by bad book-keeping. There is hardly one bankrupt in fifty who can tell with any exactness what has become
of the property which he has had in his possession, what he has
lost in his trade, and what he has spent in his family,—in short,
whose accounts are not in a muddle. Out of forty-one bankrupts' estates in Great Britain, as returned by an official
assignee, twenty-nine kept no proper books and eleven none at
all. Hence in that country, as in France and the Dominion
of Canada, every mercantile person is required by law to keep

proper books of account, without which, says a high authority, "it would be almost impossible to trace the insolvent's transactions in nine cases out of ten."

Again, a not infrequent cause of failures in business is *partnerships hastily and inconsiderately entered into* with men of whom little is known. It is astonishing how thoughtlessly men contract this relation with those by whose incompetency or knavery they may be suddenly ruined. But we have space only to hint at this, and pass to another fruitful cause of failures, namely, the *lack of liberality in business dealings.* Meanness in all its forms is despicable ; but especially in business matters, when it takes the form of scrubbism. There is no class of men who labour under a more perfect delusion than those who practise upon this principle ; who never risk a dollar to secure business, unless sure of getting it back again ; who never pay a cent for printer's ink, whether in circulars or advertisements ; and who think to get the weather-gauge of all mankind by cribbing sixpences from the bills they incur, passing shillings for quarters, and never giving dinners. It is true such persons meet sometimes with a degree of success which justifies their stinginess to themselves ; but in nine cases out of ten it will be found that they have succeeded *in spite* of that quality, its natural tendency being to drag them down. Their policy is like that of the farmer who sows three pecks of seed where he should sow five, and is recompensed for his leanness of soul by reaping ten bushels of grain instead of fifteen. An English shopkeeper made it a rule never to pay a porter for bringing a burden till the next day ; "for," said he, "while a fellow feels his back ache with the weight, he charges high ; but when he comes next day the feeling is gone, and he asks only half the money." This looks like shrewdness ; but never was a policy more suicidal. Selfishness is always self-defeating. When the author of such a sentiment gets wealth, it is not by his scrubbism, as he perhaps fancies, but by his industry, perseverance, caution, and other qualities that chance to be associated with his meanness, and which would insure far more brilliant results without it. There is an old English proverb that " a penny soul never came to two-pence " ; and when we consider how extreme narrowness in money-dealings disgusts the public, making enemies of those on whose good-will fortune greatly depends, and how fatal, too, is such narrowness to that spirit of enterprise which is necessary to a brilliant success, we shall not deem the old saw an exaggeration.

It is sometimes said that, if we would get on in the world we must look out for Number One, and be suspicious of our neighbours. "Till you know positively that he is honest, treat every man as if he were a rogue." Of this cynical and hardhearted maxim a late writer justly says: "If this were a condition of success, success would not be worth having,—nay, indeed, it would be wholly intolerable: commend me to a life of failure. But it is not a condition of success. To know an honest man from a rogue, and to act accordingly, is doubtless a great thing; but if we are to treat all mankind on our journey through life as rogues or honest men, why, I throw up my cap for the latter. We may be cheated, it is true; tricked, cozened, defrauded; and we may throw away that which, worthily bestowed, might have really contributed to our success. It is a serious matter to waste our strength, to squander, in this manner, the materials of success. Successful men, it may be said, do not make blunders of this kind. I am not quite sure of that; besides, who knows but that the strength may not be wasted, after all. A good deed, done in a good spirit, can never be thrown away. The bread cast upon the waters may return to us after many days. This at least I know, that if it be true, as I have said, that Providence helps those who help themselves, it is no less true that Providence helps those who help others. 'The liberal deviseth liberal things, and by his liberality shall he stand.' It was not meant that we should stand alone in the world. Whatsoever may be our strength, whatsoever our self-reliance, there are times and seasons when we need a helping hand; and how can we expect it to be stretched out to us, if we always keep our own in our pockets? And if we do not trust others, how can we hope to be trusted ourselves."

The history of business teems with illustrations of the brilliant results that flow from a generous, noble-minded policy. It was remarked of Lafitte, the celebrated Parisian banker, that though the generosity of his nature made him the dupe of whoever tried to impose upon him, he yet rose from the condition of a penniless clerk to be the first banker of his day, and one of the most eminent public characters of his country. His case

reminds one of the remark of Jenkinson in the " Vicar of Wake-
field," about his simple, kind-hearted neighbour, Flamborough,
whom he had contrived to cheat in one way or another once a
year; "and yet," said he, "Flamborough has been regularly
growing in riches, while I have come to poverty and a jail." A
similar case is that of a Mr. Fowler, a famous beer-brewer in
Scotland, who died very rich, and was believed to have owed
his wealth to a benevolent liberality of nature, which, taking a
professional direction, induced him to make his liquor unusually
good. He would go to his vats, and, tasting the infusion, say,
"Still rather poor, my lads; give it another cast of the malt."
By adhering to this course, he obtained the highest character as
a brewer, and in a few years had a large remunerative sale for
his ale throughout Great Britain, India, and the Colonies.

In a discussion some years ago by the directors of an English
railway about fares and arrangements for the public convenience, the chairman is said to have remarked that *a hard bargain
is ever a bad bargain for the apparent gainer,*—a maxim to which
all assented; and, as a consequence, its spirit being impressed
on the whole management of the line, a writer hazards the prophecy that the road will eventually be among the most prosperous in Europe. Such has been and ever will be the results
of a liberal, whole-souled policy. And is it not reasonable, and
only reasonable, that he should meet with the most triumphant
success in business who pursues his ends in this spirit, rather
than the picayune-minded dealer who adopts a selfish, extort-
ing policy? In the one case, it has been truly observed, it is
himself and a thousand minor influences wor ing to the end;
in the other, it is himself working to it, but a thousand secret
influences working against it. "Considering the difficulties
which they needlessly raise in their course, the successes of the
selfish are far more wonderful than those of the generous.
When, with competent prudence and skill, there is a genuine
natural suavity towards others, accompanied by a practical
liberality according to the measure of the understood means,
all works well, and ultimate triumph is certain; but the prosperity of the thorough scrub, attained amidst the contempt and
detestation of the public, can never be anything but a k'nd of
miracle when it occurs, and, far more probably, it is strained
after in vain."

Again, among the most fruitful causes of failures of this day is *the lack of enterprise.* We live in an age of progress, and among the proofs of it none is more striking than the change which has taken place within a few years in men's ideas touching mercantile education. That the time has come when the standard of that education should be raised, when a broader and severer culture should be exacted from the candidate for the counting-room, is conceded by the veriest fossils of the "old fogy" school of merchants. With all the keenness and sharp-sightedness of our business men, it cannot be denied that, till recently, they have thought more highly of shrewdness than of solid sense, and relied more on quick-wittedness, adroitness, and tact, than on a thorough knowledge of the laws of trade. For a long time circumstances were such as to exaggerate the value of the minor qualities of intellect, and the comic advice given some years ago by Blackwood to a trader only burlesqued an acknowledged fact. Following riches, argued "old Ebony," is like following wild-geese, and you must crawl after both on your belly ; the moment you pop up your head, off they go whistling before the wind, and you see no more of them. If you haven't the art of *sticking* by nature, it was said, you must acquire it by art ; put a couple of pounds of birdlime upon your office stool, and sit down upon it ; get a chain round your leg, and tie yourself to your counter like a pair of shop scissors ; nail yourself up against the wall of your place of business, like a weasel on a barn door or the sign of the spread eagle ; in short, only be a *sticker*, and you may get fat on a rock.

Such was the golden rule of business in the jog-trot days of " Auld Lang Syne," and almost in the present half-century. But besides this faith in the value of "sticking" talent, the ease with which blunders are repaired, and the broken arch of fortune reared again, overweening confidence in their versatility and power of self-transfer from one pursuit to another, and boundless confidence in the exhaustless fertility of their ingenuity, are all circumstances which have tended to lower the tone of culture among the merchants of this country. But now all is changed. The slow-plodding, illiterate, chicken-hearted merchant has had his day. The man who would be rich, and attain to eminence in his calling in this latter half of the nineteenth century, must discard the old-fashioned methods of getting on in the world, and be abreast with the times. A new epoch has been inaugurated, and all things are in a state of metamorphosis and revolution. Around us, on every side, the new is crowding aside the old, and "improvement" is the watchword of the day. Machinery deemed the perfection of ingenuity is transformed into old iron by new inventions; the new ship dashes scornfully by the naval prodigy of last year, and the steamer laughs at them both. The railroad engine, as it rushes by the crumbling banks of the canal, once regarded as a marvel, screams out its mockery at the barge rotting piecemeal. The cable of the electric telegraph reaches from continent to continent, and men's thoughts speed their lightning-like course below the monsters of the deep, and through realms where neither light nor sound has ever penetrated. Commerce has been leavened with the influences which have marked these mighty changes, and from a limited and easily comprehended has become a complicated and vast affair. It is no longer a mere dollar-and-cent traffic, requiring no apprenticeship; but a matter tasking the mind to the utmost, to be mastered only by the highest sagacity, and after the profoundest study of facts, circumstances, and prospects.

The growth of society, acting on the interests of trade, exacts from the merchant the broadest and severest culture. No judge or juror in civil or criminal case ever had to unravel testimony, to sift and weigh conflicting statements, more carefully than a great merchant has now to balance probabilities, and decide what and when it is best to buy and sell. Only the sharpest sagacity, the most far-reaching penetration, and the soundest judgment, will now enable one to discriminate between profitable and ruinous schemes of investment. A hundred things now affect the price of wheat, tobacco, sugar, cotton, wool, that once had no influence on their value. Within a few years articles once unknown, or deemed worthless, such as petroleum, ice, guano, etc., have created a new trade; and who can tell how far the list may yet be extended? The day has gone by when mere sagacity, dexterity, and tact would qualify a man to be a first-rate merchant. A knowledge of geography, political economy, the manners and customs of foreign countries, and a hundred other things, is indispensable; and heaven-born genius in turned-down collars is at a discount.

The times demand men of large, liberal, energetic soul; and the man who insists upon doing business in the old-fashioned, jog-trot, humdrum way is as much out of place as he who insists on travelling with an ox-team instead of by railway, or upon getting news by the old stage-coach instead of by the lightning telegraph. Under these circumstances, who can wonder that so many men who plunge into business without talents, training, or knowledge, fail to get on ?

Among the causes of mercantile failures there are some which are beyond the control of the merchant, and of these none is more disastrous than *bad and unstable legislation*. It is notorious that in no country in the world is legislation so changeful and vacillating as in the United States. Felix Grundy used to say, somewhat irreverently, that everything is foreknown but the verdict of a petit jury. He might have said, with more plausibility, "except the next Acts of Congress." Scarcely have our merchants and manufacturers adjusted their business to one policy respecting the tariff or the currency, than another policy is announced at Washington, and they find themselves making or selling goods at a ruinous loss. The conflicting views which have prevailed at different times regarding a National Bank, the Sub-Treasury System, Hard Currency, the Return to Specie Payments, the Protective System, have led to incessant changes in legislation, and made it impossible for the shrewdest merchant to forecast the future. Each political party undoes the legislation of its predecessor, and the result of this perpetual tinkering of the laws is that hundreds of capitalists are deterred from embarking in trade, while thousands who venture on its fickle sea are wrecked by financial hurricanes against which no human prudence can guard.

Still another cause of failures in business, and one the importance of which has been, perhaps, underestimated, is *the robbery by clerks of their employers*. Cases of this kind are becoming more and more common in this country, and unless something is done to arrest it, the cancer will soon have eaten into the very vitals of our mercantile society. How many establishments, doing a vast business, and seemingly prosperous, are rotten at the foundation in consequence of incessant, systematic peculation by clerks, it is impossible to estimate; but in almost every city sudden and startling failures ever and anon occur, whose secret cause is known to have been this, and this only. Confidential clerks in banking-houses in New York, who have maintained for years a stainless reputation for integrity, have been suddenly found to have robbed their employers of thousands and tens of thousands of dollars. A case occurred some time ago in Chicago, where a young man was found to have embezzled from his employer for years,—stealing not only money, but goods, on system, converting them into cash, and making regular deposits of the latter in a bank. In this case the thefts were practised with such adroitness and skill, and the whole physiognomy and demeanour of the thief, who was a clergyman's son, were so prepossessing and calculated to allay suspicion had he been suspected, that it is no wonder he baffled the ingenuity of his victim. But generally merchants and shopkeepers have themselves largely to blame when they are victimized.

Sometimes they half pay a clerk, calculating with great nicety the smallest pittance on which he can keep from starving, and then wonder that, in accepting such a situation, he should have calculated on making up the balance of fair wages from the pickings of the money-drawer. Then, again, a smart, showy appearance, a superficial varnish of politeness and a flood of small talk, are too often the ready passports to posts of trust and honour. Who can wonder that merchants are so often deceived, when they look less to the inner than to the outer man, less to the moral character of their employees than to the quality of their broadcloth or the graces of their manner, and never for an instant think of testing their honesty? The most desirable young men for clerks are not always the most prepossessing at first. There is an urbanity, the result of good principles and good breeding, which is instantly recognised by the practised eye, and which is rarely found dissociated from good sense and sterling integrity. This kind of politeness is not put on and off like a cloak, nor is it characterized by any of the dazzling fripperies of demeanour which distinguish the "swells" just referred to. Let employers learn to distinguish between the real article and the counterfeit; let them take no young man into their employment about whose antecedents they are not fully posted ; let them pay fair, even liberal, salaries ; and especially let them, so far as they can do so without establishing a system of espionage, which is always despicable, acquaint themselves with the conduct and pursuits of their officials *outside of the salesroom or counting-house*,—and they will not only save themselves from the loss of many dollars, perhaps from bankruptcy, but will prevent many a young man, trembling on the brink of temptation, from going headlong to ruin.

Finally, in addition to the causes of bankruptcy which we have mentioned might be added bad personal habits, such as intemperance, lack of punctuality, etc. ; the expenditure of capital in costly fixtures and expensive ornaments, " a device of rich old traders to monopolize a business by throwing obstacles in the way of men with limited capital ;" a lack of attention to details ; and many others upon which we have not space to dwell. But farther back—behind boundless credits, overtrading, speculation, luxurious living, and all the other causes which we have named or might name—is to be found the primary cause of mercantile failures, all these secondary ones being but the effect of elements lying deeper in the popular character. Mammon-worship,—devotion to " the almighty dollar,"—the intense, all-devouring ambition to be the Napoleon of the mart, the man who owns a greater amount of real estate, bank and railroad stocks, and solid cash or mortgages, than any other man on Change ; the impatience to attain to wealth by a few brilliant and daring strokes, instead of by tedious processes of labour and economy, by a few gigantic bounds, instead of by a slow and tedious up-hill journey ; the subordination of health and happiness, the highest interests of body and soul, to money, *money*, MONEY, which is made the end instead of the means of existence,—*this* is the root from which spring not merely the marvellous activity, but the giant vices, of the American mercantile character. The race after riches in this country is not a healthy, bracing race, but a steeplechase, a headlong, maddening rush. It is the rush of a forlorn hope to an " imminent deadly breach,"—to a breach in the citadel of Mammon with its defences of thick competition, mounds of bankruptcy, pitfalls of speculation, and files of bad debts, besieged by a magazine of capital, with the large artillery of wholesale business and the small guns of retail. The end and aim of each, captains and privates, is to be the first to mount the breach

and plant his victorious standard on the walls. Away with
the cold dictates of virtue and prudence and honour ! Fling
honesty to the winds. Extend no helping hand to your comrades sinking by your side. Think only of your own safety,
and less of that than of the glorious end you have in view,
Press on with all your energies, though the balls rain thick
and fast about your ears. Stop not to stanch your wounds.
Make a bridge, if necessary, of your dead and dying companions, and when you have carried the stronghold of Mammon,
plant your flag on its topmost battlement, look around with a
smile of triumphant satisfaction, and say, " *I'm ~ rich man !*"

CHAPTER XX.

OVERWORK AND UNDER-REST.

Steads not, to work on the clean jump,
Nor wine nor brains perpetual pump.—R. W. EMERSON.

The deepest-rooted cause of American disease is that overworking of the brain and over-excitement of the nervous system, which are the necessary consequences of their intense activity. Hence nervous dyspepsia, with consumption, insanity, and all its brood of fell disorders in its train. In a word, the American works himself to death.—JAMES STIRLING

The body has its claims,—it is a good servant; treat it well, and it will do your work; ....attend to its wants and requirements, listen kindly and patiently to its hints, occasionally forestall its necessities by a little indulgence, and your consideration will be repaid with interest. But task it and pine it and suffocate it, make it a slave instead of a servant, it may not complain much, but like the weary camel in the desert, it will lie down and die.—CHARLES ELAM, *A Physician's Problems.*

AN able London journal* has an article on the subject of Drudgery, in which it protests against the modern and absurd notion that work is an intrinsic good, or what moralists call an end. The modern revival of the dogma of the nobleness of work it thinks was well, but it has been pushed too far. The worship of work for its own sake it pronounces mere fetichism, and almost as pernicious an extreme as the antiquated and now comparatively unfashionable worship of idleness.

We deeply sympathise with this protest, which was never more urgently needed than at this hour. Everywhere men are killing themselves by overwork,—by intense, exhausting labour of hand and brain ; and the remonstrance has come not a moment too soon. The life of the present day is lived at fever-heat. There is a fierce struggle going on in all the departments of labour, and the mental wear and tear is enormous. Life, in all of the professions, is literally a battle, and men are falling by hundreds in the thick of the fight. The

* The "Saturday Review."

desire to get rich in a few years, the pride of doing "an im
mense business," or of being the leader of the bar or the medi
cal profession, leads thousands "to work double tides;" and
they go stumbling on, robbing themselves of sleep and rest
and play, till they break down into an insane asylum or into
the grave.

Welcome, then, to the later gospel, which proclaims that
work is not an end in itself, much less the highest earthly
good. Far nearer the truth is the doctrine of Moses and of
the most antient cosmogonists, that work is a primeval curse,
the result of sin. The curse may, indeed, like all human
afflictions, be turned into a blessing ; but a curse, nevertheless,
it is in itself, and only to be borne because the alternative
of idleness is infinitely worse. Work, when worshipped as it
sometimes is by its servants, or when compelled by avarice,
impatience, or early follies, too often degenerates into drudgery,
and its most enthusiastic eulogists will not pretend that it is
then a blessing. There is nothing in drudgery that is fitted
to produce happiness or beauty of character. On the contrary, its tendency is to mar all that is fair and lovely in the
most cultivated natures.

Of all the nations of the earth there is no one among whom
this doctrine of "grind" has taken deeper root than among us
Americans. From the days of the Puritans we have been ex-
cessively fond of work,—work, not as a means of getting a
living only, but in itself and for its own sake. It seems as if
we felt the primeval curse ever weighing upon us, and so we
continue to drudge like galley-slaves, even after we have provided for the ever-dreaded "rainy day," and the pressure of
bread-getting has long since passed. Hence we have so few
holidays and seasons of rest or recreation, that, when they do
come, we are quite perplexed to know what to do with ourselves. It is for the same reason that these days are grossly
abused by many in riotous dissipation, drunkenness, and otherwise swamping themselves with abominations ; for, as an old
writer says, those that seldom take lawful pleasure will take
unlawful, "and by lacing themselves too hard, grow awry
on one side." Others, again, alternate a long spell of excessive labour with a comparatively short spell of excessive repose,
—eleven months in the treadmill with one at Saratoga,—

which is about as rational as to maintain that a man who has taken a bottle of brandy one day and a quart of water the next has been drinking brandy and water.

When shall we learn that, as Aristotle long ago said, the end of labour is *to gain leisure :* and that hence it is possible to be just as immoderately and evilly addicted to work as to indulgence, and that an equal amount, though a different kind of mischief may accrue to one's self and family in one direction as in the other ? When will the old theological idea that mortals are sent here as a place of sore chastisement and mortification be scouted from our minds ? It is time that this everlasting drudgery should cease among us, and that some higher lesson should be impressed upon the brain of the infantile Yankee than the old saws about industry, money-getting, and the like. Let us abate something, at least, of our devotion to the almighty dollar, and regard the world as something better than a huge workshop, in which we are to toil and moil unceasingly, till death stops the human machine. Let us learn that the surest and best way to get on in the world is not to travel by "lightning lines" but " to hasten slowly." It is a libel on Providence to suppose that it has designed that we should live such a plodding, mechanical life, that we should be mere mill-horses treading evermore the same dull, unvarying round, and all for grist, grist, still grist, till we have become as blind and stupid as that most unhappy of all quadrupeds. Still more absurd it is to suppose that to work desperately, to be intensely employed, is in itself praiseworthy, even though it be about something that has no truth, beauty, or usefulness in it, and that makes no man happier or wiser. The truth is, that as one of the wisest of modern essayists has remarked, to work insatiably required much less mind than to work judiciously, and less courage than to refuse work that cannot be done honestly. "For a hundred men," says Arthur Helps " whose appetite for work can be driven on by vanity, avarice, ambition, or a mistaken notion of advancing their families. there is about one who is desirous of expanding his own nature, and the nature of others in all directions, of cultivating many pursuits, of bringing himself and those around him in contact with the universe in many points—of being a man, and not a machine."

"I shall die first a-top," was the mournful exclamation of Dean Swift, as he gazed on a noble oak whose upper branches had been struck by lightning; I shall be like that tree, *I shall die first a-top.*" Afflicted for years with giddiness and pain in the head, he looked forward with prophetic dread to insanity as the probable termination of his existence; and after nine years of mental and bodily suffering, the great satirist, the mighty polemic, the wit and the poet, died as he had feared and half predicted, " in a rage, like a poisoned rat in a hole."

" Dying at the top " is the disease to which a fearful number of Americans are to-day exposed. In the high-wrought state of civilization to which we have attained, hardly any complaint is more common than that of a brain overworked. The complaint is not uttered by literary men and scholars only, but is echoed by all who are striving for fame and fortune, against eager and formidable competitors. The lawyer, the clergyman, the merchant, the speculator—all are suffering from overwork ; from that strain of special faculties in the direction towards special objects, out of which comes nervous exhaustion, with the maladies consequent on overstimulus and prolongued fatigue. In every sphere of labour, the highest as well as the lowest, we behold on all sides men whose time and strength are completely absorbed by the effort to get a living for themselves and their families ; " mechanics whose life is one steady, unceasing grind in the treadmill of daily routine ; merchants who have become mere *attachés* of their counter, and clerks who are living appendages of their pens ; clergymen whose brains have been converted into a gland to secrete and discharge two sermons a week ; editors who have turned their wits into paragraphs until they are little else than walking items and talking squibs ; women who have sewed themselves into their garments until their life is but a thread."

It is in our great cities that this evil has reached the most fearful pass. A person living a quiet, leisurely life in the country can have no adequate conception of the severe and exhausting labours to which hundreds subject themselves in a second-rate city in his neighbourhood, especially in the higher walks of professional life ; nor can the inhabitant of such, groan as he may under his toils, conceive of the more burdensome duties of the corresponding classes in a great commercial centre. The brain of a leading lawyer, merchant, or business man is forever on the stretch. By day and by night he can think of nothing and dream of nothing but the iron realities of life. Anxious, perplexing thought sits on his brow as he rubs his eyes at daybreak; hurrying to the breakfast-table, he swallows his steak and his coffee in a twinkling, jumps up from his chair almost immediately, and, without having spoken a pleasant word, hastens away to the high courts of Mammon, to engage in the sharp struggle for pelf. There he spends hour after hour in calculating how to change his hundreds to thousands; dinner and supper—which he bolts, never eats—come and go almost without observation; even nightfall finds him still employed, with body and mind jaded, and eyes smarting with sleeplessness; till at length, far in the night, the toil-worn labourer seeks his couch, only to think of the struggles and anxieties of the day, or to dream of those of to-morrow. Thus things go on day after day, till the poor bond-slave of Mammon finds his constitution shattered; the doctor is summoned, and sends him to Europe; he travels listlessly;—he cannot leave thought behind him; the disease creeps on apace; the undertaker soon takes his dimensions in his mind's eye; paralysis seizes him; he lives a few years organically alive to *enjoy* the fruits of his labours, and then descends to his everlasting rest, with the glorious satisfaction, perhaps, of having gained, for his joyless days and sleepless nights, a larger "pile" than any other man on 'Change.

It has often been remarked by foreigners that the great fault of our American civilization is the terrible facility with which we exhaust life. There is no end to our ingenuity in devising plans to wear it out. We eat and drink it; we burn it with close stoves and furnaces; we blow it away in loud, vociferous talking; we exhaust it in business cares and anxieties; we smash it on railroads and drown it in steamers; we rack our invention for new ways of cutting it short. The hot, impetuous haste with which we live is the crying evil of the times. Society appears to be split into two great classes,—those who are over-anxious in the pursuit of wealth, passing their days in a ceaseless paroxysm of excitement and activity, and denying themselves all enjoyment but that of money-getting,—and those

U

thoughtless votaries of pleasure who squander their all upon
sensual enjoyment, plunge recklessly into debt, and are only
intent upon some new scheme of gratification or device to dodge
the sheriff. Between these two classes the pendulum is kept
always vibrating, and can never come to rest.

Travelling by steam at thirty miles an hour is but faintly
typical of the headlong hurry, the hot, panting haste, with which
in this country we pursue both business and pleasure. Our
very faces, furrowed with the lines of anxious thought, bear
impress of that intensity, that terrible earnestness, which is the
essence of our being. "Every American," says a late British
traveller, "looks as if his eyes were glaring into the far West
and the far future." Determined to get rich in a few months
or years, we cannot submit to the tedious process of adding one
year's patient legitimate gains to those of another, but seek by
gambling, by bold speculative combinations, by anticipation of
intelligence received by railway or steamer, to make or mar
ourselves by one bold stroke. It is no paradox to say that we
are in such a hurry to live, that living, in any true sense of the
term, becomes impossible. "Young America," especially,
scorns all limits, whether in the quest of business or pleasure.
As, when born poor, it must make a fortune in a day, so, if it
inherits wealth, it must circumnavigate the entire world of enjoyment in its gay pinnaces, with streamers flying and music
playing, before it is twenty-five. Even sleep is got through
impatiently by us, with frequent startings and consultations of
the watch, lest the morning hours be lost. We snore faster
than our fathers snored, and we grudge the hours spent in bed
as so many hours cut out of life. Our very diseases catch our
contagious haste ; the lingering consumption is growing less
and less frequent,—the instantaneous apoplexy and ossification
of the heart are taking its place. Our fevers, it is said, are running all to a low typhoid type, and men are continually sinking
down in the very noon-day of life from a mysterious lack of
vital force. Such a departure from life as that described by
Dryden two hundred years ago is now becoming more and more
phenomenal :—

> " Of no distemper, of no blast he died,
>   But fell like autumn fruit that mellowed long,
>   Even wondered at because he dropped no sooner.

> Fate seemed to wind him up for fourscore years,
> Yet freshly he ran on ten winters more,
> Till, like a clock worn out with beating time,
> *The wheels of weary life at last stood still."*

Instead of this, the toilers of to-day drop like Holmes's "one hoss shay," which

> "Went to pieces all at once,
> All at once, and nothing first,—
> Just as bubbles do when they burst,"

or, if they are permitted to linger on with a kind of death-in-life, the result of all this excitement is, by keeping the mind perpetually on the rack, to sap all the foundations of health, and pre-date old age. Hence in the great business marts are often witnessed, even in persons who have barely reached the middle of life, the haggard, care-worn face, sunken eye, hoary hair, and feeble gait, which properly belong to "weird eld." Nor can this result be surprising to those who reflect that, as a high medical authority has remarked, anxiety is but a chronic kind of fear, a sort of intermittent fever and ague, which as manifestly disorders the circulation and secretions as that which arises from the poisonous malaria of the marshes—the latter being scarcely more deadly than that of the market in these days of desperate speculation and all-grasping monopoly.

Who will say that such a life has been spent as God designed? Can there be a more pitiful failure than when the means of happiness thus swallow up the end? Were suffering to follow instantly upon the heels of transgression, were the account to be settled with Nature daily, few persons would violate her laws. Unfortunately for such fanatical devotees of business, she runs up long accounts with her children, and, like a chancery lawyer, seldom brings in "that little bill" till the whole subject of litigation has been eaten up. The poor devotee of Mammon, who thought to outwit her, finds at last that she is a most accurate book-keeper; that, neglecting nothing, she has set down everything to his credit and debited him with everything, that not the eighth part of a cent has escaped her notice; and though the items are small, yet, added up, they show a frightful balance against him and he finds himself, at forty or fifty, physically bankrupt, a broken-down, prematurely old man.

So frequent is the spectacle of strong men breaking down midway in life's race, that it may be doubted whether the best guaranty of a long life is not a feeble constitution. The men of iron frames and lignum-vitæ nerves, of muscles wrought of the the heart of oak, of giant energy and herculean endurance, are the very men who presume upon the inexhaustibility of the physical capital, and soonest become bankrupt in vitality.

This madness, this *self-killing*—for self-killing it is, as truly as if he were to cut a vein, and drain away his own life-blood, drop by drop—is less astonishing in the case of the merchant than in that of the professional man and the scholar, who makes the acquisition of knowledge the principal end of life. The latter are, or ought to be, thoroughly acquainted with the laws of physiology ; and yet the facts show that they are either ignorant of its most elementary principles or lack the self-command to act upon them. Not long since an English journal related of a leading barrister, that he acquired an income of fifteen thousand pounds, but was every night so completely exhausted by his labours, that for several hours after their cessation, he could not be addressed or approached without experiencing the acutest nervous distress. How many lawyers in our own large cities break down just as they have acquired a full mastery of the intricate science of jurisprudence, and when their faculties of mind and body should be in the highest vigour ! How many clergymen are physically insolvent, mere wrecks of their former selves, at forty ! And the scholar—who that is familiar with literary biography, does not know that half of the languages of Europe may be mastered, while the prodigy that has stuffed himself with so much learning, knows not, or seems not to know, that by perpetual study, without out-door exercise, he is committing a slow suicide ?

When Leyden, a Scotch enthusiast of this stamp, was warned by his physician of the consequences, if he continued, while ill with a fever and liver-complaint, to study ten hours a day, he coolly replied: "Whether I am to live or die, *the wheel must go round to the last. . . . .* I may perish in the attempt, but if I die without surpassing Sir William Jones a hundred-fold in Oriental learning, let never a tear for me profane the eye of a borderer." No wonder that he sank into his grave in his thirty-sixth year, the victim of self-murder. Alexander Nicolly, a

Professor of Hebrew at Oxford, who, it was said, could walk to the wall of China without an interpreter, died a few years ago at the same age, chiefly from the effects of intense study ; and Dr. Alexander Murray, a similar prodigy, died at thirty-eight of the same cause. Sir Humphry Davy, in the height of his fame, nearly killed himself by the excessive eagerness with which he prosecuted his inquiries into the alkaline metals, pursuing his labours in the night till three or four o'clock, and even then often rising before the servants of the laboratory. Excessive application threw Boerhave into a delirium for six weeks ; it gave a shock to the powerful frame of Newton ; it cut short the days of Sir Walter Scott, and it laid in the grave the celebrated Weber, whose mournful exclamation, amid his multiplied engagements, is familiar to many an admirer of his weird-like music : " Would that I were a tailor, for then I should have a Sunday's holiday." It was the same cause which struck down Sir William Hamilton in his fifty-sixth year with paralysis, and ended the life of the most brilliant and influential of American journalists, Mr. Raymond, in a cerebral crash at the early age of forty-nine. The effects of such toil in this country are far more disastrous than in Europe, for owing to climate and other agencies, work of every kind is more exhausting here than there.

It is related of Sir Philip Sidney, that, when at Frankfort, he was advised by the celebrated printer, Languet, not to neglect his health during his studies, "lest he should resemble a traveller who, during a long journey, attends to himself but not to his horse." When will professional men, business men, and scholars act upon this homely but sensible advice ? What can be more crazy than the conduct of a traveller who, having a journey of five hundred miles to perform, which he can rightly perform only at the rate of fifty miles a day, lashes his horse into a speed of a hundred, at the risk of breaking him down in mid-journey ? We are aware of the excuses given for this insanity. We know very well that the poor bond-slave of business pretends that he *must* overdraw his bank account with nature,—though every draft will have ultimately to be repaid with compound interest,—in order to maintain his position in society or on 'Change, and that the intellectual slave, besides this reason, will plead the deep enjoyment he finds in unceasing work or study. But it is simply absurd for any man to state that he is *compelled* to maintain a particular status in society, that he *must* move in this or that circle, that he *must* challenge this or that degree of respect from those around him. The argument is just that by which the Swartwouts, the Schuylers, and the whole race of swindlers, embezzlers, and defaulters, have defended and excused their crimes. There is nothing but a wretched vanity underlying all these pretences ; and he who, to gratify so low a passion, deliberately overtasks his bodily and mental energies year after year from January to December, need not be astonished if, like Swift, he suddenly find himself "dying a-top," or if the verdict of the public, the coroner's jury at large, should be, after the release of his weary spirit from the more weary body, *Died by his own hand.*

There is occasionally a business man who candidly admits that this intense and unremitting devotion to affairs, without rest or relaxation, is but a species of slavery ; but he will tell you that it is but temporary, that he endures it for the present in the hopes of earning a competency which will enable him at some day to purchase an exemption from these drudgeries. The grinding toil, the harassing cares, the exhausting brain-work, the tedious, ever-dreary monotony of the present, he cheerfully submits to, in consideration of a future which will make up for it all in one long playday,—in an indefinite period, of repose, elegant leisure, and luxurious enjoyment.

But who needs to be told how uniformly such expectations are doomed to disappointment ? Life slips through the fingers of such persons unfelt, unenjoyed, in the bustle and hurry-scurry of preparing to live. In nineteen cases out of twenty the competency, for the attainment of which such sacrifices are made, is never realized ; and even the envied few who are successful find the period of leisure, when it comes, to be one of even more misery than enjoyment. Nature, as we have already said, cannot be outraged with impunity. Though a generous giver, she is a hard bargainer; and invariably, in the long run, the man who works double tides, who crowds the work of forty years into twenty, and burns his candle at both ends, will find that he will accomplish less by attempting to over-match or cheat Nature, than by accepting her own terms. The mind is monarch of the body ; but, if it ever so far forgets itself as to trample upon its slave, the slave will not be generous enough to forgive the injury, but will rise and smite its oppressor. In all likelihood, the man who toils and moils at business, without relaxation or enjoyment, through the best years of life, with the hope of retiring at last and making the evening of life all holiday, all play, will never retire, except into an untimely grave. But grant that he is what the world calls "successful," that by ceaseless toil and self-denial he gains the high-table land which a fixed position, competency, and settled relations in life may be said to form,—who does not know what almost invariably follows, when the stimulus which has thus far goaded him up the steeps of business has lost its power? *Ennui*, world-weariness, sadness of soul and countenance, doubts "if the play be worth the candle," impatience and restlessness,—in short, all those ailments, partly mental and partly physical, which the French sum up in the expressive phrase, *maladie de quarante ans*, seize upon him, and body and mind, deprived of their wonted occupation, break down. The history of society is full of examples of retired citizens vainly seeking, in frivolous amusements and hobbies, the means of agreeably whiling away their time, until at length, unable any longer to endure a vacuity for which they are unprepared, they find it necessary to return to their former business, if not intercepted by a death of sheer *ennui* and disgust.

Nor is there anything strange in such a result. After intense and prolonged labour, rest is delightful; but after the feeling of exhaustion is gone, nothing is more irksome than enforced idleness. Who does not remember Charles Lamb's letter to Wordsworth, in which the prisoner of the India-House paints so vividly his misery on being released from his drudgery? "I wandered about, *thinking* I was happy, and *feeling* I was *not*. Holidays, even the annual month, were always uneasy joys, with their conscious fugitiveness, the craving after making the most of them. *Now, when all is holiday, there are no holidays*. I can sit at home, in rain or shine, without a restless impulse for walkings." No one who understands the force of habit would, for a moment, expect that, after having spent twenty or thirty years of his life in a round of ceaseless activity. a man could break off without giving his physical system a shock; nor is it more surprising that, after having, in his exclusive devotion to business, neglected entirely the cultivation of his mental faculties, and thus having no inward resources to fall back upon, he should fall a prey to *ennui* and melancholy, and end his days, like the Hebrew sage, in declaring all to be vanity and vexation of spirit.

But, it will be urged by another class of workers, fearful as it is to see "the fiery soul o'er-informing its integument of clay," the sword wearing out the scabbard, yet it is better, surely, to wear out than to rust out ; better to drudge at the grimiest toil than to swing in the hammock of laziness and doze life away ; better, far better, that the ship should be shivered upon the rocks, or go down beneath the waters, than rot ingloriously at the wharves ! The value of a life depends upon the amount and value of the work done, not upon the number of days to which it is prolonged. Did not Goethe deem Schiller happy in that he died in the full vigour of his days ? Is there not, as one has said, a vast difference between a half-life and half a life, considering that one may trickle through a hundred years, the other may be concentrated by force of great occasion within the limits of an hour ? Do not some men have

> " The life of a long life
> Distilled to a mere drop, falling like a tear
> Upon the world's cold cheek, to make it burn
> Forever,"

and die hoary at twenty, or like Pope, become " sexagenarian at sixteen ?"

There is much force in these suggestions, though it may be replied that these earnest and terrible workers, who have compressed the work of threescore and ten years in a half-dozen or a dozen, might have done more for themselves and for mankind, had they rested oftener and given more time to social enjoyment. That work is more likely to be well done which is done with the judgment, wisdom, and poise—above all with the reserved power—which age gives. We can estimate the loss to the world occasioned by the early death of Mr. Buckle ? Of what priceless value would ten or twenty years more of life have been to such a scholar and thinker ! Generations may elapse before another literary labourer of industry so tireless, and so colossal a capacity for generalizing colossal acquirements, shall appear to complete the noble fragment he has left us.

It is doubtless true, also, that there are men of intellectual tastes so constituted that with them overwork is a necessary choice of evils. The man whose friends deplore that he is killing himself, often bears that within him which would more ignobly kill him, if he did not throw himself impetuously into the intellectual struggle, and thus withdraw his thoughts, for a time at least, from the " Bluebeard chambers of the heart." How often do men throw themselves into the whirlpool of intellectual excitement, as a relief from deep mental anguish ! Burton, a hypochondriac, wrote the " Anatomy of Melancholy," that marvel of learning, and protracted his life to the age of sixty-four. Without mental labour, sometimes of a severe and almost compulsory character, it may be doubted whether Cowper constitutionally so gloomy-minded, would have reached the verge of seventy. Besides, there is often an enchantment, a witchery and fascination, in literary labour, which renders cessation therefrom more distressing, perhaps, than even the results of overwork.

" I must write to empty my mind," said Byron, "or go mad." When Sir Walter Scott was warned by his medical advisers, after his first attack of apoplexy, that if he persisted in working his brain his malady must inevitably recur with redoubled severity, he replied : "As for bidding me not work, Molly might as well put the kettle on the fire, and say, ' *Now don't boil.*' . . . . I foresee distinctly that if I were to be idle I should go mad." Go mad he did, from excessive labour ; but not till after many a warning and presentiment of the attack of which he died. Years before his death the reluctant conviction forced itself on the mind of his son-in-law, Mr. Lockhart, that the mighty magician of the pen was losing something of his energy. Though the faculties were there, and occasionally blazed forth with their old meridian splendour, yet his sagacious judgment and matchless memory were frequently at fault :—

> " Among the chords the fingers strayed,
> And an uncertain warbling made."

Ever and anon he paused and looked around him, like one half waking from a dream mocked with shadows. The sad bewilderment of his gaze showed a momentary consciousness that, like Samson in the lap of the Philistine, "his strength was passing from him, and he was becoming weak, like unto other men." Then came the strong effort of aroused will. The clouds dispersed as if before a resistless current of pure air; all was bright and serene as of old; and then the sky was shrouded again in yet deeper darkness, till at last the night of death closed the scene. It is said that Dr. Samuel Johnson, whose intellectual as well as his moral structure was grand and powerful, passed all his days in the dread of a similar intellectual eclipse.

How many literary labourers in our own country,—how many merchants and business men generally,—are hurrying on to a similar goal! What shall they do to counteract the fearful effects of brain weariness? Shall they be counselled for the thousandth time to take exercise,—to take long walks and breathe fresh air? Unfortunately, exercise, taken consciously and for its own sake, with no ulterior aim, does no good. The mere act of walking till the nerves have registered a certain amount of muscular fatigue, above all, a dull melancholy walk without company, degenerates into a task, and gives no relief to the mind. A man might as well train himself for a game of base-ball or a cricket-match by a night's hard study, as try to recruit his overtasked mind by a five-mile stretch on the public road. Besides, all such attempts at physical improvement, however heroically kept up for a few days or weeks, are sure of a speedy end. Shall the sufferer try the gymnasium? That, too, has been tested thoroughly, and even the most enthusiastic of its early glorifiers are now ready to admit that it has been found wanting. Gymnastics may do for boys whose frames have not yet been hardened, but are utterly unfit for grown persons, especially for hard thinkers. The hurtfulness, the exhaustion, which such recreations produce, is absolutely incompatible with much brain-work. Every man has a certain fixed amount, or capital stock, of strength; and few have so much that it will admit of being taken out at at both ends, head and heels at once. The total neglect of exercise is hardly more deleterious than too much rushed through perfunctorily. It is simply absurd to think that violent exertions for a couple of hours can atone for the want of a constant supply of fresh air; and still more to think that we can save our candle by burning it at both ends instead of at one only. Nature is not thus to be outwitted. The proper remedy for a period of unhealthy living is not working double tides, not an hour or two occupied in drawing off the remaining strength of an overtaxed system, but, as a sensible writer has observed, now and then an entire day or week or month given to renovation and merely physical improvement. In the intervals, such exercise as is taken ought to be of an easy and amusing rather than of a laborious kind. Such a change as society affords is of more value than muscular activity. But vacations, frequent holidays, though but for a day, are the true safety-valves of professional men; and he who grants himself occasional rest will not only live longer, but do more work, than he who drudges in the office, counting-room, or study from January to December.

Again, one of the worst results of overworking the brain in any exclusive direction is, that it tends, when it does not absolutely break down that organ, to produce mental deformity. As the nursery-maid who carries her burden with one hand exclusively is afflicted with spinal curvature, so the thinking man who gives his intellectual energies to one subject or class of subjects gets a twist in his brains. Those persons, therefore, who are chained to mental labour and cannot give the brain repose, should try to vary their labours, which is another form of repose. "Intense and prolonged application to one subject," says a writer, "is the root of all the mischief. As your body may be in activity during the whole of the day, if you vary the actions sufficiently, so may the brain work all day at varied occupations. Hold out a stick at arm's length for five minutes, and the muscles will be more fatigued than by an hour's rowing : the same principle holds good with the brain." There is truth in this; yet it must be remembered that even where mental labour is thus varied, there is a limit beyond which the brain cannot be safely tasked. Lands need to lie fallow, and so do brains. You may rest oftentimes by simply changing your work, as the boy at the grindstone rests by changing hands ; but the man who gets *all* his head-rest that way will suffer as truly as the boy who, with either hand, attempts an unceasing grind. To reconcile health with perpetual work, however ingeniously varied, demands, not a human constitution, not even that of a Hercules, but one of lignum-vitæ or iron

CHAPTER XXI.

TRUE AND FALSE SUCCESS.

We do not choose our own parts in life, and have nothing to do with those parts. Our simple duty is confined to playing them well—EPICTETUS

I confess that increasing years bring with them an increasing respect for men who do not succeed in life, as those words are commonly used.—G. S. HILLARD.

> To know
> That which before us lies in daily life
> Is the prime wisdom.—MILTON.

The heart of a man is a short word, a small substance, scarce enough to give a kite a meal; yet great in capacity, yea, so indefinite in desire that the round globe of the world cannot fill the three corners of it! When it desires more, and cries, "Give, give!" I will set it over to the infinite good, where the more it hath it may desire more, and see more to be desired. —BISHOP HALL

O, keep me innocent! make others great.—QUEEN CAROLINE MATILDA, *of Denmark.*

The world will be blind, indeed, if it does not reckon amongst its great ones such martyrs as miss the palm but not the pains of martyrdom, heroes without the laurels, and conquerors without the jubilation of triumph.—J. H. FRISWELL, *The Gentle Life.*

IN the preceding chapters we have endeavoured to furnish the beginner in life with some useful directions touching the art of "getting on in the world," illustrating our hints by examples of men who have succeeded and of men who have failed. In conclusion, it should be remembered that success in life is to be regarded as a means, not as an end; and that therefore there is such a thing possible as *unsuccessful success,*—such a thing as gaining every end, while the whole *life* has been a failure. For what is this success, to which we have been trying to point out the path? Viewed in the light of another world,—of that measureless existence compared with which this earthly one is but a point,—what is it, after all, but a comparatively vulgar, paltry affair? Is it anything for which a man should crawl in the dust, degrade himself in his own estimation, do violence to the divine principle within him, or stoop to the smallest mean or dishonourable action ?   Is life a scrub-race, where, at every hazard, though you have to blind the man on your right and trip the one on your left, you must struggle to come out ahead ?   Shall we subscribe to that dangerous materialism running throughout American life, which preaches that money is the great end and evidence of the possession of intellect, that a man must be a failure unless he culminates in the possession of a check-book,—a belief worthy only of a people prepared to accept " Poor Richard's " maxims as a New Testament ?   Were we sent into the world simply, in the slang phrase of the day, "to win a pile ? "   And when we have a competence, shall we sacrifice health, peace, conscience, that we may boast of our hundreds of thousands, though we know that incessant fear and nervous anxiety are often the shadows that surround the glittering heap ?   Is it nothing to have a conscience void of offence, a face that never turns pale at the accuser's voice, a bosom that never throbs at the fear of exposure, a heart that might be turned inside out and discover no stain of dishonour ?

But perhaps you regard popularity as the great test of success; you covet the *digito pretereuntium monstrari ;* you would be the focus of all eyes, " the observed of all observers," though of that kind of honour, as Cowley says, " every mountebank has more than the best doctor, and the hangman more than the lord chief justice of a city."   Then you live a life only in others' breath ; your happiness depends on every turn of the weathercock ; you are at the mercy of every wind that blows. Are you the lion of to-day, because you have burnt the heart of the world with your ardent soul ?   I am the lion to-morrow, because I balance myself on a wire over the dizzy chasm of Niagara, and you are quite forgotten.   The confounding of excellence with pecuniary success or a seat in Congress is both absurd and immoral.   Was the divinest life ever led on this earth a success, humanly speaking ?   And are you entitled to pronounce your fellow-man, who has humbly tried to copy it, a cipher, because he has not, like you, courted applause, and made some little nook or corner of the earth ring with his name ?   Has not many a man been a blessing to the world who has made no noise in it, and who has died a beggar ?   And have not thousands died rich in goods or reputation, who were intellectually and morally bankrupt? Is it not too true of the road of ambition, that, as another has said, "the higher it ascends the more difficult it becomes, till at last it terminates in some elevation too narrow for friendship, too steep for safety, too sharp for repose, and where the occupant, above the sympathy of man and below the friendship of angels, resembles in the solitude if not the depth of his sufferings a Prometheus chained to the Caucasian rock?"

Whatever you will pay the price for, you can have in this world,—that is the rule. Be rich or popular, if you choose,—bringing all your faculties, as did Bonaparte his forces, to bear upon one point, and letting your intellectual and moral nature lie fallow. But do not arrogate too much on the strength of this vulgar success ; do not expect admiration and applause, or even a tacit assent to your claims, from those who are accustomed to look below the surface. Do not deem yourself authorized to pity those who prefer incorruptible treasures to a balance at their banker's,—the "pearl of great price" to the jewel that sparkles on the finger,—and who have been successful as *men*, though they may have failed as lawyers, doctors, and merchants. The possession of 5-20 bonds, and mortgages, and corner lots does not always and necessarily reward virtuous industry ; "a play, a book, a great work, an architect, or a general, may owe success simply to the bad taste of the times ; and, again, non-success in any candidate may arise from a conscience too clear and sensitive, a taste too good and too nice, a judgment too discriminative, a generosity too romantic and noble, or a modesty too retiring." There is no possible valuation of human character which would make the slightest show in the stock-list ; and hence success, truly understood, must be sought, not in what we *have*, but in what we *are*.

All experience shows that the greatest and most continued favours of fortune cannot of themselves, make a man happy nor can the deprivation of them render altogether miserable the possessor of a clear· conscience and a well-regulated mind. Goethe, who seems to have been born to show how little genius, health, honour, influence and worldly goods can do to make a man happy, confessed that he had not, in the course of his life, enjoyed five weeks of genuine pleasure ; and a famous caliph, looking back over a brilliant reign of fifty years, found that he had enjoyed only fourteen days of pure and unalloyed happiness. An ingenious Frenchman has even written an able book to prove that no change in any man's external circumstances, bating the case of absolute indigence, can alter a man's essential feelings of comfort and happiness for more than three months. Such cynicism, which, if universal would put a sudden stop to all the wheels of the world's industry, can have but few converts; men will still continue, in spite of all the croakings of moralists, to crave and toil and struggle for the world's prizes; and it must be confessed that, in spite of all drawbacks, success, even in this vulgar sense, *is* a desirable thing. Money, and a pleasant home, and freedom from economical cares, books and pictures, travel in foreign lands, the society of cultivated and elegant men and women, the respect of the world, and the best viands, are all solid advantages, which none covet more than those who affect to despise them. Life is certainly a journey and a pilgrimage, but "if it were only a journey of a single night, travelling first-class would be incomparably more comfortable than travelling third." It is therefore a great saying that "heaven is probably a place for those who have failed on earth,"—for the

> "Delicate spirits, pushed away
> In the hot press of the noonday."

Do you ask, then, what you shall aim at in life? We answer, as we began: Aim to act well your part, for therein lies all the honour. Every man has a mission to perform in this world, for which his talents precisely fit him, and, having found what this mission is, he must throw into it all the energies of his soul, seeking its accomplishment, not his own glory. As Goethe wisely says: "Man is not born to solve the problem of the universe, but to find out what he has to do, and to restrain himself within the limits of his power of comprehension." Having found out what you have to do,—whether to lead an army or to sweep a crossing, to keep a hotel or to drive a hack, to harangue senates or address juries or prescribe medicines,—do it with all your might, because it is your duty, your enjoyment, or the very necessity of your being.

Are your intellectual endowments small, and do you despond

because your progress must be slow?   Remember that, if you
have but one talent, you are responsible only for *its* wise employment.   If you cannot do all you wish, you can at least do
your best ; and, as Dr. Arnold says, if there be one thing on
earth which is truly admirable, it is to see God's wisdom blessing an inferiority of natural powers, when they have been
honestly, truly and zealously cultivated.   Remembering that
the battle of life cannot be fought by proxy, be your own
helper, be earnest, be watchful, be diligent, and, if you do not
win success, you will have done the next best thing,—you will
have deserved it.

Is your calling one which the world calls mean or humble?
Strive to ennoble it by mixing brains with it as Opie did with
his colours.   Show by the spirit that you carry into it, that to
one who has self-respect, an exalted soul, the most despised
profession may be made honourable ; that, as we have already
said, it is the heart, the inspiring motive, not the calling, that
degrades ; that the mechanic may be as high-minded as the
poet, the day-labourer as noble as the artist.   It is related of the
celebrated Boston merchant, William Gray, that having, on a
certain occasion, censured a mechanic for some slovenly work,
the latter, who had known Mr. Gray when he was in a very
humble position, bore the rebuke with impatience : " I tell you
what, Billy Gray, I sha'n't stand such words from *you*.   Why,
I recollect you when you were nothing but a drummer in a
regiment!"   "And so I was," replied Mr. Gray, "so I was a
drummer ; but didn't I drum *well*, eh?—didn't I drum *well*?"
In the words, then, of Schiller :—

> "What shall I do lest life in silence pass?"
> And if it do,
> And never prompt the bray of noisy brass,
> What need'st thou rue?
> Remember aye the ocean deeps are mute;
> The shallows roar ;
> Worth is the ocean—Fame is the bruit
> Along the shore.
>
> "What shall I do to be forever known?"
> Thy duty ever !
> "This did full many who yet sleep unknown,"—
> Oh ! never, never !
> Think'st thou perchance that they remain unknown
> Whom thou know'st not ?

By angel trumps in heaven their praise is blown,
   Divine their lot.

"What shall I do to gain eternal life?"
   Discharge aright
The simple dues with which each day is rife?"
   Yea, with thy might.
Ere perfect scheme of action thou devise,
   Will life be fled;—
While he who ever acts as conscience cries
   Shall live, though dead.

INDEX.

INDEX.

A.

Ability generally finds recognition, 2¢, 53.

Accuracy, 161, 162.

Adam, Dr. Alexander, teacher, 203.

Adams, John, 50.

Adams, John Quincy, his punctuality, 165; his economy of time, 258.

Addison, his failure as Secretary of State, 118; his painstaking, 215, 220.

Adrian VI., Pope, 90.

Advantages, 192.

Adversity a blessing, 192-194.

Æschylus, 63.

Agassiz, naturalist, 191; on money-making, 271.

Ainsworth, Robert, his destroyed M.SS., 213.

Alexander, Dr. J. W., on sermons, 74; on faith, 56; on bits of knowledge, 262.

Alexandre, glove-maker, 95.

Allen, Andrew Jackson, 103.

Americans, too o.ten jacks-at-all-trades, 70; an imitative people, 97, 98; their impatience, 244; their haste to get rich, 289; their lack of individuality, 93; their fast living, 313, 314.

Angelo, Michael, 47; his love for his art, 68; his application, 214, 222; his proposal to fortify Florence, 235.

Application, 158-159.

Archimedes, 91, 262.

Argyle, Duke of, his elocution, 142.

Arkwright, Richard, inventor, 90.

Aristotle, his attention to bodiculture, 59.

Arnault, on rest, 259.

Arnold, Dr. Thomas, of Rugby, his politeness, 150; on energy, 183; on inferior abilities, 328.

Assurance, 172-177, 179.

Astor, John Jacob, 273.

Asylums, often an evil, 88.

Audubon, his destroyed drawings, 213.

Aurelius, Marcus, 259.

B.

Bach, John Sebastian, 44.

Bacon, Lord, 48; on books, 116; his moral weakness, 118; his note-books, 216; contrasted with Macaulay, 233; on riches, 271.

Balzac, 204.

Barrow, Dr. Isaac, 60; his studiousness, 217; his mental grasp, 233.

Beecher, Henry Ward, on mental power, 56; on manner, 138; his Indiana pastorate, 205; his drill in elocution, 223.

Beecher, Dr. Lyman, 223.

Bembo, Cardinal, 219.

Bentham, Jeremy, on happiness, 110; on habit, 154.

Beethoven, on Rossini, 87; his ignorance of finance, 119; his poverty, 119.

Bellamy, Dr., on sermons, 245.

Bentley, Dr. Richard, 69; his Phalaris controversy, 237-238.

Béranger, 219.

Blair, Dr. Hugh, his advice to Boswell, 80.

Blucher, Marshal, his decision, 134; his will, 190; his defeat at Ligny, 235.

Boerhave, 317.

Boileau, his failure as a lyrist, 69.

Bolingbroke, Lord, 115.

Bonner (of the N. Y. *Ledger*), 96.

Boswell, James, 80.

Boyle, Hon. Charles, 237.

Braham, vocalist, 77.

Brandreth, Dr., 96.

Briggs, Gov., of Mass., on failures, 287.

Brindley, engineer, 115.

Brooks, James, 206–207.
Brooks, Peter C., 293.
Brougham, Lord, his physical vigour,
63, 64; his universality, 79; on
Napoleon's attention to details, 108;
his perseverance, 187.
Brown, Dr. John, on presence of mind,
130.
Browne, Sir Thomas, on the world's
rulers, 115.
Brummell, Beau, 27, 28, 48.
Brunelleschi, architect, his attention
to details, 106.
Brydges, Sir Egerton, 232.
Buckle, Henry Thomas, 320.
Buffon, on invention, 36; on genius,
159; on style, 219.
Bulwer, Sir Henry L., on Mackintosh,
132, 133.
Burke, Edmund, his masterpiece, 18;
his early struggles, 84; his labo-
riousness, 217; his "Letter to a
Noble Lord," 220.
Burnett, Bishop, 217.
Burns, Robert, his boyhood, 45; his
bodily vigour, 63; his politeness,
151; on gathering gear, 277.
Burr, Aaron, his manners, 142; his
will, 208.
Burritt, Elihu, 258.
Burton, Robert, 40, 321.
Business, a means of mental training,
156, 157; changes of, 294.
Business habits, 153–170.
Business men not machines, 156, 157.
Butler, Bishop, 78.
Butler, Cyrus, merchant, 146.
Butler, Samuel, his common-place
book, 215; his imitators, 99.
Buxton, Sir Fowell, his advice to be-
ginners, 89, 90; on will, 183.
Byron, Lord, his imitators, 102, 103;
his irritability, 185; his first poem,
189; his motive for writing, 321.

C.

Cady, Daniel, his attention to details,
106.
Cæsar, Julius, on luck, 31; described
by De Quincey, 37; his power of
will, 181.
Calhoun, John C., 48; his faith in
himself, 92; his power of attention,
158.

Callings, all equally honourable, 15.
Campbell, Sir Colin, his decision, 134.
Campbell, Lord, 201.
Canning, George, his imprudence, 73,
74; as a gentleman, 146.
Camden, Lord, 200.
Cano, Alonzo, sculptor, 221.
Capitalists are public stewards, 271–
273.
Carlyle, Thomas, on poverty and toil,
84; his lack of courtesy, 150; on
work, 212; his destroyed M.SS.,
213.
Carnot, statesman, 48.
Caylus, Count, 41.
Cecil on method, 159.
Chalmers, Dr. Thomas, his politeness,
151.
Chambers, William and Robert, 95.
Chantrey, sculptor, 48.
Charity, 82, 83.
Charlemagne, 116.
Charles V., Emperor, his indecision,
131; on Philip II., 134.
Chatham, Lord, his manner, 142; on
impossibilities, 190; his painstak-
ing, 215; his magnetism and will,
232.
Chatterton, Thomas, 48.
Chaucer, 63.
Cheerfulness, 211, 212.
Chesterfield, Lord, on choice of a calling, 46; his son, 46; on manner,
137, 146; on the Duke of Argyle, 142; his elocution, 143; on
genius, 159; his translations, 214.
Choate, Rufus, his power of concentration, 74; his advice to advo-
cates, 74; his legal conflicts, 207;
his waste of strength, 250.
Chitty, barrister, on qualifications for
the bar, 198.
Cicero, on luck, 30; his attention to
physical culture, 59; his versatility,
68, 217.
Circumstances as a cause of failure,
26, 37, 91; the power of, 30; often
controllable, 32, 36; the stepping-
stones to success, 33, 91.
Civility defined, 149, 150; where found,
149, 150; implies self-sacrifice, 151;
how acquired, 152; a fortune of itself, 137: a real ornament, 144.
Clarke, Dr. Adam, 60, 202; on "too
many irons," 79.

Clarkson, Thomas, 45, 90.

Clay, Henry, his practice in oratory, 223.

Clergymen, their need of broad culture, 246; should economize their strength, 250.

Clerks, 305.

Clough, Arthur, 91.

Cobden, Richard, 90, 187.

Coleridge, S. T., his lack of concentration, 79; his indecision, 129; on method, 160; discovery of the "Arabian Nights," 263.

Colfax, Vice-President, 249.

Coligny, Admiral, his pluck, 36; his indecision, 131.

Collingwood, Lord, on whiling away time, 260, 261.

Colton, C. C., on ennui, 41.

Commerce, its present characteristics, 302-305.

Competition, 12, 24.

Concentration, 66-82, 211, 247; economizes strength, 74; does not imply isolation, 74, 78; nor exclusive attention to one thing, 75.

Cooper, James Fenimore, 101.

Cooper, Sir Astley, 202.

Copernicus, 90.

Corneille, 69, 119.

Correggio, 52.

Courier, Paul Louis, anecdote by, 174.

Courtesy, 144.

Cowley, on boyish fancies, 263; on notoriety, 325.

Cowper, William, 321; his shyness, 118, 119.

Credit, abuses of. 296-299.

Crichton, the Admirable, 70, 78.

Cromwell, Oliver, 31, 116, 156.

Culture, its effects when excessive, 113-116; new methods of, 230, 231.

Cumberland, Richard, quotation from, 27.

Curran, J. P., his first speech, 236.

Custom, its tyranny, 93.

Cuvier, on genius, 159; his improvement of time, 258.

D.

D'Aguesseau, on Fénélon, 142.

D'Alembert, on Euler, 184.

Dante, 69, 119.

Darwin, Dr., author, 257.

David, painter, 50.

Davy, Sir Humphry, 48; his intense labour, 317.

Dearborn, Gen. A. H. S., on failures in business, 287.

Debt, increases with riches, 274; its miseries, 282-285.

Decision, 123-135; John Foster on, 123; cannot be created, 124; Sydney Smith on, 124; necessary in battle, 126; a characteristic of Napoleon, 126; of Wellington, 128; striking example of, 128,; in crises, 129; needed by lawyers and physicians, 130; lacked by literary men, 132; lacked by Charles V. and Coligny, 131; and by Mackintosh, 132, 133; a characteristic of Ledyard, Sir C. Campbell, Blucher, and Sir T. Picton, 134; exemplified by Tacon, 134, 135.

Degeneracy, modern, 88.

De Maistre, Count Joseph, on battles, 190; his commonplace-books, 215.

Demosthenes, 46; on oratory, 142.

De Quincey, Thomas, 79, 173.

Despatch, 166.

Dessaix, Marshal, 190.

De Stael, Madame, 47.

Details, attention to, 104-111; in trade, 104; in other callings, 105; in literature and art, 105, 106; in war, 107; Napoleon's care for, 107, 108; Wellington's attention to, 109.

Dewey, Dr. Orville, on genius, 217.

Dexter, "Lord Timothy," 28, 37.

Dickens, Charles, his rules of work, 67; his painstaking, 218; on attention, 218.

Difficulty, its uses, 84.

Discouragements of beginners, 23, 29, 30.

Discretion, 22.

Disraeli, Benjamin, 115, 187, 236.

Distraction of pursuit, 79.

"Dr. Easy" and "Dr. Push," 175.

Drew, Samuel, 203.

Drudgery, 309-311.

Dryden, saying of, 24; his precocity, 47; on men of genius, 47; his failure in tragedy, 69; quotation from, 314.

E.

Easy writing, 242.

Economy, of strength, 247–251; of time, 253–263; of money, 278–280; as a habit, 279; the secret of England's greatness, 281; of nature, 282.

Edinburgh Review, on success at the bar, 28.

Eldon, Lord, 85; his early struggles, 99; his advice to a young man, 200; his study of Coke, 216.

Ellenborough, Lord, his early struggles, 200.

Emerson, Ralph Waldo, on concentration, 67, 70; on the "silent Grecians" of England, 113; not an imitator, 101; on literary imitation, 103; on tact, 118; on manner, 140; on preparatory training, 224; on success, 191; on special talents, 289.

England and the Russian war, 36; secret of her supremacy, 61; not likely to decline, 61; her sailors, 61; not a country for average men, 70.

Englishmen, their fondness for exercise, 61.

Enterprise, 99, 302–305.

Enthusiasm, 191.

Erskine, Lord, on success at the bar, 28; his first brief, 34; his early life, 189; his extracts from Burke, 216.

Etiquette, on rules of, 151.

Euler, mathematician, 184.

Euripides, 221.

Evarts, William M., 208.

Everett, Edward, his self-dispersion, 77.

Excellence, the reward of labour, 224.

Exercise, 322.

Extempore performances, 218, 241.

Extravagance of living, 295.

F.

Faber, manufacturer, 96.

Failure, its miseries, 14; excuses for, 26; of merchants, 42, 43, 286–308; in the professions, 43; as a test of ability, 49; its compensations, 85; its causes, 326.

Faraday, Professor, his gentleness, 144.

Fearne, law-writer, 72.

Fénélon, Bishop, his manner, 142; his courtesy, 148.

Ferguson, astronomer, 48.

Ferrara, Andrea, 116.

Fichte, metaphysician, 233; on resolutions, 124.

Fielding, Henry, 155.

Foote, Lundy, 146.

Fortune, 28, 35, 128.

Foster, John, on decision, 123, 131; his painstaking, 220.

Fowler, brewer, 302.

Fox, Charles James, his gallantry, 77; maxim of, 129; his manners, 141; his painstaking, 162; his practice in speaking, 222.

Franklin, Dr. Benjamin, 31, 155: his improvement of time, 258.

Franklin, Sir John, 148.

Frederic the Great, his ignorance, 116; on Joseph II., 117.

Fuller, Dr. Andrew, 60.

Fuller, Dr. Thomas, on method, 159; on the combats of Shakespeare and Ben Jonson, 168.

Fuseli, 86.

G.

Galiani, Abbé, 186.

Galton on eminent men, 34.

Garrison, William Lloyd, his will, 184.

Genius defined, 16, 17, 159, 195, 214, 217; does not dispense with labour, 195, 217, 217; old idea of, 217; works intensely, 241.

Genteel life, 282.

Gentleness, its power, 149.

George, Dr., on Frederic the Great, 75.

George IV., 35.

Getting on, 19, 20, 24.

Ghosts, 193.

Gibbon, Edward, 78, 217, 220.

Girard, Stephen, 275.

Gladstone, Sir William, his versatility, 72.

Goethe, on saying of Archimedes, 91; on authorship, 103; on human aims. 133; on use of opportunities, 259; on Schiller, 320; on his own happiness, 326; on man's mission, 327.

Goldsmith, Oliver, 119.

Good, Dr. Mason, 257.

Government and individual action, 86.

Grant, Ulysses, 18.
Gray, Thomas, 174.
Gray, William, merchant, 328.
Great men, not made by great occa-
sions, 18; Dr. Hunter on, 18; of
low origin, 86, 90; pygmies in body.
185, 186.
Great works, why written, 18.
Greatness, not attainable by all, 16-19;
the test of, 17; acquired unconscious-
ly, 18; its superiority to circum-
stances, 91.
Greeley, Horace, 206; on helps, 92;
on money-getting, 202.
Gregory VII., Pope, 90.
Grote, George, 258.
Growth necessary to professional suc-
cess, 246.
Grundy, Felix, saying of, 305.
Guthrie, Dr., on Scotch and French
manners, 145.
Gymnastics, 325.

H.

Habit, its power, 153-156.
Hale, Matthew, his laboriousness, 217,
257.
Halifax, Earl of, 212.
Hall, Robert, saying of, 178; his econ-
omy of strength, 248; his first ser-
mon, 236.
Hamilton, Sir William, 203; on men-
tal differences of men, 159; on genius,
159; his intense application, 317.
Hamilton, "Single Speech," 232.
Hammond, Dr., 47.
Handel, 40, 197.
Hannibal, his power of will, 181.
Happiness, 13-15, 155.
Hardships, 84, 87.
Harvard and Oxford boat-race, 226.
Havelock, 107, 198.
Hawthorne, on shyness, 137; his shy-
ness, 145; his painstaking, 221.
Hayne, Robert Y., his debate with
Webster, 239.
Hazlitt, William. on actors, 17; on
men of genius, 17; on choice of call-
ing, 41; on variety of pursuits,
68; on Kean's acting, 100; on busi-
ness, 156; on manner, 138; on self-
assurance, 174; on Pope's crooked-
ness, 186; his laboriousness, 220.
Health, a part of talent, 58; neces-
sary to authors, 60; often lacked by
great men, 62; essential in the pro-
fessions. 63, 64.
Helps, Arthur, on accuracy, 162.
Helps, a disadvantage, 87.
Henry, Professor, 68.
Herbert, George, on money-getting,
271.
Heyne, classicist, 217.
Hobbes, Thomas, metaphysician, 69.
Holmes, Oliver W., on pluck, 225.
Hogarth, 52.
Homer, 18.
Hooker, Dr. Richard, 217; his Ec-
clesiastical Polity," 18.
Hope, 14.
Horner, Sir Francis, 22.
Hudson, railway king, 273.
Hume, David, his scepticism, 45; on
cheerfulness, 156; his industry, 216.
Humility, 176, 177.
Hunter, Dr. John, on great men, 18.
Huntington, Bishop, on manners, 151.

I.

"If," its significance, 16, 17.
Imitation, in business, 97; in litera-
ture, 98, 103.
Incompatibility of pursuits, 79.
Indecision, 131.
Independence of thought, 83.
Individuality, 80; American lack of,
93, 94.
Industry, 20.
Ingram, Mr., publisher of "Illustrated
News," 147.
Invalids, famous, 62.
Inventions, 36.
Irving, Washington, on modest merit,
178.
Ismail, Muley, 41.

J.

Jacks-at-all-trades, 70, 82.
Jerrold, Douglas, 76; his will, 209;
on ugly trades, 225; on debt, 284.
Jesting, 140.
Jesuits, their method of education, 48.
Jewell, Bishop, 217.
Johnson, Dr. Samuel, on the elder
Sheridan, 25; on incivility, 140; his
gruffness, 150; on writing, 166;
on Samuel Butler, 215; satirized

by Peter Pindar, 250; anecdote of, 263; on opulence, 271; on debt, 283; his dread of insanity, 322.
Jonquil, painter, 50.
Jonson, Ben, 168.
Joseph II., of Austria, 117.

K.

Kames, Lord, on habit, 154.
Kane, Dr. Elisha Kent, 208; on system, 161.
Kant, metaphysician, 78.
Kean, Edmund, 17, 100; on acting, 191.
Keats, on failure, 15, 189.
Kenyon, Lord, 200.
Kepler, 90.
Kingsley, Canon, on Sir Sidney Smith, 148.
Knowledge, always useful, 77; its odds and ends valuable, 262.
Knox, John. 60.

L.

Labour necessary to happiness, 39.
Lafitte, banker, 301.
La Harpe, 130.
Lamb, Charles, on leisure, 40, 319; on his poverty, 273.
Laplace, his lack of practicality, 115.
Latimer, 60.
Law, George, 45.
Lawrence, Sir Thomas, 47.
Le Brun, 47.
Ledyard, traveller, his decision, 134.
Legislation a cause of bankruptcies, 305.
Leisure, needed by professional men. 245; sometimes a curse, 33, 40, 41, 252.
Leslie, Charles Robert, on instruction in painting, 86.
Lessing, on truth, 14; on a poetaster, 42.
Lewes, George H., on circumstances, 91.
Leyden, John, 48, 316.
Liberality in business, 300–303.
Life, 10, 11, 32, 227.
Limp people, 89.
Liston, actor, 50,

Livingston, Edward, his destroyed M.SS., 213.
Lobsters, human, 83.
Locke, John, his economy of time, 257.
Lorillard, Jacob, 293.
Lorraine, Claude, 48.
Louis XIV., 229.
Lubbock, Sir John, 258.
Lucian, fable of, 81.
Luck, good and bad, 25-38. 287; an abused word, 26; Rothschild on, 28; credited only with men's vices and disasters, 29; celebrated believers in, 30: Cicero on, 30; Cæsar on, 31; extraordinary instances of, 31; 32; fame dependent on, 32; Richelieu on, 36.
Luther, 60.
Lytton, Sir E. Bulwer, on education, 51; his failures, 186; on money, 268, 280; on poverty and neediness, 280; on the power to do good, 20.

M.

Macaulay, Lord, on the Duke of Monmouth, 116; contrasted with Bacon, 233.
Macclesfield, Lord, 143.
Macdonough, Commodore John, 74.
Machiavelli, 119.
Mackintosh, Sir James, his indecision, 132, 133.
Mahon, Lord, on Sir Robert Walpole, 115.
Mammon-worship, 307, 308.
Mann, Horace, on health, 64.
Manner, 136–152; a test of character, 137; in preaching, 138; in oratory, 139, 143; of military men, 148, 149; should be a part of education, 149.
Manners, Scotch and French contrasted, 145.
Mansfield, Lord, 201; his delivery, 142; his translations, 215.
Marengo, battle of, 190.
Marlborough, Duke of, 31; his manners, 141.
Marmontel, on the Abbé Galiani, 186.
Marshall, Chief Justice, 78.
Masères, Baron, 75.
Massena, Marshal, 235.
Matsys, Quintin, 181.

Meanness in business dealings, 300, 300.
Medical practitioners, 201.
Mediocre abilities, a reason for effort, 20; often highly successful, 21, 23, 90.
Meditation, 244.
Men of genius hard workers, 217.
Mendelssohn, his precocity, 49; on musical composition, 214.
Mental stimulants, 56.
Mercantile failures, their causes, etc., 286-308.
Merchants, the qualifications they need, 304, 305.
Metastasio on habit, 154.
Method, 159-161.
Mill, John S., on eccentricity, 93; his versatility, 72.
Miller, Hugh, 258.
Miller, Joe, anecdote from, 29.
Milton, John, as a humorist, 69; on his studies, 217.
Mirabeau, his charm of manner, 142.
Molière, 219.
Moltke, 198.
Money, its use and abuse, 264-285; useless unless earned, 85; its attractions, 265; the spur to industry, 267, 268: a means of power and influence, 267, 268; why desirable, 268; its value in the nineteenth century, 269; miseries caused by lack of, 269.
Money-getting, a legitimate pursuit, 264; a means of discipline, 268; sometimes a duty, 271; when unhealthy, 276: the art of, 277; its advantages as a pursuit, 279.
Monmouth, Duke of, 116.
Montagu, Mary Wortley, on "getting on," 24; on differences in men, 103.
Moore, Sir John, 32.
Moore, Thomas, his person, 186; his painstaking, 220.
More, Sir Thomas, 217.
Morton, Marcus, 183.
Mott, Dr. Valentine, his advice to his students, 146.
Murillo, painter, 47.
Murray, Dr. Alexander, 317.

N.

Napier, Sir Charles, on debt, 283.
Napoleon I., 47; on destiny, 37; his youthful amusements, 45; on health, 60; on war, 75; his attention to details, 107-110; his campaign of 1805, 110, 111; his decision in the field, 126; his strategy at the Lake of Garda, 126, 127; his delay at Ligny, 128; his love of system, 164; his punctuality, 160; his force of will, 182; his nickname, 186; his reserved power, 235; his opinion of Massena, 235; his Imperial Guard, 227; his defeat at Waterloo, 227.
Neander, theologian, 75.
Nelson, Lord, 31, 36, 47; his boyish amusements, 45; on punctuality, 164; his small stature, 185.
Nervous men, their need of rest, 249.
Newton, Sir Isaac, 78; his destroyed M.SS., 212: his great discovery, 262; his application, 317.
Nicolly, Alexander, 316.
Northcote, James, on French and Italian paintings, 235.

O.

Obstacles, 208.
One-idealism, 75-77.
Originality in aims and methods. 95-103: necessary in business, 96-98: and in literature, 99-103; defined, 100.
Opie, painter, 263; his self-dissatisfaction, 222.
Oratory, 222, 223.
Overtrading, 290, 291, 292.
Overwork and under-rest, 248, 309, 323; excuses for, 317-320; its effects on the brain, 323; its remedies, 322.

P.

Paley, Dr. William, 217; on habit, 154.
Parsons, Chief Justice, 241.
Partnership in business, 300.
Pascal, 47, 217; on disease, 56.
Patience, 210; examples of, 212, 213.
Patient labour, 196-197.
Patton, Dr. W. W., on reserved power, 243.

Paul, the Apostle, his courtesy, 149.
Peel, Sir Robert, 115.
Pelissier, his coolness, 129.
Penn, Sir William, on industry, 20.
Perseverance, 187.
Pestalozzi, on self-help, 92.
Peterborough, Lord, on Fénélon, 148.
Peter Pindar, on Dr. Johnson, 250.
Petrarch, 219.
Phalaris controversy, 236–238.
Phillips, Wendell, on the game of life, 33.
Physical culture, 55–65; its neglect, 55; among the Greeks and Romans, 56; Cicero's attention to, 58; English attention to, 61; Horace Mann on, 65.
Physical defects, their compensation, 195.
Picton, Sir Thomas, his decision. 134.
Pitt, William, on Canning, 73; his concentration, 73; his painstaking, 215; his division of work, 247.
Pliny, 191.
Poe, Edgar A., 101.
Poets, their physical vigour, 62, 63.
Politeness, 137, 140.
Pope, Alexander, 47; on Wharton, 80, 81; his pygmy size, 186; his industry, 257; an early sexagenarian, 320.
Poverty, its temptations and dangers, 265, 266; Dr. Johnson on, 269; relative, 280.
Practical talent, 112–122.
Praed, Winthrop Macworth, on a vicar's talk, 78.
Preachers, hints to, 211.
Presence of mind, 126.
Professions and callings, choice of, 39–54; Hazlitt on, 41; predilections for, 43, 44, 46, 47; determined by trifles or early impressions, 45; aptitudes for, 47; not to be hastily changed, 53; humble ones to be ennobled, 53.
Professional culture, 242.
Profits of trade, 302.
Property a hindrance to beginners, 85, 86.
Proverbs, 131, 132.
Punctuality, 158–162.

Q.

Quixote, Don, 70.

R.

Rachel, actress, 48.
Racine, 70.
Rahl, Count, 165.
Raleigh, Sir Walter, 35; his courtesy to Queen Elizabeth, 144.
Raymond, Henry, journalist, 317.
Readiness, 167, 241.
Reserved power, 226–252; why needed, 230; its advantages, 237.
Rest, its necessity, 323.
Reynolds, Sir Joshua, on industry, 20; on concentration, 68; on facility in painting, 235; on Rubens, 235.
Richelieu, Cardinal, on luck, 36.
Richter, Jean Paul, on the Germans, 76; his note-books, 215; on poverty, 224.
Robespierre, 187.
Rochefoucauld, 220.
Romilly, Sir Samuel, 198.
Rothschild, Nathan Myers, 274, 275; his advice to a brewer, 81.
Ross, Captain, navigator, 155.
Rousseau, 219.
Rubens, 235.
Rush, Dr. Benjamin, his economy of time, 257.
Ruskin on genius, 18.

S.

Sailors, English and French, 61.
Sainte-Beuve, on the "first talent," 46.
Salvator Rosa, 69.
Sand, George, on Anglo-Saxon shyness, 145.
Satirists, 144.
Saturday Review, on limp people, 89.
Savanarola, 187.
Savings, 278, 279, 280.
Schiller on the duties of life, 329.
Scipio Africanus, 68.
Scott, Sir Walter, his early reading, 45; his imitators, 101; on punctuality, 163; his lameness, 185; his speed in composition, 221; his excessive labours, 317, 321, 322.
Second books, 243.
Self-advertising, 171—179.
Self-help, 82, 83.
Self-instruction, 82.

Self-reliance, 82 94.
Sermons, 243.
Shakespeare, 18, 168 ; on adversity, 194 ; his reserved power, 233.
Shelley, saying of, 16.
Sheridan, General Philip, 235.
Sheridan, Richard Brinsley, 140; his first speech, 189 ; story from one of his comedies, 175 ; his "impromptus," 218.
Sherman, William T., his "Great March," 110.
Shyness, Anglo-Saxon, 145.
Sixtus V., Pope, 90.
Sidney, Sir Philip, 151, 317.
Sleep, 251.
Smeaton, James, 47, 262.
Smith, Adam, 78, 119.
Smith, Rev. Sydney, on life, 31; on choice of a calling, 43 ; his advice to public speakers, 57 ; on universality, 69 ; on Lord John Russell 81 ; on decision, 124 ; his courtesy, 148 ; his cheerfulness, 212; on the price of excellence, 218.
Social intercourse an element of success, 75.
Society, doctored too much, 88 ; tyranny of, 93.
Somers, Lord, 47, 169.
Southey, his commonplacing, 216.
Specialties, 95.
Speculation, 291, 292.
St. Bernard, 75.
Steadman, General, on General G. W. Thomas, 110.
Steele, Sir Richard, on debt, 284.
Stephenson, George, 115, 116 ; his improvement of time, 258.
Stevens, editor of Shakespeare, 263.
Stewart, Alexander, 96.
"Stickers," 303.
Strakosch, pianist, 197.
Stupidity, its compensations, 184.
Success, 13; a test of merit, 13 ; its pleasures, 11 ; its degrees, 16 ; a step-by-step progress, 19 ; how attainable, 16, 17 ; attainable by mediocre ability, 21 ; won by the meritorious, 24; at the bar, 29 ; demands concentration, 66, 70 ; demands health, 58, 66, 67 ; promoted by social intercourse, 75 ; qualities it demands, 117 : when too dear, 77, 347 ; true

and false, 324—329 ; not an end. 326 ; when unsuccessful, 324.
Sulla, 37.
Suwarrow, his will, 182.
Swift, Dean, 118, 237, 312.

T.

Tacon, chief of police, his decision, 135.
Tact. 118.
Taglioni, her labours, 197.
Taine, M., on the development of talents, 30.
Talent and tact, 118.
Talents needed more than places. 23.
Talfourd, Thomas Noon, on stupidity, 185.
Talleyrand, 185, 202.
Talma, 189.
Taylor, Henry, on money, 267.
Taylor, Jeremy, 217.
Temple, Dr. Frederic, on genius, 205.
Temple, Sir William, 250.
The will and the way, 188—238.
The world, an orchestra, 9, 10 ; a market, 80.
Thomas. General George W., his attention to details, 110.
Thomas, Judge B. F., on Webster's reply to Hayne, 239.
Thoreau, his first book, 294.
Thorwalsden, sculptor, his "Mercury," 100.
Thurlow, Lord, 200 ; on success at the bar, 85 ; denies a commissionership to John Scott (Lord Eldon), 85.
Time, economy of, 253—263.
Torstenson, General, 208.
Tournefort, naturalist, 47, 262.
Townsend, Lord, his nickname, 54.
Trifles, 140, 141.
Tupper, Martin Farquhar, 173.
Turner, painter, his conscientiousness, 106 ; on hard work, 222.

U.

Universal scholars, 66.
Unlucky persons, 19 ; their excuses. 20.
Utility the standard of actions, 21.

V.

Varro, Terentius, 190.
Vernet, Horace, 191.
Vestris, dancing master, 75.
Vinci, Leonardo da, his versatility, 68.
Violinist, first and second contrasted, 9.
Voltaire, 45; on La Harpe, 130.

W.

Walpole, Sir Robert, 115.
Walton, Izaak, on riches, 213.
Ward, Artemus, on oratory, 168.
Washington, George, his politeness, 150; his punctuality, 165; his will, 190; his economy, 281.
Waterloo, battle of, 183, 227, 229.
Watt, James, 262.
Wayland, Francis, his early struggles, 188.
Wealth, how acquired, 255; does not always confer happiness, 271, 273.
Weber, 317.
Webster, Daniel, his failure in declamation, 187; his reply to Hayne, 239; his habits of labour, 251; his use of an anecdote, 260.
Webster, Noah, 160.
Weed, Thurlow, his early trials, 205.
Wellington, Duke of, 18, 38; at Waterloo, 128; his attention to details, 109; his avoidance of quarrels, 154, 155; his will, 183; his dissatisfaction with the army, 198; his economy, 281.
Wesley, John, on whiling away time, 260.

West, Benjamin, 44.
Whewell, Professor, on great inventions, 36.
Whiling away time, 260-263.
Whipple, John, on Daniel Webster's habits of labour, 251.
White, Henry Kirke, 258.
Whitfield, George, 160.
Wilberforce, Sir William, 143.
Wilkes, John, his manners, 147.
Wilkie, David, 49.
Will, power of, 18, 180, 181, 200.
Willmott, Rev. Robert A., on singleness of purpose, 69, 70.
Wilson, Henry, Senator, his early trials, 204.
Winans, manufacturer, 147, 148.
Wirt, William, on Chief Justice Marshall, 78; on bits of knowledge, 260.
Wisdom, 115.
Witherspoon, Dr., on courtesy, 150.
Wolfe, James, his capture of Quebec, 209.
Wordsworth, William, 184.
Work not an intrinsic good, 309, 310, 311.
Workingmen, their lack of thrift, 277, 278.
Wotton, William, 237.

X.

Xenophon and Socrates, 46.

Y.

Yankees, their will, 184.
Yates, Senator, on Grant's genius, 18.

THE END.

CATALOGUE OF BOOKS

PUBLISHED BY

BELFORD BROTHERS,

60 YORK STREET, TORONTO.

These prices are in gold.   When offered on American
Railroads an extra price has to be asked.

**ANCKETILL (W. R.) — The Adventures of
Mick Callighin, M. P.,** by W. R. ANCKETILL.
Crown 8vo.; Cloth, 75c., Paper, 50c.

"The author is apparently a Milesian 'to the manner born,'
his rendition of the brogue being superior to that generally met
with in books of this class.   *   *   The humour is so rich and the
descriptive power of the author so forcible, that the reader will not
be likely to lay the work down until he has finished it."

HARLAND (M.)—My Little Love, BY MARION
HARLAND, author of "Alone," "Nemesis," "Common
Sense in the Household," etc.   Cloth, $1.00, Paper
Cover, 75c.

"The authoress of this pleasing novel is so well known, that
anything from her pen will be read with avidity.   Her new story
is well written, the plot is simple, yet perfect, and the manner in
which it has been brought out by Messrs. Belford Bros., is equal
to the high reputation of the firm."—*Ottawa Citizen.*

"This work is written in the easy flowing style for which the
author has been celebrated.   If it is not pretentious, it is at least
engaging, and will afford many a pleasant hour's reading to those
who prefer the trifles to the more solid things of life."—*London
Free Press.*

"Marion Harland's works are all worth reading, and "My
Little Love" is one of the best we have seen."—*Stratford Beacon.*

BLACK (Wm.)—Madcap Violet, by Wm. Black, author of "A Princess of Thule," "The Three Feathers," etc. Crown 8vo.; Cloth, $1.25, Paper Covers, 75c.

"'Madcap Violet' has already been variously appreciated, especially as regards the character of the heroine. * * 'Madcap Violet' is eminently readable throughout. Violet is a delightful person, even when she pretends to be dead, and her character, whether inconsistent or not, is at least interesting as a study."— *London, Eng., Pall Mall Budget.*

COOKE (JOHN E.)—Canolles; The Fortunes of a Partizan of '81. By John Esten Cooke. Cloth, $1.00; Paper Covers, 75 cents.

A remarkable romance. Each of Mr. Cooke's former works have reached the great sale of nearly a quarter of a million copies in the United States and Canada.

FLEMING (M. A.)—Kate Danton, by May Agnes Fleming, author of "Norine's Revenge," "A Mad Marriage," etc., etc. Crown 8vo.; Cloth, $1.00, Paper Covers, 75 cents.

"Mrs. Fleming's stories are growing more and more popular every day. Their delineations of character, life-like conversations, flashes of wit, constantly varying scenes, and deeply interesting plots, combine to place their author in the very first rank of modern novelists."

GAY (F. D.)—The Prince of Wales in India, by F. Drew Gay. Profusely illustrated. Crown 8vo.; Cloth, gold and black, $1.50, Paper, 75 cents.

"A lasting memorial of an interesting journey."—*Daily Telegraph.*

"Will no doubt find an extensive public, and be read by them with interest."—*Nonconformist.*

"Written in a lively and unpretentious style, and sparkling here and there with genuine humour, the book is a decidedly attractive one."—*Leeds Mercury.*

GRANT (Rev. G. M.)—Ocean to Ocean, by Rev. GEORGE M. GRANT. New and revised edition, with map and numerous illustrations. Crown 8vo.; Cloth, $1.50.

"This is, by the universal acknowledgment of press and public, the most complete work on the 'Great Lone Land' of British North America which has ever been published. The present edition has been thoroughly revised and corrected by the author, and a new chapter has been added, which brings down to the latest moment the official and other information bearing upon the vast territory so graphically and fully treated of. The illustrations have all been newly executed. It is a book of rare value."

HOLLAND (Dr. J. G.)—Nicholas Minturn. By Dr. J. G. HOLLAND, author of "Arthur Bonnicastle," "Sevenoaks," etc. 11 page full illustrations. Cloth, extra, $1.25 ; Paper covers, 75 cents.

No story of the day has as much merit as that of Dr. Holland, which has run through *Belford's Magazine* and *Scribner's* during the year. From month to month each fresh instalment of the story developed new features of surpassing interest. Its morality is of the highest order ; and as a searcher of social short comings and false philanthrophy, it has no equal since Dickens' best days. The desire to have it in book form is universal.

HARTE (BRET.)—Gabriel Conroy, By BRET HARTE. Crown 8vo.; Cloth, $1 00, Paper Covers, 75c.

"'Gabriel Conroy' is written in the author's most original vein, and altogether the story has proved to be one of Bret Harte's MAS-TERPIECES."—*Kendal Mercury.*

"Bret Harte's novel introduces many truly fine descriptive passages and heart-thrilling incidents. The writer's vivid power as a poet has long been recognized, not only in America, but in this country, and 'Gabriel Conroy' will, we venture to think, add greatly to his fame, and to a large extent increase the number of his admirers."—*Ipswich Chronicle.*

"   .   .   We have found at last *the* American novel."—*Canadian Illustrated News.*

"   .   .   The second instalment is even stronger than the first, *justifying all that was looked for.*"—*Louisville Courier Journal.*

GARNEAU (F. H.)—History of Canada from the Time of its Discovery till the Union of 1840-41. Translated from "L'Histoire du Canada" of F. X. GARNEAU, Esq., and accompanied with illustrative notes by ANDREW BELL. Third edition, revised, in two volumes. Demy 8vo.; Cloth, $4.00 set.

The press acknowledge that this is the best History of Canada published.

HABBERTON (JOHN.)—Other People's Children. Sequel to "Helen's Babies." By JOHN HABBERTON, author of "Helen's Babies," "Scripture Club of Valley Rest," etc. Cloth, 75 cents; Paper, 50 cents.

"Fully equal to 'Helen's Babies,' and sure of as large a sale." —*London Bookseller.*

HOLMES (M. J.)—Edith Lyle, BY MARY J. HOLMES, author of "Tempest and Sunshine," "Lena Rivers," "West Lawn," etc. Cloth, $1.00, Paper, 75c.

"'Edith Lyle' may fairly claim to be one of the most interesting novels of the season, and will, no doubt, as it well deserves, meet with a large circle of admirers."—*Toronto Mail.*

"The leading characters are skilfully drawn, and interest in the plot never ceases until the *denouement* is reached."—*Belleville Intelligencer.*

HOWELLS (W. D.)—A Chance Acquaintance, BY W. D. HOWELLS, author of "Their Wedding Journey." Uniform with "One Summer" and "Helen's Babies." Cloth, 75c. Boards, 50c.

"The descriptions of scenery are all fresh and artistic, and the observations of manners and people are curious and valuable."—*Goderich Star.*

"Mr. Howells knows how to describe what he sees, so that he combines genuine amusement with valuable information."—*Mount Forest Examiner.*

GLADSTONE (W. E.)—Essays on Macleod and Macaulay, by the Right Hon. W. E. GLADSTONE. Demy 8vo.; Paper Covers, 25 cents.

"Gladstone's remarks are of a peculiar interest to the student of history."—*Toronto Globe.*

"Mr. Gladstone's keen critical character is well exemplified in both essays, which the Canadian public will, no doubt, avidly seize upon."—*Toronto Mail.*

"Mr. Gladstone's pen produces nothing inferior."—*Halifax Herald.*

GUTHRIE (D. K. & C. J.)—Autobiography and Memoir of Thomas Guthrie, D. D., by his sons, the Rev. D. K. GUTHRIE, M.A., and C. J. GUTHRIE, M.A. 1 vol. Demy 8vo., with steel portrait; Cloth, $2.50, Half Calf, $4.00, Full Morocco, $6.00. Sold by subscription only.

"One of the most interesting books recently published."—*Spectator.*

"Of great interest, even as a mere piece of reading, and of no small value as a contribution to Scotch history."—*Scotsman.*

"Both interest and amusement will be found in this picture of a stirring time, in which an eager, busy nature played its part."—*Saturday Review.*

HISTORICUS.—History of King William III., Prince of Orange, by HISTORICUS, of Belfast, Ireland. Crown 8vo.; Cloth, 75c., Paper Covers, 50c.;

"The volume before us supplies a much felt want. Within the compass of an ordinary book we have here a comprehensive, intelligible, and well written history of one of England's greatest kings."—*Orange Sentinel.*

"* * * The present work gives this in short compass, and will doubtless be read by many for whom larger and more elaborate historical works would not be so convenient."—*Toronto Mail.*

"* * * Let all such purchase this work, and be able to give a logical reason for the pageantry of the Twelfth of July."—*Brantford Expositor.*

HAMILTON (J.C.)—The Prairie Province,

By J. C. Hamilton, M.A., LL.B. Sketches of travel from Lake Ontario to Lake Winnipeg, and an account of the geographical position, civil institutions, climate, inhabitants, productions, trade and resources of the Red River Valley, with maps of the North-west and Manitoba, Plan of Winnipeg, view of Fort Garry, and other illustrations. Crown 8vo.; Paper, $1.00, Cloth, $1.25, Cloth, gilt edges, $1.50.

The book contains a new map of Manitoba and the North-west, and of the Dawson Route, expressly drawn and engraved for this work. The new settlements, reserves and railway routes, and District of Keewatin, are shown on the map.

"This pleasant gossipping book, which carries one on without effort or fatigue, through an agreeable narrative of a trip through the Red River country, comes in very appropriately in this hot weather, when dry reading is almost impossible for most people."—*Perth Expositor.*

"We know of no work which contains so much useful information in so small a space. Our public men and public writers can find in it all the data they need towards an accurate comprehension of the present position of Manitoba, while for emigration purposes, we should fancy, that a cheap edition would materially facilitate the task of our agents abroad."—*Canadian Illustrated News.*

HARTE (BRET.)—Thankful Blossom, By Bret

Harte. Illustrated. Small 12mo.; Cloth, 50c., Paper, 30c.

"'Thankful Blossom' is beyond question a captivating, spirited, and well-told story. The author, as it seems to us, has never done a better piece of writing in its kind than the opening description of a freezing April evening."—*Atlantic Monthly.*

History of the Grange in Canada, with hints

on the management of subordinate Granges, rules for Patrons' Co-operative Associations, List of Masters and Secretaries of Dominion, Division, and Subordinate Granges, by Members of the Dominion Grange. Demy 8vo; Paper Covers, 25 cents.

McCLURE (J. B.)—Moody's Anecdotes and Illustrations, by the Rev. J. B. McClure. Cheap paper edition, 10 cents; fine edition, cloth, 75 cents.

The book contains 160 pages of Anecdotes and Illustrations of D. L. Moody, related by him in his Revival work. No book of the year has had such a large sale.

MULOCK (MISS)—Sermons Out of Church, by Miss Mulock (Mrs. Craik), author of "John Halifax, Gentleman," etc., etc. Crown 8vo.; Cloth, $1.00, Paper, 75 cents.

. . . "These 'Sermons' have nothing of the sermonizing style about them, but are written in a practical, popular style. They deal with the many 'blisters of humanity' in a kindly, loving spirit, and cannot but have a good influence on those that read them."—*The Journal of Education, Toronto.*

MULOCK (MISS)—The Laurel Bush, an Old-fashioned Love Story, by Miss Mulock (Mrs. Craik), author of "John Halifax, Gentleman," "Sermons Out of Church," etc. Demy 8vo.; Paper Covers, 50 cents.

"The tale is told in Miss Mulock's usual clear and forcible manner, and cannot fail to prove highly interesting."—*Guelph Daily Mercury.*

NASBY (P. V.)—Abou Ben Adhem, by Petroleum V. Nasby. Crown 8vo.; Paper, 50 cents.

. . . "Everybody will buy it, everybody will read it, and everybody will feel better for buying and reading it."—*Boston Transcript.*

OUIDA.—Cecil Castlemaine's Gage. By Ouida Cloth, $1.00; Paper, 75 cents.

"'Cecil Castlemaine's Gage,' is but one of fourteen short stories brought together in one volume. They are all as crisp as new-formed ice, and as sparkling as champagne. . . Perhaps of all the stories 'The General's Match-Making' is the best. It is full of fun, intrigue, blooded horses, coaching scenes on the road, and charming bits of description."—*The Toronto Mail.*

OUIDA.—Ariadne. By OUIDA, author of "In a Winter City," "Strathmore," "Under Two Flags," etc. Cloth, $1.25 ; Paper, $1.00.

"Ouida's new story, 'Ariadne,' is not only a great romance, but a great and consummate work of art, remarkable beyond anything which she has yet given us for the combination of simplicity, passion, severity and beauty. The work stands on an altogether loftier level than anything previously attempted by its author. . . It is as a work of art that 'Ariadne' must be judged ; and as such we may almost venture to pronounce it without fault or flaw in its beauty."—*World.*

OUIDA.—In a Winter City. By OUIDA, author of "Ariadne," "In a Winter City," "Strathmore," "Under Two Flags," etc. Cloth, $1.00 ; Paper. 75 cents.

"Keen poetic insight, an intense love of nature, a deep admiration of the beautiful in form and colour, are the gifts of Ouida."—*Morning Post.*

OUIDA.—Under Two Flags. By OUIDA, author of "In a Winter City," "Ariadne," "Strathmore," "Cecil Castlemaine's Gage," etc. Cloth, $1.00 ; Paper, 75 cents.

"This is a book which, whilst of the highest literary merit, stirs the feelings and emotions to an extraordinary degree. Than Ouida's description of the Steeplechase in it there is nothing more charming of the kind in English literature. The love stories are in the author's best style.

TROLLOPE (ANTHONY.)—The American Senator. By ANTHONY TROLLOPE, author of the "Prime Minister," "The Way we Live Now," "Orley Farm," etc. Crown 8vo. ; cloth, $1.25 ; paper covers, 75 cents.

For subtlety of thought, carefullness of literary execution, delicate and firm delineation of character and motive, and accurate elucidation of the springs of action exhibited by its leading actors, it is unsurpassed in this branch of English literature.

**OXENHAM (Rev. F. N.)—Everlasting Punish-
ment**: *Is the popular Doctrine de Fide? and if not, is
it true?* Considered in a letter to the Right Hon. W.
E Gladstone, M.P., by the Rev. F. N. OXENHAM, M.A.
Paper, 25 cents.

. . . "It may be added, in conclusion, that Mr. Oxenham's
letter deserves serious perusal at a time when men are proving all
things, and endeavouring to hold fast to that which is good."—
Canadian Monthly.

. . . "The treatise is very learned and exhaustive on the
negative side of the question, and those having an interest in the
question should not fail to read it."—*St. Catharines News.*

Rainsford's Sermons and Bible Readings.
Cloth, with fine Cabinet Portrait, 75 cents; Paper
covers, without portrait, 30 cents.

No modern preacher in Canada has captivated the affections
and conquered the hearts of his hearers so completely as Mr.
Rainsford. Thousands daily listened to his simple and yet eloquent
words in St. James' Cathedral, Toronto. They will be pleased to
have his Sermons and Bible Readings in a complete form ; while
the many thousands who only know him by reputation, will be delighted to peruse his discourses. The cabinet photographs are alone
worth the price of the book.

**SALM-SALM (PRINCESS)—Ten Years of My
Life,** by PRINCESS SALM-SALM (the Canadian Princess).
Crown 8vo.; Cloth, $1.00, Paper Covers, 75c.

.* "The present book covers some of the most exciting periods of
her life—in the United States during the American war, in Mexico
during civil disturbances, and in England and Europe during the
Franco-German war, when she was with the German army from
the beginning to the end. It is as instructive as interesting."—
Brantford Expositor.

"To many of the American officers and soldiers who were accustomed to see the Princess flitting from camp to camp on her
richly caparisoned charger, or riding around Nashville with
General Carl Schurz or some of his staff, this little book will be
of interest, as it half shows, half conceals, some facts with which
they were conversant at the time knew not the 'power behind
the throne.'"—*St. Catharines News.*

SPRY (W. J. J.)—The Cruise of H. M. S. Challenger, Voyages over many Seas, Scenes in many Lands, by W. J. J. SPRY, R. N. 1 vol., Demy 8vo., with maps and numerous illustrations, $2.00

"THE CRUISE OF THE CHALLENGER.—The Belfords have just published an interesting popular account of the cruise of the British ship 'Challenger,' written by an officer of the expedition, and PROFUSELY ILLUSTRATED WITH WOOD ENGRAVINGS. The volume, compiled by William J. J. Spry, from his daily journals, forms a concise, readable, and continuous narrative of this celebrated voyage.

"Altogether, Mr. Spry's *résumé* of all that he heard and witnessed while accompanying the 'Challenger' in her great voyage, forms a narrative that cannot fail to interest a larger audience of readers than is usually attracted by a simple volume of travel. He has avoided all technicalities. Those who have once begun to read this volume will not fail to go on to the end."—*The Mail.*

STEWART (GEO. Jr.)—The Story of the Great Fire in St. John, N.B., June 20th, 1877, with Map and numerous Illustrations. By GEO. STEWART, JR., of St. John, N.B. Cloth, $1.25.

"Its author is Mr. Geo. Stewart, Jr., of St. John, who certainly deserves credit for the terse and graphic manner in which he has executed his self-imposed task. In order to show what the inhabitants have undergone by the great devastation which swallowed up about two-thirds of the city, the author gives a sketch of its history for the past hundred years."—*Sarnia Observer.*

"Mr. Geo. Stewart, Jr., of St. John, N.B., has written a story of the great fire in that city—a volume of which, while it is a complete compendium of history, it at the same time contains a great deal of reading matter whose pathos and beauty are both commanding and admirable. . . . The style is very graceful."—*Kingston Whig.*

THEIR LATEST VICTIM.—Helen's Babies, with some account of their ways, innocent, crafty, angelic, impish, witching, and repulsive; also a partial record of their actions during ten days of their existence, by THEIR LATEST VICTIM. Small 12mo.; Cloth, 75c., Paper, 30c.